Intellectual Shamans

In traditional cultures, the shaman is the healer, the connector, and the spiritual leader or sensemaker. Today, in the management academy, some individuals use their intellectual gifts to perform a similar role – mediating between various disciplines, ideas, and theories, as well as making sense of ideas, insights, and research for others. This book, based on the work and lives of twenty-eight very well known management academics, describes what it means – and what it takes – to be an intellectual shaman. It is a fascinating insight into the career paths and the sometimes maverick behavior that has allowed these individuals to achieve success. Based on extensive interviews, *Intellectual Shamans* provides both a roadmap to junior scholars and a critique of the current system of academic career progression.

SANDRA WADDOCK is the Galligan Chair of Strategy, Carroll School Scholar of Corporate Responsibility, and Professor of Management at Boston College's Carroll School of Management. She has published ten books and more than 100 papers on topics related to corporate responsibility, multi-sector collaboration, and management education. Her recent publications include *Building the Responsible Enterprise*, with Andreas Rasche (2012), and *SEE Change*, with Malcolm McIntosh (2011).

Intellectual Shamans

Management Academics Making a Difference

SANDRA WADDOCK

Boston College, Massachusetts

CAMBRIDGE
UNIVERSITY PRESS

University Printing House, Cambridge CB2 8BS, United Kingdom

Cambridge University Press is part of the University of Cambridge.

It furthers the University's mission by disseminating knowledge in the pursuit of education, learning and research at the highest international levels of excellence.

www.cambridge.org
Information on this title: www.cambridge.org/9781107448377

First published 2015

Printed in the United Kingdom by Clays, St Ives plc

A catalogue record for this publication is available from the British Library

Library of Congress Cataloguing in Publication data
Waddock, Sandra A.
Intellectual shamans : management academics making a difference / Sandra Waddock.
  pages cm
Includes bibliographical references and index.
ISBN 978-1-107-08518-3 (hardback) – ISBN 978-1-107-44837-7 (paperback)
1. Management – Study and teaching.   2. Management – Social aspects.   I. Title.
HD30.4.W33   2014
658.4'09–dc23

                                                      2014021247

ISBN 978-1-107-08518-3 Hardback
ISBN 978-1-107-44837-7 Paperback

For all shamans.
For all the people who inspired me to use their stories.
For all the intellectual and other shamans in our world whose
  stories could not be included.
For anyone who would leave this world a better place.

Contents

Preface

For what it is worth, I struggled to write this book for several years. Unlike much of my writing, which tends to come easily and without fear, I have been afraid of this work – and that fear has posed multiple obstacles. The fear comes in the form of questions. Can I or anything I write be worthy of the twenty-eight individuals who shared their life stories and insights with me? I am so grateful to all of them, yet incredibly awed by their accomplishments and status in the world of management scholarship. How could anything I write possibly be worthy? The first fear, then, is that of failing to live up to the standards that any one of the people whose stories constitute the content of this book would have set for themselves and their own work.

Then there is the fear of success, coupled with the fear of failure. What if this book succeeds in capturing the thesis that I wanted to capture, that of how the work of intellectual shamans matters to the world – and that more of us, many more of us, need to follow in their paths? ...Followed by the fear of failure. And then what if no one listens? What, as is likely, if nothing changes? Alternatively, what if this work generates the very controversy that I hope it does? Do I have the courage to live with that?

Fears aside, I extend grateful thanks to the twenty-eight individuals who were willing – indeed, in some cases eager – to share their stories and go 'public' with them, despite my somewhat odd intuition that they were shamans – or shaman-like – in their approach to their intellectual and other work. I am also thankful for their bodies of work – for the motivation, hope, and inspiration they provide in a troubled world. Most of you are voyagers on much the same path that I tread, and I am indebted to each and every one of you for your commitments and your work, and for the examples you set.

No book is written in isolation, and support comes from many corners. Thanks are due to many, at Boston College, in the Academy of Management, and through other connections around the world, especially collaborators on other projects, including 'difference-makers' Malcolm McIntosh, Brad Googins, Steve Waddell, and Steve Lydenberg, along with Andreas Rasche (an up-and-coming intellectual shaman at the Copenhagen Business School), Charlie Bodwell of the International Labour Organization, Judy Clair at Boston College, and many others too numerous to name. You all serve as inspirations. Other sources of inspiration are long-term friends, including Priscilla Osborne, Pennie Sibley, Tish Schilling Miller, Margaret Skinner, and Laurie Pant, not to mention my music buddies, Harriet Hart, Peg Espinola, Ellen Schmidt, Jerry Wasserman (now deceased), Ed Loechler, Steve Rapson, Cindy Primett, Dorothea Juno-Johnston, and all the Summer Acoustic Music Week (SAMW) and open-mike crowds. My 'Way of Power' group, led by John Myerson, and including Barbara Ferri, Linda Thomas, and Matia Rania Angelou, played no small role in pushing me to find the courage to finally write the book.

Thanks are also due to Paula Parish, at Cambridge University Press, and anonymous reviewers for taking a risk on this 'edgy' book. I can only hope that its impact proves worth your support.

Finally, there are two who deserve special mention and thanks. My son Benjamin Wiegner, for his many gifts, including wry humor, intelligence, conversation, and love. And my friend, partner, and lover, Alan Rubin, for being who he is, for friendship, intelligence, and humor, for all the music – and for simply being there!

1   The intellectual shaman

Think for a minute about the people who attract you most. You want to spend time with them, listen to what they have to say. If they are academics, you want to read what they have written, go listen to their talks, even take their courses. In the particular context of this book, I am thinking of academics in the various disciplines associated with management, but you could be thinking of people in any field or from your personal life – or any number of academics whose stories I did not have room to include.

These people have a light that shines out and becomes a form of what physicists might call a 'strange attractor.' It is a light of intellectual curiosity, a willingness to take risks, that guides them through their work and the questions they ask. It is a light that leads them to question the status quo and provide new ways of thinking or operating. It is a light that leads them to want to make the world a better place and, in the case of management academics, to do the research, thinking and theorizing, teaching, and writing that advance that desire. It is a light that enables them to see across boundaries and make connections that others have not made – and then make sense of those connections.

I am going to call these people 'intellectual shamans.' We all know some of them. **Intellectual shamans are scholars who become fully who they must be, and find and live their purpose, to serve the world through three capacities: healing, connecting, and sensemaking, and in the process seek or come to wisdom.** I explain these ideas in much more detail as we go along. For the moment, consider the following quotations.

Healer:

> Well, . . .I'm in this very privileged profession. We get to do what we love, and I think that we want to derive meaning from our work.

1

So that's the first piece. But then there's another piece where I think that it's not just about me deriving meaning, [because] I can derive meaning actually from a lot of things. But I also think that what I do in the business school and what we are doing in the business school, what we're teaching in business is just wrong. So I think the business paradigm as we know it is broken. So it's not about me deriving meaning, . . .it's our obligation. . .to create a better society. If the business paradigm is broken, then it's our obligation to provide something to fix it.   *Tima Bansal*

Connector:

But there are no limits to human cooperation. [. . .] Because so many of the stories that we lifted up showed that perhaps business could emerge as one of the most powerful forces on the planet, I decided to [study] business as an agent of world benefit. Business as a force for peace in high-conflict zones. Business as the force for eradicating extreme poverty. Business as a force for eco-innovation. Where is it happening, what does it look like, what are the enablers, what are the ecosystems that help unleash the strengths of business and the service of our global agenda?   *David Cooperrider*

Sensemaker:

Business schools get all this stuff wrong, and I think [there will be problems] until we get business right. [Business is] a deeply human enterprise. It's how we create value and trade with each other. It's how we create meaning for each other. It's how we spend a third to half our lives. Until we come to see that as a human activity full of emotion and rationality and spirituality and sexuality and connection with others, until that's in the center, not at the edge: imagine if financiers had. . .to make the human case for their theory, rather than other people having to make the economic case for theirs. I think the world would be a much better place.   *R. Edward Freeman*

THE INTELLECTUAL AS SHAMAN?

Tima Bansal, David Cooperrider, and Ed Freeman are intellectual shamans, and I come back later to the contexts in which their ideas make better sense. They are three of the twenty-eight management academics interviewed for this project, although many others could also be considered intellectual shamans. Throughout this book I explore what it means to be an intellectual shaman and, by extension, to be shamanic in our modern world. Underlying this analysis is the idea that we can all, if we want and if we work at it, become shamans – intellectual or otherwise – and do our bit to help heal the world.

As the quotes above indicate, intellectual shamans are, through their work, healers, connectors, and sensemakers.[1] But there is more to it than that. They did not necessarily start their lives as shamans; these individuals have undertaken the task (some would call it the spiritual task) of finding and living out their core purpose in the world – and in doing that they are trying to help make the world a better place. Their implicit and sometimes explicit message to all of us is to do the same. They (and we, if we hope to achieve our full potential) have had to 'fully become who they are.' In that becoming, and in shaping their purposes, they serve the world in some important way. As *intellectual* shamans within a broadly defined management academy, they do this through the tasks of healing something intellectual or idea-based, be it theory, research, or practice; of connecting, which means mediating across boundaries or boundary-spanning; and of sensemaking. But they might be operating in any number of other realms of academia – or simply other realms.

Intellectual shamanism can be formally defined as intellectual work (theory, research, writing, and teaching) that integrates healing, connecting (intermediation or the mediating of boundaries), and sensemaking to serve the greater good.

Intellectual shamanism seems to be achieved by finding and fulfilling one's purpose in life, when that purpose is oriented toward the greater good. As I will explore in depth later, it means becoming fully who one must be. In the course of that becoming, many (perhaps not all) intellectual shamans become wise elders – sages. Wisdom, as I define it, also has a tripartite definition: **wisdom is the integration of systems understanding, moral imagination, and aesthetic sensibility in the service of the greater good**, which in the case of intellectual shamans is reflected in their healing orientation.

Too frequently in today's frantic race to achieve whatever our profession sets up as the standard, we forget to think about what it is we were really meant to be, the work we were really meant to do that will truly inspire us or others, or what will actually be useful to the world. This state can be particularly difficult and painful for intellectuals today, as the race to achieve ever higher now readily measured numbers of publications in so-called 'top-tier' journals with high 'impact factors' (meaning that other academics cite them, not necessarily that there has been any impact in the managerial or 'real' world) intensifies. Worse, too often as intellectuals we are afraid to be willing to take the risks necessary to follow our own intellectual – and healing – paths. Yet shamans, intellectual and otherwise, if they are nothing else, are healers.

Using the stories of twenty-eight well-known management academics in a range of management disciplines, I hope to illustrate the path to the healing work of intellectual shamans. This work is much needed in today's broken world, and can, I believe, be undertaken by anyone. Here I focus on the intellectual world of management academics. The lessons we draw from the intellectual shamans profiled here apply broadly to any line of work in which there is a willingness to serve the world.[1n]

SOME BACKGROUND: SHAMANS AND INTELLECTUALS IN MANAGEMENT

Very little management scholarship deals with shamanism at all, with the notable exception of two papers by Peter Frost and Carolyn Egri.[1,2] There is, however, substantial scholarship on shamanism in the fields of psychology, sociology, anthropology, and religious studies, among others. Although the subjects of this book are individuals I call *intellectual* shamans because they work as academics, I believe that we all – every one of us – have the capacity to work in shamanic ways if we find our true purpose and are willing to follow it, and if it serves the world in some way, however small. As we explore the work of intellectual shamans in the chapters to follow, I hope that you can draw from their experiences some of the principles that can help you, the reader, find your own shamanic healing path. Though this book is focused on intellectual shamans, I believe that its fundamental message has much broader implications for all of us if we want to make the world a better place.

There are twenty-eight individuals represented in this book explicitly, but there are many, many more intellectual shamans in the management academy, some of whom you probably know if you too are a management academic. Of course, there are also numerous shamanic people of other types in different walks of life. For example, in looking at the work of the individuals who built the foundations of what I call the corporate responsibility infrastructure, I termed such people 'difference-makers.'[3] In her book *Edgewalkers*, Judi Neal calls people who work in corporations trying to make a positive difference, and spanning boundaries in doing so, 'edgewalkers.'[4] Others call people who build new things within existing enterprises 'intrapreneurs.'[5,6] Peter Frost and Carolyn Egri directly apply the term 'shaman' to organization development specialists.[1,2] Further, many people today are talking about social entrepreneurs who serve in much the same capacity by starting up their own socially oriented enterprises.[7–10] Sometimes such individuals are called civic entrepreneurs[11,12] or institutional entrepreneurs.[13] Some are artists, others psychologists, others volunteers or workers in many different areas.

Not everyone in these lines of work is shamanic, for it is the healing, connecting or boundary-spanning, and sensemaking roles, that characterize the shaman. And it is the light that shines from them that helps us identify them, even though this is hardly a scientific concept. It is clear that people with a shamanic – healing, make a difference, or 'fix the world' – orientation go by many names. All these labels imply a willingness to take action and some degree of risk through initiating something new or healing for people, community, or the world. All imply a commitment to some purpose beyond the self. Typically, however, such work is not recognized as being shamanic, partly because in our Western culture the very idea of shamanism seems foreign, strange, and even slightly dangerous – or worse: weird, in the sense of mysterious or supernatural. Even with these connotations, it is the shamanic work of intellectual shamans – and, by implication, other types – that this book explores.

I cannot emphasize enough that there are many, many others who might have been part of this study. Some of those others refused to speak to me because of busy schedules; others I do not know. At some point, with a 'saturation' of data, I simply decided to start writing and stop obsessing about whether I could interview all the people, whom I so justly admire. My deepest apologies, therefore, if I have left you out and you would have liked to be included!

Perhaps you yourself are a healer, an edgewalker, a social entrepreneur (intrapreneur), or a difference-maker, and that is what intrigues you (assuming you are intrigued) about intellectual shamans. As my own shaman/teacher John Myerson[14–16] says, shamans tend to recognize each other – and I believe it is because they can somehow see the 'light' within others so inspired. Shamans know this light, with its healing orientation, when they see it.

The very different lives, specialties, and work of the people in this book suggest that there is no single path to becoming an intellectual (or any other type of) shaman, as numerous indigenous shamanic traditions likewise demonstrate. But there are common threads in the stories that I heard: all the people interviewed found, in one way or another, that they had, essentially, to 'fully become who they were' and follow their own lights to making a difference in the world. They had, in more shamanic terms, to find their own power. They had to 'own' that power and use it for what Buddhists call 'right livelihood,' 'right' speech' (writing), and/or 'right action,' although few of them might phrase it in quite this way. To follow their own paths, they needed to do the work to which they were, in a very real sense, called. Further, they needed to engage in one way or another with the three tasks that Frost and Egri have articulated as the core of shamanic work: being healers, connectors (or, in Frost and Egri's words, mediators of different realities), and sensemakers.[1,2]

It is through this framework of finding the way to one's own power, answering the call to purpose, healing, connecting, and sense-making that we explore the path to intellectual shamanism. In doing so, we move toward what I hope is a realization that we all have the capacity to become intellectual – or other types of – shamans, depending on our own gifts, power, and callings. We 'simply' need to have the courage to answer the call to become who we really are, to work in service to something beyond ourselves that tries to make the world or something in it better, and follow that call in our life's work by doing work that matters, makes a difference. The path is there before us, but it requires a strong sense of self, as well as the courage and a willingness to take risks and follow our own instincts (and knowledge) about what work is important and why it is so. We need, in short, to allow our own light to shine.[2n]

Following the path of intellectual shamanism sometimes means stepping away from the accepted 'wisdom' of well-trodden paths and 'how things are done' in this field. It means finding what matters in our own lives and work – and to the world. The management scholars in the case of individuals included in this project understand this reality. Their work is more than simply getting into the right journals and getting cited by other academics. Their work means operating in a context that sometimes seems to offer little support for the maverick that many intellectual shamans find themselves to be. Their paths are sometimes risky, and risk can mean failure (though, obviously, in the case of the individuals profiled here, it has meant great success and quite a degree of acclaim). Their paths frequently mean crossing boundaries, for one characteristic of shamans that we explore later is that they 'journey' in some way to multiple realms. Their paths necessitate putting ideas on the line with (and, in my view, this element is crucial) a healing orientation. Their paths entail a willingness to step into the light (or darkness) that new or off-the-beaten-track ideas, insights, and methods bring. And that means making sense of things that initially may seem not to make much sense.

Before going on to describe what shamanism is, I ought to confess to a set of personal motivations behind this work. First, I have long been attracted to the writings and ideas of the people I was privileged to interview. Getting to know them better through the interview process was an honor. Second, I believe that the current system of publishing and gaining reputation in management scholarship is broken, badly broken, and the words of many interviewees substantiate and elaborate this perspective (though it was not my original intention to prove this point). It was my sense, as it turns out justified, that these highly successful academics did not play the currently popular 'game of hits' – that is, of publishing only in so-called 'A'-level journals and attempting by all means to get cited by their colleagues. So finding out more about the individuals interviewed and how they experienced both work and life was an important motivation behind this work.

Obviously, of course, most intellectual shamans have had (more than) their share of notable publications and citations. But they are driven by something else: the nature of the work, a love of teaching, a desire to change the world for the better, the challenge of ideas and truth-telling as they see it – something that takes them beyond themselves and their own careers to this somewhat weird (wyrd) notion of serving the world that underlies shamanic practice. They seem, in essence, to have followed their own lights to find work that has mattered a great deal to themselves and, ultimately, to others. In following this path, many have succeeded beyond their wildest imaginings (and most exhibit a good deal of humility with respect to their successes, claiming luck or opportunity). I would argue that success came exactly because of their ability or willingness to take risks when opportunities presented themselves, to recognize the necessary connections and follow through with them, although others might claim perhaps that their success came in spite of that risk-taking ability.

Further, in undertaking this project, I wanted to hold up these people as, in a sense, exemplars. In admiring and holding up to the light their lives and work, I want to suggest (gently, or perhaps not so gently) to other colleagues that there are (yes, sometimes risky) paths to success in doing what really matters to you, especially if it is something that serves the world. Particularly for colleagues newer to today's academic and other systems, in which progress is increasingly evaluated by readily measured quantitative indicators that may or may not reflect actual contribution, such exemplars are important. Defining academic success (or performance) only in terms of the number of publications (or, worse, 'hits') in a select set of journals and getting cited by other academics is a narrowing of goals that will ultimately prove as meaningless, empty, and hollow as when companies seek only to 'maximize shareholder wealth' without regard to any deeper sense of purpose or attempting to fill a real need.

There is another, deeply personal, motivation for this work. For years I have been reading about shamans and shamanic practice. One day, in the early 2000s, then doctoral student Jen Leigh walked into my office, saying something along the lines of: 'I think you might want to meet this person.' 'This person,' John Myerson,[3n] is one of the founders of the New England School of Acupuncture, a practitioner of martial arts for over forty years, a Buddhist priest, a holder of a PhD in psychology, and a 'seer,' as well as author, shamanic practitioner, and horseman. Importantly, he is a shaman trained in an African tradition, who practices a decidedly Western form of shamanism translated for the likes of someone such as me. His main goal is helping his clients find their own sources of shamanic power. Within days I was in his office asking to learn what he could teach. Eventually, this teaching (sometimes a conversation, sometimes more like therapy) resulted in a group that John calls the 'Way of Power' group, meeting monthly, in which each member of the group helps the others find his or her own source of (shamanic) power.

From John and the other members of my group (Matia Rania Angelou, Linda Thomas, and Barbara Ferri remain in the group to this day) I learned that, while each of us has different shamanic gifts, we all *do* have gifts that we can use if we are willing to take the risks of doing so. For years I had doubted that I had any gifts in the shamanic realm. Then it finally dawned on me (after much pressure from John and the rest of the group) that my 'gift,' such as it is, is the ability to connect ideas and insights, and to 'see' the linkages that might make change or insight possible. (As an aside, in the course of this training I also became a singer/songwriter/guitar player, and have released two CDs at this writing – though my music is more a gift to me than to the world!) My particular 'gift' of seeing connections is not always a blessing, because it can mean that I see things 'before their time,' and then get impatient when others are not on board. When these connections happen, I think I can seem arrogant, too quick to judge, and somewhat hard-nosed in presenting what I think or 'see,' as well as difficult when others do not immediately (or ever. . .) 'see' things the way I do. But, for what it is worth, it this capacity to connect things – along with a lot of hard work – that has been my own source of inspiration and, hopefully, shamanic work that if not in impact at least in intent is aimed at bettering the world.

From these experiences, my belief is that management (or any other type of) scholars all have the capacity to become intellectual shamans. Further, people who are not scholars can become shamanic in whatever line of work, interest, or pleasures they pursue. To do this, we need to follow our own paths to power and use that power to better something beyond ourselves. Shamans, who fundamentally are healers, help the world, societies, organizations, or individuals heal – that is, take our power and make it a gift to the world in some way.

Shamans are in some ways the consummate insiders, but often find themselves as mavericks or outsiders. So they need to be willing to be outsiders, at least some of the time, and take risks, because the shaman's way does not necessarily follow accepted norms or paths to success. I would note that, although this approach seems on the surface to be an individualistic one, shamans, as we will see in later chapters, always work in communities and are almost always supported by extensive networks of partners, colleagues, and collaborators who tap into and share their visions. Shamanism is essentially all about healing communities, in particular the mythologies and relationships that exist within them, at a variety of levels. Intellectual shamans operate within the particular context of an intellectual and sometimes practice-based community – one that branches, in many cases, far beyond the ivory towers of academe.

There is one more thing that must be said before I go on to a discussion of shamanism in general and intellectual shamanism more particularly. That is, there is an unseen spirit behind this work, and it is the spirit of someone I met only once. One August some years back at our major professional association, the Academy of Management annual meeting, I was discussing my growing interest in shamanism and the genesis of this project with Carolyn Egri (of Simon Fraser University). Carolyn had co-authored, with Peter Frost, what turn out to be the two seminal management papers underpinning this study. She told me that, if I was interested in shamanism within the management academy, I had to meet Peter Frost, then a professor at the University of British Columbia,[4n] and now unfortunately deceased. Peter, Carolyn said, truly represented the intellectual shamans of whom I was speaking.

At the time Peter was already struggling with the cancer that eventually took him, and was presenting some of his seminal work on toxic organizations. At Carolyn's suggestion, I went to his session, listened, and afterward introduced myself to him. Shortly after that meeting he passed over, to the grief of his many colleagues and friends. But his work with Carolyn on organization development specialists as shamans, and one of his autobiographical essays, provide an intellectual grounding and framework for much of my thinking on this subject. And his approach – his essence, if you will – is, I can only hope, reflected in this book.

So it is that the spirit behind the study of intellectuals as shamans – intellectual shamans – is Peter Frost's spirit, though he and Carolyn did not use the specific term *intellectual* shamans, to my knowledge. Scholar, academic, mentor, spiritual leader, and friend, Peter Frost also, from all I can gather, epitomized the intellectual shaman. Many of the people I interviewed knew him and spontaneously spoke of him and his work and influence on them with admiration and love. Somehow, his spirit, his shining light and example, has been there guiding what has probably been the most difficult project I have ever undertaken. So, yes, there is a spirit behind this book – and my only hope is that this work on *intellectual* shamans is worthy of Peter Frost and all those individuals willing to be part of this weird (in the true sense of the word: of or related to the supernatural) project.

THE SHAMAN AND THE *INTELLECTUAL* SHAMAN

The shaman in indigenous cultures is the medicine man or woman, the healer, and often the sage or wise person. Traditional societies all have their shamans, their medicine men and women, who tend to be important community personages. In fact, Stanley Krippner,[17] who has studied shamanism extensively, notes: 'Shamans appear to have been humankind's first psychotherapists, first physicians, first magicians, first performing artists, first storytellers, and even the first timekeepers and weather forecasters.' Indeed, given how old shamanic practice appears to be from the anthropological record, it may well be that the basis of most religions, particularly those associated with mysticism, lies in earlier shamanic traditions. Christ, the Buddha, Mohammed, Confucius, and many other religious notables certainly all had their shamanic characteristics.

Frost and Egri,[2] in one of the few writings about shamanism in the management literature, point out that shamans strive for holistic balance – a connection between mind, body, heart, soul, and spirit that is one with nature, and that arguably is much needed in today's world. The idea of the shaman is a social construct that 'describes a particular type of practitioner who attends to the psychological and spiritual needs of a community that has granted that practitioner privileged status.'[1] Frost and Egri apply the term 'shaman' in the management literature particularly to organizational development practitioners, who, like some shamans, have also been called witch doctors, messianic, and sorcerers.[18] The term 'sorcerer,' it should be noted, typically refers to shamanistic practitioners who use their powers for darker or negative purposes as opposed to healing purposes. Here we are concerned with the positive – i.e., healing – features of shamanism. Despite the potential for a dark side, Krippner reports numerous studies that suggest that there is a strong ethical core and healing orientation engrained in most shamans.[17]

Frost and Egri highlight three central capabilities or roles that shamans play: healer, intermediary (i.e., mediator of reality, or boundary-spanner), and sensemaker.[2,19] In their healing capacities, shamans serve as the medicine men and women of traditional cultures. Arguably in our context, they can also serve as healers for the modern world. In their intermediation capacities, shamans bridge different realms or realities; in other words, they journey to other realms, bringing back needed information to help with healing processes. That is, shamans are connectors. Although Frost and Egri use the term 'mediators of reality,' for the purposes of clarity I will mostly use the term 'connector,' which I think better describes the linking of ideas that characterizes the work of intellectual shamanism. In their sensemaking capacities, shamans help others make sense of a complex and often confusing world. Indeed, as the medicine men and women of traditional cultures, they use these capacities to help those who are dis-eased (diseased) frequently as a result of spiritual problems in healing themselves.[20-23]

Below I briefly explore what the literature has to say about shamans in these three roles. We will look more deeply into these three roles in later chapters after we have explored the sense of purpose, calling, and becoming 'fully who one is' that characterizes the intellectual shaman, and provides a foundation for his or her work.

SHAMAN AS HEALER

Though shamans can be found in virtually all cultures,[20,21,24] the concept of shamanism is not one that generally comes to mind when we think of intellectuals, or, indeed, when we think about the developed or industrialized Western world. The term is arcane and somewhat mysterious, with supernatural – or at least spiritual – overtones that can make it seem foreign to us today. But I believe that shamanism is a construct that needs to be brought forward into our times, as some modern shamans have tried to do,[22,25–29] so that the core powers of 'seeing' and healing inherent to shamanic practice can be brought to bear on a deeply troubled world. So, what is a shaman and why do I think that perhaps some intellectuals serve in a shamanistic capacity? One useful definition of a shaman that highlights the core elements of shamanism is given by Serge Kahali King:

> [A] shaman [is] a healer of relationships: between mind and body, between people, between people and circumstances, between humans and Nature, and between matter and spirit.[24]

Based on this definition, we can see that shamans are, perhaps most centrally, healers. To heal they have to 'see,' in some sense, what others cannot, do not, or will not see. That is, they see the relationships – i.e., the connections that exist between entities – and where these relationships are troubled. 'Connecting' means seeing these connections and spanning boundaries, and operating among different relationships or different worlds. *Effectively*, the connector role involves bringing some balance to those relationships in which it is missing, for that is the healing process, which is the role of connecting, discussed in the next section. Sometimes shamans 'see' things intellectually or in other ways that others have not yet seen, and provide new insights. Sometimes they are willing, like the little boy in the fable of the emperor's new clothes, to point out when the emperor has no clothes. King identifies key areas in which balance might be needed, such as mind and body, person to person, person to circumstance (society or organization or situation), and person to nature.

Krippner defines shamanism as 'a body of techniques and activities that supposedly enable its practitioners to access information that is not ordinarily attainable by members of the social group that gave them privileged status. Shamanic practitioners use this information in attempts to meet the needs of this group and its members.'[30] Although there are some negative connotations associated with shamans (e.g., early researchers and scholars thought they were mentally ill or tricksters), in fact, shamans have been found to be healthier,[31] more creative and freer,[32] highly skilled and talented,[33–35] and less anxious[36] than non-shaman counterparts.[17]

Further, as Mircea Eliade demonstrates in his seminal book *Shamanism*,[20,21] there are as many varieties of shamanism as there are cultures – and equally so with intellectual shamanism and other forms of shamanic practice with which a reader might wish to engage. Eliade notes, 'The shaman is not a *magician*, but a spiritual guide, a physician, an artist, and he is all this thanks to his function as medium and to his spiritualistic experience.'[21,37] The central role in these activities is one of healing what needs to be healed, whether it be within individuals or the local community – the major orientations of traditional shamans – or within an intellectual community, a discipline, individuals, communities, organizations, or the world – the realms in which intellectual shamans operate.

Egri and Frost point out that shamans 'recognize, understand, and know how to enter different coexisting realities and to be able to retrieve useful knowledge from their "journeys."'[1] This useful information is typically used to help heal whatever relationship the shaman has identified as problematic, for the central role of the shaman practicing in whatever discipline is relevant is that of healer. In the case of intellectual shamans, these relationships could be between theory and practice or teaching and research, or integrating across disciplines; they could be among people in relationships, in organizations, or in the world; or they could be more macro in dealing with the bigger problems of the world.

SHAMAN AS CONNECTOR/MEDIATOR OF REALITY

Often called 'seers,' traditional shamans 'see' what others cannot by virtue of traveling or journeying to other realms, typically in an altered state of mind or a trance, and connecting what they find in those other realms to what is already known in their most familiar realm. In other words, shamans learn in and from realms beyond the day-to-day common-sense world that we know, so that they can bring back this information for the healing purposes discussed above. Eliade[20,21] emphasizes the role of 'ecstasy' in producing the trances out of which comes the information that shamans capture when entering other, usually spiritual, realms, along with 'possession,' which makes 'present, living, concrete' the spiritual world. Eliade also maintains that, though shamanism's content and orientation are context-dependent, the ritual ecstasy (trance) associated with it is widespread; in fact, he claims that such 'ecstasy' is 'an integral part of the human condition.'[21]

Krippner[30] further notes that research by Hans Hansen suggests that deconstruction of reality is a key shamanic role, because '[s]hamans break down categories, confound boundaries, especially those between worlds; and specialize in ambiguity.' These capacities enable shamans to challenge authority,[30] or, in the word used by Henry Mintzberg, one of the individuals interviewed for this project, to become a 'debunker' of accepted wisdom, if that is what is needed. It is exactly this connecting capacity to use information gathered in different realms, which can also be called intermediation or boundary-spanning, and breaking down of extant categories that make intellectual shamans' work valuable. Their work becomes *intellectual* shamanism precisely because these people use their intellectual capacities to share insight, knowledge, and even wisdom with others and make sense out of it.

The trance state is also associated with traditional shamanism, and what Krippner labels the 'shamanic sensibility' associated with shamanic practice can be found in the West as well, particularly among performing artists, musicians, poets, and some therapists.[38] Further, the 'trance' or 'ecstasy' of shamanism is very much aligned with the state that Mihaly Csikszentmihaly [39–41] calls 'flow,' that timeless, focused, concentrated experience that runners, teams, artists of all sorts, and everyone deeply engaged in virtually any experience call the 'zone.' The trance is also basically the same as the meditative state, in allowing access to 'other' realms and deeply rooted information.

Shamans access this state of trance or flow to gain what has been called 'heightened awareness,' knowledge, and insight through various means, such as drugs, dance, drumming, or meditation – i.e., to 'see' what is on the other side of ordinary or extra-ordinary boundaries. They typically use a technique called journeying, which is characterized, as Krippner[30] reports, by, 'an acute perception of their environment and by imaginative fancy.' Like flow, trance, and hypnosis[38] (which are different names for much the same phenomenon), journeying facilitates access to other (spiritual) realms, just as we shall see that intellectual shamans span various types of boundaries in their work.

Going into ecstasy, trance, or flow is a form of intermediation or boundary-spanning (i.e., liminal[38] or 'between') activity that allows shamans access to realms beyond their ordinary ones, typically spiritual realms in shamanic tradition. There they can access needed or helpful information that helps them make connections that others who do not boundary-span do not necessarily make. Such journeying allows shamans to mediate reality for others[2] because they 'operate on the *limens*, or borders, of both society and consciousness, eluding structures and crossing established boundaries.'[30,38] Shamanic journeys often occur in trance states or altered states of consciousness that one might claim allow access to what the great psychologist Karl Jung has termed the collective unconscious.

Journeying to other realms is an important part of what *intellectual* shamans do, but they do not work with drums, drugs, or other ways of inducing trance, as traditional shamans tend to do. Rather, intellectual shamans make their connections by crossing the boundaries of disciplines – theory and practice, teaching and theory – or ideas to gain knowledge and insights. Sometimes they live or have lived in multiple cultures. Sometimes they find themselves in or create what intellectual shaman Bill Starbuck calls 'nests,' collections, coalitions, and networks of interesting and influential colleagues who open up horizons beyond the day-to-day realm. Sometimes they quite deliberately create new ways of viewing old ideas, reshaping and reframing to make their insights – their seeing – accessible to others.

The capacity of intellectual shamans, difference-makers, and edgewalkers to walk at the boundaries of ideas or concepts, between the worlds of theory and practice, or at the edge of what is known constitutes a form of working between realms. The holism in the work of intellectual shamans often comes from a desire to see the world or people whole and healed and integrated. In an intellectual environment in which too much work and thinking is fragmented, specialized, or atomized, whether at the individual, group, organizational, societal, or planetary level, seeing the whole – i.e., making connections – becomes ever more important. In the case of intellectual shamans, attempting to break wholes into component parts in order to understand them is only part of the work, because making sense of the whole is needed for true understanding. Sensemaking is the third important role that shamans carry out.

SHAMAN AS SENSEMAKER (SPIRITUAL LEADER)

According to Egri and Frost,[1] shamans are not only 'experts of the supernatural, technicians of magic' but also 'sources of knowledge and wisdom, prophets of the future, and counselors,' who 'draw on both theoretical and practical knowledge in their practice.'[1] In using this knowledge and sharing it – making sense of it – with and for others, intellectual shamans serve the world in the capacity of sensemaker, or what Frost and Egri term spiritual leader.[2]

In their roles as sensemakers,[2] shamans share information gathered on shamanic journeys (trances or ecstasy) to other realms with other members of their communities.[42] In other words, they bring back information from their journeys and make sense of it for others in the process that Karl Weick calls sensemaking[43,44] and Frost and Egri term spiritual leadership.[2] They also use it to develop wisdom – i.e., to become sages. According to Roger Walsh, the 'cultivation of wisdom' is one of the hallmarks of shamanism,[33] achieved via journeying. In doing this journeying to other realms, shamans accomplish three tasks: voluntarily going into altered states, moving through different frames of experience, experiencing themselves and others in spiritual terms that go beyond physical boundaries, and purposefully bringing back information – wisdom – to heal their communities.[2]

Perhaps shamans achieve their insights because they are simply smarter than the rest of us. But perhaps, at least for intellectual shamans, it is that they do not fear their 'journeys' across disciplines, across theory and practice, from theory to teaching, or into other new realms, and the bringing forth of what they have learned. For intellectual shamans, it seems that new and potentially important questions arise out of new thinking that bridges past old ways of knowing and thinking, and then from making sense of those new ideas for others.

SHAMANS IN THE WORLD

Mircea Eliade, author of what is perhaps the seminal anthropological book on the subject, *Shamanism*, notes that shamans have been found in all cultures. Though there is little dogma associated with shamanism, it nonetheless represents the oldest spiritual traditions on Earth, in fact, underpinning most, if not all, of today's known religions.[20] The great mythologist Joseph Campbell[23] has pointed out that shamanic practices have been observed in artifacts from the Paleolithic period, well before the emergence of any of today's organized religions.

Shamans are, as we have already discovered, healers who can see beyond the ordinary – i.e., cross realms and mediate reality to make connections that others do not make, and make sense of what is needed to be done to heal the tribe (organization, society) or the individual.[1,2] The *intellectual* shaman in the management academy does this work through writing, research, teaching, sometimes consulting or working with practitioners, sometimes being entrepreneurial in various ways. In many instances, as will be discussed in later chapters, shamans are 'called' to their work, or what I earlier characterized as their purpose.

It is in this sense that I believe all of us can become shamanic – by exploring, finding, and acting on our core purpose, so long as that purpose has a healing orientation.

One description of shamans that provides important insight into the way intellectual and other types of shamans work – and that, arguably, the world needs more people to do – comes from Serge Kahali King, who states [emphasis in original]:

> Shamanism is a distinct form of healing... The outstanding quality of the shaman, regardless of culture, is the inclination toward engagement, or creative activity. Knowledge and understanding are not enough, nor does passive acceptance hold any appeal. The shaman plunges into life with mind and senses, playing the role of cocreator. There is a type of soul content to admire the shape and place of a fallen tree. The shaman is more like a sculptor who views the tree and is seized by the desire to transform it into some semblance of an internal image...or a useful tool. There is respect and admiration for the tree as it is, *as well as* the impulse to join with the tree and produce something new. This activism is expressed in the primary function of a shaman: that of a healer. Regardless of culture, location, or social environment a shaman is, by purpose, a healer of mind, body, and circumstance.[24]

As Frost and Egri[1,2] argue, there is a close analogy between traditional shamans – who helped their communities and the individuals in them when they were in need – and what is done today with organizational transformations. Frost and Egri identify organizational development specialists as modern shamans. In the developed world, labeling someone purely and simply a shaman is done only rarely, as it seems strange or weird, even problematic;[30] yet there is growing evidence that the world and many of the organizations and people in it desperately need the healing that might be provided by shamans.

Signs of ecological deterioration and human-induced climate change, called by UN secretary-general Ban Ki-moon nothing less than a 'global suicide pact,' growing gaps between rich and poor states and the rich and poor within states, the growing threat that ecosystems will be unable to support the burgeoning human population in the future, dysfunctional institutions and organizations, a global financial system that amounts to little more than a huge gambling casino geared to enhancing the wealth of the already rich, and very real threats of terrorism and war that undermine chances of peace and security are only a few of the symptoms that indicate a vast need for healing in our world. Arguably, the role of asking the 'right' question – questions that lead to healing through words as well as actions – is the primary way that an intellectual shaman works and how he or she moves the world in the direction of healing.

Intellectual shamans are able to bridge into new territories, connecting insights and ideas that others have not yet seen, because they are willing to take the risk of asking questions and potentially seeing the world (or their subject matter) in non-usual ways. Such 'insight thinking' is associated with the flow experience described by Csikszentmihaly,[19] and with traditional forms of shamanic journeying, which bring people to that state of trance that opens awareness and allows for insight. Frost and Egri[2] note that shamanism employs three basic assumptions. First, there are multiple realms or 'worlds of experience' that are relevant to shamanic – and, by extension, intellectual – work. In the case of intellectual shamans, connecting involves crossing into other realms and encompasses cross- or transdisciplinary, theory-to-practice, research-to-teaching, or sectoral boundaries. For others, it may means seeing things in new ways through the lens of some sort of art, new idea, new practice, by making connections with others, ideas, professions, businesses or other types of organizations, and in many other possible ways.

The second assumption is that shamans, including intellectual shamans, are oriented toward creating 'holistic balance' across the various realms of experience that they experience, and this creation of balance is closely tied to the shaman's spiritual quest for meaning, as well as to the healing process. Thus, the notion of seeking balance is integral to shamanic practice and is importantly related to the systems thinking that characterizes intellectual shamans, who tend to see the complexity inherent in what they study rather than trying to simplify things. Frost and Egri note:

> The human spirit and search for spiritual meaning in life play integral and essential roles in personal and community development. There is a need for holistic balance between the physical reality of the body, the intellectual and social reality of the mind, and the spiritual needs of the soul. When these three facets are out of balance either at individual or collective levels, then we experience pain and distress.[2]

Clearly, the world today is experiencing a great deal of the pain and stress that Frost and Egri write about, highlighting the great need to find ways to build in more holistic approaches to issues and intellectual problems, as well as in decisions that affect how people live and work in organizations in our modern world. More holistic approaches can help overcome the fragmentation and divisiveness in much of the way that academics approach their work today.

Third, shamans, and particularly *intellectual* shamans, understand that change is inevitable and ongoing, such that their work is in a very real sense never finished.[2] Perhaps this is why so many of the intellectual shamans interviewed who were well past normal retirement age continue to work. Through their writings and other work, many intellectual shamans have created important shifts of intellectual and boundary-spanning consciousness in their respective disciplines.

Intellectual shamans sometimes courageously walk a line between rigorous scholarship and practice, between new and established ways of doing something, between accepted practice and practice that seems radically different or novel, even 'unscientific' to some observers because of its holism or because it is somehow outside mainstream thinking. Sometimes, in their connecting capacity, they 'see' what others do not readily see – assumptions underlying existing theory and the issues those assumptions create.

They may see links between seemingly unrelated ideas, events, or theories, ways of integrating theories, frameworks and concepts that highlight new ideas and connections, and ways to link academic ideas to practice that others have not yet seen. It is this 'seeing,' of course, that is exactly the point of intellectual shamanism – its gift, and its curse, in some respects. Sometimes, as academics, intellectual shamans are accused by other academics of not being 'serious' scholars because of the applied or integrative nature of their work. Equally often, if not more frequently, it is to their ideas, sessions, and conversations that others flock and that eventually effect significant changes in thinking, research approaches, or practice – in part because they exude the 'light' (you could call it self-confidence, self-awareness, or even a degree of charisma or magnetism) that indicates they have found their own purpose.

In a world that desperately needs healing in so many relationships, the connections that intellectual shamans make among disciplines, ideas, people, and approaches, and more integrated and holistic perspectives, even if they are flawed by uncertainty, demonstrate that intellectual shamans have significant contributions to make. Too many modern academics in the management academy, and elsewhere, are focused on doing research that will help them get published in top-tier journals and cited by other academics without much regard for whether or not their work has any significance conceptually, never mind practical use or relevance. There is plenty of scholarship to support this point of view.[45–56] There is also significant evidence that far too much of today's management research, scholarship, and even teaching lacks relevance, or what some scholars have called 'actionability.'

Still, there are some scholars, some of whom are included in this book, who are the intellectual shamans, whose work takes on the holistic healing, reality-mediating, and sensemaking attributes[1,2] that are core to the work of all shamans. It is to these healers of thought and culture, sensemakers, and intermediaries we now turn to see what we all can learn from them.

WHO ARE THESE PEOPLE – AND ARE THERE OTHERS?

The twenty-eight people interviewed for this study are management scholars and scholar/practitioners. All are, within their own fields, well known, and all are highly accomplished individuals; most have been well recognized within their respective disciplines and many have received numerous prestigious awards and other recognitions. Some have had an easy life, with things synchronistically falling into place for them; others have experienced much more struggle to achieve the acclaim that now accrues to them. They have followed vastly different paths to their success, and are in different subdisciplines of management study, ranging from organizational behavior (OB) to strategy to ethics to business in society. Some are men and others are women.

Most are from the United States (simply because of the limitations of my own network and knowledge), but not all, and certainly there are many identifiable intellectual shamans beyond the United States. They were chosen because of who they are and because their work has had, in one respect or another, a huge impact. If you work in the management academy, you are likely to know most of their names and may even think of some of them as 'gurus,' although, because they approach their world and work with a great degree of humility, few would put themselves into that category.

All are, to one extent or another, teachers or scholars, and, in their different ways, they are people I call intellectual shamans. Through their work, each of them has made a difference in the world – the world of scholarship, the world of management practice, the world of ideas, the worlds of their students. As intellectuals, they have used the power of ideas, the intellect, and their teaching or research to do the work of shamans: mediating reality, sensemaking, and healing.[2] They have done so by doing what I call 'becoming fully who they are,' finding their passion and purpose in life – and following that as a calling.

In the spirit of holism that characterizes shamans, we need to recognize that everything is related. The analytical task here, then, is more narrative than anything else: the idea is to tell the stories of these intellectual shamans, and to illustrate what it means to be an intellectual shaman. In doing this, I hope to illustrate how others might, if they so wish, follow their own lights to finding their shamanic path. Further, the task is to recognize that, complicated beings that they are, most of these people would not necessarily break their experiences into the analytical categories that I have done. Nor would they necessarily claim the label of shaman, intellectual or other. And, although I adopt the framework of healer, connector, and sensemaker provided by Frost and Egri, there are clear instances when these categories overlap, making teasing apart the differences little more than impossible.

The question is, can, should, and – if so – how can more management academics, and in fields well beyond the management academy, follow the lead of intellectual shamans? Or is shamanism just too weird, too strange, to appeal to academics, particularly in the grounded and rational fields associated with management?

THE INTELLECTUAL SHAMANS

Before delving more deeply into the concept of intellectual shamanism, let me thank each one of them for his or her willingness to participate in the interviews, their openness, and their work, and let the reader know who was interviewed. The intellectual shamans will be individually introduced with biographical details (in boxes) as their stories become relevant to the broader story. Meantime, all quotes unless otherwise indicated are taken directly from transcribed interviews.[5n]

In alphabetical order, and with major affiliation listed, the intellectual shamans interviewed are as follows.

Nancy J. Adler, McGill University
Pratima (Tima) Bansal, Western Ontario University
L. David (Dave) Brown, Harvard Kennedy School; formerly Boston
   University (retired)

Kim S. Cameron, University of Michigan

David Cooperrider, Case Western Reserve University

Derick De Jongh, University of Pretoria, South Africa

Jane E. Dutton, University of Michigan

Marc J. Epstein, Rice University

R. Edward (Ed) Freeman, University of Virginia

Robert (Bob) Giacalone, University of Denver

Stuart (Stu) Hart, University of Vermont; Cornell University
(emeritus)

Andrew (Andy) J. Hoffman, University of Michigan

Josep Maria Lozano, ESADE Business School, Barcelona, Spain

Henry Mintzberg, McGill University

Philip (Phil) H. Mirvis, independent consultant and scholar-
practitioner

Ian Mitroff, University of Southern California (emeritus)

Judith (Judi) Ann Neal, University of Arkansas (retired)

Robert (Bob) E. Quinn, University of Michigan

C. Otto Scharmer, Massachusetts Institute of Technology

Edgar (Ed) H. Schein, Massachusetts Institute of Technology
(emeritus)

Paul Shrivastava, Concordia University

Rajendra (Raj) S. Sisodia, Babson College; formerly Bentley
University

William (Bill) H. Starbuck, University of Oregon; formerly New
York University (emeritus)

William (Bill) R. Torbert, Boston College (emeritus)

John Van Maanen, Massachusetts Institute of Technology

James (Jim) P. Walsh, University of Michigan

Karl Weick, University of Michigan (emeritus)

Maurizio Zollo, Boconni University, Milan, Italy

2 The path to intellectual shamanism: becoming fully who you are

One thing: you have to walk, and create the way by your walking; you will not find a ready-made path. It is not so cheap, to reach to the ultimate realization of truth. You will have to create the path by walking yourself; the path is not ready-made, lying there and waiting for you. It is just like the sky: the birds fly, but they don't leave any footprints. You cannot follow them; there are no footprints left behind.

Osho

When I let go of who I am, I become who I might be.

Lao Tzu

I think what we really [need to] talk about is: can anybody do more of what their real life intention is? That's how I would phrase it. Of course, there [are] differences in what people bring in terms of their life intention, . . .and that leads to different journeys. [. . .] So, the question is: how can we give everyone on the planet – or even just those who go to institutions of higher education – a better possibility to realize their full potential and their real life intention? [. . .] The answer is, absolutely, 'Yes.'

C. Otto Scharmer

I walk in [to the classroom] with a couple of questions and I tend to learn to trust my intuitions, which I have not. . .always done. Trust my intuitions to be able to make something happen in the classroom by doing no more than being completely, 100 percent present and engaged. Taking the students where they are, not where I wish they were. Trying to create something in the classroom together rather than 'I know some stuff they don't know; when I tell them, they're going to know it.' That's not the way I do it. That sort of creation of a life, that sort of artistic view of life, I try to do that in the classroom. I try it in everything I do, but that carries over in the classroom. I'm making it sound easier and less painful then it has been. Because discovering that is a continuous process.

R. Edward Freeman

27

These latter two very different statements carry similar messages: they signify coming to be fully yourself, and realizing the 'power' inherent in that coming to be. Yet they come from two intellectual shamans whose lives and careers have followed very different paths. Ed (R. Edward) Freeman represents perhaps the more prototypical academic. Known (sometimes to his chagrin) as the 'father of stakeholder theory,' Freeman is a consummate teacher-scholar, whose first book, *Strategic Management: A Stakeholder Approach*, provided the foundation for stakeholder theory both in academia and in practice. He has spent the bulk of his career at the University of Virginia's Darden Graduate School of Business, publishing some twenty books and more than 100 scholarly papers at this writing. His work has also been incredibly influential within the business ethics scholarly community, with which he is perhaps most identified, and also in practice, as the idea of companies needing to pay attention to stakeholders has become accepted wisdom. Companies and other types of organizations today all seem to recognize that being successful depends on the ways they deal with their various stakeholders. A professor at both the Darden School and in religious studies, Freeman has been named as the Darden School's first ever University Professor at the University of Virginia, and is a superb teacher-scholar.

R. Edward Freeman

R. Edward (Ed) Freeman holds a BA from Duke University and PhD from Washington University. Freeman is University Professor, University of Virginia, one of fewer than twenty such professors among Virginia's more than 200 professors, and is the Elis and Signe Olsson Professor of Business Administration, and academic director of the Business Roundtable Institute for Corporate Ethics at the University of Virginia's Darden Graduate School of Business. He formerly served as director of Darden's Olsson Center for Applied Ethics, and is also a professor of religious studies and faculty advisor to the University of Virginia's Institute for Practical Ethics and Public Life. Known informally as the 'father of stakeholder theory,' Freeman published his seminal book

Strategic Management: A Stakeholder Approach in 1984 (which has to date been cited more than 12,000 times), sparking widespread academic and practitioner interest in ideas about stakeholders. More recently, he has co-published *Managing for Stakeholders: Survival, Reputation, and Success,* and *Stakeholder Theory: The State of the Art,* along with about twenty other books and more than 100 articles. Recipient of numerous awards, honors, and honorary degrees, Freeman received the Academy of Management's Distinguished Educator Award in 2013, Outstanding Contributions to Scholarship Award by the Society for Business Ethics in 2010, the 2001 Faculty Pioneer Award for Lifetime Achievement by the Aspen Institute and World Resources Council, and, in 2005, the Outstanding Faculty Award from the Virginia State Council on Higher Education. Not only is Freeman a prolific and respected author but he is also an outstanding and highly creative award-winning instructor, teaching, over the years, business ethics, leadership and theater, creative capitalism, business ethics through literature, business projects, and leadership, ethics, and values. In addition to his scholarly life, Freeman is an accomplished blues musician and songwriter and holds a black belt in tae kwon do.

Otto Scharmer has followed quite a different path. Senior lecturer at the Massachusetts Institute of Technology (MIT), Scharmer is best known for his work developing what he calls 'theory U' and 'presencing.' He is also founding chair of the Presencing Institute, and chair of MIT IDEAS, which works with multi-stakeholder groups from business, government, and civil society to create societal-level innovations, among other appointments. His biography reads like that of a social entrepreneur and consultant, working on social change and innovation and leadership development globally, with rather less mention of his writing or scholarship, although he has authored or co-authored numerous papers and seven books to date. He has also received numerous grants and awards recognizing his work. Scharmer, too, is a consummate teacher, having designed an innovative approach, which is now being applied not just at MIT but also in governmental, societal, and business settings around the world, to effect social change and innovation at a deep level.

C. Otto Scharmer

Otto Scharmer is senior lecturer at the Massachusetts Institute of
Technology, founding chair of the Presencing Institute, chair of the MIT
IDEAS program, co-founder of the Global Wellbeing and Gross National
Happiness (GNH) Lab, and a founding member of the MIT Green Hub.
The MIT IDEAS program brings together diverse stakeholders from all
sectors of society to learn how to innovate systemically. The GNH Lab
links innovators from Bhutan (which first released the gross national
happiness indicator), Brazil, Europe, and the United States in order to
develop societal metrics that go beyond gross domestic product. Best
known for his work on 'theory U' and 'presencing,' Scharmer's main
focus to date is 'learning from the emerging future,' articulated in
his books *Leading from the Emerging Future: From Ego-System to
Eco-System Economies* (with Katrin Kaufer) *Theory U*, and *Presence:
Human Purpose and the Field of the Future* (with Peter Senge, Joseph
Jaworski, and Betty Sue Flowers). Internationally known for his work
on theory U and presencing, Scharmer has received awards for his
leadership and innovation programs, and worked with clients globally,
including Alibaba, Daimler, Eileen Fisher, Fujitsu, Google, Natura, and
PriceWaterhouse, as well as with governments, including that of China,
around the world. He serves as Vice Chair of the World Economic
Forum's Global Agenda Council on New Leadership Models.

As with Freeman and Scharmer, there is not necessarily a
common life or career trajectory among the rest of the twenty-eight
intellectual shamans interviewed for this study, nor, I suspect, among
others who exhibit similar tendencies. Some have followed fairly traditional academic paths, starting as assistant professors and moving on
through the ranks, frequently ending up in endowed chairs and as
professors emeriti toward the ends of their careers, if they have reached
that stage. A few are by almost anyone's assessment 'senior scholars,'
some well past retirement age, though still actively engaged intellectually and in other ways. Others, highly accomplished and in high-
status positions, are still relatively young. Of those who have passed

normal retirement age, most, if not all, are still spending significant time on activities related to their lives' work. Some were born to highly educated or privileged families and accomplished parents, while others were first-generation college attendees with less privileged backgrounds. Four are women. They come from a variety of religious and spiritual traditions (Catholic, Jewish, Protestant, Mormon, Hindu, or no particular religion, as examples). Most are or were married, but a couple never married; and most of the married shamans have children. Some have divorced; others have stayed with the same spouse throughout their married lives.

Some of these intellectual shamans have essentially spent their entire careers since receiving their doctoral degree at the same institution (though typically with excursions for brief periods abroad to other institutions), while others have been more peripatetic in terms of affiliations, going from place to place until they finally 'landed' in the institution where they were at the time of the interview or where they spent most of their career. Indeed, some stayed in scholarly tracks throughout their careers, while others have spent time in administrative positions or left academia to pursue various entrepreneurial ventures at different times, ultimately returning to academia. One or two are not academics in the strict sense of the word, coming to academia from the practice side, though most would clearly be considered fairly mainstream academics.

Each of the individuals interviewed, in his or her own way, evidenced a history of becoming – and, indeed, a need to become – 'fully who they are.'[57] They needed, in other words, to find their own source of power, and to use that power to do their best to make the world better, improve thinking in their fields, or effect social change – or to do all these things. Becoming fully who you are means, essentially, following you own lights, often as a maverick, rebel, or misfit of some sort, toward a purpose that has some element of 'beyond self' that is intended to do some good in the world. It is, in my view, this capacity that allows the internal 'light' to be lit – the light that attracts others to these people and their work, and that guides their shamanic intuition.

In this chapter, I explore how intellectual shamans go through a discovery or awareness-producing process to become fully who they are, to be true to themselves or their purpose and to the broader whole of which they are a part. This chapter also explores how the reality of taking this self-guided path meant that many of the intellectual shamans have, at some point in their lives – or throughout their lives – been, or at least felt like, rebels, mavericks, misfits, or outsiders. In the next chapter, we will look at how some of the intellectual shamans articulate their purposes – or what I call the power of purpose, and how they are called to that purpose. In following chapters, we will explore their orientation toward healing, connecting, and sensemaking – the three core shamanic activities as articulated by Frost and Egri. Following that, we will explore the particularly shamanic elements that some reveal in their stories and then look at the ways in which their shamanic work leads to wisdom – to their becoming the sages of their disciplines. We take this journey as a means of suggesting that, while the *intellectual* shaman trajectory can be useful for academics, the elements that make up a shamanic orientation are available to everyone.

Not every person evidenced the entire spectrum of this shamanic orientation. Collectively, however, there seems to be a clear pattern that leads me to argue that 'becoming fully who you are' and finding your purpose, combined with an orientation that goes beyond self or toward the greater good - i.e., the three orientations of healing, connecting (boundary-spanning), and sensemaking (spiritual leadership) discussed in the Chapters 4, 5, and 6 – are cornerstone elements of becoming shamanic. The key point here, though, is that there is no one path, as Scharmer notes in the quote at the start of this chapter. All individuals must find their own way to becoming who they truly must be and to their own particular source of power. For *intellectual* shamans, that source of power is most often found through intellectual contributions, their work, though it can also manifest itself in the linkage of work and practice, work and teaching, consulting, and, occasionally in other ways.

TRANSFORMATION TO SHAMAN: BECOMING FULLY WHO YOU ARE

Becoming fully who you are/must be is a process of learning, risk-taking, engagement with others and with issues, persistence, curiosity, and a willingness to (or inability to not) go in whatever direction your heart, intellect, or spirit leads you. Since shamans are inherently healers, it is also important that the direction be a constructive and positive one. Coming to be fully who you are involves a process of 'allowing' what is inside you – dreams, desires, instincts – to lead you to somehow, no matter in how small a way, try to make the world better. For some people, making the world better might be through scientific discovery, art or music, carpentry or building, working in a health care profession, helping people become financially better off, or in any number of other ways. For *intellectual* shamans within management disciplines (and probably most other academic disciplines), that orientation emerges largely through intellectual, teaching, and consulting contributions.

Finding the path to becoming fully one's self is a process of discovery that can happen quickly, with a trigger event or incident that brings rather sudden new awareness, insight, and direction. Equally, it can happen over time, and more opportunistically, gradually, bringing the individual to a path, a pattern of activities or work, that can be looked back on and made sense of retrospectively, but that was not necessarily planned. In the next chapter we will look at the emergent lives that some of the intellectual shamans followed, but here we focus on the discovery of the 'calling' to purpose itself.

The great mythologist Joseph Campbell has pointed out that, for many shamans, there is an actual crisis of transition, something that sparks a different awareness.[23] The crisis represents the 'call' to shamanism. We can see such triggers, crises, or transition points in the lives of many of the intellectual shamans, but not all, as for some it was a more gradual discovery process. The crisis, or, more accurately, trigger, which in traditional cultures can take the form of an illness, mental break, or vision quest, can for intellectual shamans be a moment of sudden awareness, insight, or other life-changing event. The trigger brings about new awareness and insight necessary to move towards one's source of power, one's calling. Mircea Eliade, in his important book on shamanism, points out not only that shamans are found in all cultures but that such a trigger event is common among traditional shamans, who were often believed to need to go through just such a crisis when they received the call to shamanism.[20,21]

Because of these crises, early researchers of shamanism thought that mental or other illness accompanied shamanism. But, as pointed out in the previous chapter, shamans have actually been found to be healthier and even more intelligent individuals than others. Often, though, they have gone through a trial or rite of initiation of some sort. The transition, in traditional cultures, is associated with a death-like or near-death experience in which one leaves behind the old person to become the new one, or, as I claim about intellectual shamans, to become fully who one has to be. Campbell states:

> [T]he shamanistic crisis, when properly fostered, yields an adult
> not only of superior intelligence and refinement, but also of greater
> physical stamina and vitality of spirit than is normal to the members
> of his group.[26] The crisis, consequently, has the value of a superior
> threshold initiation: superior, in the first place, because
> spontaneous, not tribally enforced, and in the second place, because
> the shift of reference of the psychologically potent symbols has been
> not from the family to the tribe but from the family to the
> universe.[23]

Of death and rebirth

Otto Scharmer articulates the death and dying process associated with this type of transition most clearly and directly, describing one of the experiences that most influenced how he became who he is today. He describes his transitions in terms of places that have deeply influenced how he lives and works:

The first [influential place] is where I was born, actually a farm.
It's an 800-year old farm [near Hamburg, Germany], 300 or 400 years
run by my family. My parents turned that [farm] some fifty years ago
into biodynamic farming. [. . .] So my parents kind of changed the
paradigm from conventional farming into organic, which is like
closed loop and diversity, symbiosis, all these things based on
biodynamic farming practices. That, of course, was a paradigm shift.
So I saw a little bit firsthand the reaction of the neighborhood and
how you have to go through a valley of death, so to speak, of all the
'nothing is working,' yet you still believe in this thing. It takes ten
years until the first successes come in, and then suddenly the
ministers are coming, the TV, and you are rewarded, and so on.

So, if you only see the tail end of that story, and the public
recognition. . . I saw firsthand also the other part, the valley of death,
and the long road, the journey of trials, really, bringing through a
profound innovation that is challenging many of the mainstream
assumptions. [. . .] I could also see on a micro level there how a
place-based community works, because every culture really is a
place-based community. So you try to cultivate a piece of land, and
you have a relationship with the larger community around, those
who take the products and so on, and how to structure these
relationships in more meaningful ways beyond markets. . .

That notion of being born to something new and dying to the old
was brought home even more vividly to Scharmer in a very real crisis
situation when he was sixteen. He describes the episode in his book
Theory U and also in the interview:

Yes, there were trigger events, sometimes more individually,
sometimes more on the collective level. I described some of them
also in my books. So one was when I must have been a sixteen-year
old. I returned from school from Hamburg and found the 358-year
old farmhouse we were living in on fire. Basically, the only thing left
was a gigantic burning heap of rubble. That kind of disruption that
happened right there, where the entire world I was living in no longer

existed, and where only in that moment I realized how much my whole old identity was attached to the physical, material possessions. All of the entire world that no longer was there. Then it feels like it pulls away the ground under your feet. You lose the old self, because these old dimensions of self are out, gone, kind of no longer there. So you drop into a state of nothingness.

But the surprising thing that happened to me at that moment was that I realized that I was not just that old self. There was still somebody standing there, taking all of that in, and out of that nowness, of that guy who was taking all of that in, something else happened that I felt like pulled up into a direction slightly, in fact kind of above my own body. I think this is commonly experienced, that also many athletes have described. Kind of suddenly, you begin to see yourself a little bit from above your own body. So I felt drawn to a direction, which was connected to a part of myself that I didn't even know that existed, which had to do with a future possibility that I could bring into reality, and that was intimately connected with my possible journey forward. So that was a very intense experience that I had never experienced before. That opened up another window, another aspect of self-knowing that ever since kind of has been become a very important guidance for me. But before that I didn't even know it could exist. So you could say that was a forced-upon experience of the U process.

So I saw that with the farmhouse on fire – the old world gone, old identities gone. Then you had to let go, I mean, unless you're in denial. There was a forced-upon letting go, and that created this space of possibility that I could connect to, that I didn't even know that existed before. So that's, in a nutshell, really what the U process is. It's letting go and letting come. But usually we are in a situation where we don't have the benefit of having our farmhouse going up in flames every noon time. So we need to find other techniques how to connect to that deeper place, other than this exterior intervention in the form of the crisis, a disruption.

David Cooperrider

David Cooperrider holds a BA from Augustana College, an MS from
George Williams College, and a PhD from Case Western Reserve
University. Currently he holds the Fairmount Minerals Professor of
Social Entrepreneurship at the Weatherhead School of Management,
Case Western Reserve University. Best known for his development of
the idea of appreciative inquiry, which is aimed at creating a positive
revolution in the leadership of change, Cooperrider is founder and
chair of the Fowler Center for Sustainable Value at Case Western, a
center whose value proposition is that sustainability is the business
opportunity of the twenty-first century – and that every social and
global issue can provide such opportunities to inspire businesses in
eco-innovation, social entrepreneurship, and new sources of value.
Named top researcher of the year at Case Western in 2005, Cooperrider
consults and advises organizations and institutions globally using the
appreciative inquiry framework, was named Faculty Pioneer by the
Aspen Institute and World Resources Council in 2007, and received the
American Society for Training and Development's highest award in
2004, among numerous other recognitions and honors. Cooperrider has,
at this point, published fifteen books and dozens of articles, including
the *Handbook of Transformative Cooperation* (with Sandy Piderit and
Ron Fry), several books on appreciative inquiry, and *The Organization
Dimensions of Global Change* (with Jane Dutton), and has been editor
of the *Journal of Corporate Citizenship* (with Ron Fry) and the research
series 'Advances in Appreciative Inquiry' (with Michel Avital).

It does not always take an actual crisis for new awareness
to emerge rather suddenly. Sometimes it happens when the individual
is exposed to a new situation and develops insight into something
not consciously present earlier. David Cooperrider, Fairmount
Minerals Professor of Social Entrepreneurship at Case Western
Reserve University and founder of the field of appreciative inquiry,
provides an example. He describes the process of gaining insight and
sudden awakening in his own discovery process when traveling to

Japan as an undergraduate at Augustana College, when he experienced an abrupt new awareness about the potentiality of life. Of this new context, which was entirely different from anything he had previously experienced, Cooperrider says:

> I received a grant to go study in Japan, a Lilly Foundation grant. [. . .] Obviously, it was a huge eye-opening cultural awakening for me, [because] I grew up. . .in a lower middle-class/poor family and had never been on a plane. But just stepping into the context of Japan. . . I can remember the first day I was there, looking out of our youth hostel from the top floor and seeing a factory across the road. All the Japanese employees and workers and managers up on the top floor were doing exercises and chanting and singing together early in the morning before they started their work. So I got interested in group dynamics and decision-making and how. . .different cultures create different societies, and so on.
>
> But the moment that had the huge impact on me as a young person was when I went to Hiroshima. It was really like an atomic bomb of awareness went off inside of my heart, inside of my chest. Oddly, instead of feeling really down, I felt an incredible sense about the miracle of life on this planet that's in our hands and what kinds of powers we had been given as a human family. [. . .] A question was born for me that never went away, and that was: 'What are we going to discover in the social sciences that's as powerful in a positive human sense as the atomic bomb is in a negative human sense?' For me, that was a question that has been with me ever since: what are we going to discover in the human sciences that is as powerful in a positive human sense as the atomic bomb is in a negative human sense?
>
> The words that came into my mind were 'the miracle of life on this planet,' and how taken for granted that had become and is. Shortly thereafter, I read a book by Albert Schweitzer called *Reverence for Life*. In it he was arguing for an ethical stance that could unite across all ethical stances. His conclusion was that the

ethic would be a reverence for life – that all wisdom traditions and faith traditions and religious traditions ultimately shared in that ethic. His belief was that ethical affirmation of life is what leads to new knowledge. I thought a little bit about that and really realized the reason appreciative inquiry is so powerful is because it does inspire research for not just what's best, but [for] what's next and what's possible. Joseph Campbell...said, 'Awe is what moves us forward as a human species.' It's when we see those higher reaches and higher possibilities that we wander beyond the data, almost like a good poet. In that sense theory might be more good theory and good social science might more like a good piece of poetry. It opens the world that Aristotle talked about the poetic; it opens the world to new possibilities.

Judith Ann (Judi) Neal, formerly director of the Tyson Center for Faith and Spirituality in the Workplace at the Sam M. Walton College of Business, University of Arkansas, also had a realization, albeit somewhat later in her life, that brought a sense of direction. Neal, now retired and continuing her spirituality in the workplace efforts, is author of the book *Edgewalkers*, which is about people who walk between worlds, at what could be called the interstices of organizations, and attempt to build bridges between those worlds. Although Neal is perhaps less well known as an academic than some of the other intellectual shamans, she is explicitly oriented to the spiritual and healing elements of shamanism that are core to the concept of intellectual shaman, helped to found the Academy of Management's Management, Spirituality and Religion Division, and uses her academic work to forward that agenda.

Judith Ann Neal

Judith Ann (Judi) Neal is the former and initial director of the Tyson Center for Faith and Spirituality in the Workplace at the Sam M. Walton College of Business at the University of Arkansas, and Professor Emeritus at the University of New Haven. Author of

Edgewalkers: People and Organizations that Take Risks, Build Bridges, and Break New Ground, and two related books, Neal edited the *Handbook of Faith and Spirituality in the Workplace*. With a PhD in organizational behavior from Yale University, Neal is a founder of the spirituality at work movement, and one of the founders of the Management, Spirituality, and Religion Division of the Academy of Management. She served as its second chair (when it was still an interest group). Neal also co-founded the *Journal of Management, Spirituality, and Religion*, and founded and directed the International Center for Spirit at Work. She created the International Spirit at Work Awards to honor organizations that are open about nurturing human spirit in the workplace. Widely published in academic journals, Neal also consults broadly with businesses about spirituality at work, and speaks publicly about the issue of spirituality and work.

Neal is atypical of academics in most respects. As the first in her family to attend college, she remembers, 'I didn't go back to school until I was twenty-eight. I started as a sophomore at twenty-eight and then graduated at thirty-one with my bachelor's degree, then went to Yale at age thirty-one and was at Yale for seven years. So I wasn't so young [when finishing the PhD].' First in her family to go to university, Neal had seen a movie when she was young in which the lead character had a PhD, and really admired that character for her strength and mystery-solving capabilities. As she remembers, 'I wanted to be like her when I grew up. So I wanted a PhD, whatever that was.'

While finishing her PhD at Yale, Neal was working at Honeywell Corporation as a manager of organizational development. Always a bit of a maverick, Neal found her professors questioning that path, because '[n]obody works full-time and goes here. You have to go here full-time.' But the work at Honeywell was on the cutting edge of experimental ways to manage, providing fodder for her research and an enormous growth opportunity, so she stuck it out, eventually earning the doctorate after seven years.

Things did not go particularly smoothly for Neal. As with other 'death to the old way' situations that some of the other intellectual shamans experienced, crisis ultimately led her to become who she needed to be. While at Honeywell, Neal faced an ethical crisis that caused her to whistleblow on certain company practices, which ended her career in business and resulted in her starting an academic career. Let Neal's words tell the story:

> Well, this is the critical turning point. I was working for Honeywell, had finished my dissertation, thought I was a fast tracker in Honeywell, in the high-talent program and getting to go to corporate headquarters all the time for special training. I really had my whole future in front of me. I worked in an ammunition plant, and I discovered that they were making faulty ammunition, and our clients, our customers, were the army, the navy. This is military ammunition. So this was really a huge serious issue, and, from the investigation that I did, it appeared that what we were doing was really dangerous to our own servicemen. So I blew the whistle. This was in '87, and in '87 you didn't hear much about whistleblowing at all, and I had no clue what to do. I just knew I couldn't live with myself.
>
> I guess in terms of boundary-spanning this is a real point of integration for me, because I had always been interested in spirituality, but I was very private. I would read something spiritual before I went to sleep and study books when no one was looking. I did not take classes or be involved in any kind of open way, because I didn't want anybody to know this is what I was interested in, other than here or there I would meet a few friends. I had some friends at Honeywell and we had conversations about spirituality. But it was something you definitely kept under the radar, and it was something you kept compartmentalized. . .
>
> So in that crisis I ended up feeling like I could no longer work for corporations, because my life got threatened. I was treated horribly, and people really attempted to cover up. I was isolated and all my job

duties were taken away. I was told that the plant might get shut down. That it would be all my fault that 200 people would be out of work. My boss said, 'You'd better watch your back, because it's going to be dangerous for you because people hate you,' which turned out not to be true at all. People were grateful that somebody [had] finally put an end to the wrongdoing. But...my trust of corporations was really destroyed. My sense of wanting to help corporations be more effective was just totally damaged, because I had been really committed to making the workplace a more meaningful place. It's like all my ideals were just smashed in the middle of this. So I just felt like I could no longer work in the career I'd prepared for, and I didn't know what to do with myself. I started selling Mary Kay [cosmetics]. It seemed like a woman's organization that had God as its center ideals.

Selling cosmetics proved problematic, and, after struggling for a year and a half, Neal came to a realization about her purpose that has shaped her career ever since:

I could continue to read spiritual literature and do my own inner work, meditate, and try to understand why this had happened in my life and what I was supposed to do. Then I really came a place of inner peace that I could just trust...that things were happening for a reason and let go of trying to understand even why. I had to just trust that my life had a bigger purpose than I understood and that I was being guided. Out of the blue a year later an offer came to teach a course at the University of New Haven, and I did, and then an offer came to apply for a position, and I did.

Saying 'Yes' to the offer, Neal pondered what her experience had taught her – concluding that working with future leaders was the key, recalling her thoughts: 'Maybe somehow I could give them the courage and strength to stick with their convictions and not get caught up in some of the unethical stuff that I saw in the workplace.' The other insight, as it relates to becoming fully oneself, was – as Neal puts it – to learn some lessons about my own integrity and my own authenticity, and stop trying to please people and be what I thought they wanted me to be. I needed to take a stand for being my authentic self, and my authentic self is somebody who cares about spirituality. So I had to stop hiding it.

Of growing awareness

Opening both the world and the self to new possibilities is following the call to intellectual shamanism, along with seemingly insatiable curiosity and the willingness to follow that curiosity. Sometimes, as is the case with Nancy Adler, now the S. Bronfman Chair in Management at Montreal's McGill University, Canada, it takes a number of related events that make the transition to greater self-, other-, and world awareness possible. Adler was born in California and attended the University of California at Los Angeles (UCLA), starting out in marine biology and eventually studying economics, in part influenced by an uncle who was employed by the City of New York to investigate how public monies were being spent.

Nancy J. Adler

Nancy Adler is the S. Bronfman Chair in Management at McGill University in Montreal, Canada. She holds a BA in economics, an MBA, and a PhD in management from the University of California at Los Angeles. Adler is best known for her research on global leadership and cross-cultural management, having written some 125 articles and ten books. She is also known for her work on culture and leadership. Among her most notable books are *From Boston to Beijing: Managing with a Worldview, International Dimensions of Organizational Behavior, Leadership Insight, Women in Management Worldwide,* and *Competitive Frontiers: Women Managers in a Global Economy.* Adler has received many teaching and other awards, including McGill's first Distinguished Teaching Award in Management (which she has actually received twice), has been named as a 3M Teaching Fellow, and is a Fellow of the Academy of Management, among numerous other honors.

Also a painter, she has written on integrating the arts into management education, and is co-author of a prize-winning paper (with Anne-Wil Harzing) entitled 'When knowledge wins: transcending the sense and nonsense of academic rankings,' along with 'Leading beautifully,' 'Going beyond the dehydrated language of management,' and 'Daring to care: scholarship that supports the courage of our convictions' (with Hans Hansen), among numerous other articles.

Adler notes, 'I was intrigued by the political and societal part of it, and economics was the vocabulary.' After facing sexist questions in a competition for a Regents Scholarship, she began to realize 'the tension around who you are as a woman if you're headed toward something professional,' particularly during the early days of the women's movement in the late 1960s when she was in college, when the 'subtle subtext was that as a woman I was supposed to get educated, then I was supposed to meet a nice Jewish man, fall in love, get married, and raise children.'

An excellent student, Adler got the Regents Scholarship and started in marine biology, then, facing registration problems, decided to switch to economics 'because economics didn't have a sequence, ...had the halo of my uncle in there, but it also had the fewest requirements of any major that were predetermined. I could study whatever...so I took all sorts of courses.' Despite being a somewhat naïve young woman who had never seriously thought about a career, Adler was one of fifty students nationwide to secure a White House summer internship during the era of protest against the Vietnam War, the beginnings of the environmental movement, and the boycott of California grapes because of labor issues, all of which 'in a huge way opened my eyes.' Going back to UCLA, eyes more open, she ran into several trigger moments that forwarded her developing awareness. Adler explained that, after getting tear-gassed during anti-Vietnam demonstrations, experiencing the first Earth Day in 1970, and being in California during the turmoil of the anti-war period, she began awakening to her Jewish identity, having taken a course from Rabbi Richard Levy during her freshman year that brought together thinking from sociologists, historians, psychologists, and other disciplines. Let Adler describe her awakening:

> [It was] the best of what our university should be doing. Help us understand where we live and how we might live here. We go to the lectures. Lectures are fine. And we have discussion. [...] I was lucky that my discussion group leader was Rabbi Levy, and he asks us to write down ten descriptors of ourselves, like woman or whatever, and then imagine what it would be like to take each one away. So how identified are you to those various categories that society uses? Good exercise, right?
>
> Well, one of the things that came out is I was the only one in the entire group who didn't have 'Jewish' on my list. Both of my parents are Jewish, but I was brought up an absolute nothing. That's a combination of mom's [an Austrian refugee who lost many family members in concentration camps and had been thrown onto the streets of Vienna by Gestapo agents][58] reaction that there can't be a God and World War II, and my father wasn't brought up religious. I was brought up in a totally Christian neighborhood. [...] It was hugely important to me in terms of 'Where are my deep roots?' and 'Where is my spiritual being?' and 'What does that even mean?'

The transition to awareness and to her life's work for Adler took even more twists and turns, however. In the next quotes, we see evidence of both the curiosity, the willingness to question accepted wisdom, and the risk-taking necessary for intellectual shamanism that characterizes Adler's career, as well as that of the other intellectual shamans. We also see the slow build of awareness, rather than the sudden insight experienced by Cooperrider and Scharmer. Adler recalls:

> So now I'm in my senior year [back at UCLA after spending an eye-opening summer as a presidential intern in Washington], and I'm in one of the advanced economics courses. But the professor is basically saying [that] the economic system works based on the

market system. I raised my hand – and picture these classes are 200
to 250 people – and I asked, 'If the market system works, then how
come the spinach and lettuce that's sold at the Watergate Safeway'
(I had been living right near the [upscale] Watergate, so we went to
the Watergate Safeway) 'is fresher, greener and costs distinctly
less than the spinach and lettuce that's sold at the Capitol Hill
Safeway?' [...] The area right around Capitol Hill is quite poor. [...]
'How come it's all wilted and it costs more?' The professor tries to
answer me. He says, 'Well, it's the preferences of the people.' I said,
'So what you're trying to tell me is that the people who live near
Capitol Hill prefer to pay more money for wilted lettuce?'

He tried to say, 'Well, the insurance in those areas...,' and I said,
'So what you're saying is that...,' repeating back to him – at which
point, in front of everybody, he says, 'You with the yellow strings
in your hair' (I had pigtails at that time with yellow ribbons), 'get out
of my class and never come back.'

So picture the kind of loops were going on inside me. I'd been
brought up to be polite. In many ways, I was brought up to fit in. That
was strongly influenced by my mom's being an immigrant; she
wanted us to be American and feel American. Also because of the
hell my mom had gone through in World War II, she very definitely
needed to believe that the US was different, was good, was just.
Originally, when she met my father, she didn't believe that she
should bring kids into the world because the world had become such
an evil place. My father, being American, convinced her that that
was not true, that America was different, that they could create a
loving home.

That meant that it was only when I got to UCLA that I began to
realize that this perfect, beautiful American world wasn't quite as
perfect and beautiful as I had been brought up to believe. That wasn't
by any means just an intellectual shift. [...] Having a European
mother, there's a definite deference to both hierarchy and certainly a
deference to educated people. So the concept that a professor
wouldn't be telling me the truth was completely foreign to me.

[...] I didn't even really have the concept of the difference between truth and false versus opinion.

As Nancy Adler's story suggests, not all the transitions that bring about the awareness needed for becoming who you must be are overt crises or sudden events. Sometimes awareness comes gradually, over time, as we will find in others as well. For Adler, coming to be 'who she truly is' was a rather lengthy process. Even in traditional cultures, shamans are apprenticed and receive training, insight, and experiences that build and enhance awareness and the healing orientation that characterizes intellectual shamans, as largely happened with Adler.

OF EMERGENT FOCUS

In traditional societies, some future shamans receive the call to shamanism because they are in a shaman's family, and others are drawn to the practice for different reasons that have nothing to do with physical or mental crisis. In the case of intellectual shamans, it can be because they are drawn to a particular issue. Still, the process is one of discovery of who one must be, and that process in many respects necessitates a leaving behind of the old self and adopting of a new self, willing to act and work in the world in new ways.

Stuart Hart was the S. C. Johnson Chair in Sustainable Global Enterprise and Professor of Management and Organizations at the Johnson School of Management, Cornell University, now emeritus, and at this writing is a chaired professor at the University of Vermont who is also pursuing his entrepreneurial instincts in sustainable enterprise and education. Hart's story illustrates yet another type of path: awareness that begins at quite a young age but then follows a rather crooked path to fulfillment.

Stuart Hart

Stuart (Stu) Hart holds a BA from the University of Rochester, an MFS from Yale University School of Forestry and Environmental Studies, and a PhD from the University of Michigan. He was the S. C. Johnson Chair in Sustainable Global Enterprise and Professor of Management and Organizations at the Johnson School of Management at Cornell University, now emeritus, and is currently the Steven Grossman Endowed Chair in Sustainable Business at the University of Vermont. Hart is also the founding director of the Green Leap Global Initiative, and is a Distinguished Fellow at the William Davidson Institute at the University of Michigan. He is the recipient of numerous awards, and president of Enterprise for a Sustainable World. He is considered one of the leading world authorities, indeed founders, of scholarship and practice on issues of poverty and sustainability, particularly in relation to business strategy. In addition to his position at Cornell, Hart was the Hans Zulliger Distinguished Professor of Sustainable Enterprise at the University of North Carolina's Kenan–Flagler Business School, where he founded the Center for Sustainable Enterprise and the Base of the Pyramid Learning Laboratory, and prior to that appointment taught strategy at the University of Michigan's Ross School of Business, where he was founding director of the corporate environmental management program. In addition to his serial entrepreneurship around sustainability issues, Hart has published seven books and written more than seventy papers , including 'Beyond greening: strategies for a sustainable world,' which won the McKinsey Best Article Award in *Harvard Business Review*, the seminal article 'The fortune at the bottom of the pyramid,' with C. K. Prahalad, which started the 'BoP' movement, and the book *Capitalism at the Crossroads*, which the University of Cambridge noted was one of the top fifty sustainability books of all time.

Hart's path to intellectual shamanism involves an emergent lifelong interest in issues of sustainability, a field he helped to found. Unlike some of the other intellectual shamans, Hart's interest was piqued at an early age and only grew more powerful as the years passed. Talking about his vision, Hart says:

> I think it is a classic case of not knowing at all that I would be where I am now. Not having any idea that this would be [my future]. There was just no way to know that. So one thing led to another kind of thing. [...] It really goes back to high school, or even a little before. [...] I grew up in western New York and we had the steel industry

and all that kind of stuff. It was pretty nasty in the '50s, early '60s, a lot of soot. [...] It was like China is now. [...] So I would ask why; when I was ten or twelve, [the] answer typically was, 'Well, kid, get used to it. If you want to have prosperity, this is the price you pay. This is the smell of money.' It just never really made much sense to me...

There were other things that just seemed to be strange. [...] Back in the late '50s, early '60s..., it was just commonplace to litter. We'd go on family vacations in the family wagon when the interstate system was just being built, and people would finish something and they'd just throw it out the window. It was just normal; that's what people did. I'll never forget: my brother and I were in the back seat; we were on one of these car trips during the summer, maybe 1959 or 1960, and we were just finishing [eating], and we had bags and paper and whatnot. My brother and I were just about to throw it out the window, and my mother said, 'No, no! Wait, wait! You can't just throw that out the window like that. You have to wad it up first, because if you just throw out loose paper like that it could blow on the people's windshield behind us.' So, she was very considerate. Stuff like that just didn't really seem to make a lot of sense, and that's probably what stoked my early interest.

Then...especially [at] college, in the late '60s, early '70s, there was a professor [who] really made a difference. He was a geology professor who was considered sort of a radical at the time. Strange for a geology professor, he taught a course on environmental issues, and that's what really did it. Then I took everything that I could possibly take at the university that remotely related. So, from there, I decided that's really what I wanted to do.

The future path was far from straightforward for Hart, however, who did his PhD at the University of Michigan after getting a masters' degree at the Yale School of Forestry and Environmental Studies, and then stayed on at Michigan as a faculty member. After a brief stint in a program called the Decentralized Solar Energy Technology Assessment program, Hart became interested in corporate strategy and began working at the Institute on Man and Science. Encouraged by his boss to get a PhD, Hart notes, 'I went to Michigan and enrolled in this interdepartmental program, but it was focused on policy and strategy. So my dissertation focused on, believe it or not, integrating external stakeholder voices in decision-making and what impact does that have on decision quality. I actually started it before Ed [Freeman] came out with the stakeholder management book.'

After finishing the PhD in 1983, Hart began working at Michigan's Institute for Social Research in a group called the Center for Research on the Utilization of Scientific Knowledge (CRUSK) – the name, as he sardonically comments, 'thinking really academic acronyms.' After a couple of years he landed in a tenure track position at Michigan, where he became involved with an intellectually challenging group that included C. K. Prahalad, a mentor and later co-author with Hart of the bottom of the pyramid concept, for which the pair are well known. Still not centered in his passion for sustainability, Hart recalls the next steps – and the risk-taking that sometimes is needed to become fully who you are:

> By the late '80s I was beginning to have an identity crisis, because,
> of course, you get swept up in all that [need for academic publications
> in top-tier journals]. The dominant culture is just 'Put your head
> down.' I was writing stuff about strategy process and had some pieces
> that came out in that domain on models for thinking about strategic
> process and its impact on performance. It was moderately interesting.
> Then teaching the core course in strategy, but by the late '80s I had
> tried on a few occasions to try to bring environment stuff in, and then
> was just roundly [resisted]. One person said, 'Kid, just forget it. That's
> a career ender. Just put your head down, publish your articles. Teach
> the [traditional material]. Don't question that. If you do that, get
> tenure, everything will be great.'

But, as Hart's story continues, it becomes clear that, for people following their own inner light, their own instincts, simply doing what others say needs to be done – following the traditional path – is insufficient. Hart illustrates the importance of having a mentor or 'teacher' to guide the burgeoning intellectual shaman:

> By the late '80s I was miserable. I really did not like what I was doing and I really didn't like what I was becoming. So I made a very conscious choice, and it was because, certainly at Michigan, C. K. [Prahalad] was a major factor there. Very few other people there counseled me in any other way than 'Put your head down and keep writing the eight journal articles [needed for tenure].' C. K. was one of the people that said, 'Look, you've got this weird background, why wouldn't you go for this? If you don't, you'll look back in twenty years, and you'll regret this for the rest of your life. You should go for it. You should always go with what your passion is.' Not many other people gave that advice. [...] Back then there was still that pretty significant split between social issues and environment. [...] I spent a fair amount of time talking to [Tom Gladwin and Paul Shrivastava, two of the very few management scholars oriented to the natural environment], in 1989/1990. That really also helped me make the call, which I made as a very conscious choice in 1990, that I was going to devote the rest of my professional life to bridging the connection between business strategy and environment.

Taking the path to inner guidance (or spiritual guidance, as Judi Neal might say) is fraught with risk, as Hart found out when he was subsequently denied tenure at Michigan. Ultimately, as we will see when we pick up his story later, the risks proved worth taking, but the path is not guaranteed and certainly not easy.

OF WINDING ROADS

Two other stories illustrate the complexity of paths that can be taken to intellectual shamanism, along with several points that will be elaborated and explored in greater depth later on: the emergent and unplanned nature of many of the intellectual shamans' lives, the numerous types of influences that can help to shape the intellectual shaman, the healing orientation, and the 'outsider' status that many feel at some point in their lives. Dave Brown's story of his early life illustrates not only the complexity of the 'call' to intellectual shamanism but also these other elements. Note that Brown's story also illustrates the 'dying and rebirth' theme characteristic of so many shamans, as he tells how he transformed from 'dork' to 'preppy' to Peace Corps volunteer to law student and, ultimately, to intellectual and change-maker.

L. David Brown

L. David (Dave) Brown is senior research fellow, Hauser Center for Nonprofit Organizations, Harvard Kennedy School, having retired from his position as lecturer in public policy and coordinator of international programs in 2009. He holds an undergraduate degree from Harvard, and PhD and JD degrees from Yale. Prior to joining Harvard Kenndy School, Brown was Professor of Organizational Behavior at Boston University's School of Management for nearly twenty years. During that time he also served as president of the Institute for Development Research (IDR), a not-for-profit research/consulting center for development and institution-building in developing nations, where he worked alongside his wife, Jane Covey, who ultimately ran the IDR when Brown left Boston University for Harvard. Brown is best known for his research and practice-based consulting on large-scale social transformation and institution-/capacity-building in developing nations. He continues active engagement with the Hauser Center's research on civil society organizations in China and related projects. Author of numerous books and articles at the intersection of consulting, scholarship, and practice, particularly around large-scale change projects, Brown was a Fulbright lecturer in India, and served in the Peace Corps in Ethiopia in his youth. Among his best-known books are *Managing Conflict at Organizational Interfaces* and *Creating Credibility: Legitimacy and Accountability for Transnational Civil Society*, and he has co-edited the books *Transnational Civil Society* and *Practice–Research Engagement for Civil Society in a Globalizing World*.

Brown details the background that brought him to where he is today, and some of the transformations – 'little deaths' that took place in that process:

It probably makes sense to go back to being a kid, because I sort of grew up with a foot in different places. My family moved to Maine when I was seven, I think, so I grew up in Bangor, which is a small town in middle Maine. Then I went off to high school, to boarding school. Growing up in Bangor I was a prototypical brain. I was overweight, had braces on my teeth, got straight 'A's, and had heavy glasses. When I went away to school, I wanted to be something different. I didn't want to be a dork. So I worked hard at not being a dork, while doing well in studies, but trying to be a different person than I had been up to then. Then went off to college and gradually decided I didn't like very much what I had been in prep school, which was a sort of classically cynical, sarcastic prep school kid. But I didn't really catch fire on anything when I was in college. I spent a lot of time singing and spent a lot of time at 47 Mt. Auburn St. [now Club Passim, a famous folk club in Cambridge, Massachusetts], listening to Tom Rush and Joanie Baez and so on.

Then Kennedy invented the Peace Corps when I was a senior in college. [...] So I was an undergraduate [at Harvard] and sort of wondering what the hell I was going to do when I finished. I thought at some point I would probably go to graduate school, but had no idea of what I might want to go to graduate school in. The Peace Corps seemed like a very good way to take some time off after college and stop studying and do something interesting and not be in the military. So I went to Ethiopia with the second group of volunteers to go there and spent a couple of years [as] a community development, a community organizer volunteer. [...] I don't think I did much for Ethiopia, but Ethiopia did a lot for me. I got pretty committed to the notion of development and trying to make that happen. My father was a surgeon and very committed to doing right by his patients and my mother had been a teacher and was sort of a lefty Democrat. My grandparents were Quakers, so there was a sort of long tradition in the family, but I don't think I was very aware of it at the time. But I think a lot of my work has been shaped by concern with doing something about the world in terms of social justice and fairness and development and sustainability and so on.

As with many of the intellectual shamans, Brown took his time finding his way to purpose. Returning home, Brown found himself faced yet again with an uncertain future. Having taken the law aptitude test, and been influenced by some Peace Corps members who were lawyers, or, as he later realized, 'probably refugees from the law,' he decided to go to law school. He remembers:

I walked off the boat from Ethiopia, and two weeks later was in law school and sort of walked into my first class, which was torts, and had no clue what a tort was. As soon as I found out what a tort was, I thought, 'Who gives a rat's ass?' A lot of law school was difficult. People were very excited about what seemed to me extraordinarily abstract and silly points, when the real question of the world was 'Is there enough food and water for most of the people in it?' I think there were three ex-Peace Corps volunteers in my class, and we were all sort of wandering around like 'What the hell is going on here?'

After a number of what he terms 'encounters' about the role of lawyers with a distinguished legal scholar named Eugene Victor Rostow, former dean of the Law School, Brown came to an insight that shaped his future: 'I was under the impression that lawyers had something to do with justice, and Gene Rostow took it on himself to educate me out of that silly notion. He persuaded me, but also persuaded me I didn't want to have anything to do with law.' This insight connected with Brown's innate curiosity to fuel his interest in many different subjects that provide a background for his later work, as he worked his way through in law school taking as many courses in different departments as possible. Then, as he recounts,

I finally took a course in organizational behaviour, and I thought, 'Hey, this is interesting!' Yale had a four-year program where you could get a master's degree along with your law degree. So I enrolled in the four-year program. [...] After the first semester I applied to and got into the doctoral program, and had the experience of having my intellectual fuse lit. I just thought, 'Holy smoke! I need to know all sorts of stuff yesterday.' So, in my second semester in the four-year program, I think I took seven courses and taught one. I just went berserk and got very excited about the substance of OB. I ended up writing a thesis for the law school that was really about conflict and did not contain the word 'law.'

Brown's wandering and questioning attitude, and his desire to take a wide variety of courses, were part of the insatiable curiosity that characterizes intellectual shamans. But it took a few twists and turns before he finally found his calling. Even after the doctoral program Brown was not clear about entering academia, but was convinced to try by his Yale mentors. With three offers in hand, one of which was withdrawn at the last minute, he, in a sense, stumbled into his first appointment at Case Western Reserve University, where he would be given the freedom to do the work that interested him. Brown recalls:

I decided to go to Case because I knew I wanted to test how I felt about doing research and writing. I thought at Case I would be under more pressure to do good practice work than to do good research. At that point I knew that I have a tendency to react badly to pressure, and I would be more likely to do my intellectual work if I weren't feeling like I *ought* to do it.

Jane Dutton is the Robert L. Kahn Distinguished University Professor at the University of Michigan, and a highly accomplished scholar of organizational behavior. Perhaps one of the best-known OB scholars anywhere, Dutton was awarded the Academy of Management's lifetime scholarly achievement award at its annual meeting in 2012 and has received numerous other awards for her scholarship. Her work is unconventional and challenging of existing theories, frequently qualitative and interpretive in nature, and constantly seeking ways to make organizations better for the people who work in them.

Jane E. Dutton

Jane Dutton is the Robert L. Kahn Distinguished University Professor of Business Administration and Psychology at the University of Michigan, Ann Arbor, where she has been since 1989. She holds a BA degree from Colby College in Maine, and an MA and PhD in organizational behavior from Northwestern University. Dutton has published more than 100 articles and chapters in top-tier journals and books, edited eleven books, and written *Energize Your Workplace: How to Build and Sustain High-Quality Connections at Work*. Best known for her work on compassion and resilience in organizations and as one of the founders of the emerging positive organizational scholarship movement, Dutton focuses on processes that build employees' capabilities and strengths. Earlier scholarship emphasized the interpretation of strategic issues, organizational adaptation, and organizational identity and change. An innovative thinker and scholar, she has received numerous awards for scholarly achievement, including the *Academy of Management Journal*'s best paper award, the *Administrative Science* Quarterly Award for Scholarly Contribution, and the *Journal of Management Inquiry*'s Breaking the Frame Award, in addition to numerous other awards for scholarly contributions, including the Academy of Management's Distinguished Scholar award in 2012. The University of Michigan named her a University Professor in 2007.

Dutton's is not a story of clear vision guiding her to her current status. Rather, just as Dave Brown did, she 'stumbled' into knowing who she needed to become after numerous twists and turns. That stumbling took place in the context of an early failed marriage, which provided the crisis and the death of the old ideas that leads to rebirth and that motivated her to action. A rather unfocused undergraduate, Dutton got serious about her studies after meeting a professor named Tom Morrione at Colby College, where she was studying. Morrione was a Herbert Blumer student, and, as Dutton recalls, 'I remember being in his class, and it really was "Whoa! I love what he's teaching us!"' Sociology was the first time I really fell in love with an academic subject, besides art history.'

The general context was the early 1970s first oil crisis, and Dutton got involved in Morrione's research to consider a four-day work and school week as an energy-saving mechanism, doing random sampling in Maine. She fell in love with the work, recalling:

> I just loved it. I loved hearing peoples' stories. I loved the process of learning from other people, and it was really fun to think it might actually have impact on policy... [S]o that was my first taste of research, but I still didn't think I would go to graduate school.

As a woman, however, Dutton faced similar expectations to what Nancy Adler had faced – i.e., that girls went to college in that time period only to find a husband. Dutifully, Dutton was married a week after graduating, and then, unable to find a job while living in Orono, Maine, she began waitressing. As with many of the other intellectual shamans, luck in the form of an opportunity taken provided impetus for the next steps and launched her on her way, almost inadvertently. Dutton continues:

> [Then] I heard that this economist at the University of Maine had gotten a grant from the National Science Foundation. I thought, 'OK, I have research experience,' so I literally begged. I hounded that guy every week. He would say, 'I don't know if I'm going to hire someone.' He did end up telling me he hired me because he just couldn't face me showing up again. [For] the first six months, he didn't know what to do with me. I spent a lot of time in the library trying to make up work, but I worked on this project for three years. It was wonderful! It was an interdisciplinary project with two sociologists and two economists on the adoption of new technology

in the footwear industry. So it was really an exposure to organizational studies. I was a secretary for a really long time, and then, by the end, I was doing all the training. I got to travel with the research group. It turned out that, when he became [US] president, Jimmy Carter made first domestic trade decision about the footwear industry, so we got to go testify. I went with them to Washington, and they testified for the Council of Economic Advisors about what we learned about what was conducive to new technology adoption in the footwear industry.

After a while, single again, and without a real plan, Dutton applied to MBA programs and ended up in the PhD program at Northwestern University, because

[t]hey had a center for science and technology there, and they were really networked colleagues. I had people who really believed in me as a researcher, so I just got in the back door.

Although there were more twists and turns before Dutton eventually landed at Michigan, the key point is that, while her intellect and ability were evident – and others certainly recognized them – moving on a straight path toward an academic life was certainly not in Dutton's early plans. It took the crisis of a divorce at a young age – and uncertainty about the future – to motivate Dutton to engage with the PhD program. By then the spark of interest in understanding organizations, particularly how to make them work better, was already ignited, only to become the flame that has supported Dutton throughout her career.

REBELS, MAVERICKS, MISFITS, AND OUTSIDERS

Almost by definition, coming to be fully who you really are puts a person outside the mainstream – because, in following one's heart or own path, an individual is less likely to do what others do or think acceptable, or what others necessarily expect of him or her. Many of the intellectual shamans discovered this reality in the course of finding their ways. In fact, Krippner in a paper on the 'Psychology of shamanism'[17] notes that, in many respects, shamans represent the 'marginalized other.' Being something of a misfit, an outsider, a rebel, a debunker, a maverick, or an otherwise marginalized person also fits the description of many of the intellectual shamans, either in the work they have chosen to do or in some other more personal aspect of their lives, making them feel as if they did not quite fit in. This element of intellectual shamanism is already clear in the stories of Dave Brown and Jane Dutton.

A core aspect of becoming shamanic is discovering what your own source of 'power' is – i.e., what it is that you will bring to serve the world in some way. This power is the gift that shamans – intellectual or other – offer to the world. The process of discovering that gift or power may not be straightforward or easy – and this may be why 'outsider' or 'misfit' status, for at least part of their lives, is so common among the intellectual shamans.

Their power, or what I will call the power of purpose in the next chapter, combined with the strength to pursue that purpose, make many of the intellectual shamans not quite fit the normal academic mold, not quite follow the accepted path, or not quite adhere to common wisdom. In becoming fully who they are, they also set out, whether deliberately or not, to find their own paths, their own ways of thinking, doing, and being in the world. Thus, often they do not necessarily desire to conform to what is expected, either by mainstream academia or by others. For example, many successful academics would today claim that the path to success lies in publishing primarily in top-tier journals (or, in some fields, books), doing quantitative and rather narrowly defined, strictly discipline-based research, and staying within an accepted canon of work – i.e., not questioning the system too much. Career paths are meant to be rather straightforward as well, seeking tenure at the most prestigious institution possible being seen the 'best' way of doing things, and then using tenured status to gain more prestige and acclaim through editorial appointments, more publishing, and, in management fields, sometimes consulting.

Not so for the intellectual shamans. Not quite fitting in because they following their own inner lights, they do what is important for them (not others), which often means doing things such as developing pioneering ideas that put them outside the normal stream of intellectual discourse within their fields – and then sometimes having the field center back in on what they have articulated. Or it can mean doing things that are seen by others as career killers (as with Stuart Hart's interest in sustainability early on in his career, a similar story that we will explore later with respect to Andy Hoffman's career).

Collectively, the twenty-eight individuals studied have pioneered new ideas and sometimes even whole fields, followed 'crooked' career paths, published their work in whatever ways seemed appropriate to the work, and questioned both the system and many of the commonly accepted ideas within their disciplines or fields. This need to follow one's own way means that intellectual shamans are sometimes rebels, mavericks, misfits, and outsiders, at least at some points of their lives and careers. Not quite fitting in can be deliberate or inadvertent; it can mean questioning the status quo, or doing things differently from what common wisdom or the accepted path suggests. Of course, it (almost) goes without saying that all of them worked incredibly hard, so their success, while never guaranteed, is at least in part a product of hard work – not just being different.

Indeed, in some respects it seems that many of the intellectual shamans had to be misfits, because, quite often, they simply see things differently from how others do (my cousin calls this skill 'seeing around corners'). 'Seeing' things differently – and it is 'seeing' that all shamans do – sets one apart from others. Shamans, in their healing, connecting, and sensemaking roles, the key roles that Frost and Egri identify, need to 'see' or somehow sense what needs to change. Almost by definition, they do this in ways that others cannot yet see. I would note here that, in my own shamanic practice, we have identified two main modalities – seeing and 'feeling' – as key paths of insight and healing. Both are important and equally powerful. It seems that some people are better 'seers' and others are better 'feelers,' though everyone uses both types of sensing to some extent and both sets of skills can be developed and enhanced through practice. From what I can observe in the interviews, it also seems that most of the intellectual shamans interviewed tend to be seers, in part perhaps because of the nature of their work – or perhaps they have chosen intellectual work because they are seers. Otto Scharmer also talks about such 'seeing' in his book *Theory U*,[57] as a core aspect of coming to be one's realized self – and in my view it is key to becoming shamanic, and also to gaining wisdom.[59,60]

We have already observed how Dave Brown felt like a misfit (in his words, a 'dork') as a youth and how he transformed himself several times. If we follow his career forward from where we left off, we find that there were several points at which he took significant life/career risks to be able to carry out the social change and development work that he wanted to do. These risks include leaving Case Western Reserve to spend a year in India, returning to Boston (not Cleveland, where Case Western Reserve is located) without a job, and ultimately joining Boston University where he gained tenure and full professorship. At the time he joined Boston University, he also become president of a then foundering non-profit organization, the Institute for Development Research, and then ran it for nearly twenty years with his wife, Jane Covey, who has been both life and work partner and, in his view, central to his success. With his heart in the development work, in 1990 he gave up his full professorship at Boston University to become senior lecturer at the Harvard Kennedy School's Hauser Center for Nonprofit Organizations, where he believed that his work on social change and development could be furthered better. Hardly a prototypical academic career!

Brown is not alone in this respect, though, as most of the intellectual shamans, at one time or another, found themselves in some way outside the accepted canon, academic (or life) norms, or career paths. That these individuals have achieved as much career status as they have, however, can be attributed to the impact of their ideas and work; they have earned what Peter Frost, following Edwin

Hollander,[61] calls 'idiosyncrasy credits.' That is, they did enough good and well-accepted mainstream work in what Thomas Kuhn calls normal science,[62] or good enough out-of-the-mainstream work and writing that they transformed thinking in their fields, thus earning their credibility, their own idiosyncrasy credits.[63] Despite the risky nature of what many intellectual shamans did, these idiosyncrasy credits ultimately allowed them to simultaneously be successful and go off the beaten track.

Philip Mirvis, organizational consultant and winner of the 2013 Academy of Management's Scholar-Practitioner Award (one of four major awards granted each year), is someone who did not follow a traditional academic path yet has made significant academic contributions over the years. Denied tenure at Boston University, his first academic appointment in the early 1980s, he became an organizational consultant who continued doing research and publishing, following what can only be called a crooked road throughout his career.

Philip H. Mirvis

Philip (Phil) Mirvis holds a BA from Yale University and a PhD in organizational psychology from the University of Michigan, and has, over the years, taught at Boston University, Jiao Tong University in Shanghai, China, the London Business School, and in the Leadership for Change program at Boston College. Author of ten books and dozens of articles, Mirvis focuses on large-scale organizational change, workforce and workplace character, and business leadership in society. A fellow of the Work/Family Roundtable, board member of Citizens Development Corporation, and former trustee of the Foundation for Community Encouragement, and Society for Organizational Learning, Mirvis' books include *The Cynical Americans* (with Donald L. Kanter), *To the Desert and Back: The Story of One of the Most Dramatic Business Transformations on Record* (with Karen Ayas and George Roth), and *Beyond Good Company: Next Generation Corporate Citizenship* (with Bradley K. Googins and Steven Rochlin), among others. Mirvis is best known for bridging between the world of ideas and practice, having

worked closely on issues of organizational transformation with the
Royal Dutch Shell Group, Ben & Jerry's, and Unilever, as well as other
major corporations including PepsiCo, Mitsubishi (Japan), and the SK
Group (South Korea), to name a few. His 2008 *Academy of Management
Learning and Education* paper 'Executive development through
consciousness-raising experiences' won that journal's Best Paper
Award. In 2013 Mirvis was awarded the Academy of Management's
Scholar-Practitioner Award.

As an independent organizational psychologist and consultant,
Mirvis has made a career out of being what he calls a gadfly and a
raconteur or storyteller: 'The last twenty years I have been self-
employed. I move into different environments and go back and
forth between being a gadfly, provoking and stirring things up, and
a raconteur, watching what happens and reflecting on it. I haven't
been intentional in what I do. I look up and things just come in over
the transom...'

It seems Mirvis was a 'rule-breaker' right from his days in
Catholic grammar school, when his teacher, a nun, wanted him to
show all his math calculations in long division. He recalls, 'I said,
"No, that takes too much time; I'm not interested." And the nun
said, "Well, that doesn't matter, these are the rules." I guess I've
been a rule-breaker ever since. I don't follow stupid rules. So I was
ultimately expelled from elementary school.'

More provocation and confrontations with rules met Mirvis
when he next moved into public school, in the early days of racial
integration in Columbus, Ohio, and met his first black teacher.
He remembers an internal shift that took place amidst prejudice, racial
conflict, and questions about 'Whose side are you on?':

I had never met a black man in authority before. I had met some
black women who were maids, but here I had black and white
friends, with riots going on all over the country, and a black teacher
who I really admired. I caught fire around questions: 'What's going
on here? Why are these kids different? Where do I fit in? What does it

all mean for me?' Next thing I knew, I was editing an underground newspaper, *The Truth*, and got suspended for it. This began a gradual shift in my understandings of America the Beautiful, and in my view of who am I. 'Am I just a good kid and everything will turn out right? Or am I sort of caught up in this and is there any possibility of contributing to social change?' [...] A lot of my motivation was a kind of anti-authoritarian, knee-jerk reaction to what was happening, and a certain amount of anger...but beyond that was the sense that it's not right. There may be some injustice here, and certainly there's a better way to deal with it than what we're doing now.

Accepted at Yale for his undergraduate studies, during its first year of co-education and more open admission policies, Mirvis had his eyes opened by the trial of Black Panther Bobby Seale in New Haven, the Kent State shootings, and the general anti-Vietnam-War movement. All this turmoil left him, as he notes, 'with a mission to reform things' - a mission that ultimately became his professional identity. After taking courses in organization psychology and reading about organization development and change, his mission focused on 'saving the worker,' to use his term. After graduation he worked at the US Department of Labor to develop methods for the 'Behavioral economic analyses of Worker Discontent,' and then moved to Ohio, where he joined a former Alcoa executive named Barry Macy to begin fieldwork. There he had a flash of insight that further shaped his future: 'I could actually do something useful with the knowledge that I was producing. I wasn't at the barricades fighting the establishment. Instead I was generating knowledge out of a logical base...to effect change.'

Leaving Ohio to continue his studies in organizational psychology at the University of Michigan, Mirvis worked with Edward Lawler at Michigan's Institute of Social Research (ISR). There he was 'slotted' as the behavior economics expert, and worked across twelve different change projects (instead of, as the rest of the researchers were doing, sticking with one primary project). While the ISR was well known for survey research and rigorous quantitative studies, there was tension among the graduate students between those who saw themselves as 'testing theories' from a detached observer role and those, such as Mirvis, who were more grounded in action.

Mirvis recounts his personal resolution of this 'Whose side are you on?' division after attending a seminar led by psychoanalyst Michael Maccoby (author of *The Gamesman*) about a change project in an auto-motive supplier plant. The change agents had invited assembly line workers to take classes in subjects ranging from math to pottery-making and worked with managers to explore their character using Rorschach inkblot tests and free association techniques. Not all the grad students could discern the 'theory' behind these interventions:

> I remember vividly, at the end of the seminar, a good friend of mine –
> a really good guy, but the champion, or at least an adherent, of the
> positivists' approach – said to me, 'Wasn't that awful, just awful?
> That he would come here and present this tripe to a group of social
> scientists!' I remember saying, 'You know, you're wrong! This is
> good! Here's a guy who is making a difference, on a journey to frame
> his own theories.' [...] It's not like I said, in a moment, 'That's who
> I want to be,' but I did say: 'That is going to be my path. I'm going
> to be exploring stuff and letting it unfold and just continually
> questing and being. That's my game.' It was a real identity
> crystallization for me that, on the academic side, you could do this
> kind of things as a scholar (small 's'), and that as an activist (small 'a')
> you could also take a big bite out of the world.

This encounter focused Mirvis' growing sense of purpose. After completing his PhD he negotiated a joint appointment between the Sociology and Psychology Departments and the School of Management at Boston University, working through the Center for Applied Social Science with Robert Chin. He launched several survey feedback and action research projects at the Center, and also joined the faculty union as the steward for the School of Management, running afoul of the university's then president, John Silber. Denied tenure at least in part as a response to his campus activism, Mirvis recognizes that he was replaying old scripts and 'not following the rules.' He admits that he had not yet 'figured out how to deal with authority figures [as I was] thumbing my nose at them, as opposed to being able to engage them, even in confrontation, with a measure of empathy.'

Jane Dutton provides a similar example of this sense of being outside the mainstream. Though today few could question her scholarship, mentoring of others, and status as a mainstream and important scholar, she took many risks in her career that might have thwarted less persistent, more risk-averse, and less intense scholars. For example, Dutton says:

> I finished the PhD in 1982, and got pregnant in 1980, and [my daughter] was born in 1981, so I collected my data really pregnant. In fact, I think that's why I was able to get lots of good confidential data. At that time having a dual-career couple and then having a baby was considered really weird – the kiss of death for your career. So, again, I felt like I was doing stuff that really didn't fit.

Highlighting both the 'odd woman out' feeling, and the hard work and persistence necessary for her accomplishments, Dutton further admits:

> Yes, I've gone part-time lots of times, . . .like the year that we went up for tenure. [. . .] I am a driven kind of gal. [. . .] I'm a doer. [. . .] I think probably, at different times, different things are motivating me, partly fear about not living up, never good enough, got to work harder. There's that terror. I know that's part of it. Loving certain aspects of what I'm doing. We talk about the maniac factor, like just a dog to a bone when you see a deadline. I'm really good at just going for it. Just, 'All right, let's go, roll up our sleeves.' [. . .] So I think different things have motivated me at different times.

The feeling of not quite belonging, not quite fitting in, and also the humility that seems to characterize many of the intellectual shamans, also is present in Dutton's words:

Since the moment I arrived here [Michigan] I have felt I don't belong.
I love Michigan on an intellectual level. [But] I'm the kind who
would never have gotten in. [. . .] The people that are here. . .just have
a level of smarts of a particular kind that I totally respect but I do not
have. I have other things, but I do not have that.

Robert Giacalone

Robert (Bob) Giacalone holds a bachelor's from Hofstra University and a
PhD from the State University of New York at Albany. Currently the
Daniels Chair in Business Ethics at the University of Denver, and
previously professor in the Fox School of Business at Temple University
in Philadelphia's Human Resources Department, Giacalone has also
taught at Bryant College in Rhode Island, the University of
Southwestern Louisiana, the University of Richmond, and the
University of North Carolina (UNC), where he held an endowed chair.
Known for his research on behavioral business ethics, exit surveying
and interviewing, employee sabotage, and impression management,
Giacalone has authored more than 100 papers and published seven
books to date, and has guest-edited numerous special journal issues,
including ones on business ethics, new paradigm thought, and ethics
education. He serves on multiple editorial boards and is co-editor of a
book series entitled 'Ethics in practice.' Not afraid to express his
opinion, Giacalone has published several notable papers in the
Academy of Management Learning and Education, including 'Taking a
red pill to disempower unethical students: creating ethical sentinels
in business schools,' 'Academic rankings in research institutions: a case
of skewed mind-sets and professional amnesia,' 'Business ethics
and social responsibility education: shifting the worldview,' and 'A
transcendent business education for the 21st century.'

Some of the intellectual shamans know when they do and do not
fit in – and choose quite explicitly to try to find places where their more
offbeat interests (and sometimes personalities) may be better accepted.
Bob Giacalone, Daniels Chair in Business Ethics at the University of

Denver, has followed such a path. Starting out wanting to be a poet, he quickly realized the general impracticalities associated with earning a living this way. Giacalone was also discouraged by several well-meaning people from entering a psychology PhD program. That type of discouragement became something of a theme in his life. He recalls this feeling of being an outsider – and how persistent he was in finding his own path to both self-knowledge and self-expression:

> I went to Hofstra and became interested in a whole bunch of different stuff, so I dual-majored in English so I could continue to do my creative writing and in psych. I decided that I was going to be therapist. Then I also realized that it wasn't going to be easy to get into a clinical program. [...] That's where I first ran into the phenomenon that has chased me my entire life. That is, people said, 'You can't do that, Bob.' I just looked at them and said, 'Really, why not?' 'Well, there are plenty of reasons. ...[Y]ou can't get into a graduate school.' 'Well, OK, maybe I can't get into a clinical program, [but] I can get into another psych program.' 'No, no, no. You just can't get into a psych program. It's difficult.'
>
> So l left there and I thought, 'Oh, the hell with you. I'll do what I want.' So I applied and I got in. I got into a social psychology program, a top twenty-five program, and when I got there I was the last student in. I was basically treated like garbage. You know, they figured that I wasn't going to make it through; I didn't have the highest GRE [Graduate Record Examination] scores. I didn't come from a prestigious school. People would look at me like I was the dumb brother that you keep in the back room. The funny part about that story is I'm the only one who graduated in my class in social psych that year. Everyone else dropped out.

As with so many of the intellectual shamans, Giacalone's story is one of persistence and willingness to take risks, to do the hard work necessary to succeed in following a dream, an idea, or a set of interests. Sometimes, as with Giacalone, this path means making choices that are difficult, and that can mean dying to one early dream so that another can emerge. Giacalone tells one story that illustrates this point vividly. Applying for a position at Harvard Business School, he found himself uncomfortable at the affluence there prior to his interview with a famous professor. He recalls what happened next:

> [He] looks at me and he says, 'Why do you want to come to Harvard?' So I, being who I am, looked at him and said, 'I'm not really sure I do.' [His] face almost hit the ground. I don't think he had ever been told in his entire life 'I'm not sure I want to come to Harvard.' He said, 'Well, why are you here?' I said, 'I don't know. Investigating. Seeing if I like it. I need a job, but the truth of the matter is, I walk around this place, professor, and this isn't my world. There's a lot of wealth here. I grew up relatively poor and don't know if I can be comfortable here. To me quality of life is important.' He said, 'So you need a job, so tell me what you do.' He said, 'You don't need me. Go apply for a job in business. You'll get one. I guarantee you you'll get one. Apply to as many places as possible. Go there, retool. You're already taught psych, you got the dissertation in leadership. You're going to get a job, you don't need me.' So I left. So I passed up Harvard because I told the truth. I never regretted it.

In his next steps, Giacalone went to teach at a small business school in Rhode Island, despite the fact that he was told he 'would never leave here' once he had made the commitment. Soon, however, he found himself changing positions for the University of Southern Louisiana, followed by the University of Richmond, and the University of North Carolina, before joining Temple University as a full professor, and ultimately the University of Denver in endowed chair. In these moves, contrary to common wisdom, he was able to move from somewhat less to somewhat more prestigious business schools, in part because he had amassed a considerable publication record that made him desirable. Indeed, he was also offered and accepted an endowed chair at UNC, leaving that behind when offered the post at Temple. Further highlighting his outside-the-mainstream status, Giacalone states:

I think the accomplishment that I would tell you career-wise has been that I'm able to do creative things. I never published in *AMJ* [*Academy of Management Journal*, one of the most prestigious mainstream management journals], and never will. In some ways I'm proud of that. It's not because *AMJ* is such a terrible journal, but it's defined by mainstream, and I never wanted to be mainstream. It took me a long time to figure that out. I never wanted to be mainstream. So I'm really proud of the fact that I was able to do really what my heart told me to do.

Like Giacalone, John Van Maanen always seemed to understand that what he wanted to do and who he wanted to be were not necessarily mainstream, yet he has spent his entire lengthy career at a very mainstream institution – the Massachusetts Institute of Technology. Celebrated for his ethnographic, qualitative studies of police, fishing, Disney, and other cultures, Van Maanen bucked a considerable cultural norm at MIT by doing qualitative research in one of the world's most prestigious – quantitatively oriented – technical institutions.

Highlighting his independence and free-thinking spirit – the spirit that allowed him to be who he truly is – Van Maanen early on in his career (1978) published what is now a classic article entitled 'The asshole,' which scholar Bob Sutton calls 'delightful and insightful.'[1n] Sutton in his blog sums up Van Maanen's impact far better than I could:

Van Maanen didn't just talk to cops, he went through the police academy, rode along with them on patrols (and got involved in all sorts of crazy things like chases), and was otherwise embedded with them for a year or so. He has since gone on to become among the most renowned organizational researchers. John had a huge impact on my generation of organizational researchers because, when we first started graduate school, qualitative methods were generally treated as unscientific, obsolete, and so biased as to be enticing but not anything that should ever be published in a top academic journal. Due in large part to John's example and leadership, by the time many of us had graduated with our PhDs, there were many corners where qualitative studies had become acceptable and encouraged. And even once exclusively quantitative researchers were starting to do qualitative studies. There is still controversy about them in my field, but also a fairly widespread acceptance now that such methods are useful for describing organizational life in rich detail and for generating theories and hypotheses that can be tested with quantitative methods.[2n]

John Van Maanen

John Van Maanen is the Erwin H. Schell Professor of Management and Professor of Organization Studies at the Massachusetts Institute of Technology's Sloan School of Management, where he has spent his entire academic career. Renowned for his ethnographic studies on the culture, socialization, and power relations of police officers, Gloucester fisherman, Disneyland ride operators, high-tech industries, and London detectives and their supervisors, among others, Van Maanen was a pioneer in bringing ethnographic and qualitative research into more general acceptance. Holding a BA in political science from California State University, Long Beach, and MS and PhD degrees from the University of California, Irvine, Van Maanen is acclaimed for his classic book *Tales of the Field: On Writing Ethnography*, and numerous papers, many of them methodological, as well as other books on ethnography including *Qualitative Studies of Organizations*. His expertise and writings span career development, change management, cross-cultural awareness, cultural differences, dispute resolution, leadership, and employee motivation. Van Maanen received the 2014 Academy of Management Scholar-Practitioner Award.

Van Maanen's path was both straightforward, in his affiliation at MIT, and less so, in that he always did the type of research that suited him best. In the process of following his own lights, he helped to establish ethnography and qualitative research as credible. From the start of his work he was clear about the nature of the work he wanted to do: interdisciplinary, qualitative, and impactful. In his words, it is

relatively easy to see Van Maanen's determination to do the work that
he wanted to do, whatever the consequences. He spent seven years in
the 1960s at the University of California, Irvine, to end up that institution's first PhD, graduating from an interdisciplinary program started by
James March,[3n] who became, in Van Maanen's words' something of a
mentor. Drawn to ethnography, Van Maanen became deeply interested
in studying the culture of 'cops because they were topical and there were
very few, if any (well, there was one) ethnographies of American police.
So I managed, by hook or crook, to do that.' He recalls:

> I guess in some ways my interest in ethnography, participant
> observation, was really colored by all the stuff that I thought was
> interesting to read in graduate school. I was bored to death by the
> journal articles, the quantitative work. That was a big piece of
> everybody's graduate education, certainly, in the '60s, and
> particularly at Irvine, which had a modeling tradition that March
> brought in. But it was boring. At least to me. I wanted to do
> something [that] for its time was different and then, once you get
> caught in it, it has its own dynamic.

Luckily, Van Maanen was recruited to MIT, where there was
already an established applied management tradition, and where he
was given freedom to pursue his interests his way. The independence
to follow his heart in doing the type of work that he liked – and finding
his way to being fully himself – was a major motivator for Van Maanen
even in the selection process of an academic career in the first place.

> Well, the motivator was I could call my own shots. [...] There is
> authority in universities but it's hard to find, and if you're halfway
> savvy you can avoid it most of the time. MIT was a great place for
> that. Teach whatever I wanted. Nobody gave me a syllabus. These
> days it's a little different because we have a much bigger MBA course
> and we didn't even have an MBA for the first twenty-five years I was
> here. A little small MS course and a little bit of undergraduate
> teaching, but mostly PhD teaching or research-oriented.

Sometimes the stumbling blocks that the intellectual shamans face are internal – yet they still lead to the intellectual shaman realizing him- or herself fully. Emeritus New York University (NYU) scholar William (Bill) Starbuck, now affiliated with the University of Oregon, whose career path took him to numerous different places before he settled on NYU, talks about another kind of maverick status. It is one that is linked to the very idiosyncrasy credits that Peter Frost has mentioned, discussed earlier. At this writing, Starbuck has published over 160 papers and edited or written some nineteen books, gained fellowships in three prestigious scholarly institutions, and earned several honorary doctoral degrees, all of which recognize his scholarly achievements.

William H. Starbuck

William (Bill) Starbuck is at this writing Professor in Residence at the Lundquist College of Business at the University of Oregon, having retired from New York University. With an MS and PhD in industrial administration from the (now) Tepper School of Business at Carnegie Institute of Technology (now Carnegie Mellon University), Starbuck also holds an AB in physics from Harvard. Having had a rather peripatetic career, Starbuck also was a faculty member at Purdue University, the Johns Hopkins University, Cornell University, and the University of Wisconsin–Milwaukee, as well as a visiting professor at multiple European institutions including the Universities of Paris, Oxford, Cambridge, and numerous others. Recipient of many honors, Starbuck is a fellow of the American Psychological Association, American Psychological Society, and the Academy of Management, which he also served as president, in addition to having been editor of the prestigious journal *Administrative Science Quarterly*. Author or co-author of more than 160 articles, Starbuck has written two books and edited another seventeen, and has received honorary doctoral degrees from three European universities. He is known for his contributions to a wide range of managerial and psychological topics, including self-designing organizations, organizational design more

> generally, decision making based on 'noisy' or unreliable data, bargaining, business strategy, human–computer interactions, scientific methods, and social revolutions.

Maverick from the start, Starbuck never actually wrote a formal dissertation of the type that PhDs were then expected to write. He attended then Carnegie Institute of Technology (now Carnegie Mellon University), and worked with, among others, Richard Cyert, economist and statistician and ultimately president of Carnegie Mellon University, and James March, organizational scholar, then at Carnegie, currently the Jack Steele Parker Professor Emeritus at Stanford, who are themselves perhaps best known for their seminal book *A Behavioral Theory of the Firm*. Starbuck tells the story:

> I never wrote one [a dissertation]. I was unable to write a dissertation. There were various issues. [But] I did [get the doctorate]. As I sat at Purdue, I wrote articles and sent them off to journals. I kept thinking that these were steps toward a dissertation, but in fact they never added up to any coherent thing. Eventually, I had published a lot of articles, including a chapter in the *Handbook of Organizations*, which drew a lot of attention. [...] So, I gave up. I was going to go become an architect. I sat in my house drawing pictures of buildings. I actually architected two buildings. I had given up on an academic career, and then one day Dick Cyert called me up. He said, 'Why don't we just give you the degree without a dissertation?' I said, 'That would be fine.'

All that was necessary, said Cyert, was to change the university's rules. With the support of Herbert Simon [professor at Carnegie and a member of Starbuck's dissertation committee, Simon was a political scientist, economist, sociologist, psychologist, and one of the twentieth century's most significant social scientists], March persuaded the faculty to vote that Starbuck could use a collection of his papers, which had to be meticulously retyped in the days before computers, in lieu of a dissertation. When the dissertation was ready, Starbuck called Cyert, as he recalls:

I called up Cyert and said, 'OK, I've got all these things retyped, they're all ready to go; now what should I do?' He said, 'Have them bound into a book.' I replied, 'But, nobody on my dissertation committee has actually looked at them.' Cyert said, 'I know, but I figure that, if you have them all bound, the committee can't ask for any major revisions.' So that's how my dissertation got done and, in fact, it was a bound volume with an errata page pasted in.

Starbuck's studies became, effectively, the prototype for a type of dissertation research that has become increasingly common today: the multi-paper dissertation. At the time, however, he and his committee were carving out new territory to accommodate the fact that his leanings were toward articles rather than book-length manuscripts. Starbuck would have switched out of academia to architecture, because of the lack of 'fit' with traditional academic norms, had his committee members not been so creative – and believed in him so much.

Another intellectual shaman is Maurizio Zollo, who is Dean's Professor in Strategic Management of the Sustainable Enterprise in the Department of Management and Innovation, Bocconi University, Milan, Italy, visiting scholar at MIT, and head of the Global Learning and Development Network for Sustainability (GOLDEN). Known for his entrepreneurial ability to gather the intellectual and monetary resources necessary to launch large-scale projects, as well as his academic work on mergers and acquisitions, organizational learning, and dynamic capabilities, Zollo has recently turned his attention to issues of corporate responsibility and sustainability, particularly through the GOLDEN program.

Maurizio Zollo

Maurizio Zollo is the Dean's Professor in Strategic Management of the Sustainable Enterprise, in the Strategy Institute, at Bocconi University in Milan, Italy, and the director of the Center for Research in Organization and Management (CROMA). Zollo holds PhD and MSc degrees in managerial science and applied economics from the Wharton

School, University of Pennsylvania, and the Laurea degree in economics from Bocconi. Zollo previously had appointments in strategic management at INSEAD, Fountainebleau, France, the Wharton School, and the Advanced Institute of Management in the United Kingdom, and was visiting professor/scholar at MIT for the 2012–14 academic years. Best known for work in the field of strategic management on mergers and acquisitions, dynamic capabilities, and organizational learning, Zollo has in more recent years turned his attention to how organizations learn to change in a responsible way. He headed up a European-Union-funded project called RESPONSE, and currently directs an innovative global research initiative called GOLDEN, the Global Organizational Learning and Development Network for Sustainability, which brings together people from around the world to study how companies make the transition to sustainability successfully. Editor of the *European Management Review,* and former president of the European Academy of Management, Zollo has published nearly thirty articles in prestigious academic journals, ten managerial publications, and two books, as an academic, and previously was a management consultant at McKinsey & Co., a major consulting firm, an associate for Kidder Peabody Italia, and a financial analyst for Merrill Lynch Capital Markets.

Zollo's RESPONSE project, funded by the European Union, found, among other things, that teaching managers to meditate was a more powerful learning mechanism than traditional instruction for more ethical and responsible behavior. Willing to take the risk necessary to raise funds for global-scale research by a global network of scholars, in GOLDEN, Zollo is both an academic and an entrepreneur, and is also currently working on neuroscience as it relates to managerial ethical decision-making. As he tells it, Zollo deliberately chose his current institutional affiliation at Bocconi so that he could follow his own instincts about research rather than having to toe the line of traditional research. But he made these moves having already earned his idiosyncrasy credits in more traditional forms of research involving strategies of mergers and acquisition, and dynamic capabilities.

I think the other concern [in deciding to go to Bocconi] is the fact that INSEAD basically was not really well organized to entertain the possibility of doing innovative – really deeply innovative – research. So I was lucky essentially to get all this money from the European foundation, the European Commission. I could spend it the way I wanted really because the design was my own. So INSEAD was very helpful in getting us access to companies, for example. But…at Bocconi there's suddenly a lot more space, a lot more freedom, being the director of my research institute (CROMA) and having a[n endowed] chair.

Derick de Jongh

Derick de Jongh is the director of the Albert Luthuli Centre for Responsible Leadership, University of Pretoria, South Africa, having previously served as the founding director of the Centre for Corporate Citizenship in the College of Economic and Management Sciences, University of South Africa. De Jongh holds B Com, M Com, and doctorate in commerce degrees from the University of Pretoria. He came to academia after serving in the human resources department for a major South African bank, then as CEO of the consulting firm Knowledge Brokers International, which offered training and consulting to South African and UK businesses. Then he became general manager of group strategic marketing at a major South African bank, where he established a foundation and started integrating the bank's strategy with corporate social investment. De Jongh is also vice chairman of a nongovernmental organization (NGO) called Heartbeat, which attempts to address the HIV/AIDS pandemic's effects on orphans in Africa. He serves on the editorial boards of the *Journal of Corporate Citizenship* and the *Journal for Innovation and Sustainable Development*. In addition to his work in South Africa, de Jongh has become a leading voice for the transformation of MBA education, working with the global 50+20 Initiative, the European Foundation for Management Development (EFMD), and the UN Global Compact's Principles for Responsible Management Education initiatives to do so, among other appointments and entrepreneurial activities.

Derick de Jongh is more of an academic entrepreneur than a distinguished scholar, though he works within the university context. He treads a fine line between the rigors and realities of academic life at the University of Pretoria, South Africa, where he is director of the Albert Luthuli Centre for Responsible Leadership, and his entrepreneurial instincts to make the world a better place, about which he is quite explicit. 'Not quite fitting the mold' of any one thing, particularly today's demands on academics, sets de Jongh apart from many of the other intellectual shamans. His work, which is focused on corporate citizenship, corporate responsibility, and responsible leadership, is realized mainly through his center directorships. De Jongh is quite clear about his priorities – and the outsider status that they sometimes give him, as he comments on the opportunistic events that gave rise to his moving toward his vision:

> It was...both vision and opportunities. Being a bit of an academic entrepreneur and – finding myself many times in a very hot seat, because universities in general don't cater very well to academic entrepreneurs. We constantly poke the system, if that's the right way [to say it]. We're irritating because we say what we think, but we're not happy with the silent mentality; we're not happy with the way you teach finance or economics. So they don't always like us.
>
> So you might want to call me a bit of a rebel, which I am in my heart. When the system resists me I become even more persistent to make sure to do what I can to change the system, even though it takes a lot of emotional energy... It's a question of if I don't do it, who will do it? [...] So being an entrepreneur, coming up against the resistance that I've come up with over the past ten years in academia, sometimes led me to a point where I became very disgruntled and at many times asked myself, 'What the hell am I doing?' I know why I want to do this [work on corporate responsibility and responsible leadership], but is it worth the effort to constantly being in conflict with bloody historic and (what's the right word?) people who come from the Stone Age, almost? So I find

it very hard. I think that's where my business brain, being private sector, also kicks in. I just can't understand why people are so dinosauric in their attitude.

Sometimes being an intellectual shaman means taking the risks necessary to do the initial work to open up a field. Just as Van Maanen was willing to risk doing ethnographic work in management scholarship, Ian Mitroff has taken many such risks over the course of his career. Mitroff is Professor Emeritus and former Harold Quinton Distinguished Professor of Business Policy at the Marshall School of Business and Anneberg School for Communication at the University of Southern California. Sometimes called the 'father of crisis management,' he was one of the pioneers studying crisis management, and among the first to recognize the importance of studying spirituality in the workplace, among numerous other topics he has addressed in more than 350 papers and over thirty books.

Ian Mitroff

Ian Mitroff is Professor Emeritus and former Harold Quinton Distinguished Professor of Business Policy at the Marshall School of Business and the Annenberg School for Communication at the University of Southern California (USC). Officially retired from USC, he has also served or currently serves as Adjunct Professor at St. Louis University, and Adjunct Professor in the College of Environmental design, University Professor at Alliant International University, and senior investigator in the Center for Catastrophic Risk at the University of California Berkley, and is president of Comprehensive Crisis Management, a consulting firm. He holds a BS in engineering physics, an MS in structural mechanics, and a PhD in engineering science from the University of California Berkeley. Named a Fellow at the American Psychological Association, the Academy of Management, and the American Association for the Advancement of Science, he has received numerous awards, including a gold medal by the UK Systems Society for lifetime achievements and contributions to systems thinking. Recipient of numerous awards and an honorary doctorate, Mitroff serves on numerous editorial boards, and is also a public intellectual, writing for *The Huffington Post* and appearing in numerous newspaper, television, and radio outlets. Over his career Mitroff has published more than 350 papers and thirty books, some pioneering in areas as diverse as organizational crisis management, corporate culture, spirituality at work, applied epistemology (complex problem-solving), and the philosophy of science, among other areas. He is known as the 'father of crisis management,' and was also among the first management scholars to recognize the importance of spirituality at work.

Studying for his PhD under noted philosopher and systems scientist C. West Churchman (professor at the School of Business Administration and Professor of Peace and Conflict at the University of California Berkeley), Mitroff gained insights into both systems thinking and philosophy of science that he has carried throughout his career. He is typically clear about his ideas and insights, and willing to express them openly. Below, he talks about the reactions that he received when first addressing the issue of spirituality in the workplace, a topic he helped to pioneer, and his response to those reactions:

So, coming from the way I grew up, not really finding very many competent adults, I didn't have much respect for authority. I had some, or I would have been in trouble, which I never really was. But I was a maverick from the get-go, not to *be* a maverick, but, because when I was in high school I loved everything from art, literature, science, math, I was absolutely horrified that that's not what universities were about. You had to specialize, and if you liked math you thumbed your nose at art, and vice versa. That's atrocious! That's why we really fail to truly be interdisciplinary. But then I have to view specialization as [meeting] psychological safety needs. I think that's what it really is. It's not fully cognizant; it's unconscious. It's a defense mechanism [for some people], and that's why it's so hard to change, because you cannot just change your purely rational arguments.

Willingly assuming the status of maverick gave Mitroff a sort of freedom, along with the idiosyncrasy credits he had earned by publishing prolifically, to do the work he wanted to do without questioning himself too much.

Although I could continue with examples of other intellectual shamans who are also mavericks, rebels, misfits, and outsiders, I will, at this point, let Mitroff's words close this chapter. The core notion of this chapter is that intellectual (and other) shamans take the risks, assume the mantle of outsider, and do what is important to them – because, in a sense, it is what they *must* do as they come fully to themselves. Mitroff states about his pioneering work on spirituality at work:

> That's why when I first went out and gave talks on my book *Spiritual Audit of Corporate America*, [which was] not the first but one of the early empirical studies of. . .spirituality at work, . . .the first question I was invariably asked after all these academic presentations was not about the methodology and all that kind of crap but. . . 'Why aren't you afraid to do such a study?' I fed into it because I knew what they were going to ask. 'Well, what do you mean?' 'Well, weren't you afraid of going to study spirituality?'
>
> I looked and laughed, and said, 'I've been out of the mainstream my whole life. If that's what you're worried about you'll never do anything really creative or groundbreaking in your life.'

3 Beyond the self: power of purpose

In the last chapter, I explored how becoming an intellectual (or any other type of) shaman means having the courage to become who you really are. Intellectual – or any other form of – shamanism involves allowing a sense of inherent power to emerge out of deeper purpose, taking the individual beyond self, beyond pure self-interest, to attempting to do something for the world. Finding and realizing that calling or deeper purpose to become fully who you can be is what the psychologist Abraham Maslow calls 'self-actualization.'[64]

To accomplish the task of fully becoming yourself, it is important to come to understand what your unique purpose in the world might be. Coming to purpose also requires having the courage to follow that purpose and the willingness to go at least somewhat off the beaten track if necessary. Heeding the 'call' to purpose can come in any number of ways. Some paths are subtle, others more obvious; some are clear straight away and others take a roundabout and lengthy path. We saw in the last chapter, for example, how David Cooperrider and Otto Scharmer experienced sudden transitions and awareness, built on a range of prior life experiences, while others, such as Nancy Adler, Jane Dutton, and Dave Brown, perhaps more typically, took circuitous routes. Heeding the call to purpose also means acknowledging the power that is associated with purpose – sometimes simply the power to do the work to which one is called.

In this chapter, I look more deeply at the variety of ways in which purpose manifests – and how the intellectual shamans studied have heeded their particular call to that purpose, while having the courage to accept that power. The call to *intellectual* shamanism, in effect, means answering the call to power through the *intellectual* work that one does, which also can manifest itself in different ways. In the book

Habits of the Heart, Robert Bellah and colleagues suggest that answering a calling to make the world a better place is one of three general approaches to work that people can take: a material and security orientation, a careerist orientation, and the calling orientation,[65] which is where intellectual shamans fit.

Michael Novak[66] finds that there are certain identifiable characteristics to callings that seem relevant to the work of intellectual shamans. He identifies four key characteristics. First, callings are unique to the individual, and, second, they require the talent, love, and dedication necessary to succeed in that arena. Third, working in the context of a calling energizes rather than depletes the individual, despite the hard work or sometimes even drudgery involved. This aspect of calling helps explain why many of the intellectual shamans continue to work long past what would be considered normal retirement age. Fourth, finding the calling is not always straightforward or easy. Indeed, although understanding their purpose was straightforward for some, such as David Cooperrider, Otto Scharmer, and Bob Quinn (see below), most of the intellectual shamans followed what I call a 'crooked path' to ultimately becoming fully themselves – i.e., till they found their purpose. In this section, we look at some of the intellectual shamans' journeys along that sometimes – though not always – crooked path.

PURPOSE: HEEDING THE CALL

The idea of a calling – finding life's purpose and the 'power' associated with working toward fulfilling that purpose – is most often associated with the call to religious or spiritual life. While the idea of finding a calling certainly has spiritual overtones (and related historical legacy), the notion of calling can also be found in the context of work or other interests that draw one to them – especially when that call contributes to the individual's work of making the world a better place. In this sense, the concept of calling is secular and can be found in just about any context.[66-68] Importantly, first the call must be heard, and then it must be heeded.

The famous educator Parker Palmer has written about the power inherent in finding one's calling, while acknowledging the difficulty in that task:

> Vocation does not come from willfulness. It comes from listening. I must listen to my life and try to understand what it is truly about – quite apart from what I would like it to be about – or my life will never represent anything real in the world, no matter how earnest my intentions.
>
> That insight is hidden in the word *vocation* itself, which is rooted in the Latin for 'voice.' Vocation does not mean a goal that I pursue. It means a calling that I hear. Before I can tell my life what I want to do with it, I must listen to my life telling me who I am. I must listen for the truths and values at the heart of my own identity, not the standards by which I *must* live – but the standards by which I cannot help but live if I am living my own life.[67]

Another interpretation of vocation, calling, is possible given the root word 'voice' in the word 'vocation.' The idea of voice is particularly *à propos* in the context of intellectual shamans, with the implication that finding vocation or purpose means finding and using voice to give expression and meaning to that purpose. As scholars in the management academy, the intellectual shamans studied here use 'voice' in writing, research, teaching, public speaking, and consulting, and sometimes as public intellectuals translating academic work for public consumption as well. Much of the source of intellectual shamans' power somewhat naturally revolves around the use of voice in writing and speaking. Other shamanic people use a form of voice in various forms of art or other expression, such as music or painting, or through work as psychologists, doctors, leaders, or in other professions.

Heeding the call to purpose takes courage and some degree of risk. We have already seen at the end of Chapter 2 Ian Mitroff's strong statement about stepping outside the mainstream to do the work that you are called to do: 'If...you're worried about [being outside the mainstream], you'll never do anything really creative or groundbreaking in your life.' That courage to step outside the mainstream, to speak out about, or voice, what the intellectual shaman sees as needing to be done, whether in practice, in research, or conceptually, is much needed today in an academic world in which conformity to norms, disciplinary traditions, and, seemingly, a 'one way is best attitude' is increasingly notable. Indeed, outside the mainstream is the only place where what Thomas Kuhn has called 'paradigm shift' can take place.[62]

In management research, such 'mainstreaming' is increasingly evident, with the promulgation of 'A' journal lists, citation counts, impact factors, and similar quantitatively based approaches to assessing faculty research ever more dominant. These data are often used to assess research 'quality,' without anyone actually taking the time to evaluate the significance, contribution, relevance to anything useful, or importance.[49,52,53,69–72] Intellectual shamans seem not to be fazed by or much interested in such measures of success, however, perhaps because most were working long before these measures became available. More importantly, possibly it may be because they typically view such measures as essentially meaningless to doing or assessing the work that they believe they were meant to do. In other words, through the way they have lived their academic lives, they implicitly support Mitroff's statement.

Intellectual (and other) shamans need to find their sources of power by living out their purpose in life or their calling. Simultaneously, they need to find the courage to do what they must to serve the world in their particular ways. Following the path of service to something bigger and being true to self constitute the basis of the success of intellectual shamans. It is not in following formulas about getting published in the right places, doing the work that others might want them to do, or being afraid to step outside the boundaries of what is currently popular or accepted. As Mitroff's comment implies, it is hard to do work of significance if you are afraid to really be yourself. It is hard to do the work that is important to you, especially if it is outside the mainstream of what is currently considered acceptable, unless you are willing to risk following your own call. Yet that may be the way to finding true purpose – and true power in one's self – and one's call to shamanism.

Andrew (Andy) Hoffman, Holcim Professor of Sustainable Enterprise, jointly at the Ross School of Business and the School of Natural Resources and Environment at the University of Michigan, directly addresses the issue of work as vocation or calling in his comment below:

> When I think of a career, I think of the idea of a calling or a vocation. I think of something bigger. I like to talk to kids and say there is a question that we all get asked from a very early age: what do you want to be when you grow up? I think that's the wrong question. The correct question is: what are you meant to be when you grow up? For me there is a God piece of this but there doesn't have to be. I actually happen to be a Catholic and am motivated by the idea that we have a purpose; that we have a set of skills and gifts and that we should use them to the benefit of society as best we can. That's what I'm trying to do.

Andrew J. Hoffman

Andrew (Andy) Hoffman is the Holcim Professor of Sustainable Enterprise at the University of Michigan, Ann Arbor, where he holds joint appointments at the School of Natural Resources and Environment and the Ross School of Business. He joined Michigan in 2004, after spending several years at Boston University's School of Management. Also the director of the Erb Institute for Global Sustainable Enterprise, Hoffman has published nearly 100 articles and nine books on corporate environmental and social strategies. Holding a PhD in management and civil environmental engineering, an MS in civil and environmental engineering, and a BS in chemical engineering, all from the Massachusetts Institute of Technology, Hoffman worked at the US Environmental Protection Agency, Metcalf & Eddy, and Amoco prior to becoming an academic. Named one of the 'World's 50 best business school professors' by Poets and Quants, Hoffman has received numerous awards for his pathbreaking research on companies and the natural environment, including the Breaking the Frame Award from the *Journal of Management Inquiry*, for work (with P. Devereaux Jennings) on the BP oil disaster in the Gulf of Mexico, awards for case writing, and for teaching. His 2010 autobiographical book *Builder's Apprentice* (winner of the 2011 Connecticut Book Prize for best memoir/biography) details the two years he spent as a young man building mansions. A public intellectual frequently quoted in popular and business media, Hoffman, as Poets and Quants suggests, 'found his muse...[w]here environmental awareness and business collide.'

Note the direct emphasis in Hoffman's words on finding one's purpose, and giving back in some way to serve the world. Hoffman also suggests that 'what you are meant to be' is core to finding purpose. In other words, becoming fully yourself involves both identifying your core purpose, which sometimes can happen retrospectively, by looking back at actions you have taken, and using what Hoffman labels the 'gifts' that have been given – and it is in those gifts that the power of the shaman lies.

In an article entitled 'Purpose: the starting point of great leadership,' Nikos Mourkogiannis makes the link between purpose and the ethics of making the world a better place. He writes: 'Purpose is so powerful because it is founded on deeply held ideas about what is right and what is worthwhile.'[73] Mourkogiannis further argues that embedding purpose into companies (and here I argue into the work of intellectual shamans too) involves four approaches: discovery, excellence, altruism, and heroism.

We can see in the lives of the intellectual shamans the process and lifelong engagement of discovery as part of the work of the intellectual shaman, the desire to give back that could be associated with altruism, and the search for excellence in the types of intellectual, research, and consulting contributions that these individuals make. We see somewhat less in their stories of the element of heroism, for, at least with respect to telling their own stories, they exhibit remarkable humility, and few would consider themselves heroic in the traditional sense of the word.

Some degree of what Mourkogiannis calls altruism, alternatively expressed as desire to give back or to make the world a better place, is apparent in the lives of intellectual shamans. We will see this sense of 'beyond the self' in the next three chapters, when I talk about the three core roles of shamans: healing, connecting, and sensemaking. In the rest of this chapter, I focus on how purpose manifests and how intellectual shamans speak about it. James P. Walsh, a professor in the Ross School of Business at the University of Michigan, speaks explicitly about purpose. Walsh believes that his purpose arose from family ethos and a core ethic about giving back. That upbringing established a kind of standard for how to live. His challenge was to find a career that would enable him to serve, and maybe even to make the world a better place.

James P. Walsh

James (Jim) Walsh is Arthur F. Thurnau Professor, the Gerald and Esther Carey Professor of Business Administration, Professor of Management and Organizations, and Professor of Strategy at the University of Michigan's Ross School of Business. Walsh holds a PhD from Northwestern University, MAs from the University of Chicago and Columbia University, and a BA from the State University of New York at Albany. Author of dozens of papers in top journals, Walsh is best known for his research in three areas: managerial and organizational cognition, corporate governance, and his work on the place of the corporation in society. Holding research and teaching chairs at Michigan, he is dedicated to the scholarly combination of research, teaching, and service. In fact, a service orientation frames almost all his work. Some of his formal roles include serving as the sixty-fifth president of the Academy of Management and the fifteenth dean of the Academy's Fellows Group. He helped edit (in various capacities) the *Academy of Management Review, Organization Science*, and the *Strategic Management Journal*. He also served as a founding co-editor of *Academy of Management Annals* during its first five years of existence.

Walsh is characteristically unassuming about his numerous accomplishments, but quite clear about the sense of purpose that has driven him over the years. Indeed, the opening of his official biography on the University of Michigan's Ross Business School's website reads:

> Research, teaching, and service define my professional life. Two qualities define much of my work. I'm fascinated by cross-level relationships: the influences between and among individuals, organizations, and society really engage me. And as romantic as it may sound, I think we are all called to try to leave the world a better place. The desire to better understand these cross-level relationships, done with a clear eye on enhancing our well-being, animates nearly everything I do.[1n]

Early influences shaped the sense of purpose experienced by Walsh, who says in his interview:

> I think I have a sense of those influences. In fact, this is the kind of question I ask everybody on job interviews. What is the story of your life? Why are you here today, looking to become a professor? In that light, what do you hope to accomplish with your career? As for me, it is hard to know where to pick up the thread. I guess I'll start with my family and adolescence.
>
> I was raised by parents who each in their own way tried to leave the world a better place. My father was both a World War II and a Korean War veteran who saw a great deal of combat. My mother's family was hit hard by the [Great] Depression. She went to work very early to help support her family. They were both devout Catholics. I suppose that their efforts were always oriented towards a higher purpose. This was the air I breathed as a kid, and, by the way, the air I am back to breathing today.
>
> I also came of age in the 1960s and early 1970s. Of course, that was a period of incredible change and turmoil. I grew up in Albany, the capital of New York state. It seemed like there was always a protest march or peace vigil to attend. The city also experienced some very

bad race riots. So, I was very attentive to politics. Very early on, I remember sending Christmas and Easter cards to President Kennedy, and then, later, looking for a ride to the Albany airport to welcome our governor home from a trip. Later, I paid pretty close attention to the civil rights movement, the women's rights movement, Watergate and of course, Vietnam. . .not to mention the loose promise of the counterculture lifestyle and all. So this idea of trying to serve, to leave the world a better place, was baked into me early. The challenge was to figure out who I was, take my place in the world, and then try to make some kind a difference.

Walsh graduated from the State University of New York at Albany, and, in his words, 'didn't quite know what to do.' He did heavy construction work through college and beyond for a while, following what he terms a 'Norman Rockwell existence' as a child and youth. He started out studying counseling at Columbia and obtained a master's degree, but notes: 'I was very naïve about that world. I was just following the impulse to try to better the world. I didn't have any real sense of what that work entailed. In a quiet moment, I would have confessed that I didn't really know what I was doing there.' After recognizing rather quickly that counseling psychology was not going to be his career, he notes:

> I started thinking in terms of levels of analysis and what determines behavior. Sure, I was in a psychology program and focusing on individuals, but, even so, context matters. As we talked about how individuals are affected by, say, their family, school, and community life, I started to think about work. Even at Columbia, I started to say to myself, 'If you want to leave the world a better place, go to where people are spending all their time. Shape the work context.'

With this insight, Walsh went to the University of Chicago, where he earned another Master of Arts, this time focusing on organizational psychology, noting:

> I graduated from Chicago in '80 and then enrolled in an organization behavior doctoral program at Northwestern that fall. I did not find

enough organization in my organizational psychology studies. At Kellogg [Northwestern] I could study individuals and their business context directly. The rest is pretty much history. At that point, I'm in our world. I liked the life of mind and I liked the potential for the kind of work we could do. I started to learn the craft of scholarship and, of course, began to appreciate business and my new business school world. In retrospect, I can see three different intellectual moments in my career.

Walsh summarizes the three 'moments' that defined his research career in the official biography posted on his website:

Looking back, I see that at least three broad themes define my research life. I've investigated the relationship between individuals and organizations for many years. My early work on managerial and organizational cognition was fueled by a desire to understand how cognitive heuristics might blind leaders to their decision environments and in so doing, leave them vulnerable to mistakes that might bring harm to their organizations. I then shifted gears to look more directly at firms and their governance practices. I considered whether and how leaders' self-dealing might be responsible for problematic firm performance. In time, I realized that I simply assumed that wealth creation would best serve society. And so, I moved to take a closer look at the fundamental questions of corporate governance – what is the purpose of a corporation and to whom is it accountable? I am now interested in how and how well corporations serve society.[2n]

In Walsh's case, the desire to serve the world was manifest not only in his broad choice of research projects but also in his teaching and service. His teaching journey is not covered above but it is clear that his counseling impulse might have found an outlet with his students. Particularly drawn to action-based learning, he tries hard to connect personally with his students. Further, his years of service to our academic journals were complemented by his broader service to the profession. For example, he has been intimately involved with the Academy of Management's recent work with colleagues in Africa. Otto Scharmer, founder of the Presencing Institute and senior lecturer at MIT, whom we met in the previous chapter, also discovered his core purpose early on – and almost inadvertently.

Below, Scharmer tells his own version of this story. Asked what his purpose is, Scharmer, who was born in Germany when the country was still split into eastern and western segments, responds:

> I have no idea, but I can tell you a story that gives the answer. [. . .] I was, for a number of years, active in a grass-roots peace movement in East and West Germany and Europe, and got to read a lot of things. Most of them were illegal, of course, given the laws in East Germany back then.
>
> I came on the blacklist and could no longer enter East Germany after that. So, when the wall came down, they had these archives, the East German Stasi [Ministry for State Security (German: Ministerium für Staatssicherheit, MfS), abbreviated Stasi], the East German KGB. They opened the archives so you could access your own file, and after a while I also sent a request just to find out what was it that they knew, what they didn't. It turned out that they knew much less than we thought they would have. But, like good German bureaucrats, they had these typewriter-set sheets [with] all these different dimensions of observations, where they have evidence, and what the data are that they collected on you. At the top of the page there is a larger piece. It's one paragraph: who is that person? It said, 'He inspires leading circles of the grassroots opposition movement.'
>
> When I read that I thought, 'Wow, that's exactly it!' So. . .it's inspiration? Leading through inspiration, and then circles? It's not just one. It's the collective dimension of leadership. That is the grassroots movement from the bottom up. When I saw that I thought, 'Wow, that's exactly what I tried to do!' It would have taken me hours to explain that to anyone, or to myself, and of course I would

not have claimed that I really did that. Maybe in my better moments some of that, but that's exactly what I had been doing. When I read that sentence, I knew, that's it! That's exactly it!

Demonstrating the enduring quality of such a core purpose, Scharmer continues:

> I think it's still true. [...] What I've changed is, back then it was just the opposition movement...that I hung out with and connected with and worked with. Now it's really a grass-roots level and the top level, and, at the heart of the organization, the mid-career people. Now I'm working all these levels, and I enjoy that. It's really about connecting these dots and helping these three levels to connect with each other more effectively to help them to transform their systems. So it morphed a little bit, but the essence of what these East German KBG Stasi people wrote is still true.

BEYOND SELF

The call to purpose comes from a deeper place than materialism, deeper than simply finding work to do for a paycheck, deeper than status-seeking, deeper than trying to scrape by, and deeper than living out someone else's agenda. Living the call to purpose is almost something that 'must' be done – or, at least, that is how many people experience it. As noted above, I am not using the words 'call to purpose' in the religious sense most often associated with the idea of a calling. Though I am personally mostly agnostic and consider myself a secular humanist, I do have to admit that there is a spiritual element to receiving and following the call to try to make the world, in one's one special way, a better place. It is fundamentally about finding meaning in one's life and work.

The deeper place from which the 'call' to purpose emanates can be like a small voice guiding the way toward something bigger than one's self or self-interest alone. Alternatively, it can be something discovered in retrospect, by looking back at the path one has followed and, as intellectual shaman Karl Weick would say, making retrospective sense of it.[43] That small inner voice is easy to ignore if you get caught up in the day-to-day frenzy of earning a living, competitiveness with others, or fighting for prestige. For intellectual shamans, whether they would claim this voice as a 'call' or not, there is something that draws them to do the field-, social-, organization-, or meaning-changing work they have done, an internal need to do something beyond the self. It could, of course, be the self-confidence that comes of a successful career and retrospective sensemaking. But it seems to be more than that. It seems that these individuals were drawn to the work that they did. Indeed, Michael Novak contends in his book *Business as a Calling* that the calling can be viewed as a person's identity.[66] We will let that drawing towards identity – to what I have termed becoming fully who you are – stand as the call to shamanism, whether it is made sense of prospectively or retrospectively.

The call can seem to come from a god or God (as a couple of the intellectual shamans articulate), the universe, or a higher power. More simply, it can come from some internal source and understanding that provides passion and compassion, meaning, and direction. Or it can derive from a set of values that appeal, perhaps because of family circumstances or being in situations with admired others. The call amounts to something that defines purpose in one's life. However it manifests, it is this call to purpose that drives the passionate pursuit of ideas, social or organizational change, or other quests of the intellectual shaman. I am guessing that similar calls to action and passions drive the work or interests of other types of modern shamans as well. These calls seem to be hard to ignore once they are recognized. Yet they could conceivably be easy to ignore if the busyness of day-to-day life does not allow some way of recognizing and listening to that call, some time for reflection, even some degree of failure that forces reconsideration of a path from time to time. It may well be that the difference between becoming shamanic and not lies in the capacity to hear – and actually listen to – one's personal call and a willingness to take the necessary risks to move forward toward it.[67]

Robert E. Quinn

Robert (Bob) Quinn holds the Margaret Elliot Tracey Collegiate Professorship in the Faculty of Management and Organizations at the Ross School of Business, University of Michigan, Ann Arbor, and is a co-founder and, at this writing, director of the Center for Positive Organizational Scholarship there, and also of the movement known as positive organizational scholarship. Quinn holds BS and MS degrees in sociology from Brigham Young University and an interdisciplinary PhD degree in organizational hehavior from the University of Cincinnati. Prior to joining Michigan, Quinn served on the faculty at the State University of New York at Albany for more than a dozen years. One of the originators of the 'competing values framework,' a Fellow of the Academy of Management and World Business Academy, Quinn is author of nearly twenty books and dozens of papers. His research focuses mainly on issues of leadership, vision, and change. Known as an innovative teacher, Quinn also consults widely with many Fortune 500 companies to help them design large-scale change projects. Among his notable books are *Deep Change: How Ordinary People Can Accomplish Extraordinary Results*, *Building the Bridge as You Walk on It: A Guide to Change*, *Lift: Becoming a Positive Force in Any Situation*, *Diagnosing and Changing Organizational Culture*, and *The Deep Change Field Guide*.

Sometimes the call is quite distinct and clear, as Robert E. Quinn, Margaret Elliot Tracey Collegiate Professor of Management and Organizations at the Ross School of Business, University of Michigan, articulates:

> Yes, the vision is this absolute commitment to transforming human beings in unleashing human potential. If you look, look at the movie *Stand and Deliver*, you watch that movie and say to executives, 'What's the vision?' Well, the first answer was, 'To teach calculus.' Well, no, that's not the vision at all. The vision is exactly the same thing: to unleash human potential. Calculus is just an arbitrary tool to do that.

Quinn is particularly well known for his work on leadership, vision, and change, having written (among many other books and articles) about *Deep Change*, a book about individual transformation for everyone, and for developing what is called the competing values framework.[74–76] The competing values framework addresses the effectiveness of organizations and leaders, in settings ranging from business to education to other social systems, on two continua: from flexibility to control and from internal to external orientations. Applied in a wide range of contexts, the competing values framework helps organizations define their culture and leaders define their style. Quinn also currently serves (along with Jane Dutton and Kim Cameron, also part of this project), as one of the founders of the Positive Organizational Scholarship (POS) movement. For Quinn, who is Mormon (i.e., a member of the Church of the Latter-Day Saints), there are two faces to his call: the one to do the scholarly work that helps unleash human potential, and the other to his church.

Just after he and others (including Dutton and Cameron) began work on POS, he received a literal 'call' from the Church that both disrupted and opened up his personal calling. He relates the story:

> About thirteen years ago we did a book about positive organizational scholarship and started the Center for Positive Organizations. The notion was to flip the lens from a focus on the middle of the curve to the far right of the curve, to examine excellence, or what we often refer to as positive deviance. We wanted to know what organizations, groups, processes, and people look like at their best. The positive lens can be applied to any topic, and, over time, a lot of scholars became involved. It was exhilarating to see the subfield grow. Then, in 2006, I got a call from my church asking me to take the next three years and go to the desert of Australia, and be a mission president. So, we went to Australia. It turned out to be a spectacular experience. I had to transform. My old identity and my status did not matter to Aboriginals or impoverished immigrants. No one cared about who I used to be. I had to go deeper and find the

real me. From six in the morning to ten-thirty every night, for three years, with no days off, I had to be fully and authentically present. I had to keep learning and keep digging for the most authentic version of myself.

The return to the United States three years later created significant adjustment issues, as Quinn notes:

Australia turned out to be a spiritual feast. Then suddenly I had to get on a plane and return to Ann Arbor. It required a big adjustment. I remember when someone asked me to turn in a syllabus for a class I was slated to teach. I felt panic. I wondered if I could write one. I wondered if I could still teach the old content. Everything was petrifying. The interesting thing is that I began to engage in those former activities but I did so with new eyes. I ended up doing the old things in new ways.

In this more vulnerable state, Quinn received a call from a research organization that studies public school teachers. Interestingly – and related to our conversation about the importance of calling – here is what Quinn discovered:

The researchers were involved in trying to understand the practices of value-added teachers, people who were objectively identified as exceeding expectations in the classroom. They contacted me because the practices they were documenting seemed to fall neatly into the competing values framework. What captured their attention was the fact that the highly effective teachers seemed to have the ability to cross the boundaries of the framework and integrate perceptually differentiate behaviors.

I knew what they were talking about. As people move towards the mastery of a given activity they become less mechanical and more creative. They become more cognitively and behaviorally complex. To someone with a mechanical view of the activity, more masterful people seem paradoxical, because they are transcending the categories of normal observation and logic.

So I told them I would like to talk to them. We ended up reviewing videos of the highly effective teachers and then doing in-depth interviews. In those interviews the highly effective teachers were fully present and the conversations fully authentic. Often there were tears. One of the first things that became clear is that they did not have jobs. They had callings. Their purpose was not to transfer information but to transform their students, to turn them into life-long learners. The highly effective teachers were full of stories about transforming unlikely kids and unlikely classes. There were operating at a different level than what we normally expect.

Quinn's comments illustrate both the complexity and the inherent power of responding to the call as he talks about the teachers he was studying, who are shamanic in much the same way that intellectual shamans are:

I was interviewing one of the teachers. She said that, to really succeed, a teacher has to do something difficult. They have to learn the individual needs and interests of each child and teach to those needs. This made sense. She was advocating individual consideration – a factor in the research on transformational leadership.

Then she said something that stunned me. She said that, after you learn to care for individual needs, you can go to the next level. You learn that all the kids are the same. Each one, no matter what they claim, wants to be respected. They all want to succeed. She said that, when you learn that, you can teach any group: gifted or special education, urban or suburban, old or young.

She was articulating something I now call 'generalized consideration.' In pursuing her calling and her purpose, she had to go an extra mile and learn individual empathy. In doing this over and over, she evolved to a high level of complexity. She moved to a universalized practice theory that leads her to believe she can teach anyone. It is a complex theory of teaching that accelerates the learning of her students. Again, I found this stunning.

What Quinn discovered, from the framework of intellectual sha-mans, is the power of listening to and answering the call to purpose – and having the courage to live that purpose. The teachers he studied follow the insight that shines a light on the paradox that these teachers uncovered. The very different students whom they taught all funda-mentally have the same needs, and it is those needs that teachers need to satisfy. With Quinn we see that answer both in his excitement about this new research and in the very subjects that he is studying, who, in their own shamanic ways, are answering their call. What looks almost magical, and certainly sounds mystical, has ultimately to do with taking the call to purpose seriously. Quinn concludes:

> I find her comments stunning because of the learning process that is reflected. A novice goes to the university and reads books about teaching and eventually does some student teaching. The emphasis is on mechanics and all the students are the same. Real teaching begins and the teacher starts to see differences. A committed teacher learns the differences and works with them. That learning can open the door to more learning and the transformational insight that the differences can be integrated, all the students have the same needs. This jump in understanding leads to mastery, the ability to perform at a level that exceeds expectations. What a beautiful notion.

PURPOSE AND INTELLECT

Some of the intellectual shamans find their core purpose in trying to understand deep intellectual questions. Pratima (Tima) Bansal, profes-sor and J. Allyn Talor/Arthur H. Mingay Chair in Business Administration, at the Richard Ivey School of Business, University of Western Ontario, and executive director of the Network for Business Sustainability, among other appointments, discusses the question guiding her research and sense of purpose. Having earned her MPhil and DPhil degrees in economics from Oxford, Bansal worked for seven years as an economist and international consultant, during which time both the feeling of sometimes being an outsider and a nagging question helped shape her sense of purpose. As she says:

> [I] ...was motivated by an interest, why economic models didn't really hold up in terms of explaining why firms would be environmentally responsible. I was curious about [the] limitations of economic models. That gave me more of a critical lens. I think that critical lens also applies partly because I am Canadian, and I think Canadians tend to be a little bit more willing to embrace diversity, [as you know, I am of] Indian origin although I'm completely Canadian. My parents are Indian, so there's this aspect of always feeling like you're a bit on the outside.

Pratima Bansal

Pratima (Tima) Bansal is professor and J. Allyn Taylor/Arthur H. Mingay Chair in Business Administration at the Richard Ivey School of Business at the University of Western Ontario, London, Ontario, Canada, director of the Cross-Enterprise Leadership Centre on Building Sustainable Value, director of Ivey's Sustainability Leadership program, and the executive director of the Network for Business Sustainability, all at the Ivey School. Awarded the Aspen Institute's Faculty Pioneer Award for Academic Leadership, she has also been named Faculty Scholar by Western Ontario University and a Fellow of the Oxford University Centre for Corporate Reputation. Working predominantly in the arena of sustainable development and international business, Bansal has published numerous papers in prestigious journals, including the *Academy of Management Journal, Organization Science, Strategic Management Journal*, and the *Journal of International Business Studies*, has co-edited several books, including *Business and the National Environment*, and co-authored some two dozen teaching cases. Something of a public intellectual, she is frequently quoted in the popular press, and also serves as associate editor of the *Academy of Management Journal*, and has served on several other editorial boards. Raised in Canada, Bansal holds a bachelor's degree from the University of Calgary, an MA from the University of Western Ontario, and MPhil and DPhil degrees from the University of Oxford in economics. In 2012 she was named to the prestigious Tier 1 Canada Research Chair in Business Sustainability by the Canadian government.

Bansal relates her purpose to her interest in making a difference in practice, bridging between theory and practice – another route for intellectual shamans beyond research that exists within management disciplines. A pioneer in studying business and ecological sustainability, Bansal sees her purpose in the importance of boosting sustainability in business as (in her words) a matter of some urgency. As she notes:

> Going back to the meaning of one's work, if I didn't believe in what I was doing, I'd probably just say, 'Yeah, moving on.' I really do believe that there's something bigger than me here. It's not just me following a fad [on the issues of sustainability and business]. It's believing that it's important work. My husband's a mathematician, and he does pure math, and this stuff [that] no one can talk to anyone about because there's maybe a half dozen people in the world who understand what he's saying. His work is going to end up in a journal that nobody will probably ever read yet he still finds it incredibly satisfying. At the same time he's driven by this internal drive, and if he doesn't feel like working he doesn't. I am not driven entirely by this internal drive. I'm driven by an urgency that, if we don't solve these issues first, then more...harm is going to come. So what sustains me is this external drive of wanting to help, wanting to help.

Josep Maria Lozano

Josep M. Lozano is professor at the Department of Social Sciences, ESADE Business School, Barcelona, Spain, and senior researcher in corporate social responsibility (CSR) at the Institute for Social Innovation, and part of the academic team of the Chair in Leaderships and Democratic Governance, at ESADE. Founder and former director of the Institute for the Individual, Corporations, and Society at ESADE, and director of the Observatory for Socially Responsible Investment in Spain, he also co-founded Ética, Economía y Dirección, the Spanish network in the European Business Ethics Network (EBEN). Lozano has served on the consortium of European universities that developed the European Academy of Business in Society (EABIS), on the Catalan government's Commission on Values, Forum of Experts on CSR for the Spanish Ministry of Employment and Social Affairs, and on the Taskforce for the Principles for Responsible Business Education of the UN Global Compact, among other appointments. Holding a doctorate from the University of Barcelona, and degrees in theology from the Theology Faculty of Catalonia and arts from the University of Barcelona, Lozana serves on multiple editorial and advisory boards, and has received numerous awards and honors. He has (co-)authored or edited numerous books and articles in both Spanish and English on corporate social responsibility, business ethics, organizational values and leadership, and spirituality in management.

Like Bansal, Josep Maria Lozano, professor at the ESADE Business School in Barcelona, Spain, is guided by a general set of values to do his notable work in corporate social responsibility and business ethics. Asked whether he had a vision, Lozano's response is:

> Good question. It's always a question. Even with my wife I will discuss that. If you understand vision as a clear design of the future, of a clear idea [about] what the future should be, I think the answer is 'No.' If you understand vision as clear consciousness, a clear awareness of some basic attitudes or some basic frameworks, that something is really important, I think that at this point I have a vision. For me, what is really important is that it is related to the Jesuit [ESADE Business School was founded by a Jesuit university] tradition of discernment. It is not so much a matter of having a clear idea and a vision of the future, but of developing attitudes and sensibilities that allow you, through the connection with your fundamental values, to respond in a suitable way to what the events you live through confront you with.

Here we see a general sense of values, or what he calls attitudes and sensibilities, guiding the work in business ethics and corporate social responsibility undertaken by Lozano, rather than a clear vision. These attitudes and sensibilities shape the direction of his scholarship and the academic programs with which he has become involved over the years, as his biography attests. His interest in spirituality and ethics led him to found a program at ESADE called the Vicens Vives program, which integrates 'values, civic commitment, and leadership' in a hands-on, highly interactive year-long program for emerging leaders. This sensibility also caused Lozano to become involved with the 50+20 group, which is trying to reform management education globally so that it develops more responsible leaders who are equipped to cope with a diverse, changing, and challenged world.

Paul Shrivastava

Paul Shrivastava is the David O'Brien Distinguished Professor and director of the David O'Brien Centre for Sustainable Enterprise at Concordia University, Montreal, Canada, and also leads the International Research Chair in Art and Sustainable Enterprise at ICN Business School, Nancy, France. Best known for his pioneering work in sustainability and business, Shrivastava now merges artistic with scientific approaches to sustainability and particularly to sustainable development. Co-editor (with Matt Statler) of *Learning from the Financial Crisis*, and author of *Bhopal: Anatomy of a Crisis*, among other books, he has published over 100 articles and seventeen books at this writing. Prior to joining Concordia, Shrivastava was the Howard I. Scott Chair in Management at Bucknell University, Lewisburg, Pennsylvania, and prior to that he taught at the Stern School of Business, New York University. He received a Fulbright Senior Scholar Award to research Japanese companies' sustainability at Kyoto University, and has taught at the Helsinki School of Economics. Shrivastava, who holds a bachelor's degree in mechanical engineering from the Maulana Azad National Institute of Technology, Bhopal, a Post Graduate Diploma in Management from the Indian Institute of

Management, Calcutta, and a PhD from the University of Pittsburgh, co-founded two academic journals, *Industrial Crisis Quarterly* and *Organization & Environment*, along with the Organizations and Natural Environment (ONE) Division of the Academy of Management, among numerous other accomplishments and interests.

Paul Shrivastava, currently the David O'Brien Distinguished Professor and director of the David O'Brien Centre for Sustainable Enterprise at Concordia University, Montreal, Canada, talks about the influence of his childhood and family in shaping his own sense of purpose. Shrivastava, who was born in India, comments:

> I think one of the sustaining influences has been that I grew up surrounded by a very open view of the major problems, social problems, in India with regard to poverty and underdevelopment. Then, as I came to the United States and lived there, I've always had a sensibility to social problems and a need to justify my own existence in terms of how much I'm influencing them or making an impact on them. I don't feel that being a professor or being at the university is a privilege to be taken for granted. It is something that you need to return back in terms of thinking and writing, your engagement with the community. So part of the influence, definitely, is from my home, from my upbringing, from my mother. I grew up in a single-parent home in India, which was very, very unusual in those days. My mother was a physician, a doctor, and she practiced the kind of barefoot medicine that was about helping people. She would go out and put herself into a risky situation to help people who were desperately in need of help. That has been an enduring influence. I've always seen that, as humans, that is part of being a full human, to connect with people and to do things that affect the community.

Others, such as Dave Brown, who gave up a tenured full professor appointment at Boston University to become senior lecturer at the Harvard Kennedy School, where he thought his social and economic development work would have more impact, offer clarity in their articulation of the retrospectively 'discovered' sense of purpose, which might not have always been evident for them. Brown puts it this way:

> When push comes to shove, doing something about fairness, justice, making the world a better place is more important to me – is most important to me. Now I'd like to be a professor, I'd like to have a chair and so on, and be recognized as a contributor to intellectual capital. But I want to contribute to intellectual capital that makes a difference, that people can use, that is going to contribute, to. . .more inclusive institutions, both political and economic. Maybe I've never outgrown my Peace Corps days, or maybe the Peace Corps happened to be the right fit for somebody like me.

Similarly to Brown, Derick de Jongh, who heads the University of Pretoria's Centre for Responsible Leadership, articulates a clear sense of drive to make the world better – and has, accordingly, surrounded himself with like-minded people in this Center:

> The one thing that all of us [working in the Centre] have in common [. . .] – and it's going to sound very, very corny – but it's a basic, deeper calling. It's something much deeper in us: why are we doing this? What I believe in and what I live every day, and what I do, are all in alignment with my constant realization that things aren't well at the moment. Saying I want to make a difference the world sounds very precious, but it's true. So that's what's driving me. I've got a constant – how can I call it? – something that almost haunts me. I'm never satisfied with anything. There's always that something out there that forces me to say: 'But this is not what it should be.'

Some of the intellectual shamans, even very renowned scholars such as the University of Michigan's Karl Weick, would claim not to have a sense of core purpose at all, even while implicitly articulating one. Weick is perhaps best known for work on retrospective sense-making and enactment, which argues that people look back on actions to make sense of what they have done, and the theory of loosely coupled systems, which explains how organizations can operate when they are not tightly coordinated.

Karl Weick

Karl Weick is the Rensis Likert Distinguished University Professor at the Ross School of Business, University of Michigan. Holding a bachelor's degree from Wittenberg College (Springfield, Ohio) and MA and PhD degrees in psychology from Ohio State University, Weick is known for his work on sensemaking, enactment, loosely coupled systems, and mindfulness, particularly with respect to organizations. Named a Fellow of the American Psychological Association, the Academy of Management, the American Sociological Association, and several other major professional associations, Weick has been at the University of Michigan since 1988, and has also served on the faculty of Seattle University, Cornell University, and the University of Minnesota, and as a visitor at Stanford, the State University of Utrecht, the Netherlands, and others. Weick is recipient of numerous honors, including honorary degrees, the Levinson Award from the American Psychological Foundation, and best book or article, and best scholar, awards from numerous associations, and has served on numerous journal editorial boards, including serving as editor of *Administrative Science Quarterly* from 1977 to 1985. Weick has published (or co-published) more than 200 articles and chapters, more than eighty book reviews, and numerous books, including perhaps his most famous books, *The Social Psychology of Organizing*, *Sensemaking in Organizations*, and *Managing the Unexpected*.

Modest by nature, Weick has informed organizational theory through the years by studying phenomena and assessing how people make sense of those phenomena. Of his own work, he says:

> I think it's that cognition lies in the path of the action. I suppose, if there's any mantra that I believe, it would be that one, and that's been with me for a long time. I'm not a particularly active person,

though. So maybe that's a wish that I could act my way into more feelings or do more different actions and arrive at different kinds of feelings or cognitions. But the theorizing really does follow that kind of thread going through. You could call that a vision. I don't think I would. I don't feel a lack because I don't have a vision. I certainly am around people who have them, people like Jane Dutton or Noel Tichy or Bob Quinn and other ones who act that way. [...] I'm more opportunistic, probably more eclectic, or I've just been really lucky that people have asked me to do terrific things or things that turn into terrific projects.

Kim S. Cameron

Kim Cameron is, at this writing, the William Russell Kelly Professor of Management and Organizations in the Ross School of Business, Professor of Higher Education in the School of Education, and associate dean, executive education, at the University of Michigan, Ann Arbor. With BS and MS degrees from Brigham Young University, and an MA and PhD from Yale, Cameron has published over 120 articles and fourteen books. He is known for his work on organizational downsizing, effectiveness, and culture, and also on leadership excellence. A co-founder of the Center for Positive Organizational Scholarship and leader in that emerging field, Cameron has also been dean of the Weatherhead School of Management at Case Western Reserve University and associate dean of the Marriott School of Management at Brigham Young. He is a Fellow of the Academy of Management and has received the David L. Bradford Outstanding Educator Award from the Organizational Behavior Teaching Society, in addition to numerous other recognitions and honors, and serves on multiple editorial boards, including those for the *Academy of Management Learning and Education Journal*, the *Journal of Management Education*, and *Human Resource Management*, among others.

Similarly to Weick, Kim Cameron, William Russell Kelly Professor of Management and Organizations at the Ross School of

Business and Professor of Higher Education in the School of Education at the University of Michigan, who is also at this writing associate dean for executive education, claims not to have a vision. Yet Cameron has published pathbreaking work on compassion in organizations, organizational effectiveness, and virtuousness in organizations, and, with Bob Quinn, the competing values framework discussed above. Cameron, speaking about a vision underlying his work, comments:

> I think not. I could never have predicted that I would be doing what I am doing now having accomplished what I have accomplished now. So I am on the other end of the continuum from my friend Bob Quinn. Bob says you should plan your life out, a vision statement, and work toward it and be very clear and don't get deflected and all that stuff, and he is inspiring. Many people just think he walks on water when he gives that kind of message. I think it is wonderful. It just doesn't characterize my life. My philosophy is that I feel like my job is to prepare and to be prepared, and then opportunities will be presented to me and I should take advantage. I have to be thoughtful about which opportunities I select, but my job is to be prepared; my job is not to set the agenda. Things will unfold. So I have had a different career path in that sense. There are people, like Bob, who has been very careful at crafting what he wants to do, and I have not.

'I GOT LUCKY': OPPORTUNITY AND THE RIGHT INFLUENCES/NETWORKS

The 'I got lucky' theme articulated by Karl Weick and, in a sense, Kim Cameron, above, is not unique to them, nor is the humility with which they speak about their own work. As must be clear from the examples we have already seen, not all intellectual shamans see their paths as deliberately chosen – or necessarily as coming about because of their particular skills and abilities. Many view themselves, despite the hard work that has led to their success, as extraordinarily lucky, opportunistic, or as having been in the right place at the right time. They have clearly been willing to follow opportunities as they arise and take the associated risks. As Parker Palmer notes and Dave Brown's retrospectively stated sense of purpose suggests, the 'call' to living one's one life purpose can be subtle – and understanding what that call is can sometimes be a long time in coming. Perhaps it is that subtlety that can sometimes make finding the way to being wholly oneself seem like 'luck' or serendipity – something that might have easily been missed without close attention.

Ever the philosophical pragmatist, the University of Virginia's Ed Freeman highlights his orientation toward teaching as his core purpose and the path that took him to his present position, as University Professor at the University of Virginia, as partly attributable to serendipity or pure luck – even happenstance. Talking about his vision or sense of direction, Freeman's response is:

> Serendipity. A lot of people who teach in business schools like Darden, if they weren't teaching at Darden (Darden's a very business-oriented type of school), would be in business. I would be teaching eighth grade math. What I've known for a long time is that teaching was what I wanted to do. The only temptation not to do that was when I sort of fell in love with Freud and the psychoanalytic literature. But that meant you had to go to medical school, and I wasn't about to do that. There are lots of similarities between the role of the teacher and the role of psychoanalyst. Once I learned more about teaching, [I realized] I'd get all the psychoanalytical stuff I'd need from relationships with students and colleagues.
>
> I knew pretty soon after I read the *Credo*, the *Apology*, Plato's *Republic*, that I wanted to do philosophy, that I wanted to teach philosophy, and I always have. Which, in a business school, it's in courses called 'management' and 'strategy.' But, make no mistake about it, it's philosophy. But philosophy in a very different sense than professional philosophers would see it, where I think I would not be seen as a real philosopher. Because I took Socrates seriously, that this is about how we live our life. Philosophy has to be practical in that sense. It has to start with experience. That's what I've always tried to do.

So there hasn't been any sort of vision. [...] I've said to Maureen, my wife, 'Look, one of the things I know is that you fell in love with me, not my prospects, because I didn't have any.' 'Cause there are no jobs in teaching philosophy. So I just got lucky. I mean, I got lucky being at Wharton. I got lucky working on this stakeholder idea, and the time was right. So there's no grand plan. There's stuff I've always stood for, around teaching, around trying to teach philosophy. A part of that is ethics. But whether I did that at a business school or a philosophy department, [...] I just fell into kind of a lucky way to do it.

Freeman also acknowledges the serendipity that took him to the Wharton Business School at the University of Pennsylvania early in his career – and the many influences there that made possible the early work on stakeholder theory that has made his reputation. Implicit, as with other intellectual shamans, is Freeman's recognition that no one achieves success single-handedly; networks of influential others, friends, and family play essential roles. Freeman noted that one of his advisors in his PhD program at the Washington University told him he should apply for a postdoctoral position. He recalls:

I was very young. I was maybe twenty-three, and I didn't really know much. I'd gone straight from Duke, where I did math and philosophy, to Washington University, where I did the PhD... I had a sister who'd done a postdoc in psychology. Postdocs seemed to be great. I didn't know what they were, but it was fine. I said, 'Where?' He said, 'Well, Pittsburgh,' which had a great philosophy department, and he said, 'But, given what you're interested in, you should go to Wharton.' I said, 'What's that?,' because I had never really heard of Wharton. He said, 'It's a business school,' and my face fell. I thought they taught typing and shorthand. So I said, you know, 'Is it a good one?' He said, 'Well, it's one of the best.' So I said, 'But it's a business school.' He said, 'Yes.' 'Where is it?' He said, 'Philadelphia, Pennsylvania.'

I said, 'Well, I might be interested.' Because my girlfriend – now my wife of thirty plus years – was going to grad school in city planning there. So I went off to Wharton, interviewed, got a sort of research position. About a year into that a bunch of us decided to start our own research center called the Wharton Applied Research Center. We had originally been working with a group called the Busch Center – [management theorist] Russell Ackoff was really one of the pioneers of systems theory. A hallmark of his approach was using stakeholder analysis as a way of analyzing, a way of sort of categorizing things. He wrote about this in a book he published in the early '70s called *Redesigning the Future*. That was written at Wharton. Eric Trist was there; Howard Perlmutter – a whole bunch of people who were thinking about this stuff. We started this new research center. We had projects with companies and then we had development areas – areas that we wanted to take forward as kind of intellectual activities. I sort of picked the stakeholder area as one I wanted to do something with. There's a lot of stuff about it, but no one had ever really, I thought, thought about it in a systematic way. So that's what I set out to do.

So how did I start this? It was honestly just kind of chasing after a young woman. And going to Wharton. I was young, I didn't know any better. Wharton was a place in those days – Russ Ackoff always said Wharton was like an 'A' student that got 'B's. That's before it started to get 'A's, which it does now. But it was a place that was intellectually open enough that it could take someone who had a PhD in philosophy, who had never worked, had always been an academic and could find a place that had enough respect for ideas and people. [...] So...Wharton always has a very special place in my heart because of that.

Happenstance, or opportunism in terms of others around to create the right kind of intellectual atmosphere and luck in terms of being in the right place at the right time, can provide fertile ground for hearing the call to purpose and the power that it brings. John Van Maanen of MIT followed his heart to do the inductive ethnographically based research to which he was called, and for which he is rightly famous. Van Maanen highlights some of the serendipity of being in the right place at the right time with the influence of mentors in recalling his own history:

> Well, I came from a sort of working-class background, first in my family to get an undergraduate degree. Went to Long Beach State, grew up in California. Backed into graduate school because I didn't want to get drafted. [...]
>
> So that's been helpful [being at MIT]. But, no, there wasn't any grand vision. [...] Then, once [in graduate school], gosh, it was really interesting. But I had no idea what I was getting into. I think that's true of most fieldworkers. I guess you think you know what you're stepping into, but it very rarely meets your expectations. It usually turns out to be something quite different. 'When did you burn your research proposal?' is the sort of question people ask.

Although he was following his heart in doing the type of research he wanted to do, Van Maanen was unclear about steps beyond the PhD until several influential people took him under their wing. He remembers:

> I was in the field for a year, and as I was writing up my thesis, which took me two years, but one of my [University of California] Irvine people, Lyman Porter, sat next to Ed Schein [of MIT] at some event that they were at. He said he had this student that was doing unusual work in organizations. Ed then said, 'Well, we're hiring, so maybe we could have an interview.' Then I think Argyris, Chris Argyris [late, of Harvard Business School], was at the same table. So they decided they would split my airfare and I could interview at Harvard and I could interview at MIT. I had lived on Long Island for six months in the winter once, but I'd never really been east.
>
> So I came to Boston, and I came to MIT because my bookshelf was filled with Ed Schein's work and other people's work who were here then. The organization studies group seemed like a perfect place to be for what I wanted to do, which was to continue doing fieldwork,

continue writing about police. I was getting increasingly interested [in what] we later came to call occupational communities. But my work was socialization. Ed worked with socialization. Then we said, 'Well, socialization is a kind of little slice of it. Maybe we need to look at careers.' There was a Chicago school tradition of career studies, and my police work kind of led to that, because I kept going back at three- to five-year intervals for the course of my cohorts, the people I went through the [police] training academy with, for their careers. So I sort of followed them out for twenty, twenty-five years.

SOMETIMES A CROOKED PATH: WHEN PURPOSE SNEAKS UP ON YOU...

The path to purpose is not always so straightforward. As we have already seen, it is sometimes a crooked path, in which purpose is eventually revealed – or only retrospectively makes sense. Below, we will look a couple more examples of intellectual shamans who both 'got lucky' in the sense that Ed Freeman described in the section above, and also had the good fortune to uncover their purpose after a long period of moving from task to task and job to job without any particular sense of purpose.

Rajendra S. Sisodia

Rajendra (Raj) Sisodia is the F. W. Olin Distinguished Professor of Global Business and Whole Foods Market Research Scholar in Conscious Capitalism at Babson College, Wellesley, Massachusetts, which he joined in 2013. Formerly, he was Trustee Professor of Marketing at Bentley University, Waltham, Massachusetts, founder and chairman of the Conscious Capitalism Institute (CCI), and one of the founders of the conscious capitalism movement, as well as founding director of the Center for Marketing Technology and chair of the Marketing Department at Bentley. Holding a PhD from Columbia University, an MBA from the Bajaj Institute of Management Studies in Mumbai, and an electrical engineering degree from the Birla Institute of Technology and Science, Pilani, India, Sisodia was previously Trustee

> Professor of Marketing and founding director of the Center for
> Marketing Technology. Cited in 2003 as one of fifty 'Leading marketing
> thinkers' by the Chartered Institute of Marketing, Sisodia has written
> more than 100 articles and seven books, including co-authoring *Firms of
> Endearment: How World-Class Companies Profit from Passion and
> Purpose, Tectonic Shift: The Geoeconomic Realignment of Globalizing
> Markets, The Rule of Three* (with Jag Sheth), and *Does Marketing Need
> Reform?*. Sisodia received the Award for Excellence in Scholarship from
> Bentley University in 2007, the Innovative Teaching Award in 2008,
> was named one of 'Ten outstanding trailblazers of 2010' by Good
> Business International, and one of the 'Top 100 thought leaders in
> trustworthy business behavior' by Trust Across America in 2010 and
> 2011. At this writing, his most recent book is *Conscious Capitalism*, co-
> written with John Mackey and Bill George.

Raj Sisodia, one of the founders of the emerging conscious capitalism movement and author of a book entitled *Conscious Capitalism*
(with Whole Foods CEO John Mackey and Bill George, released 2013),
is F. W. Olin Distinguished Professor of Global Business and Whole
Foods Market Research Scholar in Conscious Capitalism at Babson
College, and also founder and chair of the Conscious Capitalism
Institute. Previously, Sisodia had been Trustee Professor of
Marketing at Bentley University. Unlike others who knew or at least
sensed their purpose relatively early on, Sisodia followed a more traditional intellectual path before writing up a research project and associated seminal book that helped open his eyes to his own sense of
purpose, *Firms of Endearment: How World-Class Companies Profit
from Passion and Purpose*. In Sisodia's story, we can see both the
influence of mentors, or caring other people, and serendipity, that
sense of being in the right place at the right time with the right people.
Sisodia explains the somewhat opportunistic nature of his journey:

> I had a rough start. I describe my journey as an accident or
> opportunity; actually, I refer to it as opportunistic drifting, because
> there was never a grand plan. I also did not have the sense of higher

purpose or mission or something that truly excited me. It was always at every stage just doing what seemed to be the next best choice in a sort of pragmatic way. That went all the way back to high school. I went into engineering because I happened to be good at math, not because I had a passion for engineering.

This was in India. It's a place called Birla Institute of Technology and Science. It's one of the IITs [Indian Institutes of Technology] in India. Then, after I became an electrical engineer without having any real passion for engineering, I worked for about a month and then got into business school, because in those days in India business schools were much better than being an engineer in terms of career options. It was very tough to get into those schools, so, if you got in, you pretty much took the job. There I took marketing because I didn't like finance or accounting. So I kind of backed into that.

Opportunistically, one day Sisodia ran into a group of friends about to register for the Graduate Management Admission Test (GMAT) at the American Consulate so they could apply to PhD programs in business. Sisodia continues:

So I went and got the forms and a few weeks later they gave the GMAT exam, and a few weeks later we got the results. Out of that group of ten, I'm the only one who ended up actually coming for a PhD to the US. Again, the motivation was, it seems like a fun thing to do, go to the US. Not that I had a passion for research. I did enjoy writing and I did enjoy teaching to some extent. I did a little bit of that with my fellow students, helping them with things that they needed help with. So I ended up in a PhD program and...did OK academically and drifted into a dissertation topic. The point is that, at every stage, it was never some internal drive, but it was always just external pragmatism. I became a professor [at Boston University] and after a slow start I did OK with that. Actually, I only stayed [at Boston] three and a half years, because I was still doing my dissertation. I got a very slow start on my research, so it really wasn't an option for me to stay beyond that.

Sisodia notes that it took some twenty years to 'figure something out, to get into something that truly excited me [i.e., *Conscious Capitalism*].' To that point he was involved in interesting work because he had connected with Jag Sheth, Kellstadt Chair of Marketing in the Goizueta Business School at Emory University, who brought him into interesting and high-profile projects. The sense of purpose for Sisodia thus emerged slowly and only in the context of doing interesting new research and asking questions that he had not previously asked. This research opened his eyes to wholly new ways of seeing and engaging with the world and with his work, particularly his work with colleague and mentor Jag (Jagdish) Sheth, world-renowned marketing scholar. By the 1990s Sisodia was engaged in the world of telecommunications, what he terms a 'brave new world coming into shape.' But the field of marketing was becoming more frustrating, because,

> well, it is a discipline that evokes a lot of mixed feelings in people. It's not an inherently self-justifying profession, if you will, a socially valuable profession. It's seen as a thing that consumes a lot of resources. It tries to convince people to do things that may or may not be necessarily in their best interests, focuses a lot on wants and desires and so forth. So a lot of my work within marketing was focused on marketing efficiency and effectiveness. Is it actually contributing to a better world? Asking that question.

Through this work, however, Sisodia noticed that, as marketing productivity increased, customer satisfaction and loyalty were decreasing. He recognized that

> [i]t just seemed like a lot of money being thrown after not very noble ends and not being very successfully done in what they were trying to achieve. That in a roundabout way led to a project called In Search of Marketing Excellence, which was about companies that did it right, that had positive impact on the world, had high customer satisfaction and loyalty, and spent reasonable, not excessive amounts, of money on marketing.

That then led to the discovery of these companies that...actually were equally loved and trusted by their employees and communities and so forth [documented in Sisodia, D. B. Wolfe, and Sheth's book *Firms of Endearment: How World-Class Companies Profit from Passion and Purpose*]. So they were clearly stakeholder-oriented, but beyond that they also had the sense of something special about them, higher purpose, etc., and a different kind of leadership that really cared about that higher purpose and about the people and the planet and so forth. So that's really when I started to feel fully alive, doing what I do. The book came out in 2007, so let's say around 2005. So, literally twenty years after I started teaching and writing, I felt now here was a project that I could really get excited about, because here are businesses that are truly having multiple positive impacts on the world. It's not just about making money, not just about selling things, etc. It's about having multiple kinds of benefits all around.

From this start, Sisodia then met Whole Foods CEO John Mackey, stakeholder theorist Ed Freeman, and others interested in the type of company that they had studied, and moved to found the Conscious Capitalism Institute, a movement to try to reform capitalism along the lines of the firms of endearment companies. The CCI represents a group of managers, leaders, and scholars interested in forwarding a new vision of business. Ed Freeman, a trustee of the institute, powerfully states the importance of purpose – for companies as well as individuals, and, in this case, for intellectual and other shamans – on the group's website and in talks that he gives:

> We need red blood cells to live (the same way a business needs profits to live), but the purpose of life is more than to make red blood cells (the same way the purpose of business is more than simply to generate profits).[3n]

NOT ON YOUR OWN: THE IMPORTANCE OF MENTORS,
NETWORKS, AND OTHER INFLUENCES

In Sisodia's and others' experiences, we have already seen the important
roles that mentors, networks of like-minded individuals, family members, and other influential people play in the individual shamans'
ultimate success. Mentors, networks, and influential others provide
opportunities that might not otherwise be discovered, and also play
crucial roles in shaping ideas, attitudes toward the profession, and the
orientation toward the work that the intellectual shaman eventually
adopts. For those intellectual shamans who started out without a clear
sense of direction, mentors and influential others can be essential com-
ponents of an eventually successful career. Of course, the individual still
has to be capable of and willing to do the hard work necessary to take
advantage of the opportunities given. When these intellectual shamans
say they 'got lucky,' or that they took advantage of opportunities that
fell into their paths, it is often through the auspices of mentors and other
influential people, as well as the support of spouses, that these opportunities came to be or could be taken, even though it is through their
own auspices that the hard work got done. We have already seen how
this kind of 'happenstance' influenced the careers of Dave Brown,
Nancy Adler, Ed Freeman, Ian Mitroff, Raj Sisodia, and others.

   That same element of being in the right place, at the right time,
with the right people thinking new and innovative thoughts influenced the career of intellectual shaman Ed Schein, now Sloan
Fellows Professor of Management Emeritus at the MIT Sloan School
of Management. Schein gained international renown for his work on
organizational careers and cultures, and for research that was both
informed by and informed practice.

Edgar H. Schein

Edgar (Ed) Schein is the Sloan Fellows Professor of Management
Emeritus at the MIT Sloan School of Management, with which he has
been affiliated since joining the Sloan School in 1956. Schein holds a

PhD in social psychology from Harvard University, and a masters' degree in psychology from Stanford University, and served as chief of the social psychology section of the Walter Reed Army Institute of Research, and as a captain in the US Army, from 1952 to 1956. He became Professor of Organizational Psychology and Management at MIT in 1964, served as Undergraduate Planning Professor, Chairman of Organization Studies Group, and was named the Sloan Fellows Professor of Management in 1978 (through 1990), and now holds that title emeritus. A productive author, Schein is known for his work on careers, organizational culture, and process consultation. He studied the culture of the Singapore Economic Development Board (published as *Strategic Pragmatism*), and worked for many years with Digital Equipment Corporation, culminating in the book *DEC Is Dead, Long Live DEC: The Lasting Legacy of Digital Equipment Corporation*, and served as founding editor of the Society for Organizational Learning's journal *Reflections*. His latest book is *Helping: How to Offer, Give, and Receive Help*. Schein is recipient of many awards, including the Lifetime Achievement Award in Workplace Learning and Performance of the American Society of Training Directors, the Everette Cherington Hughes Award for Career Scholarship of the Careers Division of the Academy of Management, the Lifetime Achievement Award of the Organization Development Network, and the Distinguished Scholar-Practitioner Award of the Academy of Management, among others, and is a Fellow of the American Psychological Association and Academy of Management.

Like some of the other intellectual shamans, Schein admits that there is a degree of serendipity in how he came to be fully himself, and credits others with providing significant opportunities that influenced his ultimate choices. In many ways, his journey to finding his full power is typical of other intellectual shamans, so it is worth telling his story in some detail. Schein, who was in his eighties at the time of the interview and still active, though officially retired from MIT, starts his description of his journey:

Well, the basic way to put it is that I think I was always very much driven by circumstances rather than by design or plan. So one of the earliest influences I can remember is at the University of Chicago, not knowing what I wanted to do. At that time there was a very general education program where we took big courses in philosophy, science, etc. In the biology course there was a little segment on psychology. At that time the person who was just evolving his theory was [psychologist] Carl Rogers. What I remember was caricaturing him. My friends and I would go around repeating to each other what the other person had said [a therapeutic technique pioneered by Rogers], and we thought that was really funny that anyone would make any sense out of just saying back to the person what they had just said.

After three years in Chicago Schein determined that he actually was indeed interested in psychology, not the physics path chosen by his father, so he applied to Stanford and was accepted for a two-year bachelor's and master's degree. As Schein describes it, his move from individual psychology to social psychology was more of a drifting toward the area than a clear decision that he made, and it was shaped by interactions with key influencers and mentors. At Stanford, he was influenced by Harry Helson, a psychologist known for 'adaptation level' theory, which explores how context affects human perception and judgment, and began working with Helson on whether social pressures could influence perceptions – e.g., of how much something weighed. After two years, having taken all of the relevant psychology courses at Stanford, Schein was again faced with the 'What's next?' question. Fortunately, he landed at Harvard, where influences and important mentors were many, as he recalls:

It was the best decision I ever made, because Harvard at that time had combined psychology – social psychology, clinical psychology, sociology, and anthropology – into the Department of Social Relations. So, right off the bat I got influenced by this whole range of fields, and this was in '49, '50, '51, which was probably the heyday of social relations [theory], because at that point all the major figures decided to work together, . . .just the whole array of people who were very active in the field.

Soon after joining Harvard, Schein realized that he had to undertake a year-long clinical internship to get the PhD. Combining that requirement with the fact that the draft was still in existence, he decided to join the army's clinical psychology training program as a second lieutenant, and with a three-year postgraduation commitment to the army as a psychologist.

During his training internship at Walter Reed Hospital's Institute of Research, Schein again found himself in circumstances that opened pathways that more or less opportunistically shaped his future course. Of course, none of these opportunities would have been meaningful unless Schein himself had taken advantage of them – and had the creativity, training, and insight to know what do with them. The stint in the army shaped his choices and opportunities, and, like others, he seized those opportunities – and made the most of them, guided by his own intuition and instincts about what would be both interesting and useful to study. Schein's early work in the army following his PhD was on the socialization processes used by internment camps with prisoners of war. Below he tells how that research came to be:

> Then it was time to pay back the army, so they sent me back to Walter Reed, where they had a very nice research lab run by the psychiatrist David Rioch [David McKenzie Rioch, ultimately director of the Walter Reed Army Institute of Research Division of Neuropsychiatry, 1951–1970].[77] He was the head of something called 'Chestnut Lodge,' which was a famous hospital in the Maryland area for severe schizophrenia, and autism, and his wife, Margaret Rioch. He was one of these people who really believed in interdisciplinary work. So, in the research lab at Walter Reed, he had an ecologist, biologist, Skinnerian, experimental psychologist, several psychiatrists who were studying what was then called shell shock, but what we call today post-traumatic shock, me as a social

psychologist, a statistician. We were all supposed to just sort of work on problems that interested us.

I had, while I was at Harvard, taken a course at MIT taught by Alex Bavelas [who founded the Group Network Laboratory at MIT], who was one of [Kurt] Lewin's [often called the founder of social psychology, and founder of the National Training Labs (NTLs) at Bethel, Maine; known for work on 'sensitivity training'] main students when Lewin was doing the research center for group dynamics. I loved Bavelas' experiment, the one-way, two-way, communication experiment: the broken squares experiment. Hal Leavitt [Harold Leavitt, Stanford University, known for his work on group dynamics, communication, and social networks] had just finished his communication stuff. So at Walter Reed I started a kind of comparable set of experiments on leadership and communication. Then one day I got a telegram saying to report to Travis Air Force Base [AFB] in forty-eight hours. If you're in the army, you do that. So I packed my bag. I had no military training. They had told me to go down to the army base here on Summer Street and buy a uniform and a manual and learn how to salute, because at Walter Reed I had to be in uniform and act like a real solider. By then I was a first lieutenant, so well paid for a first postdoc real job.

Following orders, Schein flew to Travis AFB in California, where he joined a group of psychologists, social workers and psychiatrists, who were shortly flown to Tokyo. The armistice with the North Koreans and Chinese had been signed, and some 3,000 repatriated prisoners of war were coming out of prison camp. With the government worried, as Schein put it, about whether US troops had 'all been brainwashed' (to which he replied: 'Well, let's find out. Let's put a team on board ships to interview the men, do any counseling that was needed, and find out what had gone on'), he found himself on one of the debriefing teams. What happened next illustrates how a combination of opportunity combined with the willingness to follow his own instincts shaped Schein's future:

We spent a week in Tokyo, flew on to Incheon, Korea. At that point, we're supposed to board a ship with several hundred repatriates and come back. They were coming through by the truckload into this army base and I learned that my ship was delayed for three weeks, so what to do? Here I am having just studied imitation, an experimental social psychologist, and there's all this talk about brainwashing. So I decided just to start pulling people at random off this repatriation line, and sitting them down and interviewing them in a very straightforward [way]: 'Tell me from the moment you got captured what had happened to you.'

This is where David (Rioch) comes in, because he had been mentoring a lot of us, and somewhere along the line we had been talking about interviewing. He said something that I've never forgotten: 'When you're really trying to find out something that may conceivably be in any way socially sensitive, do not ask about it. If you want to find out something, don't ask about it.' It was a paradoxical advice, but of course it made complete sense. If I was going to ask a repatriate 'Why did you sign a confession? Why did you collaborate with the enemy?,' there's no way you'd get anything approximating the truth. Versus saying, 'I'm interested in your story. Tell me from the day you got captured what happened.'

They started telling me about how the Chinese soldiers were friendly and would say things like 'Congratulations, you've been liberated.' Then the interrogator would point out how unjust the war was, and why were we in North Korea anyway? If a leader in the camp said 'Don't pay any attention to this bullshit; they're just trying to get you to collaborate,' pretty soon that leader would disappear and be moved somewhere else. So I began to piece together the whole array of techniques that the Chinese communists had evolved in their own movement and were now using in prison camp because they wanted the propaganda. They wanted to show that their version of communism really was the right version.

Schein returned to the United States and wrote up his study, which eventually was published in the journal *Psychiatry*, to considerable acclaim (despite initial problems in getting it published). Then it was time to leave the army and figure out what to do next. With an offer from Cornell Psychology Department in hand, Schein made a 'crooked' turn in his career path, taking a significant risk by joining a fledgling business program instead. Unexpectedly, he had received a letter to apply for an assistant professorship in the business school at MIT from Douglas McGregor. McGregor was a well-known humanistic psychologist, who applied some of psychology professor Abraham Maslow's humanistic ideas about managing and leadership to business in a book entitled *The Human Side of Enterprise*, which articulated 'theory X' and 'theory Y' orientations to management. The story again highlights the serendipity and networks involved in some choices, the necessity of taking risks, and the impacts of influential others on choices available:

> In '56 it was time to leave the army, so what to do? I had a pretty good offer from Cornell's Psychology Department. Then out of the blue this letter arrives – again, circumstances – from a man whose name I had read in articles, from Douglas McGregor. [. . .] It was an invitation to consider an assistant professorship in the School of Industrial Management at MIT. I'll tell you, I literally did not know at all what this meant, 'industrial management' – brand new idea. At MIT I had taken the courses with Bavelas, but that's all I knew.
>
> So it was a dilemma. My mainstream career was to go to Cornell, but I liked Bavelas's stuff. Bavelas was still here [at MIT], so I decided to at least look into. It came to be that McGregor and the school were trying to hire disciplinary people, rather than management people. So McGregor had gone to Gordon Allport [a well-known psychology professor at Harvard, known for his work on trait theory and a founding scholar in the area of personality theory] and said, 'Do you know of any social psychologist, because we're looking for one here?' So Allport, who had been my thesis advisor, said, 'Well, try Ed Schein.'

So they sent me this letter. I came and interviewed and thought long and hard about it, but I also went to Cornell. I think I had gotten, without realizing it, Charles River fever [the Charles River flows by MIT between Boston and Cambridge]. This was an unknown job, and it was risky, but MIT, Cambridge – I had done my work here. Cornell was sort of way up in the woods. I wasn't sure I wanted to be there. So I decided to gamble and come here. [...] It was called the School of Industrial Management [now the MIT Sloan School of Management]. It had grown out of an undergraduate program in industrial management, and they had had a grant from Alfred Sloan creating the Sloan Fellows program, which was operating in the School of Industrial Management.

For Schein, the challenge of joining MIT's new program, despite its fledgling status, proved a powerful career choice. At MIT he picked up on the different opportunities that presented themselves, which will be discussed in a later chapter.

POWER OF PURPOSE: UNIQUE TO THE INDIVIDUAL

The call to purpose is also related to the power that comes from finding one's purpose in life. There is a transcendent quality to finding that purpose and integrating it with one's life, thereby creating meaningfulness in one's life[68,78] that could well be associated with self-confidence and clarity about what one is doing and why. Goals, directedness, and meaningfulness are all associated with having purpose in life, as are aspirations,[79] particularly for what I have elsewhere called difference-making – making the world better for others in some way. Below, I briefly explore how some of the intellectual shamans experience that sense of power in finding their purpose – a purpose that inevitably is unique to the individual, and cannot be imposed by someone else.

The University of Michigan's Andy Hoffman, for example, started his career in chemical engineering without much sense of direction, though he had already developed an interest in the environmental issues around which his life's work later formed. He notes,

'I was really looking for a deeper purpose, and Love Canal happened [a neighbourhood in Niagara Falls, New York, that became notorious as a toxic waste site in the 1970s]. I was really struck by that, and thought, "OK, this is what a chemical engineer can do: trying to make sure that doesn't happen again."' But, as he notes, when he graduated from the University of Massachusetts Amherst in 1983 'environmental issues just weren't in vogue,' so finding work in that arena was difficult. One recruiter actually said to him, 'Yeah, that's the chic thing to do nowadays, but we're not interested in that at [this company],' so he went to work for the Environmental Protection Agency for a couple of years, then applied to graduate schools. Instead of going to Harvard or Berkeley, where he had been accepted, he 'answered an ad in the paper looking for carpenters and flew to Nantucket and took a job as a carpenter. I then had to sit down with my parents and say: "I'm not going to Harvard or Berkeley. I'm going to pound nails." That was a hard conversation.'

Hoffman later wrote about the years he spend building mansions and learning the building trade as a very young project manager in an autobiographical account called *Builder's Apprentice*. Despite enjoying building, Hoffman felt a call do more on the environment, and went to MIT for a master's degree. Once he finished he was offered the opportunity to stay and run an environmental consortium. When that possibility fell through at the last minute, he accepted a fellowship for the PhD program at MIT, though, as he recounts, his future path was far from straightforward. It is clear that he already had a sense of personal power, a clear sense of self, confidence, and groundedness – and the need to use it for what Buddhists call 'right work':

> Two weeks before classes began I started a PhD, and all through the PhD I kept saying, 'I'm not going to be an academic. I want to be in the real world.' Then, at the very end, I was using Amoco as a case study in my dissertation and I had to give a presentation to the board. I just had this epiphany that, to be in a company like Amoco, which was fairly progressive, and get to a position to effect change, you're

going to have to toe the party line for about ten or fifteen years. I just wasn't willing to do that, so at the last minute I decided to go into academics.

Hoffman immediately ran into a problem. Coming out of MIT with a joint degree in management and civil and environmental engineering, he discovered that 'I had to be legitimized in business schools. I had a dual degree. People didn't know what to do with that.' For Hoffman, there was a degree of unexpectedness and serendipity in his ending up in a chaired professorship in a business school. As he notes, 'So, a lot of people laugh, and I laugh myself that I'm actually sitting where I'm sitting. I was not the person you'd expect to be in an endowed chair at the University of Michigan. I never would have predicted this to happen.'

Hoffman's purpose – to do something to help businesses improve their practices with respect to the natural environment – and his hesitancy with respect to an academic career also lent a certain power to the choices that he was able to make, because he was and is not tied to any particular path. He recognizes this sense of power in the following comment:

> I think it's because I backed into everything in this career. I didn't set out at the beginning to be an academic. If I did, I would have been fully wedded to the process and the outcome. I've seen the terror of some friends and colleagues who are totally committed to academia when they go for tenure. If they don't get tenure, they're in trouble, because they don't have a set of skills that are as broadly applicable. But I knew I had options and was not so concerned. My ambivalence was genuine. I just sort of backed into this and that ambivalence is a very powerful thing. Deb Meyerson [and Maureen Scully in an article in *Organization Science* on 'tempered radicals'[80,81]] talks about the idea that ambivalence for tempered radicals is truly empowering, if you really are [ambivalent]. It can't be feigned. It has to be real, and it was real for me. It would have stung if I'd gotten denied tenure, of course. But I would have picked myself up and kept on going. It wouldn't have been hard.

THE COURAGE TO BE YOURSELF

As with Hoffman, for many of the intellectual shamans, following their own lights, path, or sense of purpose is almost unavoidable, even when it leads to crooked paths or gets them into what William Torbert characterizes as 'trouble' with others. Intellectual shamans work toward being themselves despite others frequently telling them how foolish their path is. It is simply what they must do. They are often willing to do what others have not done, say what others won't say, think new thoughts, do new types of research that are not in the accepted canon.

One person who has consistently done that intellectually and in other ways over the course of his career is William Torbert.

William R. Torbert

William (Bill) Torbert is Professor Emeritus of the Management and Organization Department at Boston College's Carroll School of Management, where he served as graduate dean from 1978 to 1987, and director of the Organizational Behavior PhD program, among other roles. Author of ten books and nearly seventy articles and book chapters, Torbert has served as chair of the Organization Development and Change Division of the Academy of Management, a board member of Trillium Asset Management and Pilgrim (and Harvard Pilgrim) Health Care, and currently as the founder of the Action Inquiry Associates and Fellowship for Collaborative Developmental Action Inquiry, as well as Distinguished Visiting Professor at the University of San Diego School of Leadership and Education Sciences. Known for his development of the theory of action inquiry, Torbert holds bachelor's and PhD degrees from Yale University. He participated in the Gurdjieff work [a form of spiritual work] for twenty-five years and consulted widely with business over the course of his academic career. His multiple books include *Action Inquiry: The Secret of Timely and Transforming Leadership* (with associates), *Personal and Organizational Transformations* (with Dalmar Fisher and David Rooke), *The Power of Balance: Transforming*

THE COURAGE TO BE YOURSELF   129

Self, Society, and Scientific Inquiry, and *Managing the Corporate Dream*. Among his numerous awards and honors are the Outstanding Scholar Award from the Western Academy of Management and the AESC Annual Award for Best Published Research on Leadership and Corporate Governance for his *Harvard Business Review* article 'Seven transformations of leadership' (published 2005).

Torbert, Professor Emeritus in the Management and Organization Department of the Carroll School of Management, Boston College, served as dean of the graduate programs from 1978 to 1987. He majored in politics and economics at Yale, which, as he says, 'was largely an excuse to take as few classes as possible and to do the most independent work that I could.' After writing an undergraduate thesis on the relationship between blue-collar work, labor, leisure, and politics, which later became his first book, *Being for the Most Part Puppets,* Torbert entered the PhD program at Yale with 'such a strong interest in particular questions that I did not think in terms of a career, particularly.' Torbert chose Yale because he wanted to study himself leading something (that is, being both the researcher and the actor) and in so doing create what he called 'action science' – a term later adopted by his then advisor Chris Argyris (deceased, Harvard Business School). Although it turned out that Torbert's original dissertation idea did not fly at Yale, and he ultimately did another thesis project, he wrote a book about the experience later on.

Recipient of a Danforth Fellowship that supported his PhD study and helped expose him to interdisciplinary scholarship and teaching through scholars such as psychologist Erik Ericson, leadership theorist Warren Bennis, and others at Yale at the time, Torbert recalls: 'I did have a lot more freedom, and, because I had written something that was already becoming a book, I had a lot – probably – more confidence than a lot of graduate students do that I could basically do it.' Unlike some of the other intellectual shamans who did not discover their vision or sense of purpose until later in their careers, Torbert remembers being driven by his vision to make particular types of choices. For example, on finishing the PhD he decided to take a position at Southern Methodist University (SMU) in Dallas, Texas, 'because that was an educational experiment, the way the dean was talking was different, and it seemed like an exciting opportunity to do what I was training myself to do.' Although he stayed only two years at SMU, his experience organizing and running an innovative course there enabled Torbert to begin implementing some of his ideas about what he later came to call action inquiry, the theory for which he is best known. Then Torbert left for the Harvard School of Education, drawn because of scholars such as Lawrence Kohlberg and Chris Argyris, by then at Harvard, and later getting to know other developmental theorists including Carol Gilligan and Robert Kegan.

Leaving Harvard after several years without another position, because, as he puts it, 'I didn't have a career orientation,' Torbert 'wandered around the country in a pine green VW camper, with a wooden bumper on the back.' He applied for jobs unsuccessfully in California, before returning east to run what he called the 'Theater of Inquiry' in the Boston area for a year, still without a formal position. Then he applied for and got the graduate dean's position at Boston College, and, 'to everybody's amazing surprise, lasted thirty years, and retired in 2008.' During the whole period Torbert intensified and deepened his interest in action inquiry, or, as he puts it, 'You might say I started to get deeply into first-, second-, and third-person research, although I didn't come up with those terms for another thirty years, but I was doing that work way before I had put a name to it.' In the sense that no matter how strong the orientation to a particular type of work, other influences are also important. Torbert recollects:

> The one motivation [for going to Yale] was the particular teachers.
> I found an enormous number of incredibly important teachers.
> I usually reduce it to three: Bill Coffin, the Yale minister; Chris
> Argyris; and a man named Lord Pentland, who was my teacher in the
> Gurdjieff work. He was in the British House of Lords. People did call
> him Lord Pentland. I called him Lord Pentland. But these three were

bigger-than-life characters, each of them in their own way, in their own very different ways. They had a tremendous influence on me. All of them, somehow, were trying to bring thought and action into relationship with one another. So that became very important to me.

AMBIVALENCE AND OPPORTUNITY

Just as ambivalence about the future path can provide a sense of power because it allows a variety of outcomes to be acceptable, so potentially does the ability to realistically appraise one's self and not take yourself too seriously, no matter what work you are doing or how well recognized that work is. One of the best-known management academics in the strategy arena, Henry Mintzberg, Cleghorn Professor of Management Studies at the Desautels Faculty of Management, McGill University, is an example of that ability. Mintzberg started out as an undergraduate in mechanical engineering at McGill University, where he also ended up spending much of his career. After two years of operations research with the Canadian National Railways he decided to become a consultant to small business, then ended up applying to MIT for its Master of Science program, rather than an MBA program, because 'it didn't sound like a business school.' Mintzberg notes, 'When I got there, I slipped completely over to what was called the policy side. Rather than getting a real job, I guess I kind of liked the atmosphere. My grades got a bit better, so they mistakenly let me into the PhD program.'

Henry Mintzberg

Henry Mintzberg is the Cleghorn Professor of Management Studies (and previously holder of the Bronfman Chair) at the Desautels Faculty of Management, McGill University. Mintzberg holds PhD and SM degrees from the Massachusetts Institute of Technology, a bachelor's from Sir George Williams (now Concordia) University in general arts, and a bachelor's of mechanical engineering from McGill. Internationally known for his work on management and strategic management, particularly for its practical bent, Mintzberg has written more than 150 articles and fifteen books, including *The Rise and Fall of Strategic Planning*, and recent work criticizing management education in *Managers, Not MBAs*. A two-time winner of the McKinsey Award for the best article in *Harvard Business Review*, Mintzberg has written numerous books considered essential to the management literature, including his first book, *The Nature of Managerial Work*, for which he shadowed executives to find out how they really spend their time, *The Structuring of Organizations*, and *Power in and around Organizations*. Known for his iconoclastic thinking, Mintzberg is the recipient of numerous awards and prizes. He was named an Officer of the Order of Canada in 1998, and the first management faculty Fellow of the Royal Society of Canada, as well as being named Fellow of the Academy of Management, the International Academy of Management, and the World Academy of Productivity Sciences. The Academy of Management awarded him the Distinguished Scholar Award for Contributions to Management, and the George R. Terry Award for the best book for *The Rise and Fall of Strategic Management*. He has received honorary degrees from well over a dozen international universities, among numerous other honors has served as president of the Strategic Management Society, and has held visiting professorships at multiple institutions, among many other accomplishments.

In his seventies at the time of the interview, Mintzberg is still active in writing and scholarship, and, indeed, is writing a pamphlet for the general public called 'Rebalancing society: radical renewal beyond left, right, and center,' which he has made publicly available on his website.[4n] Asked whether a vision guided him in his work, Mintzberg responds:

> Wow, what a question! Did I have a vision for what I did? You mean, like way back when? I certainly have a vision for each step, like what I'm doing now in this pamphlet; I have a vision for this pamphlet, for sure. But whether I started with a vision – no, just insight, I think; trying to get at what's really going on. But, no, I would say: 'No, maybe not.'

Pressed on why he had undertaken the sometimes iconoclastic, and certainly always provocative and questioning, work he has always done, Mintzberg says:

> To be honest, I think there are two answers, sort of the noble answer and the personal answer, in a way. As sort of truth, although I don't think there's any such thing as truth, but I think we get closer and the idea of getting theories that are useful, and by that I don't mean to change things directly. I mean to understand things, so 'insight,' I guess, is the better word than 'truth.' Yeah, delete 'truth.' Insight; I'm driven by insight, and I love stories that, or even jokes that, sort of come up with the unexpected.

Mintzberg has told a story relevant to his way of viewing the world that highlights both his sense of humor and the way insight develops for him – through observation of what is actually happening in managerial situations. This ability to observe and gain insights was evident in Mintzberg's earliest and pathbreaking research, his dissertation, eventually published as *The Nature of Managerial Work*. In this research he shadowed five executives to see how they actually spent their time, rather than assuming, as most academics did during that time period, that executives 'planned, organized, coordinated and controlled.' Rather than accept this common 'wisdom,' Mintzberg looked to see what executives actually *did* with their time. As he wryly notes:

> Yeah, well, it was pathbreaking because it said the obvious and nobody else said it. I mean, I said managers get interrupted a lot, and that was considered pathbreaking, because everybody thought managers planned, organized, coordinated and controlled, which is four words for 'controlling.' So, the only reason this was so successful was because people are living with old myths and never compared them with what they saw before their own eyes or what they saw in themselves as managers. Everybody was living with a myth.

Mintzberg highlights the insight that comes from actually observing the phenomenon of interest and trying to strip it of assumptions as his way of approaching intellectual and managerial problems. He tells the following story:

> I think to challenge, not necessarily for the sake of challenging (that would be contrarian), but to challenge what seems to me wrongheaded, and simply say 'It's not A, it's B,' based on just going out and looking. So you watch a manager in his office or her office (but they were 'his' in most cases), and you see that they get interrupted a lot. That doesn't sound like planning, organizing, coordinating, and controlling. So, you just look at what's going on, and you look at strategies. You know how IKEA came up with its strategy of selling unassembled furniture? A worker...had trouble putting a table in his car, so he took the legs off, and somebody said, 'Gee, maybe our customers have to take the legs off, too.' I love those stories. So I love this kind of IKEA story, just because it makes a bit of fun of a bunch of executives sitting around the boardroom inventing strategies.

He goes on to detail what he calls debunking myths and 'things that kind of twist around,' recognizing the need not to take himself too seriously, saying:

> So I like things that kind of twist around. I guess my favorite quip ever is by Groucho Marx, who said: 'I'd never belong to a club that would have me as a member.' [...] So, I like to debunk things and I like insights. I guess my ego is fairly big, in the sense that I like to be successful and known and considered important and all that. [...] The sort of official side is insight and debunking. The personal side is ego-driven, although I don't think I take myself that seriously. I can laugh at myself as easily as I can laugh at anyone else.

FINDING PURPOSE

The varied paths of the intellectual shamans interviewed clearly indicate that there is no one right way to finding your purpose. They also signify that purpose is unique to each individual. If an individual is not lucky enough to 'discover' his or her purpose with a transition or insight as some did, purpose must be uncovered gradually through the course of living. Perhaps, as Karl Weick would say in many of his writings,[43,44] purpose is retrospectively made sense of.

MIT's Otto Scharmer synthesizes the point of these stories in the concluding comments in this chapter, which also set the stage for our discussion of the healing, connecting, and sensemaking roles of intellectual shamans – and suggest that such pathways are open to just about anyone:

> I think what we really need to talk about is: can anybody do more of what their real life intention is? That's how I would phrase it. Of course, there are differences in what people bring in terms of their life intention, and what that is, and that leads to different journeys. For some of us, for example, for me, what I saw my parents doing and what I saw in my environment, the political economic environment of the '80's and '90's, [made me think:] 'Well, we actually are moving in the wrong direction. We need to entirely rethink the foundations of the economy of economic theory in our society.' So I saw that with my own eyes. Then I was looking for places that would be conducive for me to do this type of work, basically recreating the foundations based on which our civilization is operating. So you go to places where you find some nurturing context for that. But that's not everyone's piece of cake. So is it true that, in order to give everyone on this planet, or everyone who goes to school or institution of higher education, a better possibility to realize their full potential and their real life intention, what they bring, is that possible? So the answer is, absolutely, 'Yes!'

So, we are left with a question. Can anyone find the power of purpose as these intellectual shamans have done? I would answer 'Yes,' with courage, conviction, the willingness to take risk, and a desire to work 'beyond the self' – that is, for the betterment of the world in some way. We simply need to listen carefully to hear what our purpose might be, follow the sometimes subtle and sometimes overt signals we see, and 'live' that purpose by orienting ourselves and those gifts or powers that we have toward healing some things or some ones in the world. That work can be done in the context of family, in the context of organizations, as Judi Neal has shown in her book on the 'edge-walkers,'[82] or in the context of society, as I showed in my previous book on the 'difference-makers' who built today's corporate responsibility infrastructure.[3] Or it can be done, as in the case of intellectual shamans, in an intellectual context through writing, teaching, consulting, and informing practice. In the next chapters we look at three crucial roles of intellectual shamanism: healing, connecting, and sensemaking.[1,2]

4 Healer

The only work that ultimately brings any good to any of us is the work of contributing to the healing of the world.

Marianne Williamson

The art of healing comes from nature, not from the physician. Therefore the physician must start from nature, with an open mind.

Paracelsus

In this chapter, I explore the healing function of the intellectual shaman. As intellectuals within the management domain, their purview goes beyond the individual patient (or, sometimes, local system) that is the focus of the traditional shaman and even the psychotherapist. Healing is generally considered to be the central role of the shaman.[2,83,84] Jeanne Achterberg calls shamans the 'master healer[s] of the imaginary realms,'[85] and this insight is supported by many other observers.[2,22,84,86–89] As Frost and Egri point out in their seminal paper on organization development specialists as shamans, shamans also play important roles in mediating different realities – or spanning boundaries or realms of various sorts, which I call connecting, and in gathering information and then making sense of that information for others in the sensemaking process, which will be explored in Chapters 5 and 6.

As noted earlier, shamans are found in virtually all human cultures, historically as well as today, though their identities in modern society may be less central and overtly visible than in some more traditional societies.[20,27,88–92] Fundamentally, those individuals who take this path of healing, connecting, and sensemaking, and its associated risks and trials, can emerge with visibility and impact, whether in intellectual life, as with the management academy, or in other realms. In this process, it is the healing role that takes center stage.

Importantly, the etymologies of the words 'whole,' 'health,' 'healing,' and, perhaps more strikingly, 'holy' are quite similar. 'Whole,' as defined in the *Online Etymology Dictionary*, means 'entire, unhurt, healthy,' 'undamaged' 'salvation and welfare,' with a reference to 'see Health.' Clicking on 'health' brings up definitions from the Old English of 'wholeness, a being whole, sound or well,' as well as 'uninjured' and 'of good omen,' with further references to prosperity, happiness, welfare, preservation, and safety. The word 'holy' means 'consecrated, sacred, godly.' The *Online Etymology Dictionary* further notes that the primary pre-Christian meaning of holy probably was 'that must be preserved whole or intact, that cannot be transgressed or violated.' 'Holy' derives from the Old English word *hal*, from which the word 'health' is also derived, so their roots are the same. It is this sense of sacredness in the work of intellectual shamans that suggests, as explored in Chapter 3, that they are answering a call to purpose and to finding their source of power, whether expressed in spiritual terms or not, and that they are becoming somehow 'whole' in doing the work they do.

Certainly, the focus of interest of *intellectual* shamans is different from that of traditional shamans. Unquestionably, modern shamans of any sort live in vastly different cultures and times from those of traditional shamans. They do, however, serve similar core functions. Intellectual shamans, in particular, operationalize their healing and other activities dramatically differently in their focus and in how the work is done from the ways of traditional shamans. Yet, in one sense, they are all similar: core to the traditional shaman's healing role is to heal whatever myth is causing the illness or, often spiritual, dis-ease of the subject, typically an individual, sometimes a group. James Dow, exploring 'Universal aspects of symbolic healing,' argues that, in the psychotherapeutic context of traditional shamanism, healing takes place in the setting of a cultural myth that the patient accepts. The shaman considers the myth disordered, needing to be brought back in order to help the patient regain health – or become whole and ordered again through the shaman's healing rituals.[83]

Similarly, the intellectual shaman deals with changing a form of dis-order or dis-ease (hyphens deliberate to imply a lack of order, and uneasiness) that he or she perceives as needing correction. For the intellectual shaman, these dis-eases occur in the various cultural myths that surround management intellectuals, theories, research methods, management and consulting practices, teaching, the role of business in society, and the natural environment being predominant examples. Sometimes the dis-ease is with theories or practices advocated in those theories (think of Karl Weick, Henry Mintzberg, Nancy Adler, and Tima Bansal, for example). Sometimes it is with the methods of research or approaches taken to understand what is happening in practice or theory (think of John Van Maanen, Dave Brown, and Henry Mintzberg). Sometimes it is in inventing new ways of teaching or reaching learners (think of Ed Freeman or, below, Marc Epstein). In many cases, we can think of the intellectual shamans as performing a healing function that attempts to correct some sort of cultural myth that they perceive has gone wrong.

The intellectual shamans may not be doing this myth-healing deliberately as a traditional shaman does. They seem to do it because it is what they are drawn to do. The term 'cultural myths' is used here in much the same way that John Meyer and Brian Rowan argue that formal organizational structures serve as representations of institutionalized myths that ultimately shape organizations.[93] Myths in the context of management scholarship, teaching, and practice include notions and ideas, representations, norms, and standards about what proper theory (and theorizing) is, what accepted theories and ideas are, and how to frame them. They also encompass assumptions about the correct explanations for individual, organizational, and social phenomena that comprise various theories, and about what constitutes 'good' research and teaching. For example, myths in the form of theories shape what variables need to be included in research studies, what is acceptable as a research subject, how it should be approached, what should rightly be worthy of publication, and what is outside the norm, among many other variables.

Theories seen as myths also shape managerial practice and consulting by academics and others to organizations and individuals, and even societies. Consider, for example, the large-scale impacts of the myth or belief that the purpose of the firm is to maximize shareholder wealth above all other considerations, a myth that Ed Freeman's work on stakeholders has attempted to counter. Think of myths about how it is that managers do their work or develop strategies, which some of Henry Mintzberg's research has addressed. Myths also shape research practices and norms. Consider the dominance of quantitative methods over qualitative as more 'rigorous.' Cultural myths similarly frame teaching and pedagogical approaches. In management education, lecture-based and case-based pedagogies help to frame current mythology about effective teaching.

Of course, the construction of new theories, research agendas and protocols, teaching approaches, or consulting practices by intellectual shamans in a sense creates entirely new stories or myths that need to stand up to the questioning of others. Today's management academy is, for instance, fraught with myths about measurement that arose in the early 2000s with the advent of new technologies that permit, for example, easy citation and publication counts, the creation of so-called impact factors, and similar measurement tools. Student evaluations, numerically quantified, also now play crucial roles in assessing faculty teaching performance, despite the fact that their unreliability and lack of validity are well known. All these devices (and any other that one could devise) represent 'stories' or myths that we believe provide adequate assessments, just as we believe that the grades that students get on tests somehow measure their ability, insight, or knowledge.

All the norms, cultural variables, 'do's and don'ts,' and practices associated with a given set of ideas or theory, a way of doing business, accepted norms and standards of research or management practice, and consulting approaches shape the way scholars approach their work, and can be viewed as myths. Essentially, these myths represent the story that we tell ourselves about what is appropriate and what is not in a given context, or even what 'is' and 'is not' happening. Each myth shapes thinking and, ultimately, behavior – in management practice, in the ideas and practices of the scholars who promulgate those mythologies, or in teaching and consulting. Yet, because each of these sets of norms is essentially a story, a myth, and because the world sometimes refuses to conform to these stories, there is the potential for dis-ease with the stories or myths. It is this dis-ease that intellectual shamans, in a wide variety of ways, seek to heal, essentially by creating new stories that will likely themselves work for a time only to be replaced in a later time and context, when new myths are needed.

HEALER, HEAL THYSELF

Often the first step to becoming a healer is to first heal the healer, as the Bible was perhaps the first to point out, and as most psychotherapists and social workers know. Indeed, there is an informal sense in the research community that we as scholars frequently work on the issues that most personally affect (as well as interest) us, sometimes as part of a healing process. As Dow points out, 'In many systems of symbolic healing the healer must first be healed.'[83] Certainly, this need for healing the healer is well known in psychotherapy, and in the saying 'Healer, heal thyself.' This need for self-healing is apparent with many intellectual shamans, who work to heal the system as they heal – or find – themselves and their calling, as we saw in the last two chapters. As they found their ways to their central purpose or calling, they were, in a sense, healing themselves.

Bill Torbert is perhaps most explicit in the healer healing himself orientation. In discussing the development of his theory of action inquiry, he recalls:

> I guess the idea [behind action inquiry] was, if you wanted to do better in the world, what is the science that you would study? We now have design theory, but design theory is rather an intellectual version of this and doesn't really touch one's behavior. But, if you actually wanted to be a better leader, then what kind of knowledge

and practice would you put together to be that better leader? It seemed to me that there might be a science about that, naïve as I was. That was what I wanted to begin discovering, because you couldn't very well discover it without doing it, given the idea. The question was, could it transform the way I and others lead people? Could it change the way professionals and anybody begins to act? Because people would use this [idea] like self-help books, in a sense, and could it make everybody's behavior more inquiring, more mutual, and more effective? If you could do that, that would be pretty impressive.

Asked what his motivation was for moving in this direction, Torbert further evidences the desire for self-healing, along with healing the broader world, in the following:

Well, of course, I assumed that I was going to be relatively famous, because I was intent on doing something very big. I was doing it instead of doing other things that would've made me famous; some were more sort of conventional. [...] That now looks very funny to me, because now, although I want to do a piece of work that becomes famous, I don't want to be famous any longer. [...] Well, of course, part of the motivation at the beginning was to know the truth. So the big question was about how to know the truth, and whether the kinds of analytical procedures that most of the academic disciplines were getting themselves into, more and more, led to truth. Or whether there was some more synthetic combination of theory in practice, and questioning, and so forth that would put them together. All these people [who influenced me] pushed me toward the non-analytic and the multidisciplinary, ...but it, in part, was to know the real truth and the truth that made a difference to me, not just intellectual truth. I had to make my life better and other people's lives better.

For the shaman, healing the self is an important step, necessary to gain the ability to heal others or, in the case of the intellectual shamans, theory, the world, research, or practice. Phil Mirvis talks a bit about his own healing process, which happened in part through a connection with M. Scott Peck, MD, author of the hugely popular book *The Road Less Traveled: A New Psychology of Love, Traditional Values, and Spiritual Growth* and numerous related books. After attending a workshop that Peck ran shortly after Mirvis was denied tenure at Boston University, Mirvis began a fifteen-year friendship with Peck. Mirvis recalls the healing process:

> Don Kanter and I had written *The Cynical Americans*, and it was big hit. I was on talk radio a lot and got the biggest laughs when I played the cynic. I was sore about what happened at Boston University and sour about what was going on in business – corporate raiders, the shareholder's rights movement, the downsizing, and so on. So I adopted a snarky persona on the radio and in my life...that sort of passed for cool, for me.
>
> With Peck and his crowd, I began to heal. With Scotty, I was learning to deal with powerful men and authority figures in particular. In this community, there was a sense that you don't need that [cynical persona]. Here, you could refind yourself, maybe at a more mature stage of development. What was extraordinary about [the experience] were three things.
>
> One is, it left me open to the possibility of spirituality and a larger force at work in the world. I had read and talked about spirituality when working with futurist Don Michael at Michigan and then got to know Willis Harmon, Peter Frost, Dave Cooperrider, and others who had deep thoughts on these matters. So I could entertain a new set of ideas, but I wasn't yet living them. From my elementary school days, all I knew about God involved molesting priests, wicked nuns, and lots of rules. This [work with Peck] opened up a whole sense of possibility and some conceptual framing and even direct experience of connection with the beyond.
>
> Second, it put me in touch with a lot of spiritual people, some of whom were absolute fruitcakes...but incredibly diverse fruitcakes,

coming from lots of different traditions. Then seeing and meeting shamans of all stripes. That really opened me up to diverse ways of knowing and being, and stimulated me to begin to experiment with community-building in business

Third, I began to write about 'soul work' in organizations. If I look at scholarship, initially you sort of stand on the shoulders of giants and rewrite what they said, and then gradually you find your own voice, and discover you might even have something distinct to say. That was what happened with Peck. I learned from him and then found my own voice in this space. Now, I don't know that I had anything significant to say in that particular realm, but I certainly found it an incredibly enriching, personal experience.

Healing can take place through experiences, as happened with Mirvis, or in a moment of sudden insight and recognition (as when Cooperrider discovered his passion for appreciative inquiry in Japan, described earlier), or over time, as Torbert describes. Jane Dutton's awareness of positive organizational scholarship took place as the result of sudden insight at a conference, supplemented afterward by the tragedy of the 9/11 terrorist attack on New York City's World Trade Center in 2001, when her work on compassion became immediately useful. She recalls being invited to the first positive psychology conference in Akumal, Mexico, by Amy Wrzesniewski, now at Yale and then a relatively junior scholar. In 2001 Dutton had already been working on her compassion in the workplace research for a couple of years, yet she was amazed to find an array of senior scholars from psychology and related areas presenting work on positive psychology. The field of positive psychology was then very new, spearheaded by Martin Seligman (psychology, University of Pennsylvania), who had recently introduced the concept in his capacity as then president of the American Psychological Association. Dutton's reaction to seeing this positive orientation to scholarship, people, and organizations for the first time was to be overwhelmed by it – and, in a sense, healed. She puts it this way:

I remember listening to all this stuff and thinking, 'Oh my gosh!'
These people were really passionate. I [was] thinking, 'This work is
going to be so important, but, in organization studies, you can't get
there from an individual level. If we can understand organizationally
how this worked, we could really [make a difference].' It was a real
on-your-knees kind of moment. [...] I started crying. [...] I knew
I was supposed to build a bridge between the positive psych world
and organization studies.

Coming back to the University of Michigan after the conference,
Dutton had been changed by her experience. She very much identified
as an organizational studies scholar, and also saw herself as what she
calls 'an organizational studies bridge across areas.' Her Michigan
colleague Kim Cameron had recently returned from Case Western
Reserve, where he had been dean and was then doing work on forgiveness. Bob Quinn, also of Michigan, was interested in these new ideas
as well. Along with some of the pioneers Dutton had met at the conference, which had focused primarily on individual psychology, this
group began thinking about positive organizational scholarship.
Dutton recalls what happened next: 'We had coffee in June of 2001.
I had just come back from this meeting and said, "We should have a
conference. Let's just have a gathering."' Quinn and Cameron agreed,
saying, 'Yes, that would be fun!' But events intervened and pushed both
the idea and the research forward in ways that few could have imagined. Dutton relates the story of how POS began to gain traction
much more quickly than any of them might have expected – as a result
of many people's need to heal from the traumatic events of the
9/11 attacks in the United States on the World Trade Center and
Washington, and the plane crash in Pennsylvania, all engineered by
terrorists:

Then 9/11 happened. We were going to have this conference in
December, and, on 9/11, I was supposed to give a talk at the business
school on compassion. It's the most terrifying thing, because you
present to the whole faculty group. I didn't sleep the whole night of

9/10, because all I could imagine were the finance faculty seeing this girl, this OB [organizational behavior] professor, get up and start talking about compassion and saying, 'What does this have to do with business?'

Because I was supposed to give a talk on 9/11, which I never gave, this new dean we had knew I was doing work on compassion. So he e-mailed me on 9/11 and said...: 'I know, you're doing work on compassion. Prepare me a memo by tomorrow about what your work says I should do as a leader. Then come in and talk to my management group.' I thought, 'Oh shit!' [There was someone else] in our compassion lab who was talking to the executives. I was the one working with the doctoral students and writing the abstract stuff that nobody practiced. [...]

But, 9/11, you're doing anything [to help], so I did this three-page document, and had my doctoral students helping me, too, and they found it really useful. I remember going into this room and it was so serious. Everyone really wanted to know: 'What could we do? How should we think about this?' [There] was this urgency. Anyway, they found it really useful, and they ended up saying, 'Can we share this with the deans?' They ended up sharing it with the whole alumni. So I got, in a very short period of time, a lot of feedback about how useful this [compassion work] was. [...]

We had a group of people who were already prepared to go to the conference, so I sent this three-page [document] to everyone, and said, 'If you can write up a three-page paper from your research on what managers and leaders should do at this time, send it to me, and we'll create a website.' So we created this website called 'Leading in trying times,' in a really short period of time. We got about 25,000 hits really fast. This [event] was such a strong jolt to this POS movement. If [9/11 and the subsequent follow-up] hadn't happened, I think it would have been more of an intellectual exercise, but 9/11 gave us a strong sense that this way of seeing is actually really helpful. It gave us a lot more courage, so we ended up redirecting the whole conference around 9/11.

This conference was also the beginning of what has become known as the POS movement, spurred in part by a subsequent book by Cameron, Quinn, and Dutton that intellectually framed positive organizational scholarship.[94]

Notice that, for both Torbert and Dutton, the healing process within themselves allowed them the courage, confidence, and conviction to move forward on an intellectual issue they believed important but that went against mainstream thought – or current mythology. In Torbert's case, the myth was about leadership; essentially, that you could study traits of leaders, attributes, or behaviors externally, without first looking at your own leadership – something that much of Torbert's work has tried to deal with. In Dutton's case, it was learning the usefulness of applying principles of then incipient positive psychology to organizational scholarship and to a crisis event. This new knowledge enabled Dutton and colleagues to build on what might otherwise have been scholarly work that received little attention except by other scholars, with far less from practicing managers. By breaking the myth that compassion and positivity did not matter at work, demonstrated so vividly in the aftermath of 9/11, Dutton began to courageously and more fully than ever embrace the work that had had such a strong emotional effect on her at the Akumal conference.

Dave Brown tells another story of self-healing through his research. Recall that Brown had transformed himself several times during his youth as he tried to find his place in the world – transformations that, in his case, continued throughout his life. The context of his dissertation work drew in part from his own experience as a high school student in a difficult school culture, providing both a basis of insight and understanding personally and in terms of the scholarship that he undertook. Brown explains:

> One of the things that emerged out of the dissertation and a later book with Clay Alderfer [then at Yale, then Rutgers from 1992 to 2006, now a consultant, who was Brown's dissertation advisor, and is best known for his work on ERG or existence, relatedness, and

growth theory, and later on group relations and organizational diagnosis] was looking at trying to change what Erving Goffman [one of the most influential sociologists of the twentieth century, known for his work on the presentation of self] would have called total institutions. The boarding school that we did this project at had a very intense socialization process. What we were trying to do was loosen up the culture to allow much more diversity and much less pressure by the kids and the faculty to be one kind of cool. I'd gone to a school much like that. Clay had gone to public high school.

We used our two experiences to help do the diagnostic work at this school. Over time – we worked with them for four years – the quality of the school's culture changed radically, I think largely because we recruited the kids into changing their own culture. So we worked with the school long enough so the kids who were freshmen when we started were seniors by the end. As freshmen and sophomores, they made an explicit decision to stop hazing the underclassmen and then police themselves. There was a fair amount of faculty support for this, but the faculty was never as engaged as the students were. So Clay and I wrote a book about the experience with the school and looked at what are the implications of being what I later called over-organized and too tightly organized?

One more experience highlights the variety of approaches that incorporate self-healing with the desire to do good in the world, and also highlights how the healing and learning process is ongoing. Ed Freeman, whose 1984 pioneering book on stakeholders is one of the most enduring books and concepts in management, talks about the work that is core to him and his own sense of self in the context of important relationships at work:

> Actually, the way I've come to think about it is, what's interesting is the set of relationships in which you're enmeshed, and in trying to figure out how to help junior colleagues get tenure. How to help doctoral students do interesting work. How to help colleagues become better teachers and better researchers. The temptation is to

work on the institution, not the relationships. Whenever I've tried to work on the institution, I've not been very successful. So, if you work on a set of relationships in which you're enmeshed, it's a much more 'How you want to live every day' question than 'What do you want to do?' Institutions and deans and presidents like to announce things – things that the institution's going to do. Nobody likes to announce, 'Well, we're going to try and live in a way that's kind of a role model for our students.' I mean that's not an announceable thing.

So the 'How?' is more important to me than the kind of 'What?' you end up doing. Then what happens is there are milestones that take care of themselves. So you keep publishing books and articles, but those are things that are outcomes. I've learned to see out of the 'How you want to live' versus 'They're the reason that you live.' I think a lot of young faculty, especially in today's world, in business schools, where the mania is to publish in 'A' journals, get caught up in the chase for the outcome. It's real easy to lead a damn miserable life. I think if I were starting today with the skills I had, my '84 stakeholder book would never have been published. I certainly couldn't get tenure anywhere and I would not be very successful. I think there are some issues [with that].

What Freeman is fundamentally speaking about is treating – and seeing – people as whole people, a way of interacting that is, at its core, a healing process for both individuals. He also highlights that the learning and changing process is a lifelong experience rather than a 'once and done' activity. Changing yourself so that it is possible to see the whole person changes your interactions with others – and, ultimately, is what can lead to transformation and healing. In the next section, we will focus on other ways that intellectual shamans undertake healing activities.

HEALING AS HOLISM AND THE SACRED

For the intellectual shaman, it is typically an *intellectual* dis-ease or dis-order of some sort that needs healing – i.e., fixing or changing.

For the management scholar, the dis-order often falls within the realms of theories and conceptions about managers and leaders and their practices, how organizations do or should operate, and how societies do or should function, and, of course, the interactions of each of these systems on the system as a whole. The particular focus of change could be a theory or set of ideas in need of correcting or improving, an approach to research needing improvement, or management practice that needs to be changed to create more effective concepts/ideas, research outputs, or organizations. Obviously, intellectual shamans in management disciplines, instead of dealing with individual patients as traditional shamans do, tend to focus on something larger, such as leaders or managers in general, organizations, and systems.

One person who has experienced a number of such transformations is Paul Shrivastava. He noted earlier his orientation to social problems coming out of his childhood experience in India, then at New York University early in his academic career, when the Bhopal disaster happened in his hometown in India and thousands of people were killed and hundreds of thousands hurt and displaced. He recalls:

> That was a big watershed for me in terms of my own intellectual development. I got to see a side of technology that I had until then taken for granted, that technology's only good, and it provided all these benefits of infrastructures and hospitals, etc., etc. But there I got to see what happens when something goes wrong. Also, it was a lesson in understanding organizations, because [it] became very, very apparent and clear in how this technology was applied in this social cultural setting and what could've gone wrong.
>
> That led to a very prolific period in my writing: several books and papers on industrial crisis management, and launching a journal on that topic. I did that for a good, probably, ten years – eight, nine years, at least – and the more I got convinced that the industrial and technological crises were a serious issue, the more resistance I found from corporations. They would say, 'Look, this is [a] one in a billion

chance kind of event. That's not something that is going to happen to us; don't bother us with this.'

The other thing that was happening around the same time, the mid-'90s, was [that] this whole area of environmental crisis and the debate on sustainability was becoming quite salient. So, instead of resisting and pushing an angle that managers are not willing to accept, I reframed my question in terms of sustainability. What is it going to take for these organizations to become ecologically and socially sustainable? That has been my quest since the mid-'90s. In '95, with a group of people from the academy, we established an organization and the Natural Environment [ONE] Division [of the Academy of Management].

Shrivastava also points to the healing – holistic – aspect of working on the bigger problem of sustainability and trying to change the ways in which companies relate to the natural environment, as he continues:

In trying to understand technology in the context of society, one thing that became absolutely clear to me was that this sort of...holistic understanding could not occur within disciplinary silos. There were just too many things outside that we, within our own silo, would think of as irrelevant that were actually quite centrally involved in the occurrence of these kinds of events and these crises. By the end of the decade of the '90s I was convinced that this disciplin[e-based] inquiry was actually harmful. It was part of a career game that I had unwittingly been playing myself, along with a lot of my colleagues, and I needed to get out of it. I was so disenchanted with academics that I took a leave of absence for three years, which turned out to be four years, and went and started a company. I wanted to put into practice some of the ideas that I'd been talking about, and I created an online education company called eSocrates.

This passion for holistic approaches to problems has stayed with Shrivastava over the years, and morphed into a passion for integrating the arts into management, much as Nancy Adler has been trying to do. For Shrivastava, as with Adler, it has also transmuted into a need to rethink the way that management education is delivered. Shrivastava explains the need for more holistic thinking in management, and particularly in management education:

> I want to put a significant amount of my energy into rethinking management education, not just from [a] sort of investor in business school concept, but broadly. Humanity needs management; there's no question in my mind about it. It is very fundamental. Today you can't even operate your own house if you can't manage a television and a cooking system in a house – intelligent, smart house – and so on. So, management is required. But the kind of narrowness that we have forced management thinking into within business schools is now starting to hurt us, both individually and intellectually.
> I think a wholesale rethinking is necessary. This critical aesthetics project is one platform to start it on, but we want to take it to the accreditation bodies, to the funding organizations, the education ministries, etc., to try to change [management education]. In that change, I think one of the big elements that is going to have to come in is that you can't just talk about managing organizations and the companies, that this happens in the context of an overall economy. If the economy is going into a degrowth mode, or the kind of economy that we had in the past is not what we want in the future [because] it's not sustainable, then we, as management thinkers, have to stretch our own frameworks and start talking about managing the economy rather than just managing organizations within it.

For Shrivastava, the healing orientation also includes the element of the holy, the sacred, integrating the core elements of what the etymology of the word 'healing' suggests. Shrivastava treads this ground explicitly but carefully:

> The other [element] is the need for – I want to frame this cautiously, because I'm going to use the words 'spiritual' and 'spirituality.' In

general, it's a suspect term. To me, it is a fundamental requirement for us as thinkers to get in touch with this element of our lives, our spirit, both collective and individual, and find ways of theorizing it and including it in our explanatory schemes – whatever we call science. I think science without the spirit and without spirituality is barren and destructive.

A SACRED PATH?

Holistic thinking, which we will look at even more closely in the next chapter, characterizes intellectual shamans and their work, as exemplified by the quotes from Paul Shrivastava above, as does the healing orientation. The language of holism and healing has another implication, because, as noted earlier, the roots of these words are also associated with the word holy – i.e., sacred. Traditional shamans are frequently associated with the sacred – or holy – as well, with some observers even claiming shamanism to be a 'religion.'[92,95] Given shamanism's many varieties and ubiquity, however, to the extent that it is a religion at all it is one without any particular doctrine or set of beliefs demanded, which varies in its manifestations throughout the world. Better, I think, to perhaps suggest that shamanism represents a calling to purpose, as Chapter 3 outlined, and that the purpose involves healing and some element of spirituality, especially when that spirituality is expressed as seeking meaning and purpose. Here it is important to make the link between holism and healing.

As intellectual shamans attempt to 'heal' what they perceive is wrong with the world, the field, thinking, research practice, teaching, or management practice, they are also working for greater internal coherence, conceptual coherence, and identity – i.e., greater wholeness. They may or may not deliberately engage followers, but their writings, commentaries, and intellectual contributions of various sorts have the effect, ultimately, of changing the system itself. In the traditional shaman's case, as Dow points out,[83] family systems or social problems, as related to the cultural myth surrounding the dis-eased person, are presumed to have affected the patient's health. In the case of the intellectual shaman, it may well be that it is the social system of relevance, theory, or practice that needs to be healed – and it is that system on which the intellectual shaman focuses.

Although intellectual shamans may not think explicitly of their work as healing work, Dow argues that shamans live in the context of a mythic world that is somehow out of order. He demonstrates that, in the context of psychotherapeutic treatment, there is a similarly developed mythic world that therapist and patient exist in. Similarly, there is a mythic world of thought, accepted wisdom, theories, common beliefs, and practices of various sorts in which the intellectual shaman exists – and that he or she ultimately alters through intellectual contributions.

Dow also articulates the importance of the therapeutic encounter between healer and patient, noting: 'In the encounter, the healer gets the patient to accept a particularization of the general mythic world as a valid model of the patient's experiences.'[83] In a sense, the intellectual shaman is doing just the opposite: taking the accepted wisdom and turning it upside down or inside out, so that a new mythic world is, effectively, created. Intellectual shamans do this through a process of what Dow calls 'manipulating the symbols,' which are 'communication devices between different levels of a hierarchy of living systems.'[96] Society, academia, research norms, theories, and management practice are all relevant systems that can be and are manipulated by intellectual shamans who are stepping away from commonly accepted wisdom.

This approach to holism is reflected in Jim Walsh's words. He saw that management scholarship was becoming ensnared in an audit culture of its own making. In his 2010 Academy of Management presidential address, he urged us all to 'embrace the sacred in our secular scholarly world.'[97] Walsh talks about how and where he finds inspiration in his life:

> I can talk about my inspiration. I am very aware of the people that
> I keep around me. I try to keep the company of people that have

some kind of special quality. They're authentic, they're genuine, and they've got passion. Sure, they're smart and all of that, but there's something real about them. You get this palpable sense of something else. You can feel it. I can't really articulate it, but it's there. You'd know that's it's there too. I think of them as having a light that shines from them. These people inspire me to find that same kind of light in myself, to honor who I am, honor the moment, and essentially ask me to aim higher and reach farther. I really am inspired by all manner of people.

Curiosity matters too. I'm always looking for something new. I love meeting new people, learning, and jumping over boundaries. I like crossing them for my own benefit, and I really like working across them to pull people together to make the Academy better, to make the journals better, to make our students better, and so on.

Walsh, who received the Academy of Management's Distinguished Service Award in 2013 for his many contributions, gives a concrete example to illustrate how he brings these two qualities to life in his work:

I took a group of undergraduate students to China three times over the years. Each trip was pretty compelling, but I was getting a little restless. I was reconnecting with too many established friends and connections. The trip was always new to the students but it was getting a little old for me. I met a friend of a friend of a friend in a restaurant in Accra, Ghana, when I was there doing some Academy work. This fellow is someone special. Long story short, he helped me bring about thirty students to west Africa for two weeks. I am sure I will take my students to Africa again next year.

I love working across cultural boundaries, paradigm boundaries, sector boundaries (you know, business, government, and civil society), and, of course, class, race, gender, age, and 'you name it' boundaries that seem to divide so many of us. To me, that's where our lives come alive. Mix together my curiosity, a 'make a better world' orientation, a boundary-crossing reflex, and a nose for extraordinary people, and there you have it: the story of my life!

Marc J. Epstein

Marc Epstein is at this writing the Distinguished Research Professor of Management in the Jesse H. Jones Graduate School of Business at Rice University, Houston, where he teaches management control and technology commercialization in developing countries, and advises student Action Learning Projects. Formerly Visiting Professor and Hansjoerg Wyss Visiting Scholar in Social Enterprise at the Harvard Business School, Price Waterhouse Visiting Professor of Accounting and Control at INSEAD in France, and Visiting Professor at the Graduate School of Business at Stanford University, among other appointments in a peripatetic career, Epstein is known as an outstanding teacher and has written or co-written some twenty books and more than 100 articles on a wide range of topics, mostly related to measuring social and ecological impacts in business. Among other appointments, he has been editor of *Advances in Management Accounting* and series editor of *Studies in Managerial and Financial Accounting*. His book *Measuring Corporate Environmental Performance* received numerous awards, including the prestigious AAA/AICPA Notable Contributions in Accounting Literature Award. Epstein consults and lectures widely to a variety of companies. Educated in accounting, Epstein is also known for his work on corporate strategy, corporate environmental performance, and environmental management. Recent books include *Making Sustainability Work, Corporate Social Environmental and Economic Impacts,* and *Making Innovation Work: How to Manage It, Measure It, and Profit from It.*

Marc Epstein, Distinguished Research Professor of Management at Rice University's Jones Graduate School of Business, has focused much of his academic career on measuring the impacts of environmental, social, and other non-financial indicators in business, paying attention to corporate responsibility issues and company impacts through the lens of accounting. As does Walsh, Epstein evidences both a healing and a sacred orientation as he describes the source of his motivation:

> I am not sure I can tell you [the source of my passion] going back to when I was a child. But when I was in college this passion grew around activism and the role of businesses in society; maybe it was even earlier. My father was in a small wholesale business selling tobacco products. I was pretty vocal to him about what I thought about selling tobacco products, and I am not sure I was that different than many other teenagers would have been. I know I said it in ways that were probably not as diplomatic as I should have, as a teenager might. Again, maybe some of it goes back to my religion. I was active in Jewish youth groups as a teenager and a big part of that is what is called *tikkun olam*, or saving the world, and I was involved in social action work as a teenager. I guess I am still trying to do that.

Nancy Adler was also influenced by her heritage in much the same way, and she displays a similar sentiment in integrating the work she does in the world with the sacred (or holy), as shamans do. Speaking of her activist youth in the late 1960s and early 1970s, she recalls:

> At times I got burnt out or discouraged, frustrated, or overwhelmed, along with a lot of other people at that point..., whether your concerns were Vietnam issues, war and peace issues, poverty issues, civil rights issues as they were playing out then. One of the things that...the Jewish community [gave me] was the honoring of Shabbat. They honored the Sabbath. That's where I first understood what today is a central part of my Judaism as it plays out in the world. Six days a week you work to make the world a better place. One day a week, which is Shabbat, Friday night Sabbath, you live as if it's the messianic time. You live as if the world is perfect. So you get together with the best people, you have the best food, you drink the best wine, you have the best music. You dance. In the Torah [the Old Testament of the Bible], there's actually a *mitzvah* [a rule] that you're supposed to make love on Shabbat, but they're focused

on the fact that you're supposed to be married to the person that you
make love to.

It was interesting because of the whole notion that 'You won't
remember what you're working for unless you come back to the
Shabbat.' So, if you're just out there working, working, working,
it's not the vocabulary of burnout, but you'll forget what it is that
you're trying to do. [...] Judaism doesn't believe in an individual
heaven. It doesn't believe that, if I do X number of good things
(or say enough 'Hail Mary's), I'll personally get sent up to heaven.
[In Judaism] it's either all of us win or none of us win. So, the concept
is a heaven on earth. So you work for everybody, and it's not just
for the good of the few.

As she elaborates, Adler explicitly notes an element of being
guided by a higher power in doing the work she has done over the
years – including her turn toward painting in recent years:

People used to refer to me as a perfectionist, but I've translated that
into 'artist.' They mean the same thing. I knew that, whatever I did,
I wanted to do it very well. I feel more like I've been guided. So
that would, in some sense, be opportunistic, but I think underneath
all of it there's very deeply etched in me that I somehow wanted to
contribute to 'Never again' – the World War II experience of my
mom, that people could commit such atrocities. On all the puzzle
pieces it comes back, whether it's celebrating diversity – of course,
that's the opposite of disparaging it. I could never stand the phrase
'Tolerating diversity.' Sorry, not in this lifetime. I don't feel I can
honor people by merely tolerating them.

So it's always been in the way I teach, whether executives or at
McGill, and the way I write. I always have the image that I wanted to
support people. I fought like mad at McGill to get my global
leadership course for all the new incoming MBAs to be the first week
of the term, and for it to be pass/fail rather than [be] graded, because
how could I be a coach and support people and get them to be honest
with their real desires and images [if they were being graded]? In

Judaism, the phrase for what you're supposed to do for six days a week is *tikkun olam*, to 'fix the world.' Even if I didn't grow up with that phrase I think I grew up with that notion. But it's strange saying it, because at a deep, deep level, especially right now, I am not completely sure I believe it's possible. It's almost like it's what I'm supposed to be trying to do, but...

As she tries to frame her meaning, Adler relates an illustrative story that links healing, the spiritual, and her work:

I heard an interview once with Elie Wiesel [Nobel Laureate, writer, peace activist, professor at Boston University, and Holocaust survivor] on the one day the United Nations, which doesn't have a particularly good relationship to Jews, was holding its first all-day event against racism..., and for once they were including anti-Semitism as part of their definition of racism. Of course, they asked Elie Wiesel to speak. The interviewer asked if he was hopeful, and his answer was, 'No,' that, if the Holocaust couldn't teach people 'Never again,' couldn't teach people that we should never commit that kind of murder, that kind of horror, ...then what would one speech do at the UN? Then he paused, as only Elie Wiesel can do, and he said, 'And I'm coming to New York and I'm going to speak.'

One other intellectual shaman, who links her work explicitly with the sacred, perhaps not surprisingly given that the core of her work is spirituality and management, is Judi Neal. Neal founded the Spirit at Work organization and awards by the same name (now called the Faith and Spirit at Work Awards). Neal claims:

The spiritual principle for me in all of this work is that what you pay attention to grows. It's like the law of attraction. So, what you give energy to expands. In the field of business, and even in business education, we tend to give energy to what's wrong with organizations. Look at our case studies, [in which] it's 'Well, figure out what's wrong and how to solve the problem.' There's only recently been [work on] appreciative inquiry and positive organizational scholarship and other fields that are looking at what's right with organizations. But, starting back in 1992, I wanted to look at what was good and highest and best and most inspiring about organizations.

Inspired by the power of business to shift consciousness and by the power that businesses have as institutions in the world today, as well as by the work of Willis Harmon, Neal created the Willis Harman Spirit at Work Award in 2001, recalling her insight: 'What if we created an award so that companies actually wanted to be recognized for being very value-centered and very humane and really more transcendent in their approach to business?' Neal shares her vision for the awards and, ultimately, for her work linking healing with the spiritual:

> The vision is that there are so many of us around the world who are trying to make a difference. I realized that my role in this is not for me personally so much to make a difference, but to build community, to help people find one another, to help people know they're not crazy if they see this kind of vision and have this kind of inner drive, that they are a part of something bigger. Once I knew that there's one other person as crazy as me, it gave me courage. 'OK, I may be crazy, but I'm not the only one. So let's go do some crazy stuff together.'
>
> That's been my vision of pulling together and connecting people who are crazy enough to think they can change the world, as [Apple founder Steve Jobs said], 'because only the people who are crazy enough to think they can change the world are the ones that can.' [...] It's that intersection of academia and spirituality and business, like a braid. I feel like I'm weaving this braid of those three strands to hopefully make something strong enough that the world might be a little bit better place as a result.

Neal also applies her sense of healing and holism to the ways in which management education is taught – and to the need to teach not just disciplines and not just to the intellectual aspects of the learner, but the whole person. She sums up:

The process [in management education] is – we still get students sitting in seats pretty much and listening to people lecture. That's not how people learn. So [we need] much more experiential education, but also more holistic. [I talk] about how management education ought to incorporate body, mind, heart, and spirit. We do some creative things around mind, and we do some creative things even around [emotions,] emotional intelligence, and people's hearts to some degree. It's sort of the leading edge now, but what about their spirit, their spirituality, and what about their physical well-being? There was a study I read in *The Wall Street Journal* about [how] the most successful executives have incredible physical endurance. What do we do to help students have physical endurance, or even value that? Nothing. So I think there's a whole lot more that we could be doing with management education that would incorporate the whole human being.

HEALING CULTURAL MYTHS

Intellectual shamans emphasize the mythologies or social constructions associated with, say, fields of study, ways of doing research, theoretical lenses, how management is practiced or taught, or how organizations function – or even how society itself functions. Such constructs can also be viewed as forms of cultural mythologies, in what some call the 'imaginal realms': realistic-seeming social constructs developed by a set of practitioners and theorists that shape the way disciplines develop, are understood, and are promulgated – and thus a natural subject for intellectual shamans.

The term 'imaginal' was coined by Henri Corbin, writing about the distinction between the imaginary and what he termed the imaginal, derived from the phrase *mundus imaginals*, meaning 'imagined world.'[98] A self-described interpreter of Arabic and Persian texts, Corbin needed a word that encompassed a degree of realism, or strong belief, yet went beyond the imaginary to capture what he termed the imaginative consciousness, or, alternatively, the cognitive imagination. Corbin argues that the imaginal, derived from the Latin *imago* (image of god, typically meaning an idealized image of another person in modern usage), is an order of reality between the experienced 'real' world and the pure world of intellect or imagination. Derived from the word *imago* in the same way that the word 'original' is derived from the Latin *origo*, the imaginal is related to the soul, while the real is related to the body and the intellect/imagination to spirit, in Corbin's view.

For intellectual shamans in management disciplines, the imaginal can be considered to be the world of theories, ideas, research methodologies, and managerial practices that constitute what I am calling cultural mythologies. That is, we can consider the imaginal realm a construction that somehow attempts to reflect reality, albeit comprised of ideas. Although ideas about these elements of the work of the intellectual shaman are intellectual creations, they become, in a sense, reified or made real by the belief systems that surround them – at least, until some new set of ideas or mythologies comes along to replace them. We can extend this notion to other types of shamans, who create or visit 'real' imaginal worlds, from which they bring back information to help with the healing process (a boundary-spanning process to be explored more deeply in the next chapter).

In discussing the healing processes used by shamans, Dow articulates the important role of such mythologies in what he terms the therapeutic encounter:[83] 'In the encounter, the healer gets the patient to accept a particularization of the general mythic world as a valid model of the patient's experiences.' In other words, the shaman gets the patient to accept that the imaginal world he or she describes is real or believable, that this world is dis-ordered, and that the shaman can bring order back into that world, thereby healing the patient. These healing features of shamanism are increasingly well accepted today in the health professions and in some forms of psychological therapy.[84]

In a sense, the intellectual shaman is doing much the same thing as the traditional shaman: taking the accepted wisdom and turning it upside down or inside out so that a new mythic world is, effectively, created. The intellectual shaman thereby shakes up some aspect of both the accepted wisdom and its adherents that he or she believes to be problematic and in need of healing (or at least change). Perhaps this alternative-to-the-norm perspective, very real to intellectual shamans, helps to explain the maverick/outsider status of many intellectual shamans, explored in Chapter 2, which is also common among traditional shamans.

Traditional shamans accomplish their healing through a process of what Dow calls 'manipulating the symbols.' In the case of intellectual shamans, these symbols might be associated with how society, academia, research norms, theories, management practice, and the like are defined. Such symbols constitute the imaginal world of the intellectual shaman as management academic, and, of course, such analogies could be extended to numerous other realms of work and experience by shamanistic individuals in those fields. The intellectual shaman perceives that something is wrong, something is not being properly conceived or accomplished in practice, within these systems of belief or cultural norms, and creates a new way of approaching them. The shaman thereby performs much the same function as the traditional shaman: healing what is dis-ordered and bringing greater order to it, somehow healing what is wrong and making it (more) 'right,' at least to the intellectual shaman's point of view. The healing role of the intellectual shaman is to somehow correct the situation, often by upending common wisdom or accepted norms and creating something different and new.

As noted above, the traditional shaman is the 'master healer of the imaginary realms'[85] (or we could say, following Corbin, the imaginal realms), while the intellectual shaman works in the worlds of (management) practice, thought, research, and teaching, though with much the same (sometimes implicit) agenda of healing these realms. The work of intellectual shamans often has a decidedly affirmative element to it as well, much of it fitting in well with emerging ideas about positive psychology, positive organizational scholarship, appreciative inquiry, and sustainability.[94,99,100] Indeed, as already noted, several of the individuals interviewed are directly associated with that movement, in particular Jane Dutton, Kim Cameron, and Robert

Quinn, and others such as David Cooperrider, Tima Bansal, Stewart Hart, Judi Neal, Paul Shrivastava, and Ed Freeman have formulated alternatives to existing ideas that also focus on positive elements.

Cooperrider has developed the concept of appreciative inquiry,[101–105] an approach to organizational or social change that emphasizes what is already being done well in an institution. Cooperrider recalled his interest, while still an undergraduate at Augustana College, in doing something with a positive or healing orientation. In addition to his experience of the potentialities of life when studying in Japan and visiting Hiroshima, discussed earlier, he remembers other major influences that shaped his emergent ideas on appreciative inquiry:

> I think one [influence] was that experience that emerged in Hiroshima, the miracle of life on this planet that's in our hands. So the language of life [came] from there. The other was this book called *Reverence for Life* by Albert Schweitzer. It's probably the most profound small text that anyone could read. The third was, when I was beginning to craft this notion of an appreciative inquiry into organizational life, I was very impacted by my wife. Nancy is an art history major and she was an art teacher. Her bookshelf was filled with books on art history. One of them by an author, Melvin Rader,[106] was a whole anthology of articles on art and aesthetics, and articles by John Dewey trying to understand the aesthetic, by Nietzsche, by other folks like Santayana. Anyway, this editor made a distinction that was very powerful. He talked about the difference between art and science. Science he called communities of interpretation and art he called communities of appreciation, where appreciation meant valuing those things of value in the world.
>
> A sudden insight went off for me: why are those two separate? Why not an appreciative science? Why not an appreciative inquiry? So [I began] drawing on the language of art, which was filled with the language of life. [I was] starting to realize that we do live in worlds that our language creates, and [that] this language of life was very

powerful in helping me see things in organizations that I hadn't seen before, that would kindle the imagination and mind, and that would lead to new and better theoretical propositions for the future. Anyway, I think it was shortly after that that I started saying, 'This isn't about positive or negative. It's about what gives life. It's not Pollyanna-ish. It's not putting a paintbrush on a troubled world. It's searching for those things of value, worth valuing for everything that gives life to living systems when you're most alive.'

The healing orientation of appreciative inquiry becomes explicit as Cooperrider continues – and as he makes links among the philosophers' famous trio: the good, the true, and the beautiful. As we will see more fully in Chapter 8, wisdom can be defined as a combination of moral imagination or the ability to see the ethical implications of system (the good), systems understanding or the ability to see things as they 'really' are (the true), and aesthetic sensibility or the capacity for coherence, beauty, and wholeness (note the relationship to healing) (the beautiful),[59,60] in the service of making the world a better place. Cooperrider provides a similar set of thoughts:

> The idea [of appreciative inquiry] is a little bit artistic, in the sense that as a theorist you're taking these images and moments and narratives and examples and the texture of actual. . ., these ideals that are in the texture of the actual. These [ideals] visit utopias that are right there in front of us and lift those up in a way that nourishes the theoretical imagination in mind for what's possible. Inquiry into the good, inquiry into the true, inquiry into the better, inquiry into the possible, inquiry into those things of value, worth valuing, inquiry into what gives life was very special in terms of igniting the inspiration needed to see new and better futures.

The 'utopias' that Cooperrider speaks of are the imaginal worlds that the appreciative inquiry process constructs – and then attempts to make real, by doing what all shamans do: dreaming the world you want into existence. That is, by healing the cultural myth, or changing the myth and the words surrounding it, you begin to change thinking and, ultimately, reality. Cooperrider provides an example of how these qualities of 'good,' 'true,' and 'beautiful' merge – into an appreciation of a better future in which many of the problems that the world is facing today could potentially be resolved and healed:

> One of the stories [in the Business as an Agent of World Benefit initiative started by Cooperrider and his appreciative inquiry colleagues at Case Western Reserve University] recently was about this Netherlands company called OAT [which makes] 'shoes that bloom.' It's amazing! After I saw the story, which one of the students submitted, I went to visit them. [The company] literally is an image of what the next stage of our economy could look like. Imagine you're a designer, and someone comes up to you and says, 'We'd like you to design a shoe that young people are going to love, won't require any advertising, creates an incredible social media buzz, and is completely sourced in renewable ways. It's completely developed and designed in renewable energy factories, for example, and more than just being designed sustainably, so that after the shoe is worn out, instead of landfill or decomposing more rapidly, how about you design a shoe that actually regenerates and serves as a regenerative force for the planet?'[1n]

Reflect back to the discussion on the imaginal – the imagined world made real. Cooperrider's vision highlights how the intellectual shaman attempts to do what traditional shamans – and, in this case, social entrepreneurs – also try to do: dream the desired world into existence. He concludes his story:

> So, literally, these are shoes that bloom; you plant them in your backyard when you're done and they turn into a tree. I love that. It's a wonderful story that came in from one of our students. It's a seed image of what the whole economy can be, where we're saying that the economy is not just growth or no growth in the economy, but it's good growth. How do we create that?

Other intellectual shamans also see the current economic system as broken with respect to its sustainability, and view their work through that lens. Tima Bansal, for example, in 2013 was awarded a Tier 1 Canada Research Chair, the highest honor a Canadian academic can receive, for her work on sustainability. She is one of only a dozen business professors in all of Canada to have been so designated. Bansal, who heads up the Network for Business Sustainability, among other activities, articulates her sense of duty to serve the world combined with a sense of how lucky we are as academics to do the work we do. Ultimately, she expresses a healing orientation for the world:

> Well, my personal goal is that I think I'm in this very privileged profession; that we get to do what we love. I think that we want to derive meaning from our work, and so that's the first piece. Then there's another piece, where I think that it's not just about me deriving meaning. (I can derive meaning, actually, from a lot of things.) I also think that what I do in the business school and what we are doing in the business school, what we're teaching in business, is just wrong. So I think the business paradigm as we know it is broken. So it's not about me deriving meaning, it's that it's our obligation, as people who had the privilege of being funded by public resources, . . .to create a better society, and, if the business paradigm is broken, then it's our obligation to provide something to fix it.

The University of Michigan's Andy Hoffman takes up a similar challenge. Hoffman articulates how he hopes to link his academic work to move ideas about sustainability in academic papers that speak mostly to other academics into the world of practice. In expressing this point, Hoffman alludes to the cultural myths that surround climate change. He uses work on understanding the perspectives of climate skeptics and their particular cultural mythologies, which contrast distinctly with his own, to illustrate how the cultural mythologies or imaginal world of climate skeptics play into the climate debate:

I'm getting to a point now where I'm trying to write more and more for the intellectual debate in this country. My next goal – and I don't know if I'm going to be able, don't even know how to achieve it – I would like to start publishing in places like the *New Republic*, *The Atlantic Monthly*, *New Yorker*, and *Harpers*. This is where the intellectual debate is taking place in this country. It's not in *ASQ*, *AMJ* or *AMR* [*Administrative Science Quarterly*, *Academy of Management Journal*, and *Academy of Management Review*], though I will still do that as a way to test my ideas. But that can't be the end.

The end has to be in the public debate. I'm finding in my work on climate skeptics that the theories we use are a way of presenting a clear view of the world. For instance, looking at the climate change debate through the lens of organizational theory shows that it is not about CO_2 molecules. It's not a scientific debate. It's a cultural debate. It's a debate about your beliefs about the role of government, the faith in the market, our place within the global environment. Are we [humans] really at a point where we can affect the global climate? I think we are. But that is a cultural, even an existential, question.

These are the deeper ideological questions that are at play. I'm finding that I'm saying something that people are responding to. They say, 'That's really interesting. I've never thought about it that way before.' That makes me feel good. I couldn't have got here without taking my cod liver oil and developing my theoretical foundations. There's a benefit in earning your bones. But it gets you to a point where you now have the license to really say something important. The people who don't take advantage of that license or don't recognize that license miss a real opportunity to use the power of the academy to make a real difference in the world.

Stuart Hart, emeritus from Cornell, also a sustainability expert, expresses a similar sentiment about his status as emeritus professor, and his new role at Vermont, where he is helping to develop a sustainability-oriented MBA, as a way to shift his energy to work that he believes will really make a difference in the world. Also discussing the imaginal realm of climate change, he comments:

Well, there are people trying to say either [climate change] doesn't exist or it's a 2030 or 2040 or 2050 problem. It's not. It's right here now. So what's been a continuous source of motivation is that realization. Now it's all the more pressing, which is why I am really backing down on the academic side, because I figure, if I'm ever going to make something stick, now's the time. Plus the condition of the world requires it.

I'm not arrogant, . . .but I see my role as creating the model that could take us down that different path. As I say, sort of creating the lifeboats. Because there will come a time, in the not so distant future, where [climate change] will become widely recognized by everyone, including the man or woman on the street, and all the people at the Academy [of Management] meeting. That that's the reality! If we don't have viable alternative models. . .the government can't create them; the government can only kind of get the billows out and put wind behind the sails of stuff, lifeboats, that are already there. So I view my role as creating those alternative models.

Bill Starbuck, too, Emeritus Professor at New York University and now affiliated with the University of Oregon in what for many would be retirement years, is concerned about the state of the world. He is particularly interested in healing the world of scholarship, although he also points toward the world of practice in his remarks. Starbuck reflects on the current state of management scholarship in his typically pull-no-punches manner:

I spent a long time trying to start an organization that would sponsor more applied forms of management research. But that never came to fruition. I am proud that I tried to do it, but I would have to say it didn't work.

Asked for the reasoning behind this effort, Starbuck replies:

Oh, I think that most professors are wasting their time doing things that are of value only to themselves and not to anyone else. I admit that maybe most people aren't capable of doing anything that's of value to anyone else, but, if even 10 percent of the effort put out by management professors was devoted to trying to make lives better or to solving the world's problems, we might be more useful to someone.

Starbuck recognizes the irony in articulating such strong opinions, because as a scholar he is not working, in a sense, in what many call the 'real' world to effect change but, rather, in the imaginal world of scholarship theories and ideas. He has devoted much effort to trying to persuade management professors to change their research methods. One of his books focuses on ways to improve research, and for many years he has participated in workshops that aim to replace traditional research methods with ones he advocates.

Despite his claim to not be trying to save the world, Starbuck encompasses a healing orientation in his thinking. Pressed on the rationale for giving more power to corporations, he responds:

> There's one irony to observe. There's a Wikipedia entry about me. Somebody anonymous wrote into it, 'Although Starbuck preaches this kind of stuff, if you actually look at what he does, he doesn't do any of it.' I think that's a legitimate criticism, as I'm not out there trying to save the world. I have tried to write some things about why we should give more power to big corporations. I think that, if I actually would publish these ideas as a book, it would offend so many people that nobody would actually pay attention to what it said. I don't think I have figured out for how to do something like that.
>
> I think, however, we can't just change corporations. We have to somehow create a different kind of corporation than exists at present. We need a modification of the current corporations that would make corporations less destructive and less sociopathic. The only ideas I've come up with have to do with their governance. Maybe we could get some leverage by encouraging corporations to have a much more diverse collection of people in their top management. For example, we could require that no more than 15

percent of the board of directors or 15 percent of the managers have the same nationality. In other words, my dream would be to get people to act in their own self-interest, but while thinking in terms of their children and their homelands where they grew up.

Starbuck summarizes his point cogently, linking his perceptions of the world's problems – his own imaginal world – with his healing philosophy:

My basic agenda is: I don't think it's a good idea for people to kill each other. It seems pretty clear to me that people kill each other largely over economic issues, and we have to have more equality of economy. At this moment a sixth of the people in the world are actually starving to death, and close to half of the world's population has inadequate nutrition. As long as the world is in that shape, I don't think we can ever deal with the problems. People are going to keep on killing each other until we find a way to make them more equal. Perhaps they'll keep on killing each other anyway, but we can reduce the frequency of it.

Derick de Jongh of the University of Pretoria's Centre for Responsible Leadership also focuses on the nature of the modern corporation:

Unfortunately, the real examples out there of significant, almost transformational, shifts are very few and far between. [...] Those companies out there [that are transformational in the sense that Starbuck had mentioned] – they're almost boutique-style businesses. Patagonia [the clothing and sports gear company] is an example: Patagonia and the story of [its founder and CEO] Yvon Chouinard – of doing business in a way that really fully supports sustainability. You know, [these businesses risk] being seen by the majority of the mainstream businesses out there as catering to the greenies, and they're not really part of the bigger mainstream business fraternity, as much as Yvon Chouinard would argue that being good also means you make a lot of money. It's like the two are mutually exclusive.

Asked what drives him to focus his work on responsible leadership and responsible companies, de Jongh emphasizes the element of calling to purpose discussed earlier, as well as the almost spiritual nature of some of this work of healing the world. He highlights the reality shaping the imaginal realm that surrounds the corporation and its purpose, and shows how leadership can take place and can be undertaken from numerous perspectives, not just those of management academia:

> It's an interesting question, and a question that [we focused on] when I did my strategic planning session at my Centre. I've got a nice team of about eight academics in the Centre at the moment, and they are coming from a variety of backgrounds: environmentalists, ethics specialists, I even have a theology person who's from a spiritual point of view. I've got the law people from the legal background. So it's a really cross-functional, cross-disciplinary group of people. I asked them the very same question. The answer comes from a much deeper place than (and it sounds very precious) . . .the eye can see.
>
> The one thing that all of us have in common is (and it's going to sound very, very corny) . . .a basic deeper calling. It's something much deeper in us. Why are we doing this? What I believe in and what I live every day and what I do are all in alignment with my constant realization that things aren't well at the moment. So, saying 'I want to make a difference in the world' sounds very precious, but it's true. So that's what's driving me. I've got a constant (how can I call it?) something that almost haunts me. I'm never satisfied with anything. There's always that something out there that forces me to say, 'But this is not what it should be like.' So, I can come up with a lot of other reasons, but it's really something very deep.

One more intellectual shaman illustrates the healing orientation that arises from trying to change extant cultural myths. Josep Lozano of ESADE Business School in Barcelona, Spain, and an ethics scholar, provides an individual-level example and, like Stu Hart above, expresses humility as he thinks about his possible healing role in the world:

> Let me say that I am talking about these things really from a humble attitude, because otherwise it could seem pretentious. One of my concerns is that humanity is really at a crossroads. A crossroads. We have also enormous possibilities and enormous dangers. On the other hand, there is so much suffering in the world that creates in me the need to do something that creates conditions...to change this kind of situation, and I'm convinced that we need not only to change our practices, we need to change also our understanding, our mindsets, even our assumptions, about how to confront the world's problems.

Note that Lozano is directly confronting the imaginal world and its associated cultural myths, with which scholarship inevitably intersects. He continues, framing how his teaching attempts the healing process:

> The other point that motivates and moves me is the real importance of education – education understood not just as teaching, but education understood as a creating a space where people at different stages of their lives can be involved in a fruitful dialog related to something that really helps them to grow, to improve by increasing skills, and to go further to the core. So, frankly speaking, for me the teaching practices are (just let's say) a tool, an instrument to create a deeper relationship between people in the classroom, in other settings, and in creating that helps people to question themselves and to achieve a critical outlook to the world and their life.

Lozano creates his own imaginal world to illustrate how shifting mindsets can shift practice and help to begin the healing process – and in addition he takes us to the notion that healers must also cross what look like rigid disciplinary boundaries and heal themselves too. Speaking about the future of business schools, Lozano argues:

I can imagine that colleges and the schools are clearly defined as, for example, law, as medical schools, and so on. But maybe business schools should not have such clear borders. Probably, [business schools] will be a space that will be more open to other contexts. That's why it's important that business schools are within a university. But it's not just as an academic incorporation of new departments closed in on themselves, but a space that takes advantage of the different contributions from different areas of knowledge, from other faculties, to help to answer this basic question that at the end is: 'What kind of world are we constructing with our organizations, our business, and so on?' Humanity is emerging, companies contribute to that emergence, and business schools should see themselves as a servant of these processes of creating and transforming the world through organizations. Finally, business schools have to practice what they preach: if they speak of transparency, accountability, dialogue with stakeholders, good governance, then to what extent is that also true within the business schools themselves?

BEYOND SELF

A recurrent theme in all the interviews with intellectual shamans is that what needs to be healed goes beyond the self to some aspect of the broader world. So, while the shaman often has to be healed before his or her work can be effective, the orientation to healing that characterizes intellectual shamans is a 'bigger than self' one.

Bob Giacalone states this orientation openly in discussing a paper he published in the *Academy of Management Learning and Education* journal called 'A transcendent business education for the 21st century,' which represents one of his proudest accomplishments. In the paper, Giacalone describes the imaginal realm of management education that he believes needs to be fixed, integrating the healing, spiritual, and holistic elements associated with shamanism:

We promulgate a worldview that facilitates questionable decisions. We create brilliant tacticians who know how to play the end game of

wealth creation, where financial success is defined without
transcendent responsibilities. We teach a path without a heart
where tacticians can cheat themselves and others of good lives.
We are proud, excellent drill sergeants teaching tactical
reductionism: The worthiness of a tactic depends on whether it
results in profits for oneself or one's company. But in search of a
personal or corporate gain, proponents of this instruction aid and
abet physical, psychological, and spiritual toxins for our students,
the organizations they work for, and society at large.[107]

In the paper, Giacalone goes on to argue for the basics of what
he calls a transcendent business education founded on five goals:
empathy, generativity, mutuality, civil aspiration, and intolerance of
ineffective humanity. Giacalone recalls the intensity of his feelings
about the paper and the reasons for that intensity:

When I wrote that article I wrote with an enormous amount of
fear. I wrote it thinking, first of all, 'This is never going to get published.' That usually didn't bother me; it should have been the cue to
me. Usually I laughed about rejections. I thought, 'Oh, so what? Who
cares?' But for some reason, had this paper been rejected, I felt it would
have crushed me in some way, because there was something about
my heart and soul in this paper, about how I viewed the world, and
how I thought students should be educated.

Giacalone goes on to create a new cultural myth of self-
transcendence and a better world, a world beyond the self:

What has guided me all along is an idea that, if people really
understood, if they really understood, what the good life was about,
we'd have a happier world. We'd have a world with less conflict.
We'd have a world with ethics. We'd have a world where people can
go to work every day and do the things they love to do and feel
inspired. They'd come home with a sense of purpose and ability to
embrace their kids and their spouses and be there in that moment.
That's really what has guided me: the fact that I think that we can
make things better.

Acknowledging that, despite this revelation, there are still dark days and dark thoughts, Giacalone highlights his belief that, 'if we changed the dominant ideology, we'd have a much better world.' MIT's Ed Schein also illustrates how the healed presence of the intellectual shaman can operate to effect positive change. Schein was influenced early in his career by Richard Beckhard's work on sensitivity training and psychologist Carl Rogers' humanistic (client-centered) approach to therapy, which developed what are known as T-groups (alternatively, encounter groups or human relations training groups). He began to think about how these approaches fit into his own work. He recalls asking himself, 'What is the impact of low-key facilitative intervention? I realized [the impact] was enormous.' Schein elaborates:

> Now, what I realized is that I've always taken that for granted, but I never thought of it as a possibly controversial statement, that, when Rogers first articulated [his ideas about therapy], apparently people said, 'What, you're not telling people what to do? You're just letting them figure this out? This is crazy!' It took years for people to come to terms with it. Then, here, I see in the T-groups the same phenomenon, the trainers sitting there helping the group to help itself. I've often thought of myself as, kind of, a lazy scholar-consultant, because it's really easier to do less. It's sort of comforting not to come in all geared up to do stuff, but to come into a situation and see what you can do. That appealed to me.

For years, Schein continued to go to the sensitivity training or T-group sessions in Bethel, Maine, as he points out, putting in his 10,000 hours[2n] of practice and really absorbing the idea of what he calls low-key facilitative intervention, which ultimate became his trademark approach to organizational change. As time passed, he found that 'after a while you don't realize that you begin to have trained eyes and ears from all these hours, and hours in the groups.' When he was invited into what was then Digital Equipment Corporation (DEC) by founder and CEO Ken Olsen, Schein found that Olsen wanted him to 'come and sit in the meetings and be paid for it.' Schein recalls the experience, which has been documented in his book *DEC Is Dead, Long Live DEC: The Lasting Legacy of Digital Equipment Corporation*:[109]

> I didn't realize at the time what a gift that [invitation] was. I didn't know how unusual it was, but that's what he wanted. They were a bunch of engineers. 'We think we probably have communication issues. You're an expert, so come on in and see what you can do.' [...] In the Digital book, I've described in a lot of detail how learning to consult at Digital was a traumatic experience because I thought I ought to be telling them what to do. I knew what groups should be doing, and they always thanked me and never changed until I finally learned to figure out apropos of David Rioch's advice 'Don't ask about it. Just watch.' The notion of humble inquiry (I hadn't labeled it that but that's what it really was) was the successful way to intervene. So I got hooked on it.

Schein expands further on how what he now terms 'humble inquiry' shaped his way of dealing with organizations, his consulting, and, ultimately, his writing and research:

> I think the closest thing to beginning to formulate a vision probably was process consultation, where I had been working as a facilitator, trainer. In consulting I was evolving something that was different. The difference was, the job of a consultant is not to make recommendations or tell people what to do but, working with a human system, was to help the client figure things out for themselves. Again, even today it's widely accepted and totally controversial that many consulting books say 'If you haven't given a recommendation, you haven't done your job.' I'm saying that, when you're working with human systems, that's absolutely, totally wrong.

Schein has more fully developed these ideas in recent years into a theory of 'helping,' published in 2009 in a book by that name.[110] Below he discusses his view of helping (i.e., healing) in organizations – and with other types of human systems for facilitation, inquiry, catalyzing action:

> I learned the best word just a few years ago. I was up at Dartmouth Hitchcock [health care system in New Hampshire], where they have this big coaching program. They said the best metaphor for helping in their view is a midwife. That fits perfectly, because it makes it bell clear. No matter what you do, it's not your baby. You can jump, yell, scream, and wish it were yours, but only the client can produce the baby.
>
> I had never used that term before, but I'm going to use it more. I think my form of consulting is midwife. I can help someone sort out what they need to do, and in that process I can make suggestions. I can make recommendations, but I shouldn't ever for a moment assume that I can actually make something more than what they're willing to do. Then it hit me just the other day that this is what Carl Rogers was saying: that people have the capacity to help themselves, and your job is to elicit that and help them help themselves. So that grew into the helping book.

Yet this insight, present in Schein's work throughout the years, also gestated for many years until crystallizing:

> [This perspective] grew out of going all the way back to the NTL [National Training Laboratories' sensitivity or T-] groups to the consulting experiences to finding over and over again that, if I got assertive and thought I knew what to do and suggested it, nine times out of ten didn't work. Or people said, 'We've already thought of it.' So I've kind of learned by being negatively reinforced to stick to this sort of low-key facilitative thing. It keeps getting reinforced all the time, both positively and negatively. If I deviate from it I get negative reinforcement. If I stick with it I get positive reinforcement. I have to keep reminding myself that you can only get people to do what they're willing to do.

Ed Freeman relatedly summarizes the transformative aspects of aesthetic sensibility in creating an imaginal world that goes beyond the self to holism. In discussing an innovative course in leadership and theater he developed at the University of Virginia's Darden Graduate School of Business, Freeman gets to the fundamental issue, the holy/sacred core, that ultimately faces scholars, teachers, and, indeed, all of us:

> The thing that becomes more important is trying to use our imagination to understand what our view of human beings is. We need to develop that more and in a more robust way. I went to see recently *The Merchant of Venice* with Al Pacino. You leave that changed. Here, you're just watching the performance, and it's an unbelievable way that the performance was staged to speak to us. Not just engaged, you leave that changed. Imagine what it would be like if you had to perform that. So you had to not just be a spectator of the creative arts, but you get to actually do it. That changes things. It deepens our idea of what a human being is, and what's possible for human beings to do in business.

5   Connector

Our life is composed greatly from dreams, from the unconscious, and they must be brought into connection with action. They must be woven together.

Anaïs Nin

Though knowledge itself increasingly ignores boundaries between fields, professors are apt to organize their pedagogy around the methods and history of their academic subculture rather than some coherent topic in the world.

Steven Pinker

Underpinning and enhancing the healing orientation of the shaman discussed in the last chapter are two other key roles, as articulated by Frost and Egri: mediator of reality (or boundary-spanner), which I call connector, and sensemaker. Connecting means linking ideas, theories, methodologies, and pedagogies across traditional boundaries. Connecting inherently means making links. The success of intellectual shamans comes in part because they see holistically and are able to make links that others have not yet made.

By their nature, then, intellectual shamans cross boundaries to find new ideas, insights, and practices – and then make new connections. Seeing holistically, they are seldom content with the current state of things in their intellectual or other aspects of their work lives – i.e., they see where healing is needed or holes exist that new connections will help mend. They integrate and bring together ideas in new ways, so they are constantly pushing at the edges of existing (e.g., disciplinary) boundaries to find new ways of thinking, being, and acting in the world. They cross into new realms to find out how things are done there and bring back that information to their own discipline, providing insights and new perspectives. This capacity is what Frost and Egri call shamans' ability to mediate reality,[2] or, more simply, boundary-spanning.[111] I call it connecting.

Connecting enables intellectual shamans to create order where there is dis-order or dis-ease by gathering information and insights from different realms to support healing of the relevant cultural mythology. Intellectual shamans, in one sense, engage with multiple different realms, then create bridges among those worlds as they make connections. In doing so, they both seek new information, which can be brought back to their own particular realm of experience, and develop new types of connections – and information.

Because they engage with multiple 'worlds' – i.e., disciplines, theories, ideas, functions, practices, or research endeavors – intellectual shamans also 'see' things in ways that others do not see. Their views of the issues and ideas they are generating are generally rather more holistic than fragmented or atomistic. Taking this holistic stance provides insight into the issues with which they are dealing; that is, they 'see' holistically, not in fragments, and thereby attempt to provide a more realistic, truthful, grounded, and dynamic sense of what is going on within a system than might be possible with a more fragmented perspective. Below, we explore these aspects of intellectual shamans as connectors.

BRIDGING MYTHOLOGIES: WALKING BETWEEN REALMS

Charles Laughlin and Jason Throop define myth as 'the corpus of sacred stories that constitutes a highly symbolic, but coherent, description of a people's origin (cosmogamy), as well as the origins of significant aspects of the environment (animals, food plans, changes in the weather, social roles, institutions, and so on).'[112] In today's secular societies, where the intellectual shamans tend to work, natural or social science's understanding of the origins of the world – or management and leadership systems, in the case of these academics – frames the cultural mythologies that help explain the world to others.[112]

Myths serve many purposes in society, including providing a 'charter for many of the society's important institutions,' creating moral order, explaining how the world works, and serving as a place where cultural knowledge is preserved.[112] In a very important sense, the sciences and social sciences represent today's core cultural mythology, as science is said to explain whatever needs to be explained in the physical world, just as economics is often thought to explain what needs to be known about the business world. What Ramakrishna Movva[111] terms the shamanic consciousness plays a central role in articulating, shaping, and healing these myths. Sometimes, like the cultural mythologies of traditional cultures, these modern mythologies need to be healed – or exploded.

Relevant cultural myths in the management academy include theories, best practices, research frameworks, ideas, and the like. It is these myths with which intellectual shamans deal. As Laughlin and Throop note, 'The stories are primarily concerned with transmitting knowledge about the primal relations upon which the existence and well-being of the people depend. They form the primary warp and woof in the fabric of a people's "field of tropes," a field of interconnected meaning in which each of life's significant experiences has a location, much as a patch has its appropriate place in a quilt.'[112]

Although cross- or multidisciplinary – i.e., integrated – approaches are now emerging in some arenas, the management disciplines (like a lot of other disciplines) have become specialized and narrow, creating sub-myths within each subdiscipline. Sometimes scholars work on similar issues albeit with different names without communicating across (sub) disciplinary boundaries. Because of their narrowness and specificity, sometimes these cultural myths are problematic. It is such dis-orders and lack of linkage that intellectual shamans attempt to bridge, bringing information from multiple realms to bear on questions and issues of interest to them. Frequently, they work between or among various sources of somewhat different mythologies – i.e., disciplines or subdisciplines – to connect them more holistically, thereby changing the relevant myths in new and insightful ways.

In bridging among various realms, including creative imagination, experience, and reality, myths also serve two other important functions, '(1) the transmission of socially salient vicarious experience and (2) the coordination of individual conceptual systems relative to socially valued experience,' and thereby inform the 'collective consciousness' initially framed by Émile Durkheim.[112] These functions of myth are important here because the mythologies associated with theories, best practices, research approaches, consulting, and other elements of the intellectual shaman's work take on much of the same character as myths themselves do with traditional peoples. For example, as noted by Laughlin and Throop, myths in the view of traditional peoples are said to be 'stories about reality' (citing Mircea Eliade),[20] descriptions of 'the world as problem' (citing Paul Tillich),[113] or 'transcendental experiences and the boundaries of a people's view of multiple realities' (citing Alfred Schutz).[114] So too are myths about theories, research, and practice thought to be reflections of reality.

Like mythologies in traditional cultures, theories, practices, and research orientations frame actions, create explanations for various phenomena of interest, shape perceptions of how the world is and works, and shape values, mores, and norms for the worlds that they affect in our modern management culture. As Laughlin and Throop argue, following Joseph Campbell,[115] myths 'become the "collective consciousness" of a particular people – a collective representation that is keyed to both the local and the global realities within which people are embedded.'[112] In scholarly communities, theoretical, consulting, practice, and research myths frame ways of working and thinking, generating communities of scholars (and others) around particular interest arenas.

Some intellectual shamans were greatly influenced by others who were spanning across different cultural mythologies and making a difference in their particular domains. Others simply were not satisfied with studying a narrow discipline, and found themselves moving between worlds to satisfy their intellectual curiosity. One intellectual shaman who has studied the boundary-spanning capabilities of research subjects from an explicitly spiritual perspective is Judi Neal. Neal described individuals (and organizations) she calls 'edgewalkers' in her book by that title as taking risks, building bridges, and breaking new ground. Neal describes her thought process in researching these individuals:

> I had started interviewing people who had a very strong spiritual life and who were also business leaders. I asked them how they integrated their spirituality and their work, and I began to see patterns in that. At the same time, I was studying with a shaman. He had been talking about walking between worlds and taught me techniques for walking in the upper world, in the middle world, and the lower world. So I put that together as I began to see that these leaders who had a strong spiritual life were walking between worlds. That might not have been their language, but they would get their inspiration and their support and their guidance from the spiritual world and would be able to use that to be effective in business in a very humane and value-centered way.

Neal observed shamanically oriented managers quite deliberately seeking information from one realm, such as meditation, contemplative practices, or other sources, and using it in their management practices. Like Neal, David Cooperrider emphasizes a link between theory and practice in much of his work, and the desire to span across realms started early in his career. He remembers:

> I really felt like I wanted to be in a field that had its feet in both theory and practice. I was searching for a field that might be called applied social psychology. Well, I didn't find such a field, but then my dad told me about a field called organization development that was just being born. He gave me some books by Warren Bennis and a few others, and I was absolutely inspired. One of the books was Carl Rogers' book that recounted his experience in South Africa. It was a book on the T-group, the encounter group. He called it the most important social invention of the twenty-first century because it made human relatedness amenable to inquiry, to change, and to development. This book really spoke to me about what this field might be about. [...]

[Reverend] Dale White[1n] is the one who invited Carl Rogers to South Africa during the really intense period of time – and to introduce to the T-group. Dale told me that in Carl Rogers; first T-group one of the members was Steve Biko.[2n] Steve Biko gave voice to the black consciousness movement during that T-group, and then went out of that T-group setting and began to create a movement, the black consciousness movement.

Well, we know what happened to Steve Biko. He got killed. Carl Rogers; book speculates about the power of the T-group for helping us surface the highest growth-promoting relationships possible where we are who we are because of other people and how to create those growth-promoting contexts where the relationships come alive. Then Rogers speculated and talked about this breakthrough of the T-group and how many applications it had from interpersonal relations, to family relations, to group and team and organization, and he said it has implications all the way up to international relationships. I thought, 'This is a fascinating new field being born that can make a difference in the human condition of the world through this kind of merging of inquiry and action and in the here and now of human interaction.'

Similarly to Cooperrider, organizational scholar and psychologist Karl Weick was drawn early on to integrative approaches to thinking and scholarship. He remembers some of the early influences that have shaped his work:

I suspect that [my connecting] really did start at Ohio State, because I was admitted into the industrial psych program. That didn't seem particularly attractive. Then I switched into counseling psych, and then into clinical psychology. I did a one-year internship at a VA [US Department of Veterans Affairs] hospital. Really got depressed in that experience. I said, 'Boy, this clinical stuff's not for me,' and then finished up the fourth year in a major that was dreamed up on the spot, a combination of social and organizational psychology. It was probably one of the first – best we call tell, it's either the first or the second PhD that was granted in an area you'd call organizational psych.

The transdisciplinary orientation that drew Weick to organizational psychology was fostered by an experience during his graduate school days, which he recounts:

> One of the first graduate courses we had at Ohio State was a proseminar that was fabulous. Each professor in the department, and there were probably fifty, had one week over the course of a year to give it his best shot. We'd say, 'Professor, you've got one week. You've got five hours, and you can pretty much assign anything you want people to read on strategy [or specialty topic]. Give us your best shot on that.' Then, the following Monday, somebody else walks in the room and says, 'This is my life. These are my great ideas. This is why I love my field.' Geeze, that was just so wonderful to get that much wide exposure. It was really tough to choose a specialty, no real desire to choose one, as long as you read on your own time. I know this is not a crisp answer, but it's like browsing the stacks.

Jane Dutton talks about one of her most notable and well-recognized papers, 'Keeping an eye on the mirror: image and identity in organizational adaptation,' a study of the homeless in New York's Port Authority area.[116] She explains how unexpected connections between people and situations created an opportunity to research a typically unstudied area. The study also helped her connect to her sense of needing to make a positive difference in the world by addressing real-world problems. In addition, as Dutton explains, the project to study the homeless in the port authority area linked her to individuals in different realms, and helped to bridge between her home life and her work:

> That was a total gift. [...] My best friends from college called ourselves the dirty dozen. One of them got a job at the port authority. I was commuting in with her...and I remember her saying to me, 'Jane, I don't know what to do. I just got this job as

head of the homeless task force.' I'd been studying issue interpretation in organizations, and, on the other hand, I'm struggling just like everyone was with the human despair that was everywhere in New York at that time. [...] I would go in to teach on Sundays, and, going through the bus terminal, you would go into the ladies' room, and, literally, you couldn't even find your way to the toilet, because there were so many women sleeping on the floor. [...]

So there was intellectual argument, I'm doing my stuff on issue interpretation and threats and opportunities and all that stuff. Then there is this, like, daily experience of human misery. Then Deb, my friend, said, 'I'm head of the homeless task force.' It was just one of these things, 'Oh, we've got to study this. This is a way to link these things.' [...] [Co-author] Janet [Dukerich] and I were commuting on the same train, too. What are the odds of that? She had children she sometimes would leave with our nanny, so we were linked personally, too, which enabled a lot of stewing time about 'What this is about?' [...] The separation between my work life and my non-work life was all blurry and intertwined... I feel like I'm always sort of picking stuff from these different spheres, and sometimes they enhance each other.

For Dutton, part of the motivation to study the homeless was to integrate her personal values and sense of injustice with her work on issue interpretation in organizations, as she walked between the different worlds of work, friendship, life, and values. Values also propelled Maurizio Zollo to begin a huge multidisciplinary research project integrating the study of companies' sustainability at multiple levels of analysis and across multiple functions, industries, and other realms. The project, called GOLDEN for Sustainability (the Global Organizational Learning and Development Network for Sustainability), is attempting to accelerate business and society's transformations toward sustainable enterprise.[3n] Zollo describes the rationale for walking between the numerous worlds that GOLDEN's scope encompasses:

Now, GOLDEN is by far...the most experimental, the most innovative, the most ambitious thing that I've done so far. It will probably be one of the most crazy things I will do in my life, so I want to make sure that it works out well. [...] It is about studying how companies learn to change themselves, to transform themselves in fundamental ways, connected to their *raison d'être*, to why they exist, to what they can do. What is their purpose, their strategies? How they should be conducting their business, how they should compete and collaborate. Obviously, how the culture of the organization should evolve towards a model of sustainable enterprise. So, it's about innovation in business models toward sustainable business models basically. Toward embedding notions of sustainability across all the various functional activities, of the firms, and across levels. So very ambitious, very deep.

Zollo explains the different realms that the GOLDEN project spans, and notes that part of the rationale for the project is to seek and protect truth for healing the world – by examining crucial issues through a number of different lenses and across what many could consider traditional boundaries. Such boundary-spanning is innovative and unusual in an academic world typically bounded by cultural myth-ologies that limit the nature and type of research agenda, as well as the scope, to fit within conventional research boundaries:

There are a number of taboos that we're breaking with this project. One taboo is that you're not supposed to mix inductive and deductive research designs. Of course, we're trying to do both if we can. Another – it's not a taboo but it's really a practical constraint, doing either large-scale but very superficial quantitative analysis or deep case studies but with very few companies. Here we're trying to do very deep data collection inside the company throughout all the main functions, also looking at subsidiaries in different countries and so on. So, really deep and longitudinal, with sustained access for about three years. At that same time we are trying to do that with a large – fairly large – number of firms, 100 to 150 firms, across the world.

So we want to access key regions of the world, across sectors, and really look at the way that companies across all the various functional areas [and different industries] understand and make sense of the sustainability issues. [We are looking at] the way that they make decisions to tackle these issues, and, even more importantly, the way that they deploy their decisions, their initiatives, and scale them up – which is a big, big issue. We're trying to look at the entire sequence, the life cycle of the sustainability issue, as the company tackles it, from the beginning, when they're kind of not sure, all the way to the deployment and the scaling up.

In describing the research process that underlies the GOLDEN concept, Zollo is articulating the rationale that drives many of the intellectual shamans' pathbreaking work:

Doing that across industries and across cultures, across the institutional context, is fantastic, because – clearly – it allows us to not only understand the processes inside the firm but also how firms try to figure this out: what are the barriers, what are the enablers? We also try to understand the impacts of all these processes and the role of the context – the role of the industry context, the role of the cultural context, the role of the institutional context – in facilitating or inhibiting the learning and change processes inside firms.

To the notion of seeking and protecting 'truth,' discussed below, Zollo adds the following points about the fundamental purpose for him personally undertaking an enormous project such as GOLDEN:

Well, the goal is very clear: the goal is to make this world a better place, obviously. I think the clarity of the goal has developed, has evolved. Clearly, at the beginning, when I was working in investment banking or doing consulting, there was no awareness, or very limited awareness. I must say I was very, very happy when I switched to a PhD program, not only because I could have time for learning, but also because – well, because I started asking the deeper questions. So I started meditating. I started my own personal development quests, even spiritual quests. All those dimensions started putting things together right, various pieces of the puzzle that slowly were falling in the right place.

Walking between worlds suggests inter-, multi-, or transdisciplinary work, or work that integrates theory and practice, home and work life, or other realms. In crossing the boundaries that exist between worlds and making connections between them, intellectual shamans also seek and discover information that can be helpful to them as they work to heal the particular mythologies of interest to them. I delve more deeply into this bridging of worlds and associated connecting in the next section.

BRIDGING WORLDS

As Frost and Egri have pointed out, a core function of shamans is that of mediating realities to accomplish connecting. The mediator is the reconciler of differences, standing in a middle position between competing or conflicting myths; in this case, he or she attempts to resolve these differences in creative ways, often by bringing information from one realm into another in creative ways. This creativity often sheds new light or insights that could not be gained by staying within a single old mythology or from a single realm. Mihály Hoppál explicitly articulates the mediating or boundary-spanning role that shamans making connections enter. Typically, traditional shamans span boundaries or go to different (spiritual) realms while in trance, in so-called journeying states. Hoppál comments, 'The shaman as a mediator is a specialist in ritual communication and in maintaining the fragile state of social/psychological equilibrium by symbolic mediation between worlds of ordinary and non-ordinary reality' – or, as he and Mircea Eliade put it, between the 'sacred and profane worlds.'[29]

Hoppál further notes that traditional shamans – and, I would argue, intellectual shamans as well – are explicitly connecting figures, bridging different worlds. In the traditional shaman's case, the worlds are described as the real world, the underworld, and the heavens. These worlds are accessed in trance through journeys to those different realms to create balance when things are out of order (dis-ordered), dis-eased, or unbalanced. The job of creating balance and the ability to access the information that helps create balance and coherence (i. e., healing) is a source of power for the traditional shaman,[29] and also for the intellectual shaman. In bridging worlds, the traditional shaman serves as a mediator 'between the cultural heritage of the past and the present situation.'[29] Similarly, the intellectual shaman takes present knowledge in whatever realm or discipline he or she is working in, and bridges between that accepted knowledge and new ways of thinking, knowing, and acting.

Intellectual shamans do much the same work in crossing disciplinary, intellectual, theory/practice, and teaching boundaries as traditional shamans do in bridging spiritual worlds – and for much the same reasons. Bill Torbert describes such bridging work as interweaving:

> I ended up working in a management school [at Boston College] for a long time, but I was the graduate dean, so I was interested in the educational process there and studying that and making that the research. Also, I was influenced by [Harvard scholar Chris] Argyris' model of not seeing teaching and research as opposites, but seeing teaching, consulting, action research in the outside world, and theory-building, and then testing it again through action research, as a way of – instead of making teaching and scholarship competitive, you interwove them. I think I took it further than he took it, because I took it outside of formal situations and into my whole life.

Another person whose research has bridged multiple levels of analysis, from individual cognitive biases and 'blinders' to group-level knowledge structures, and decision-making processes to memory processes as constraint and heritage, to strategy and to the study of business in society, is Jim Walsh. Thinking about crossing levels of analysis and past/present/future boundaries, Walsh comments on his transition into field development and service to the profession that has characterized so much of his work:

In very broad terms, I was interested in memory both as an enabler and constraint to decision-making and action. Knowledge structures both enable you to see the world with cognitive efficiency and, at the same time, run the risk of blinding you to it. I had done some conceptual and empirical work at the individual, group, and organization levels of analysis when, for my own purposes, and maybe for the field's as well, I decided to try to take stock of the entire managerial and organization cognition 'movement' in our world. Too many people seemed to be working 'alone together' in this new area. I wanted to try to wrap my mind around where we were in our quest to understand these issues, and, hopefully, to help move us all along.

It turned out that this project dovetailed with my first foray into the world of professional service. Bill Starbuck worked hard to create the precursor to what is now the Managerial and Organizational Cognition Division of the Academy of Management. Somehow I found myself in his world, and became one of the first officers of this new interest group [divisions originate as interest groups in the Academy structure]. That was hugely important for me. I saw that you could advance the field both with your writing and with your service. You can do the research yourself and, at the same time, you can bring others together and help them do it too. The two reinforce each other. In retrospect, I can see that this opportunity changed my life.

His interest in cognition was fundamentally motivated by a quest to figure out when and how senior leaders' cognitive processes might blind them to their decision environments and in so doing leave them vulnerable to decision mistakes that could harm their firms. Walsh's review convinced him that the conceptual and empirical challenges of working with cognition in the field, as opposed to a psychology lab, would leave him working on the psychology of decision-making for years. He might never look at leaders' actual decisions and their effects on organizations. So he moved to study corporate governance. Walsh recalls how this stream of work forced him into an interdisciplinary research stance:

> There I was, in the 1980s, puzzling and struggling over the nuances of group- and organization-level cognition, and how these processes might compromise firm performance, when the reality of the merger wave hit me in the head. My finance and economics colleagues were all abuzz about agency theory. They told me that all of this restructuring was due to, essentially, the misbehavior of firms' senior managers. The only way to deal with these entrenched and self-dealing individuals was to buy their companies and fire them. I said to myself, 'Oh, really? Do you really mean to say that the actions of a few individuals are behind all of the control changes and turmoil we see today?' I realized that this was my cross-level question. Of course, I now had to shift gears and look at firms and then reason back to individual behavior, rather than look at individuals and make the connections to firms. My life changed dramatically at that point.
>
> Instead of spending my time in the psychology literature and hanging around with fellow travelers who wanted to explore applied psychology in the world of strategy and business, I started to spend my time in the economics and finance literatures. I wrote my first paper in this area with a political scientist and then formed a really important connection with a friend and colleague in finance. Jim Seward and I wrote a number of papers together. He was clearly my teacher. I owe him a lot. I then branched out to work with others in the worlds of economics, finance, accounting, law, and, eventually, ethics.

Walsh's work took another turn when, just as before, he paused to take stock of his work and, ultimately, his commitments. This time the stimulus was a grant from the Sloan Foundation.

> At this point my wife and I had more or less recovered from the chaos of not only moving from Dartmouth to Michigan but also from

adding two more children to our family. I was doing my research but being more and more drawn to editorial work and service. My passion and enthusiasm for learning all about these new fields and exploring the power and reach of agency theory had cooled some because so few of these agency theory predictions proved to be as robust as people imagined. Plus, the world was changing. We all learned that the merger and acquisition wave of the '80s was actually a part of a bigger globalization story.

The Sloan grant came at exactly the right time. Joe White, our dean at the time, was instrumental in landing the grant. The operative word was 'ventilation.' The idea was to 'ventilate,' or to breathe some fresh air into, our understanding of the purposes and accountability of the firm – especially in light of all the changes brought by globalization. We put together a team that included a lawyer, an international economist, and a finance professor who has a joint appointment in the law school to examine the extent to which neoclassical economic thinking holds in the face of the challenges of globalization. We put together a big seminar series and offered a joint course for what turned out to be 120 business and law students. We, basically, educated ourselves about these challenges. We ended up writing a law review paper about all of this. So now I found myself in the world of law. You really can't look at these questions seriously without going there. I even audited a course in the law school to try to bring myself up to speed.

Walsh talks about what it takes to make these types of transitions in research agendas, bridging into new disciplines and research arenas as he has done periodically throughout his career:

It is interesting to see this kind of pattern and think about it. I never sat around and said: 'Well, enough psychology; it's time for finance,' and then: 'Enough finance, it's time for law.' I just followed the questions and my intuition. Having said that, I see that I pretty much thrive on crossing borders. [. . .] So, yes, I guess it doesn't surprise me to see that I moved from psychology departments to business schools and from cognition to governance. I don't make these changes for the heck of it, but, if I see a reason to move, I really don't think twice about moving.

Walsh comments on the underlying rationale for this shift – and much of his other research:

My question is really broad. I am really interested in cross-level relationships that, when understood, might make the world a better place. I want to know how people make a difference. The cognition and governance questions were all about how people can mess up the world, either with their cognitive mistakes or by their self-dealing. That Sloan project really changed things. Forget the specifics of the project but just look at the last line in our paper. We said, 'The deepest challenge then is to find a way to enact communitarian sentiments in a contractarian world.'[117] We, basically, tried to ask and answer the question 'Can you organize an economy around communitarian principles?' and came up short. The contractarian perspective seems to provide the spine that allows people to organize, but it has its limits. So the question then, is: how do we breathe the communitarian sentiments into that world?

I think it was Niels Bohr who said something like 'The opposite of a great truth is often another great truth.' In my mind, anyway, both of these supposedly competing perspectives are right. It just took me a while to see that, but, when I did, I decided that I had to look at a fundamental assumption I had been carrying around with me for years and years. I would have flinched if you ever told me that I was a 'What's good for General Motors is good for America' kind of guy, but, at base, I never seriously questioned the place of the firm in society. I guess I casually imagined that, if our business leaders were free of cognitive bias and overweening self-interest, then we would all live happily ever after. I decided that I needed to look at another cross-level relationship, this time at how and how well corporations serve society.

Walsh reflects further on this shift and what it meant for another boundary in his life, the research–teaching frontier:

> Looking at bridging this contractarian–communitarian divide, and doing it with a clear eye at how and how well the corporation can serve society, pretty much led me right to the corporate social performance/corporate financial performance literature. This is the first place you go when you are looking to see if a firm can both 'do good' and 'do well.' I've wandered about that world for some time now but, in doing so, I guess I found that there may never be a research idea or finding that will forever bring flourishing and prosperity to all. We are going to have to watch out for our mistakes and, maybe more importantly, beware the temptation to profit at others' expense.
>
> I was as struck by what a Buddhist priest told Richard Feynman [the famed physicist who helped develop the nuclear bomb]: 'To every man is given the key to the gates of heaven; the same key opens the gates of hell.'[1] We need leaders who are quite aware of their power and alert to the fact that they can use this power for the greater good – or not. I found myself developing a course that would teach the questions we have about the place of the corporation in society and at the same time entertain what it really means to 'do good.' I want to help our future leaders know how to use the key we give them in business school. That course now has me thinking across three levels – individuals, corporations, and society – and connecting the worlds of research and teaching. I guess the quest continues.

Tima Bansal, of Canada's Ivey School of Business, bridges worlds too. She has made a significant impact bridging between the world of ideas and theories and the world of practice, albeit in much the same domain of thinking about fundamental economic questions and the system as a whole, particularly with respect to sustainability issues. She articulates her rationale for doing so below:

> With the basic philosophy that I have, that the business paradigm is broken, then how do you fix it? What I think I need to do is really

understand the problem. To understand problems you have to be embedded in the problem itself. So that's part of it. I think that the community of practice understands the problem, and so, in a way, it's that emic [internal perspective] view. I have to understand the culture of the issue of business, and the environmental issues. So that piece of being with the practice means something to me. The other piece is that I want to influence practice. That sounds really arrogant, and it drives me a bit crazy when my students come to me and they say they want to go to Kenya and go help those poor women in the fields or whatever. I'm thinking, 'Oh my goodness; these poor women in the field actually can teach *you* a lot!' So, in a way, for me to say I want to influence practice, it's more that I should be learning from practice. But I think that there's an aspect that I really do want things to change.

With an interest in business and sustainability, and a recognition that separating these realms is problematic, much of Bansal's work is aimed at creating linkages across arenas that are typically separate. She describes this bridging function and its rationale in the initiative she heads, the Network for Business Sustainability:

Business sustainability is often defined as the triple bottom line – environmental, social, and financial performance. But we need to go beyond that. We need to think about sustainability as the long-term future of the firm, and that means that firms have to think not just about making money in the short term but how are they going to make money over the long term. The Network for Business Sustainability is a collaborative between business, academics, nonprofits, and governments to try to achieve sustainable solutions. The Network for Business Sustainability is really intended to break down the silos that have been erected; so it is allowing people the space to collaborate. I think that people in organizations everywhere care about the world. What's different now than before is that they have a voice that they didn't have before. So they feel that they can speak out, and that business is moving in the ways that they want [it] to move.

Underpinning this work is a fundamental integrative question, whose answer requires the building of numerous bridges, as Bansal points out:

> My area of study was motivated by an interest: why economic models didn't really hold up in terms of explaining why firms would be environmentally responsible. So I was curious about limitations of economic models. That gave me more of a critical lens. That critical lens also applies partly because I am Canadian. Canadians tend to be a little bit more willing to embrace diversity, [and I am also of] Indian origin, although I'm completely Canadian. My parents are Indian, so there's this aspect of always feeling like you're a bit on the outside. I think that this critical orientation is part of interdisciplinarity. One always feels that their discipline can't always explain everything. The other piece that's been a big influence is that, when you're looking at environmental issues, they're often rooted in science and they cross disciplines. So I was looking at innovation within firms; it would be very much a firm-related concept, whereas environmental issues are rooted in the natural sciences. Looking at organizational responses to [environmental issues] means that I have to understand the science of it as well as the organizational response. Then also that leads to theories that are sometimes rooted in the sciences, like complexity or the systems view.

Like Walsh and Bansal, Maurizio Zollo addresses questions related to the foundational purpose of business through much of his research. Zollo comments on the core reasons for his integrative or bridging work in GOLDEN and in past projects, simultaneously previewing the sensemaking role of intellectual shamans that is addressed in the next chapter:

> It's not just a question of interdisciplinarity; it's really a question of aligning, integrating, converging – facilitating the conversations and the knowledge development process, because we've not been doing

this very well. We've been suffering a lot across all social sciences and natural sciences from increasing levels of specialization without the bridging, without the links. We're building these huge towers of knowledge without any link between the various towers.

It's actually quite scary, quite problematic, because, first of all, you're missing a lot of huge potential for discovery. More importantly, you actually end up making wrong decisions – also, potentially, wrong conclusions – because you only see the trees and don't see the forest. Or you don't see the interconnections between different disciplines, different approaches. Generally speaking, I think it's really important that we start doing this interdisciplinary research. Everybody talks about it, but actually doing it is a lot more difficult.

Zollo is realistic, however, about some of the problems associated with doing inter-, trans-, or multidisciplinary research that the GOLDEN project demands in a world of specialization, and, in particular, specialized outlets for that research. He continues:

Think about publishing. [...] Generally speaking, reviewers in strategy have no clue about how to evaluate a paper on strategic decision-making using fMRI scanning – right? So it's not easy [to publish that work], and it's nobody's fault. It's just that there is only very limited experience or academic endeavors in really doing the multidisciplinary and interdisciplinary work – not just doing the work, but in going through the processes of publication and dissemination.

A similar agenda has shaped much of the work of Josep Lozano, of ESADE Business School, in ethical leadership development and business in society. He emphasizes the interdisciplinarity of two of the major initiatives that he has helped to found and shape:

At this time I was strongly involved in [corporate social responsibility] development. I founded an institute at ESADE called the Institute for Individuals, Corporations, and Society. The idea was to stress the importance of linking the personal and the social dimensions of business and management. We were involved basically in practice, research, teaching, and consulting activities. One of [the activities] is to work with companies, helping them to introduce CSR in the management practices. The most important change was in research. We even created an observatory on social and responsible investment in Spain. We translated into Spanish the key CSR documents for SMEs [small and medium-sized enterprises]. We published studies on business and human rights, on accountability and innovation related to CSR. We created, let's say, really important work on introducing CSR issues in public policies – not centered just in big companies, but also we worked on the issue of the public policies related to CSR, because I think that there are political dimensions related to CSR. We collaborated with the Spanish parliament and the Catalan government in this sense.

Bridging across traditional sector boundaries in the Institute for Individuals, Corporations, and Society led Lozano to found another bridging initiative focused explicitly on social innovation, which quite deliberately spans across issues, functions, and types of enterprise. He recalls:

When I moved to co-create this new institute with a broader approach, it was my opinion that it fitted with ESADE's new strategy and priorities. We called it the Institute for Social Innovation. The idea, social innovation, here [in the institute] is not understood as a specific and well-defined term. It's understood as an umbrella that covers any initiatives that really help to create social innovation in any kind of organization.

In this institute there are four basic lines of activity. The first one is CSR. This institute concludes the experience coming from the previous Institute for Individuals, Corporations, and Society, because we understand CSR as a way to innovate. [...] Innovation is not just related to technology and business processes. Innovation is also related to values. Innovation is also related to understanding – understanding of the professional life.

The second focus is that this institute receives all the experience we have at ESADE related to working with and teaching to NGOs, because. . .it is important to be a management school. So, at the center of the business school, the main programs are the MBA, undergraduate program, and an executive program, but we also have an Institute of Public Management. . .and important programs for NGOs. So we have teaching activities with the three sectors. [. . .] The third focus is the consequence: to produce just the relationship between business and NGOs, and all these kinds of situations and practices that it creates.

The fourth focus is social entrepreneurship. We have created a specific project for sharing capacities as an ecosystem that put together MBA students, consultants that work with these social enterprises for free, professors, and social entrepreneurs. Again, our idea is to create something that we call an ecosystem for social innovation. We don't want just to work with social innovators individually considered, but we want to create a real network in order to promote social entrepreneurship. So that's why, for us, the Institute for Social Innovation includes CSR, NGOs, companies, their relationships, and social entrepreneurship.

Underlying these multi-sector and multi-level initiatives is a core rationale that drives Lozano in his work:

[One point] that motivates me is that our society, or societies, are organizational societies. The solution of their challenges is through organizations. So we need to change or create new organizations, but we need to work from an organizational point of view. [. . .] Our society will change or perish as a result of organizational activity.

In his role as quasi-academic and mostly consultant, Phil Mirvis is perhaps best known for his work in bridging theory, research, and practice. One of his better-known projects, detailed in his book *To the*

Desert and Back, chronicles his work with Unilever, the huge Dutch consumer goods company. While spending a year at the London Business School, having been brought in by Sumantra Ghoshal (renowned strategy scholar and author of a seminal paper entitled 'Bad management theories are destroying good management practices,' published posthumously), Mirvis received a call from Unilever. He recalls:

> Mid-year I got a call from this guy, Tex Gunning. He said, 'I wanted to reach Scott Peck, but he's not available, and he says you're over in London, I should talk to you.' So this crazy Dutchman...came over and said, 'I have some ideas. I'm in business, I'm running the Dutch side of Unilever Foods, and I would like to create a community here.' I said, 'My God, you've got some interesting things here, but I don't know what the hell you're talking about. There's community, spirituality, organization transformation, etc.' So, after we had a good, sharp set of exchanges, I said, 'Well, let's take a look.'
>
> We designed a set of community building retreats, going to the Ardennes for the first one. It was just incredible. One of the tensions here was between the old guard and the Young Turks who wanted to boot them out. At the retreat, this older guy gets up, weeping because his father had been a collaborator with the Nazis and he had been ostracized as a result. That opened a deep conversation about whether we could operate as a community in the midst of dramatic transformational change. We went later to Scotland, then to Jordan and Israel, and that became the story of the desert book. But it was also for me a chance to understand large-scale change not simply as a set of strategies and tactics but as a series of performances and soulful experiences.

When Gunning moved to Asia, Mirvis started collaborating with Karen Ayas, whom he had met at the Society for Organizational Learning, and who is a Dutch professor who speaks six languages. The two created another set of learning journeys, which became a whole stream [of work] of using journeys for learning, community services, and consciousness-raising, which I really didn't fully grasp until some anonymous reviewer (of a manuscript) came back and said 'You've got something else going on other than service learning.'[4n]

Ed Freeman also bridges between research and management practice in his thinking about stakeholder theory. In fact, Freeman is explicit about the practice–theory link and why this type of bridging is important:

> Stakeholder theory is not informed by practice; it starts with practice. It has to start there. Seeing the distinction, theory, informed by practice, is a way of framing it which, I would say, is mistaken. [John] Dewey told us all intellectual life, all life, starts with our experience. Where intellectuals make the mistake is that they try to start with the abstract. It's not that you don't make abstractions from experience, it's just that it all has to somehow get grounded. That's where management theory's gone off the tracks.

In undertaking their bridging of worlds and walking between realms, intellectual shamans are oriented toward more holistic perspectives than siloed disciplines permit. In the next section, we look at the ways in which this holistic perspective emerges, and think about some of its implications.

SEEING HOLISTICALLY FOR COHERENCE AND GENERATIVITY

Gaining a holistic perspective seems to be one of the particular gifts of intellectual shamans, especially given the relationships between healing, holism, and holy (the sacred) discussed earlier. Developing theoretical or practice-based research, teaching, and consulting that focuses on achieving system coherence could be said to constitute the core healing practice of intellectual shamans. Part of what intellectual shamans try to do is to understand the system as it is to develop systems understanding.[118] Holistic or systems thinking is naturally boundary-spanning, because of the need for making connections across different realms. Real-world problems, often 'wicked problems,'[119,120] do not come neatly packed in disciplinary boundaries. Rather, such problems demand more comprehensive, expansive, and integrative approaches, more holistic or systemic in nature.

Such integration necessarily involves 'seeing,' making the shaman a seer. Shamans see across and into boundaries that others may find more rigid or impenetrable, and, as Chapters 2 and 3 discussed, are willing to take the risks associated with seeing things differently from others. 'Seeing' often takes place in the imaginal realm, a realm of reality different from the traditionally accepted 'normal reality,' related to more to the mythopoetic level that Laughlin and Throop[112] describe.

The varied realities that intellectual shamans span offer different types of insights, explanations, and action strategies from those that discipline-specific ideas would. Just as myth can generate action,[112] so too do the mythologies associated with theories in different spheres or disciplines, highlighting what is considered to be best practice in management, leadership, teaching, and research. As with traditional myths, the (mythological) constructions of intellectual shamans 'provide an imaginative explanation of the unseen vectors of causation and energy that run between all objects and events in the universe.'[112] In crossing boundaries, intellectual shamans use their ideas to perform another of the functions associated with the mythologies that shamans in traditional societies attempt to heal: that of making the hidden visible.[112]

Mike Money notes that traditional shamans deal with 'cognitive [spiritual] variables including beliefs, values, imagery, social and individual definition of events and circumstances, and the fundamental attribution of meaning to situations and circumstances, profoundly affect[ing] the functioning of this complex system.'[84] Here Money's specific attribution is to a field called psychoneuroimmunology, which is the study of how the mind affects health and disease resistance. The analogy to sick social systems or intellectual/research traditions is also apropos of intellectual shamanism. Even so, Money argues that it is the immune system (of the patient) that shamans attempt to influence, which raises a question about what the social or theory-driven equivalent of the immune system is.

Could it be in our Western culture that the immune system equivalent is our fragmented thinking – and that the intellectual shamans' tendencies toward more holistic approaches and ways of thinking represent efforts to bring order and coherence to what is otherwise a disordered system? Here I adduce that when an immune system is disordered it lacks coherence, and when our understanding of systems is fragmented we cannot think clearly about reinvigorating the system holistically. Thus, when theories, practices (including research, teaching, and management practices), or perspectives are disordered or out of line with what is effective or lack holism, there is a lack of coherence that produces dis-order – the opposite of order or coherence – in that system. If this observation makes sense, then it is the attempt to bring order and coherence to thinking, practice, teaching, and theory that represents the intellectual shaman's witting (or unwitting) attempt to heal. Accomplishing that task often necessitates moving from disciplinary, fragmented, or atomistic thinking about the issues involved to a more holistic framing.

Connections across different realms provide a source of power to the traditional and the intellectual shaman alike because of their bridging function, allowing information to be carried across traditional boundaries. They also allow people from different arenas to connect in new ways over ideas informed by multiple rather than single disciplines and perspectives. This type of work is inherently integrative and inevitably more holistic, rather than atomistic or fragmented. Shamans, then, find ways of making the myth or system with which they are dealing more whole, more coherent in a sense, and more integrated – and consequently more healthy, more holy (and more whole?).[121]

Traditional shamans 'go into trance to contact spirits thought to affect living people.'[95] The trance state, while characteristic of traditional shamans, does not necessarily apply to intellectual shamans, at least not as a deliberate act, though they do search out knowledge, wisdom, and information – seeing – across disciplinary, sector, research, and theoretical boundaries in their quest. Perhaps they do, however, enter the state that Mihaly Csikszentmihaly[122] calls 'flow,' in doing their work. Flow, a form of trance, is a state in which the individual is completely involved or absorbed in the task at hand, when time seems to slow or simply disappear, and that provides a sustaining source of energy – a state that certainly appears to characterize many of the activities of the intellectual shamans.

Flow is found in all manner of activities, including running and other sports (think of the runner's 'high'), musical and artistic endeavors of all sorts, teams that are functioning well, and engaging and involving work, as examples. As Csikszentmihaly also points out, flow is an intense state that highly creative people enter when they are undertaking their work and are deeply immersed in it.[41] Being in flow, because it is energizing and life-enhancing, allows people to sustain their work and themselves over long periods. It also may well explain why many intellectual shamans seem to continue their work long past what is traditionally considered normal retirement age.

Ian Mitroff is an example of someone working well beyond normal retirement on holistically oriented issues. Mitroff started off studying engineering, but was soon attracted to the philosophy of science as a broader discipline. He remembers:

> I studied philosophy of science, psychology, sociology of science. People often select fields, like physical scientists – fields they are often running away from emotions. Social scientists are really trying to solve their emotional/social problems, only it's deflected and they really don't solve them. So it's hidden. Early on when I was studying philosophy of science, which was highly unusual, we read a lot of Freud and Jung. [...] I was attracted to not just psychology but psychoanalysis, really deep stuff, because I don't believe any of the surface stuff really explains much of what goes in human behavior.

That's why to me too much of organizational behavior and strategy research is just superficial. It doesn't really get to the motivations that drive people in organizations. I learned early on that it's denial that really keeps people from doing crisis management, because crisis scares the living shit out of people. It raises too much anxiety.

Unless you've been through some concerted course of study or therapy, you will not have the emotional fortitude, not only when you study crises but, I think, everything. You'll just remain at the surface. So I have to view a lot of academia, I'd say the majority, as just a gigantic defense mechanism. So, if you want to talk about changing the academy and how people are educated, yeah, they need to be given philosophy and really study psychoanalysis, and stuff like that. But they really need to go through, however they get it, their own therapy, or they'll never get through their own demons and really be able to take the enormous anxiety that comes with studying things that are new and uncertain.

Mitroff continues in his reflections on the broad set of influences that shaped his thinking and interdisciplinary research – and his understanding of the holistic nature of the problems that scholars face:

I studied for my PhD in engineering. The College of Engineering never really understood why I wanted to do it, because I loved engineering, but I couldn't stand engineers. They're too narrow, too limited, and all the rest of that. I really wanted a deeper education. It was really liberating, but I'm glad I had both the math, physics. Can't be bamboozled by all that crap. But philosophy [of science, which Mitroff ended up studying] really teaches you how to think about thinking. It's foundational. Unfortunately, most people, whatever field they're in, do not really truly have the background to really study what they purport to study. You can't just have the tools and the silos and all that kind of stuff. The phenomena that we are now faced with cut across every known field, profession – everything. So the philosophy of science I studied was highly interdisciplinary, way, way in advance of its time, highly systemic.

For me, doing academia was a chance to get back out and see if you can help in some of these great problems that humanity faces. They're not disciplinary problems; they're interdisciplinary.

Along analogous lines, Concordia's Paul Shrivastava reflects on his own history of integrative – or bridging – work, and his struggle to find his way in an academia focused on subspecialties:

When I was at NYU, which was my first job, I was trying to do this 'publish or perish' thing. For about three years much of my publication was mining my doctoral dissertation and conventional stuff about technology, strategy, and how to make it more socially useful. Then this big Bhopal disaster occurred. It was in 1984. I graduated in 1981, so two and a half years, three years, into my first job. Of course, Bhopal was the place where I had grown up and also got my engineering degree. I had a lot of contacts there, so I went to study the impacts of technology when things go wrong.

That was a big watershed for me in terms of my own intellectual development. I got to see a side of technology that I had until then taken for granted, that technology's only good, and it provided all these benefits of infrastructures and hospitals, etc., etc. But there I got to see what happens when something goes wrong. Also, it was a lesson in understanding organizations...

That led to a very prolific period in my writing: several books and papers on industrial crisis management, and launching a journal on that topic. I did that for a good, probably, ten years – eight, nine years, at least – and the more I got convinced that the industrial and technological crises were a serious issue, the more resistance I found from corporations. They would say, 'Look, this is [a] one in a billion chance kind of event. That's not something that is going to happen to us; don't bother us with this.'

It was not just the Bhopal crisis that shaped Shrivastava's bridging across disciplines. He gained insight into the sustainability crisis, which was just beginning to emerge into the public spotlight during the 1990s. He remembers the transition this way:

> The other thing that was happening around the same time, the mid-'90s, was [that] this whole area of environmental crisis and the debate on sustainability was becoming quite salient. So, instead of resisting and pushing an angle that managers are not willing to accept, I reframed my question in terms of sustainability. What is it going to take for these organizations to become ecologically and socially sustainable? That has been my quest since the mid-'90s. [. . .]
>
> In trying to understand technology in the context of society, one thing that became absolutely clear to me was that this sort of. . .holistic understanding could not occur within disciplinary silos. There were just too many things outside that we, within our own silo, would think of as irrelevant that were actually quite centrally involved in the occurrence of these kinds of events and these crises. By the end of the decade of the '90s I was convinced that this disciplin[e-based] inquiry was actually harmful. It was part of a career game that I had unwittingly been playing myself, along with a lot of my colleagues, and I needed to get out of it. I was so disenchanted with academics that I took a leave of absence for three years, which turned out to be four years, and went and started a company. I wanted to put into practice some of the ideas that I'd been talking about, and I created an online education company called eSocrates.

The formation of eSocrates, bridging the worlds of academia and practice, provided not only an enormous learning opportunity for Shrivastava but also an ongoing orientation toward a more holistic perspective on the role of management, leadership, and social innovation. Shrivastava continues:

> For about six years I ran [eSocrates] before we sold it. The idea was very simple. If you added up all the classroom seats in the world, in every university and college, that total was only 2 percent of the

population that needed education, so there was no way that people sitting in a classroom was going to be the final solution for education. So what this company was doing, eSocrates, was trying to establish a way of delivering online education to the masses.

We were partially successful in what we originally intended, but, as happens in the case of many startup ventures, it changed form, it changed goals, missions, the funding, etc. After six years I'd had enough of it. I learned a lot and learned two important lessons with regard to transdisciplinarity. The first thing was that creating business is not a technological or a financial or an organizational or a leadership challenge. It is a challenge of passion. With all these guys – I was in an incubator with nineteen other startup companies in Allentown [Pennsylvania], and every single one of them was running because of the passion of the entrepreneur. The entrepreneur had a vision and sort of seen the light and was pushing for it morning, evening, and night, eating, drinking, and breathing the stuff.

Toward the more holistic understanding needed to do the systems-oriented work of intellectual shamans, Shrivastava, discussing the transformative nature of his entrepreneurial experience for his academic work, adds:

The other thing I learned was that the conviction that I had about the irrelevance of discipline became absolutely transparent to me. Nothing I did in the company was in a disciplinary mode, or even in a functional mode. Since we were a relatively small company (we never had more than sixty, seventy employees at our highest), we did not operate in the disciplinary mode. So, I went back to Bucknell [University], and started doing different kinds of thinking and trying to build this platform of transdisciplinary science and reading about the latest philosophical developments. I realized that there was a lot of stuff that had gone on in the past twenty years with regard to developing a philosophy and epistemology and ontology of transdisciplinarity. Since then I've been trying to architect projects that are explicitly transdisciplinary in nature, encouraging my doctoral students to think in terms of transdisciplinary solutions.

The University of Vermont's Stuart Hart, also operating in the social innovation and sustainability spaces, discusses his own emerging vision of how more holistic and better-integrated models of sustainability in management education can provide a better path forward than initiatives that 'hang off the side' of existing institutions:

> I have really been focused on trying to have more global impact over the past several years doing a lot of work in China, in India, Latin America and Africa. There is a new center at Tsinghua University called the Tsinghua Center for Green Leap Research, of which I am the co-chair with the vice president of Tsinghua.
>
> We will develop and launch a new business institute in India focused completely on disruptive innovation for the base of the pyramid – the 'green leap' kind of stuff. It is called, right now, the Indian Institute for Sustainable Enterprise. So, I am the founding, managing director. It will be based physically in Bangalore but the objective is to start a new global model. I've done three 'hang off the side things' in business schools, Michigan, UNC, and Cornell, and I feel proud of those. But here it is twenty years later, and they really had, if I'm honest with myself, no real impact on the core of the business school itself. They hang off the side; they attract good students, interesting students. They benefit the business school because about half of the students that apply to the Johnson School [at Cornell] now mention sustainable enterprise as either the main reason or one of the main reasons that they apply. [...] But they haven't had any impact, any fundamental impact on the core of the business school itself.
>
> So the idea behind this new institute is to start something that from its very beginning, with its core DNA, is completely 100 percent focused on the green leap, incubating tomorrow's clean tech lifeboat: businesses that could get us to a more sustainable future,

and the skills it is going to take in order to do. I think of it as creating corporate lifeboats, entrepreneurial lifeboats. Then, when the time comes, you need to get out giant billows – but, unless you've got models, we're sunk. So, you go back to the Paul Gilding argument [about the potential for a 'great disruption'],[123] and I think he's right: that over the next decade the [environmental and sustainability] shit's going to hit the fan.

The holistic perspective on the troubled state of the world that Hart – and the other intellectual shamans – take means that they see things from a higher level of analysis or abstraction, or 'bigger picture' perspective, than more discipline-based scholars. As seers and truth-tellers, intellectual shamans often see and verbalize what others do not, will not, or cannot see – and that does not always make them popular. Hart makes this point as he continues:

> If you are a dot-connector by nature, it's hard to not see it. But, most people don't see it, or willfully don't want to see it. So, that's really my focus now: . . .how do we get to beyond greening? We can't be just doing incremental, continuous improvement projects on what already exists. We need to leapfrog disruptive next-generation models that take us to regenerative, clean technology, and start with the underserved. If we don't lift the base of the pyramid, it's game over. But we've got to do it in a way that makes sense. [Some people are] convinced that can't happen just through the growth model. [. . .] But this is all we['ve] got to work with right now. So I'm hell-bent on figuring out how you tap into the entrepreneurial process, intrapreneurship and entrepreneurship, to drive these next-generation businesses forward. I view that as the leverage point.

Raj Sisodia of Babson College discusses the start of the Conscious Capitalism Institute and associated movement. He fortu-itously met Whole Foods CEO John Mackey just as his book *Firms of Endearment* was about to be released, when Mackey had somehow obtained a pre-publication version of the manuscript. He recalls the conversation:

> [Mackey] said, 'This book is exactly my philosophy of business. What can I do to help?' So, in that connection, I ended up meeting him. He had been talking about conscious capitalism as a phrase to describe what we had been writing about. He had a fledgling non-profit called FLOW that he had been funding for a few years. So we started to meet, and then we started to enlarge the group, . . .and that ultimately became the non-profit Conscious Capitalism Inc.

Sisodia's vision, shaped into ideas of conscious capitalism, emerged from what he characterizes as idealism as a child. He discusses his holistic perspective on the ways that companies can succeed through conscious capitalism:

> As a child I was always called too idealistic. My father would say, 'You're not practical.' It was very affirming in the long run to be able to learn that these ways of being actually result in success in the long term – that it's not that 'nice guys finish last,' and all of those messages that are honed into us; that the good companies do win in the long term. They win in a much richer way, as defined by all the kinds of good value that they create for everybody. It was a very affirming message to me to say that this is something that actually works. It's not just idealism – the idea of businesses built on love and care – that they can actually be stronger businesses. They can actually succeed and compete better *because* they're built on love and care.

Moving beyond thinking about companies that care for their stakeholders, Sisodia's perspective on conscious capitalism is considerably more encompassing, including individual consciousness as well as the ways in which societies themselves function. As he has developed his thinking about conscious capitalism, his vision has correspondingly grown more holistic:

I think, as we bring consciousness into business and capitalism, we're going to figure out ways to create value for all of us – 7 billion of us now – in ways that do not erode the planet and don't make it unsustainable. Because we've had these different schools of thought around the world and different ways of living and approaching things, I think it's coming now to a higher-level hybrid of the best of what we as humanity know. So, blending the best of Eastern wisdom, effectiveness, and that understanding with the Western efficiency, and systems, and so on allows this [initiative] now to be kind of a universal operating system that works. [...] It seems to appeal across cultural and even across sort of income levels: poor countries versus rich countries, and so forth.

Taking an integrative – arguably, a shamanic – perspective on how a new vision of conscious capitalism can shape the world, Sisodia continues, implicitly recognizing the paradoxes inherent in systemic thinking and the need for a both/and versus either/or logic:

There's a higher level integration here. It's not one versus the other. It's really a combination of everything; north, south, east, west. Not to say that we have understood it to that degree, or that we currently think of it as sort of the final thing. It's something that will evolve, and our understanding will deepen. We use a certain language to describe it right now. But part of the journey that's exciting and interesting is to bring in people from different traditions and backgrounds.

So, in India, for example, we have a group called the Chittasanga or the Consciousness Collaborative, which is about thirty, thirty-five people, about twenty different organizations. Most of them are management development or consulting-type practitioners. These are all people who have been doing some kind of consciousness and business interface type work, some for two or three years, some for twenty years. They all come with a strong business background. Most of them have degrees from some of the leading business schools. Essentially, they've created a collaborative. Even though they have separate companies, they come together three or four times a year and they share ideas and perspectives, and they learn from each other and they grow. Now we've injected this conscious capitalism idea within that group, and so for them this has kind of become a rallying point, sort of the common theme, that all of them are ultimately in that same domain. They have a lot to offer. They have existing frameworks and ways of thinking about things, and they're highly sophisticated and highly evolved in some of those dimensions.

What we're doing with them Chittasanga is, really, co-creating. We're saying, 'OK, here's the skeleton that we've put together so far based on what we understand.' They're helping fill in a lot of that with some richness of their own understanding. I think there'll be some interesting learning that will happen out of [South] Korea, and in Brazil there's a group of people whoe are starting to think about this [approach]. So everywhere we're finding this kind of interest. We're not saying: 'Here's the formula. This is just a franchise.' We're just saying that only as a general philosophy. Let's first of all adapt it to the specific environment, but also enrich it with some wisdom from that environment. That collective – the knowledge-sharing and -deepening of understanding – really flows in all those directions. So that's our vision for how this could and should evolve.

Derick De Jongh, of the Centre for Responsible Leadership at the University of Pretoria, South Africa, similarly talks about the need for both 'pushing' and 'pulling' future and present leaders along, providing insight into some of the system forces that hinder change:

Consider the complexity of the economic situation that the US is in at the moment. It's very hard for any senior business leader to actually criticize the system though the system is very fragile. [. . .] It's very difficult at the moment to get current leaders to challenge the very system that feeds them, so you need that pulling force. The pulling force is those out there who 'get' it, to take their comrades and their peers to say, 'Listen; there is an alternative out here.' You need a few of them. Of course, the pulling part is legislation, like Sarbanes–Oxley [the Public Company Accounting Reform and Investor Protection Act of 2002, which set new standards for US companies' boards of directors] and new sets of codes of standards, etc. But that pushes the mindset issue.

Discussing climate change as an issue in which change is needed but difficult to achieve, De Jongh continues:

[For] the current leaders of the world, politicians, what are the chances that we'll come up with a treaty or a deal that will really favor the planet from an emission point of view and from a sustainable future point of view? [. . .] We're not convinced that it will happen. It's a lot of political rhetoric and then hogwash. [. . .] The pushing part of this is the issue around a new generation. It's where we have the opportunity to develop leaders of the future who will end up in businesses that will be able to actually argue for a different regime to create ways within the business that show the benefit of being responsible, accountable, and so on. So, it's an emerging new generation, almost. So that's, I guess, where the 'push and pull' principle comes in.

De Jongh elaborates how this cadre of new leaders can be developed, not just in South Africa, where they are needed, but in other emerging nations of the world as well:

So, the Centre for Responsible Leadership's goal is basically to develop the next generation of responsible leaders. [. . .] It's a very, very complex point. It's a point of deep tension that exists. For political and business leaders to deal with, this is not easy. Where the Centre comes in is to try and understand that tension and build a body of knowledge that supports new understanding of what kind of leadership it takes to lead organizations into the future, with the ability of not only meeting their shareholders demands but also much wider society at large, and the national requirements that are placed on business to survive.

David Cooperrider, the final example in this section, discusses the holistic and future-looking elements of his initiative Business as an Agent of World Benefit, which is built on his appreciative inquiry framework, and the developmental nature of some of this work:

There are no limits to human cooperation. There was a whole series of work that unfolded over a period of time that then led to my current interests around the specific role that [the business] system plays. So many of the stories that we lifted up showed that perhaps business could emerge as one of the most powerful forces on the planet. I decided to do a next stage of that study, and that next stage was called the study of business as an agent of world benefit: business as a force for peace in high-conflict zones; business as the force for eradicating extreme poverty; business as a force for eco-innovation. Where is it happening, what does it look like, what are the enablers, what are the ecosystems that help unleash the strengths of business and the service of our global agenda?

With the insight that business resources, strengths, and clout could potentially be harnessed for the greater good, Cooperrider struggled to develop a theory of change and business practice that would encompass these emerging ideas. As he notes below, however, the process is one of co-creation with those in practice, rather than that an academic theorist sitting in an 'ivory tower' office developing a theory unlinked to practice:

That was a challenge for me: to articulate how [business could be an agent for world benefit]. I think we're starting to emerge a full-blown theory of this kind of change. It's exciting, because it's not saying that the other approaches are wrong, but they're very limited. So this [initiative] is leading to whole new applications of appreciative inquiry.

For example, one of the applications of appreciative inquiry is to say it's not just us as theorists that should be doing the theorizing, that we should be in a participatory theory-building sense, be lifting up new theory with the groups that we're working with, so that they are building theory alongside of us, or vice versa. There's a lot of great work happening, participatory action research, so [this initiative is] in that tradition. But it's taking it a step further and asking the people of the system to not just be using new behavioral sciences to improve their system but to help build theory together. I call it corporate theory, 'corporate' meaning the whole body corporate, or cooperative theory-building.

Appreciative inquiry, in Cooperrider's view, provides a framework, an approach to change, and a methodology that allows this co-creation process to build in a holistic fashion, using what he characterizes as a strengths-based approach to heal the particular cultural myth that surrounds the nature and purpose of the modern corporation:

> One of the ways we do that [corporate theory-building] now is in very large group configurations of the whole system of strengths. I call it the appreciative inquiry summit method, where we'll bring anywhere between 500 to 1,000, 2,000 (we've done 8,000), people together going through this kind of grounded theory-building process, where we're lifting up the DNA of what gives life to that living system and using that to dream and design and imagine propositions and prototypes for the future. It's really a form of cooperative theory-building, collaborative theory-building. It's based on this whole root metaphor that we live in this universe of strengths, so why not bring that whole universe together? So, if you're working with a trucking company, why not have the truck driver and the dock worker and the customer and the supply chain partner sitting around the same table with the CEO, planning and designing and theorizing about the possibilities for the future?

Bringing the entire system into the room in this manner,[118] as Cooperrider explains, provides a rationale for a wholly different sense of possibilities for the future:

> That's a next step in this whole idea of participatory action research, where we're really operating from the assumptions of, not only is

the glass half full, but that we live in this universe of strengths. To do good theory-building about what's possible, we need to create conditions where we do it with that whole universe of strengths in the room.

INTEGRATION: SEEKING AND PROTECTING TRUTH

In exploring the healing function of shamans, we can see that articulating the truth as they perceive it is central to that function. Thinking about crossing multiple realms of mythologies associated with different theories, disciplines, and practices, intellectual shamans use their own holistic understanding of various myths to bring the world close to truth. As Laughlin and Throop point out, 'Myth operates as a truer of cognitive operations... '[T]ruing refers specifically to the inherent epistemic faculty of the brain to produce a cognized world in a dynamic and veridical way in conformation to reality.'[112] These authors further point out that 'truing' happens in two primary ways – 'through intuition and through action in the world.'[112]

Speaking about brain physiology, Laughlin and Throop comment: 'One of the most common reactions people have to the intuition of truth about reality is to feel as if they knew it already. In a very real sense they do know the truth before they hear it.'[112] Just as, for traditional peoples, seeing the world in accord with their mythologies is consonant with how the world actually is until intellectual shamans begin to bring together information from different realms to reshape thinking and practice, what is embedded in older ideas and practices is frequently just how the world seems to be. Yet the 'Aha!' moment – in effect, the intuition that so often comes when an insight is generated because new ideas or information sources collide, making the new idea seem completely obvious in retrospect – is exactly the 'magic' that intellectual shamans work in their connecting capacity.

Taking these ideas one step further, Edwin Loeb argues that what he terms 'inspirational shamanism' (as opposed to a non-inspirational type of shamanism) has two important cultural traits: exorcism and prophesying.[124] In exorcism, the shaman (or priest) drives a bad spirit out of the person who is ill; in intellectual shamanism, we can think of a similar action taking place as shamans attempt to drive out bad ideas, practices, or theories. The shaman as 'seer' is tasked with going to other realms beyond the day-to-day or normal realm, seeking and seeing new information, new 'truths,' and bringing that information back to whatever his or her normal realm or discipline is in order to get outdated or no longer functional 'truths' out of the way. Traditional shamans claim to get this information from spirits, who then become guides in helping the shaman use the information gathered. Though Loeb makes a distinction between the true shaman, through whom the spirits speak, and the seer, with or to whom the spirits speak, for intellectual shamans it seems that the speaking through and speaking to activities are combined into one individual.

Intellectual shamans often do perform this 'seeing' role in their boundary-spanning or connecting roles as part of their desire to 're-vision' the world, their discipline, research, and practice in the interest of making it better. Indeed, seeing what they perceive to be a better way, a better version of truth, is a major source of new insights and ideas. As we have seen above, intellectual shamans accomplish this task of seeing, and, in a sense, protecting truth, by drawing from sources in other realms than may be traditionally accepted within their domain of inquiry – such as from practice (Schein's inspiration from the T-groups and his experiences in companies, particularly Digital Equipment Corporation), from other disciplines (e.g., Adler's inspiration from her art for her research), from theories beyond their own discipline (Hoffman and Hart's drawing from ecology and sustainability science as well as management theories), or from a variety of teaching practices different from accepted pedagogies (Freeman's theater course; Epstein's action-based social entrepreneurship courses that combine engineering and business disciplines).

Henry Mintzberg, famous for his views on strategy, organizing, and reforming management education, has turned to more holistic endeavors in the later stages of his career that seek and convey the truth as he sees it. Mintzberg's thinking is shaped by a concern about the state of the world and its societies, as he explains:

Concern. I think things are falling apart and I don't hear any solutions. I hear lots of complaining [but] I don't hear anybody saying 'How do we get around this?' But that's sort of bass ackwards [sic] in a way, because right from the beginning, that was my kind of focus. ... We've been going out of balance on the side of markets, or the private sector.

Mintzberg discusses some of his hopes for a holistic perspective on the state of society:

Right now, I'm finishing a monograph called 'Managing in health care,' and turning to something much bigger, a pamphlet called, 'Rebalancing society: a radical renewal beyond left, right and center.' The 'Rebalancing society' is essentially bumping that [thinking] up to the societal level with pretty harsh criticism of economics, which I claim is sitting in the clouds. Economists don't generally understand how organizations work at all. Otherwise, we wouldn't be inundated with this shareholder value nonsense. Yet, they have an enormous influence in what's going on, and it's killing us. I don't think the current problem is an economic problem at its heart, and I don't think economists are going to solve it. . .because they don't understand organizations. The problem is at the organizational level. The trashing of American enterprise is the real problem, to my mind. As an example, I'd say any chief executive who accepts to be paid 400 times as much as workers in that company is not a leader. So the Fortune 500 companies have virtually no leaders.

Tima Bansal also has an agenda to seek and protect the truth, particularly around issues of sustainability:

The Network of Business Sustainability is part of [changing mindsets], and the social movement idea is that maybe we can all work together. That's the reason I invite people to give talks, some in the mainstream world, because if you can get them to understand these issues and they have the influence then they can influence them. It's by inviting people into our own constellation as a friendly face, as opposed to an angry or whatever, an outsider. I think we have to be insiders.

In a video on YouTube, Bansal describes the holistic, healing, and truth-telling philosophy behind the Network for Business Sustainability:

> Business sustainability is often defined as the triple bottom line, and that being environmental, social, and financial performance. But I think we need to go beyond that, though. We need to think about sustainability as the long-term future of the firm, and that means that they have to think not just about making money in the short term but how are they going to make money over the long term. The Network for Business Sustainability is a collaborative between business, academics, nonprofits, and governments to try to achieve sustainable solutions. The Network for Business Sustainability is really intended to break down the silos that have been erected. So it is allowing people to the space to collaborate. I think that people in organizations everywhere care about the world. I think that what's different now than before is that they have a voice that they didn't have before. They feel that they can speak out, and that business is moving in the ways that they want to move. The Network involves over 300 researchers and we collaborate, and we reach...thousands of practitioners. It's a knock-on effect, so it's not just those 1,000 people. It's those 1,000 people talking to another 1,000 people who talk to another 1,000 people. The whole idea is to put the language of research into the language of practice so that we can inform practice. It's about time that we have the barriers that have built up across industries, functions, across sectors, broken down, and using research to help facilitate the medium across that.[5n]

SYNTHESIS: WHEN INTELLECTUAL SHAMANS MAKE CONNECTIONS

Essentially, as I have argued throughout this chapter, intellectual shamans make connections in new ways. Bob Quinn of the University of

Michigan gives a striking example of the power of such connections in the concluding comments for this chapter. Describing some of his recent research, Quinn's comments highlight not only the paradoxical nature of what shamans do but also the need for 'both/and' thinking:

> This guy called me from the institute that studies public education. He said, 'We're all tied up in value-added teachers. We've been doing interviews, intensive interviews, with value-added people for three years, and we are now convinced that there are four organizing themes,' he said. 'It's the competing values model. It's the four corners.' So he got pretty persuasive that that's what it was.
>
> The interesting thing is that these teachers cross the boundaries. They cross the quadrants. I knew immediately what he was talking about, because, whenever you deal with people in excellence, they become paradoxical. When Maslow studied self-actualizers, that was one of his first observations, so they're this, and they're this. They're this, and they're this. The same thing about organizations in excellence. They cross the quadrants.
>
> So I started watching their videotapes of these teachers talking about their practice. I started getting very excited, and said, 'Look, I want to interview a group of these people myself, with you guys present, because I want to take this deeper than the questions you're asking them.' So we had two days of interviewing. We had twelve value-added teachers. Five were really good. They had good value-added scores, two out of the last four years. Seven of them were on the third standard deviation every year for four years. So you had good and great. So we conducted these interviews, in sacred space, so that they could share their deepest feelings.

It is here that the story about the value-added teachers complements the analysis of the work of intellectual shamans as described in the past few chapters:

> It was so potent. We had five observer/note-takers, and some of them were getting up, going out in the hall, and crying and coming back

in, because it was so potent. This data is just incredible! These teachers don't have jobs. They have callings. Their purpose is not to transmit information, it's to transform lives. They take some kid who is in an abusive home, comes to school almost in a catatonic state, and they spend months transforming this kid and simultaneously trying to transform the whole class. They have a whole set of characteristics that are interesting. They make discoveries of higher levels of complexity.

So, that study's got seventeen hypotheses. Each one starts with 'It is normal for a teacher to do this, these people do this, then...' So, for example, in terms of charismatic leadership, [these teachers] are enormously high...people. [They exhibit] unbelievable practices as they extend themselves to get into their lives, to know their families...and to know their deepest needs.

But well beyond that are things like when you're a novice, you go to a university, they teach you how to teach, and the books say do this. And all students are the same. You go to work, and you discover that they have differences, they're individually different. Well, these teachers are very aware of that, and they go to great lengths to recognize and teach to those individual differences. But, now just think about this: they say, 'It's deeper than that'; they say, 'When you make this discovery, then you become really effective, then you can't be stopped.' The discovery is that all students are the same. They have the same basic set of needs, and, when you teach to that, you can go to the suburban district and succeed. You can go to the inner city and succeed. You can teach special ed. [sic], gifted, you can teach adults, children, and you'll always succeed.

That's stunning. It's just stunning. It's such a higher level of mastery. Well, every kid wants to succeed, even the ones who don't want to. Every kid wants to be loved, even when they behave like it or they don't, and some related things like that, because they see the human being.

They're *fanatic* about full engagement, and they talk about their classes. The first level of full engagement is just sort of brewing it, teaching where the kid is. The second level is enriched conversation. This is where they cross the tipping point that transforms, and every kid is involved. Time stops in a kind of a collective flow notion, and they describe this in such rich language stories. It's very clear to them.

Then the next level of complexity is: I have multiple conversations going on in the classroom simultaneous, so I'm at the edge of chaos, and I'm the quarterback. I'm on the field, see, and the play is running. But the quarterback has to decide what to do, so he has to see the whole field, and over here there's this happening, and over there there's this happening. You're listening, and see there's a little noise a little higher, just a bit higher, so you know you've just got to go over there. Then you go over there and you nudge it, but you leave the other two alone, because it was just right. Then you come over here and, when I'm in the middle of this, he says, I pull out my camera, and I just start shooting random pictures. I shoot thirty pictures, and I take them home, then I lay them out on the table, and I say: 'Why is she smiling? Why is he standing like that? What's going on? What can I do to be better?'

Then they say, 'When you discover the facilitator role, teaching becomes easy. It's not work anymore. When you get them into this state, that's when all these outcomes you want happen.' Well, it has all kinds of theoretical implications. So then there's this notion of fanatic, continuous improvement. So he's taking pictures. He's analyzing. What that means is, they're living in a state of continuous productive change. They live in a state of change.

This capacity to stand in the midst of chaos and make sense of it is typical of the intellectual shaman as well as the excellent teacher. Intellectual shamans often are engaged in multiple projects, and typically, because they are looking forward, they are in the state that constitutes the edge of chaos – not quite knowing what will happen next with the practice they are observing or consulting about (witness Ed Schein), with the ideas or theories they are shaping (witness Karl Weick), or with what their research is uncovering. Reflecting the injunction for all shamans to 'dream the world you want into existence,' the teachers that Quinn is describing, like the intellectual shamans themselves, begin to live the very changes that they desire:

> Now, what is it [these great teachers] want their students to do? They want their students to convert into productive learners. So, what are they doing? They're becoming the change they want to see in the world – right? They're operationalizing Gandhi [i.e., as Gandhi said, being the change they want to see in the world]. So, they're not about telling and forcing. They're about building magnets of attraction, and they're attracting these kids to another place. So they say, 'My kids love me; when I walk in, kids surround me, and they will do anything for me,' which sounds manipulative, but it is not, because it is absolutely authentic.
>
> So the kids will take challenges. They'll take extra work. It happens because the teacher has a calling and a purpose. The teacher exercises enormous personal discipline and becomes a transformational leader living in a purpose, with authenticity, empathy and openness. The teacher is creating a positive organization in which everyone can flourish. Highly effective teachers are fully authentic people filled with the love of learning. They are inviting the students to be fully authentic people filled with the love of learning.
>
> It starts with a sense of calling and the pursuit of a higher purpose. Many of them told developmental stories of how they came to their purpose. Some were quite touching. As these teachers learned to pursue their calling they acquired great capacity to help students reach their potential.

Then, in describing the calling that the teachers have, Quinn makes the link to the third crucial role of the intellectual and traditional shaman – the sensemaker role that Frost and Egri claim is also the role of spiritual leader. Quinn continues:

> In the interview, they would speak of their calling, and I would say, 'You know, the notion of calling often has a spiritual dimension to it; is there a spiritual dimension in your life?' They would be shocked. After a pause, most, but not all, would open up and talk about how they bring a spiritual orientation to their work without being in any way intrusive or offensive. They might speak of praying over the names on their class roster or praying for inspiration on how to teach. Most of them feel that they are part of something bigger than self. That creates a deep sense of meaning. It helps when they are trying to bring others to a deep sense of meaning.

Quinn's words describing his own work reflect the higher purposes of healing embedded in the intellectual shaman's. As his description of these teachers demonstrates, the shaman's own calling is to change the cultural myths that need healing and the world out of which they derive by crossing whatever boundaries, barriers, worlds, or realms are necessary to bring about the truth – and its healing potential. They make connections that others simply do not make – as do those who learn from them – and others benefit, just as others have benefited from the work of intellectual shamans over time. Quinn concludes:

> The highly effective teachers are the kind of people you see in the grocery store. They look ordinary, but they are not; they are people of mastery. They know how to change themselves so other people can change. Talking to them is exciting. I feel elevated around them, and I feel elevated making sense of their words. The ideas just keep coming. Their stories help us understand transformative theory in a very grounded and inspiring way. Listening to them helps me cross the boundaries in my own life. I can build a theory that I can practice, and invite others to practice, so they can grow in their own cognitive and behavioral complexity. It is all about crossing boundaries.

6 Sensemaker

Where sense is wanting, everything is wanting.

Benjamin Franklin

A story must be judged according to whether it makes sense. And 'making sense' must be here understood in its most direct meaning: to make sense is to enliven the senses. A story that makes sense is one that stirs the senses from their slumber, one that opens the eyes and the ears to their real surroundings, tuning the tongue to the actual tastes in the air and sending chills of recognition along the surface of the skin. To make sense is to release the body from the constraints imposed by outworn ways of speaking, and hence to renew and rejuvenate one's felt awareness of the world. It is to make the senses wake up to where they are.

David Abrams, *The Spell of the Sensuous*

The third core function of shamans is that of the sensemaker, which combines elements of seer (or feeler, sensor, hearer, as all the senses can be useful ways of gaining information), sensemaker, and spiritual leader, though it is difficult to tease these elements apart.[2,125] There is also in the sensemaking role an aspect of the storyteller, in that the ideas generated by intellectual shamans need to be understood by – to make sense to – those who read or listen.

In the capacity of sensemaker, spiritual leader, or storyteller, as with the other functions of healing and connecting, intellectual shamans function as seers, 'seeing' into reality as it is, holistically as described in the last chapter, and taking on the role of truth-telling as they see, feel, or otherwise experience it. They serve as sensemakers, making sense for others of these new realities as they see them, essentially as meaning-makers and interpreters – i.e., storytellers of what they see, particularly with respect to the cultural mythologies relevant to their work.

Closely linked to the role of sensemaker is the role of spiritual leader, prophet, or guide, often to the future – a hoped-for better future – in terms of better theory, research, or teaching in the case of intellectual shamans. Sensemaking and leadership work take courage, a certain amount of risk-taking, and confidence in one's personal power. These abilities combine with an ability to handle what has been called 'parad-exity,' a word that links paradox and complexity and helps define some of what needs fixing in the world today.[126]

Tima Bansal's words below shape much of the content of the sensemaker role as *intellectual* shamans fulfill it:

> There's another piece...that's important: that we're in the world of ideas. Social scientists are really about telling good stories that help, are somewhat explanatory, and that capture imagination. That's the research side. I feel, if I can tell a story that captures imagination and that's explanatory, that I can change the way that people see the world. That influences actions, and that's done through research. So businesspeople don't have the privilege of being able to step back and say 'What's going on here?' because...they're in the moment, they have to perform. Now, I can step away from that moment. So I can be in their moment and then step back and reflect.

SENSEMAKING AND SEEING: FEELING, HEARING, SENSING

Seeing, as it applies to intellectual shamans, involves the capacity to 'see reality' much as it is, or, as Max Bazerman would say, 'without blinders,'[127] in the interests of being able to articulate what is going on, often in novel or interesting ways (while recognizing that there are only actually perceptions of reality that each of us have). In the case of shamans, however, 'seeing' means something a bit more than vision. It is the capacity to gain insights, make connections, or enhance under-standing by accessing different realms. 'Seeing' is not just a visual seeing but, rather, a combination of all the senses – including seeing, feeling, sensing, 'knowing,' and instinct – that are potentially used to make connections, obtain information, and create insights of the sort for which the intellectual shamans are known. Below, I use the term 'seeing' to reflect all these capacities, with the understanding that different individuals gain information or 'see' what is through all their senses, not just visually or imaginally. Whatever the particular method used, intellectual (and other) shamans need to gain information and insights – and then, ultimately, make sense of that information and those insights as they do their work.

Seeing, however manifested, is an important element of what I have elsewhere termed aesthetic sensibility (alternately, the beautiful),[60] which we explore further in Chapter 8. Seeing is also crucial to the other two core elements of wisdom: systems understanding (the true) and moral imagination (the good). Intellectual shamans, above all else, have to be able to 'see' and understand the system reasonably realistically in ways that perhaps others do not (yet) see. They also need what business ethicist Pat Werhane calls moral imagination to see the ethical issues associated with that reality.[128–130] Wisdom combining the good (moral imagination), the true (systems understanding), and the beautiful (aesthetic sensibility) will surface later as we explore – and consider – whether the intellectual shamans bring wisdom into the world.

Like the Oracle of Delphi, intellectual shamans frequently 'call' or speak their reality, their truth, as they see it. In doing so, their tendency to see connections, linkages, and insights before others do, or that others do not, is crucial. They also tend to speak their truth whether or not others want to hear it. Often their insights are future-oriented. Indeed, Nancy Adler describes a similar function for artists, who also by necessity must be seers, quoting the poet David Whyte:

> The artist must paint or sculpt or write, not only for the
> present generation but for those who have yet to be born. Good
> artists, it is often said, are fifty to a hundred years ahead of their
> time, they describe what lies over the horizon in our future world.
> [...] The artist...must...depict this new world before all the
> evidence is in.[131,132]

Two characteristics articulated by Adler as necessary for future leaders are relevant to the 'seeing' role of intellectual shamans. Both must have the courage to see reality and envision possibility.[131] Richard Noll *et al.*, in discussing traditional shamanism, points out that most, if not all, humans have the capacity to create mental imagery, while shamans cultivate particularly vivid and controlled mental images in the imaginal realm.[133] The work of intellectual shamans is different from that of indigenous or traditional shamans, in that the use of altered states of consciousness (trance states) is not typical for intellectual shamans, though they do seem to have the capacity to envision – in a vivid and controlled way – what others do not see, or at least have not yet seen. For traditional shamans, 'seeing' is enhanced by the development of 'imaginal conditioning' through cultivating the spiritual or inner eye, which enables the shaman to see spirits that may be helpers or may be distorting the cultural mythologies that surround the shaman and his or her patients.[133]

It may well be that traditional and intellectual shamans alike have cultivated their imaginal capacity in ways that others have not – and that it is this capacity that allows them to 'see' more readily the connections among disciplines, between theory and practice, or between ideas and teaching that gives them some of their cachet. Noll *et al.* suggest that perhaps shamans have particular gifts in creating imagery, what have been called 'fantasy-prone personalities,' although there is no indication that intellectual shamans necessarily fantasize any more than other people. The *intellectual* shaman also frequently seems to be driven by a central or core question that shapes his or her intellectual pursuits, and hence vision.

Elsewhere I have characterized the three attributes of systems understanding, moral imagination, and aesthetic sensibility as core elements of wisdom when used in the service of the greater good.[60] The sensemaking orientation, which integrates seeing with the interpretations associated with sensemaking, results in a form of leadership that Frost and Egri have termed spiritual leadership. Seeing, broadly defined in this context, involves gathering information and insights, often through making connections; seeing what is, what needs healing, or sometimes what might be if things were viewed differently; and making sense of what has been seen (felt, heard, sensed). It is this latter capacity that underscores the sensemaking role. Sensemakers need to make sense of something – and it is what is 'seen' that they interpret, and from which they then weave new 'stories' in the form of theories, research questions and methods, consulting frameworks, and practices.

Sometimes, as discussed in the last chapter, the goal of the intellectual shaman is to change the relevant cultural mythology surrounding a given idea or practice, and bring healing new insight into play. Typically, this healing orientation operates in the interest of serving the greater good or creating a better world that is inherent in the emergence of wisdom, and is integrally related to the spiritual leadership role discussed last in this chapter. (Of course, it is possible that some very bright and aware individuals could potentially use such insights for harm, just as sorcerers do in traditional shamanism, but that is not the population of interest here.)

The University of Michigan's Karl Weick, renowned for developing the idea of sensemaking in the management literature, discusses the connections among ideas that have framed a good deal of his writing and thinking over the years:

> I think the thrust of the argument in the '69 and '79 books [is] not to
> look at monolithic organizational structures but to look at process
> and organizing, and getting the word 'organizing,' and the whole idea
> of organizing, familiar to people. Get them comfortable with it, get
> them looking at sequences and series and so forth. That seems to be
> the one that, at least, . . .has the longest history of seeming to have
> made a difference. I love the sensemaking stuff.

We will see more of Weick's thoughts about sensemaking in the next section. Another intellectual shaman whose interests encompass the systems, ethical, and aesthetic elements of seeing is Paul Shrivastava. Shrivastava learned a systems approach to seeing the problems relevant to research or to making the world better early on from his then mentor Ian Mitroff, another of the intellectual shamans. Shrivastava, like Mitroff, was deeply influenced by studying the philosophy of science under Mitroff's influence. Shrivastava recalls:

> So, my [first job at Hindu Sun Computers] was a good experience and a cross-functional, performance-oriented understanding of organizations. From there I was somewhat frustrated, because I was still not intellectually satisfied that I understood how organizations work and what role they can serve in the larger picture of society. So I decided to do higher studies, which meant coming for a PhD to the University of Pittsburgh. My first mentor...was Ian Mitroff, who was supposed to guide what I wanted to study at Pittsburgh. His instructions were, 'You are grown up. You're an adult. You can figure out, son, what you want to study, so go out there and design a program of study.'

Following Mitroff's advice, Shrivastava designed a program of study majoring in strategic planning and policy, and minoring in the philosophy of science, building a questioning orientation that has stuck to this day.

> My quest right from the beginning has been about how...organizations and technologies serve a larger purpose in society. To me, that felt very constraining. Even in my doctoral studies, I've always stepped outside of the business school, outside of the management department, to seek other ways of viewing the phenomenon and understanding organizations in the larger societal context.

In talking about his research, Shrivastava mentions explicitly the opening of a blind spot with respect to crisis management by, essentially, telling a new story:

> If there's something [work-related] that I would claim pride in, it would have to be the bringing in of crisis – industrial,

technological crises – into the conversation of management. It was a blind spot for many, many years. We've always had these crises from the time that technology emerged, but we never spoke about it openly. We didn't have frameworks, language, or vocabulary, to do it. That work that I did between mid-'80s to mid-'90s is something I'm proud of, and I'm grateful that I was at a time and a place where I could do it, although if you look at my citation index... I think forming the initial dialogue, which started happening in 1984, '85, after the Bhopal disaster, I think that was a more challenging and more enduring contribution in my personal point of view.

In describing his work on crisis management, Shrivastava goes beyond opening eyes – seeing – through what had been a blind spot. He begins to explain sensemaking, helping others to make sense of – to quite literally see – what they had not seen before. He is particularly passionate about engaging people on seeing what their own passion is through his teaching. He understands the discovery or envisioning of passion as a process that can shift over time, encompasses multiple senses and capacities, and engages the three arenas of systems understanding, moral imagination, and aesthetic sensibility that constitute wisdom:

I don't think passion is something that is constant. It endures over time, but my current passion, and especially over the last decade... I'm most interested now in engaging community and sustainability, and all these issues, with passion. So I'm actually interested in understanding how passion emerges, and what is it that people get passionate about and how can we use that passion to change human–nature relations? I'm not so interested today in a scientific understanding of the world or a scientific understanding of organizations and their productivity and profitability. I am interested in understanding how passion is experienced by people and how that passion can help us to create a new relationship with daily humans, their organizations, and nature.

Linking passion to what I have called aesthetic sensibility, Shrivastava continues:

> One of the pathways to [passion], in my view, is the arts. Arts have always been a repository of human passion. We go and see art for the passionate experience, the emotional experience that we get out of it. Unfortunately, over the last 300, 400 years, arts have been reduced to entertainment. But, in an evolutionary sense, arts have always had a much broader role than just providing entertainment. They were a kind of way of expressing our emotional lives. I'm using arts in a scientific inquiry in a number of research projects now. One in France...is one manifestation, where we're trying to see how, through various art-based methods, one can reach a different understanding of nature and our role with regard to nature, so we use dance and music and drama and theatre and poetry, etc. to reconnect with nature if you will, in an emotionally deep way.

The sense of passion could also be considered a core element of intellectual shamanism. Passion, often for learning and knowing, fuels the deep well of curiosity and imaginative connections that allow intellectual shamans to see beyond current boundaries to frame, in the sensemaking process, new ways of thinking about things. Shrivastava expresses his understanding of the roles and importance that passion plays explicitly, integrating various aspects of the self – and the self in relation to the broader community:

> The passion part has two parts to it. One is an internal sense of who I am, myself identically, and sort of the rich, the buried, internal selves that we carry with us. It is psychological, it is emotional, it is personal, it is subjective, etc. But I also find that passion has another outlet, which is a collective. It's in the form of a collective consciousness. You can't be passionate in isolation and in a vacuum, but passion is something that connects us to the outside world and to nature. So, to me, it has both those elements: internal as well as the external.

Providing an example to illustrate the transformative potential of passion, Shrivastava continues by discussing a course he offered to Bucknell students called 'Managing with passion,' which asked the questions: 'What is it that you're passionate about? And do you have the skills to pursue that passion?' The effect, for some students was transformative, as Shrivastava recalls:

> One guy rode a bicycle from California to Maine and raised $1 million in scholarship money for Bucknell students. On the way he had, I think, 120 stops with groups, talking to them about being passionately engaged with community issues. He had his own spin on what that was, but he took one year off after graduating from Bucknell and did that. Some of them realized that, although they had paid a quarter million dollars to get a degree from Bucknell, their passion was, really, in baking pastry, so they went out and refused jobs at big accounting firms and became apprentices to a baker or something. Their parents would call me and say, 'What the hell are you doing to our kids? We're paying a lot of good money to get them to become accountants and here you're making them into musicians or bakers or what have you.'

Shrivastava reflects:

> [This idea of passion is] something that I don't think I have really cracked. I think it's a very big conundrum. Still, there are so many aspects to the search for and understanding of passion and how it manifests in our personal lives, in our professional lives, in our community lives. I still feel that it's a very powerful force, and, for the challenges of sustainability that we as humankind face now, we need that kind of power, we need that kind of mobilization that can come from passion.

Seeing what others cannot, do not, or will not see and then speaking (or writing) about what is seen is a fundamental aspect of *intellectual* shamanism. Sometimes, doing so is as simple as actually observing the phenomenon of interest rather than relying on proxy sources of data – and opening up to the new 'story' that arises from those observations. McGill's Henry Mintzberg articulates this perspective in discussing his early contributions to organizational and strategic management theories. Mintzberg's work, in which he shadowed five executives, was widely thought to be pathbreaking at the time. Having told the story of what he had actually observed – seen – managers doing, rather than simply parroting extant theory, Mintzberg made his breakthrough. He wryly comments:

> Yeah, well, it was pathbreaking because it said the obvious, and nobody else said it. I said, 'Managers get interrupted a lot,' and that was considered pathbreaking because everybody thought managers planned, organized, coordinated, and controlled, which is four words for controlling. So, the only reason this was so successful was because people are living with old myths and never compared it with what they saw before their own eyes or what they saw in themselves as managers. Everybody was living with a myth.

In his own words, Mintzberg is something of a 'debunker,' stepping outside conventional thinking, which inherently means seeing things differently from how others do, or in new ways, and having the courage to speak out about what he understands to be true. In Mintzberg's case, it meant actually observing – witnessing – what was going on, initially with CEOs, and later in company strategies and other research in which he was interested, rather than working from theory or using data that somehow 'scrubbed out' the actual process of seeing. Thinking about his orientation to what he calls debunking, Mintzberg articulates the crucial role that seeing plays in the type of pathbreaking work he has been able to accomplish over the years:

> I'm a sort of debunker. I don't think I'm a contrarian, but I do think I'm a debunker. [...] I think to challenge, not necessarily for the sake of challenging (that would be contrarian), but to challenge what seems to me wrongheaded, and simply say 'It's not A, it's B,' based on just going out and looking. So you watch a manager in his office or

her office (but they were 'his' in most cases), and you see that they get interrupted a lot. That doesn't sound like planning, organizing, coordinating, and controlling. So, you just look at what's going on, and you look at strategies. You know how IKEA came up with its strategy of selling unassembled furniture? A worker...had trouble putting a table in his car, so he took the legs off, and somebody said, 'Gee, maybe our customers have to take the legs off, too.' I love those stories.

Another of the intellectual shamans who based his pioneering work on observation is the University of Virginia's Ed Freeman, best known for his seminal work on stakeholder theory. Freeman recalls:

When I originally wrote the stakeholder book, I thought I was a strategy man. It's ironic that no one took it very seriously in strategy. [. . .] So I thought I was a strategy guy, but then the people that took the stakeholder idea seriously were mostly people in social issues and business ethics. [. . .] So I became an ethics guy, I guess. That sort of fit with my philosophical training, but I also thought it was a really forced distinction between 'This is business,' 'This is ethics.' I came to believe that that was what was actually wrong with both business and ethics, and much of business theory. That it had this sort of way of thinking about business that was nonhuman. I later called this the separation fallacy, which is probably in my mind a much more important contribution than thinking about stakeholders.

Thinking about the seeing – i.e., the observations and direct experience with companies – that made the stakeholder book possible, Freeman expresses the importance of actually seeing the phenomena of interest:

I was at the Applied Research Center [at Wharton Business School, University of Pennsylvania], and all I did for five years was stakeholder projects for companies, and try to refine how they did it and figure out what made sense and what didn't. So the empirical (if you have to talk that way) bases for the book were this set of clinical experiences. It sounds pretentious; my model was Freud, who had a bunch of clinical experiences and then developed the theory. I thought I had a bunch of clinical experiences and then tried to develop sort of a framework that made sense of those experiences. That's the way I'd say it now.

But I didn't know all the formal stuff about qualitative theory. I didn't suffer from what management theory does that I've often called methodolatry. I was just trying to do something that was interesting, based on what I saw going on in the real world, and based on what I saw happening in the journals and in the business press, and that sort of stuff. I was trying give [companies] a framework that could makes sense of all this stuff. Now it gets all caught up in this stuff – 'What's a theory?' 'What's a definition?' – and all those kinds of questions, which I think [are] not interesting.

Nancy Adler, who is an artist/painter as well as a scholar, understands the important role that seeing has played in her work. She also makes a link to spiritual leadership and explores the nature of her work, some of which has been to suggest that business schools need to 'dare to care' and 'lead beautifully,' much of which challenges conventional thinking:

> I know increasingly, when I speak, ...that I'm guided by a deeper wisdom or (I don't have a better word for it) that I say exactly what I need to say for that moment for it to work. It's not that I don't prepare really well, but the preparation is just a stage before getting out there naked and letting it go where it goes. I know, increasingly, the last four or five years, that my writing is coming from that same place, and there are times where I'm literally typing away and I'm looking over my hands up on the screen to see what I'm saying. I want to know what I'm going to say next.

In a speech given at the Academy of Management, and in another speech given at the twenty-fifth anniversary of the IEDC Bled (Slovenia)

School of Management, Adler used the phrase 'now is the time to invoke beauty,' after the era of the twentieth century, which she termed 'a long experiment in ugliness.' Thinking about the necessity of seeing and invoking beauty to contend with the many crises of our time, and simultaneously illustrating how even the intellectual shaman him- or herself can be informed by the way the story being told is shaped, Adler continues:

> For instance, now is the time to invoke beauty, but it wasn't until I said it in that audience that I totally understood that now, not tomorrow, not somebody else, now is our time to invoke beauty. Of course, beauty is my umbrella for Shabbat. It's my umbrella for what are we aspiring to. It's my umbrella for what were we meant to do on this planet. Who are we meant to be with each other? I just need to be quiet and let arrive what arrives. The whole idea of serendipity showed up in my painting and print-making. [. . .] How do I, with you, look out at the world, at what's going on in the world, at what's going on with income distribution, at what's going on with global warming, at what's going on with ([we] don't need to go down the list)? How do we, who have been the crusaders for the last decade, [look out at the world?] [S]o much of the world's in denial, . . .we can't be in denial. We need to use the artist's skill to be able to really see.

Recognizing the manifest problems of today's world, clearly seen, can create depression, and also the limitations of what one person can do, Adler comments – and in doing so reveals how her own shamanic process works as she attempts to 'see' her way forward from insight to (scholarly and artistic) action and, ultimately, as suggested above, between seeing and wisdom:

> Well, if you're not in denial, there's a good chance you're in depression. So, my own creeping depression: what if I'm right? Increasingly my biggest fear is: what if I'm right? I'm definitely not a megalomaniac. I have no sense that I'm the one who's going to go out

there and change the whole world. I do have the sense that in the domains that I work I influence people. I can touch people. I can support people in doing good in the world, but right now we're confronted with something much bigger[134] and way more evil than anything that I have the power to touch. So depression says, 'Why bother?' Then all of a sudden serendipity arrives.

What is serendipity? At least for right now it's saying, 'Can you look at this mess and transform it back to something beautiful? Can it be the catalyst that allows you to see something that you couldn't see before?' So it allows me to look at this mess and still have at least a small door out to something better. I understand completely that serendipity is, in many ways, psychologically supporting me as well as it's theoretically supporting the leadership work. [...] Rob Austin [has, with co-authors, written a major article] on accidental innovation,[134] where he talks about serendipity, and that that's where innovative discovering comes from, is the coincidences.

But the literal part of serendipity that's important is that somehow wisdom is maybe recognizing the wise moments or wise perspectives that are handed to you. It has less to do with creating wisdom and wise moments than recognizing them. Then...giving voice, literally speaking, ...in a way that people can hear and engage with that, so that the wisdom comes through me but it goes on out into the world.

SENSEMAKING AS STORYTELLING AND SPIRITUAL LEADERSHIP

Intellectual shamans, like traditional shamans, are involved in the process of sensemaking, and part of that sensemaking process involves spiritual leadership,[125] albeit in a secular (or profane, to use Eliade's word)[20] sense. Seeing (however it is done) is not enough. What is seen must be interpreted and made sense of for others to mend whatever cultural mythology the (intellectual) shaman believes needs to be changed. That is, a new story must be told that replaces or modifies the old story.

It is this interpretive and communicative role that constitutes sensemaking. The process of sensemaking involves interpreting the connections that insights, ideas, and perspectives have made and bringing these insights into forms that can be seen, read, or heard by others – i.e., in the way that academics do: telling stories, truth-telling in interpreting how the intellectual shamans see reality for others. Essentially, it involves making meaning, in the capacity that Richard Noorgard and Paul Baer call the collective bearer of cultural consciousness.[135] It is a core aspect of what Frost and Egri call spiritual leadership, as well. In this way, intellectual shamans serve much the same function as do artists and poets, particularly because they are frequently forward-looking.

Through meaning-making and interpreting the cultural myths that shape their work and the world(s) in which they find themselves, intellectual shamans raise consciousness and energize what might otherwise be abstractions.[111,136] The combined sensemaking and spiritual leadership role is a central element of the healing process discussed in Chapter 4, particularly as it relates to the interpretation and manipulation of cultural symbols.[121] Though traditional shamans attribute cultural crises and illnesses to angry gods or bad spirits, intellectual shamans are dealing with misguided theories, poor or limited practices in management or research, and the promulgation of bad ideas, rather than gods, witches, and devils. The interpretive or storytelling process also involves an aesthetic component, just as does the work of the poet or the artist. It is not surprising, then, that shamans have often been regarded as poets, 'singers of the song,' and individuals who are wise.[29] Through these storytelling means, intellectual shamans sometimes serve as prophets, guides, and, indeed, spiritual leaders.[29]

Mihály Hoppál is quite explicit about the ways in which such spiritual leadership takes place in our secular world today, which is particularly relevant for the world of intellectual shamans, though he is writing about the spiritual elements of traditional shamanism:

In our post-religious world it is perhaps more proper to speak about beliefs, attitudes, convictions, or ideological practices (*Glaubensvorstellungen*) than religion. In this sense, shamanism is a belief system which involves the acceptance of certain social roles (a healer, poet, or ideologue, or all of these together). These are no longer in the sacred sphere of culture today, but on the border of the sacred and the profane; not in that of religion, but rather on the threshold between religious and everyday beliefs.[29]

In their paper, entitled 'Collectively seeing complex systems,' Norgaard and Baer note that historically cultural knowledge, the mythologies that we spoke of in the last chapter, was collectively shared by the communities that fostered them. Today, however, much knowledge is specialized and, they argue, unprecedentedly fragmented. They note about the often indigenous communities in which shamanism is openly prevalent:

> The similarity of their lives supported a common understanding of the world around them. Of course, they did not know nearly as much about the world as we collectively know today. Yet, unlike much human knowledge today, what earlier people knew was very nearly common to all. This shared understanding meant that the knowledge available could readily inform collective action.'[135]

In contrast to these traditional shamans making sense of a common culture and mythology, intellectual shamans have to deal with a more complex situation. Much of today's knowledge is found in the silos of specialization, making 'the synthesis of multiple deep knowledges into general information that can be widely conveyed to inform public action...also difficult.'[135]

Norgaard and Baer articulate the need for scientists in all disciplines to speak/tell stories – i.e., to sensemake – across what have emerged as the boundaries of their disciplines to create the more holistic perspective that is needed for dealing with what can only be called the wicked problems that societies, our communities, and the world face today. Because intellectual shamans, by their nature, are boundary-spanners, they push the edges of their specific disciplines to integrate more and better thinking, frequently working interdisciplinarily to accomplish their own ends. This boundary-spanning becomes particularly clear in their sensemaking capacity.

As noted earlier, the University of Michigan's Karl Weick is known for his work on sensemaking. With more than fifty years of experience behind him, Weick has pioneered seminal work on the social psychology of organizing, sensemaking, and, more recently, high-reliability organizations, including looking at the ways in which wildland firefighters work. Weick explores the actual process of sense-making below:

> I can tie them all back to social psychology, and this has been a lifelong interest – in the sense of how...people deal with unsettling situations, whether you want to call them stress or whatever. So, if you think of classic dissonance experiments, those are discrepancies or things that don't quite fit together, and that would be an early influence. I think you get from that to organizing by arguing that it's people's justifications or rationalizations or explanations of the things they're doing that then lead them to do them again and again and again. We then call them organizational routines. But in the beginning you did something. Somebody said, 'Why'd you do that?' You come up with a reason, and then that reason weaves its way in, and you use the reason over and over. You do the same kind of actions, because it now seems like they were sensible kinds of actions, and you've grown yourself a routine. But it's not that you've grown yourself a static kind of structure. You just keep redoing it or reaccomplishing it, and it's a process, and it keeps coming out a little different each time. I think it's pretty elementary social psych that I've really fallen back on, and it just hasn't let me down. But I suspect it's also a social psych that would be unrecognizable these days.

In discussing his insights, Weick refers directly to the process of seeing and its important role in shaping how we understand ourselves, organizations, routines, and processes, and particularly to how he made connections among these things in telling the story of sensemaking over time. He elaborates, illustrating how interpretations have shifted the very understanding of what social psychology is over the years:

> I think the impetus in the field is more toward the more formal and less of the thinking about 'Is this the right label? What is this label keeping us from seeing? What if we treated it as something other? Let's find out what that might be.' Even going back to perceptions: how was it that I thought doubt was a big deal, and what did I miss when I first encoded that as doubt? Maybe it was fear. Maybe it was something else, and being comfortable and on your toes when you go back closer to experience. I realize that's not a recipe for a lot of publication success, but I think, to grasp what's going on or get closer to it, we have to do that. I think the narrowness [of some research questions] really holds us away from doing that. Well – but, you know, that's what I do for a living. So I'm not making a general prescription at all.

Weick uses a description of a course he taught to illustrate in more detail how the sensemaking process can work. He also illustrates how the process of really seeing what is works – and how it can potentially be taught to others (and note also the reference to Peter Frost's influence on Weick in this passage):

> I've got a course which I've done, God, forever, called just 'Craft of scholarship.' It's devoted to thinking about things that fall through the cracks in the usual methodology course. One of the things that we work on – I don't at all know whether it's correct; it's what works for me – is to say to people, and to work with people to say, 'You really know more about how the world hangs together than you realize.' Draw them out with explanations of just mundane things, and try to point out of them the twists that are in there, or the way in which that would put some existing ideas in jeopardy, or whatever it is. But it's a pretty intense one-on-one kind of interaction that

basically builds confidence as well as content on the part of people, that they have a grasp that they haven't realized or haven't articulated or could get better at doing, need to trust themselves at doing. That's a lot of what Peter Frost did. He was a terrific listener, and I think I've tried to do the same kind of thing, but then to reflect back to people something like 'You're saying more than you realize,' or 'There's more there than may meet your eye,' and let me point it out to you, and let's draw that out.

Are the people interviewed as intellectual shamans all on a spiritual quest, as Egri and Frost[1] suggest about organization development practitioners? Not explicitly so, though we can 'read' their lives and work as spiritual quest if we take into account how they live and operate. What I earlier claimed was a calling to their work that makes it something more than just passing time also suggests a spiritual aspect to the work of intellectual shamans. This sense of spiritual leadership is evident more in that Frost and Egri, citing Peter Vaill, suggest that spirit pervades everything that we do as human beings – including 'the abstract, emotional search for meaning – the how and why of existence.'[1]

Case Western Reserve's David Cooperrider exemplifies the sense- and meaning-making roles of intellectual shamans, which manifest in what can only be called spiritual leadership, in describing how his work attempts to shape holistic thinking and make connections between theory and practice, and in bridging across other domains as well:

Part of my quest as a scholar and academic has been to reunite theory and practice as one kind of integral whole. The advancement of knowledge requires us to have our feet in both worlds – the world of real practice, real leadership, real people, and a world of academia and thought and philosophy and theory and research. It's where there's that perfect interplay that the most generative knowledge is going to come forward.

So, in the early 1980s, I started writing about a kind of action research – I call it appreciative inquiry – to really argue for a world that's transformed from this mechanistic universe, industrial age, and so on to an age where meaning-making and knowledge-making in the social sphere happens between people. I started raising questions about the purpose of social science. Instead of social science just being a way to hold up a mirror to society and say 'Here's a mirror image of what we've found,' the notion is that there's a much greater role for the social sciences. It's not just to hold up a mirror to yesterday's world but to build a new theory of human potential and possibility and value to develop what I might call an anticipatory period – a period that helps open the world to great new possibilities, theory that creates propositions about what's possible.

Cooperrider wanted to frame his research in a positive and constructive, futures-oriented way. He sought to help the future by opening up new possibilities – telling a new story – rather than closing possibilities down. These elements are important to the sensemaking capability of intellectual shamans. Cooperrider elaborates:

I started noticing that the knowledge base in the field of organization theory, organization development, and change especially was so deficit-focused that pretty soon everything started appearing repetitive. Every analysis of this social system – whether people were coming at it from a critical theoretical point of view or a deconstructionist point of view or a problem-analytic point of view or a diagnostic point of view – the patterns of doing that kind of applied research [were] always in the deficit modality. What's wrong with the human being? How is the social system creating power relations over people that create oppression? How are we locked in our universe of old assumptions?

I started to feel that almost every study I was reading was boring, not motivating. It was not leading to new sense of possibility. It occurred to me that part of the reason for that is that there was an underlying metaphor that much of the research in our field seemed to operate under. That assumption is that the world is a problem to be solved. If the world as a root metaphor is a problem to be solved, then what are we searching for? We're always searching for how we are not living up to some preordained ideal. I started thinking, that's what's constraining our theoretical imagination and mind. I had just read a book by Kenneth Gergen, which I think is the most important book I have ever read, called *Toward Transformation in Social Knowledge*.[137] He looked at all of the ways in which social science was critiquing traditional science, and looking at all of the terms emerging about postmodernism and social construction of reality, and interpreted this social science and so on.

In part of the book, he joined into critiquing the assumptions of logical positivism science, but then he started saying 'Maybe we need a new conception of science.' He talked about this idea of generative theory that opens the world to new possibilities and our assumptions and so on. I started raising questions in my own mind: why are we in our field so non-generative? We don't have the great, great thinkers like a Freud or a Marx or others. Why are we not teaching theoretical imagination and mind in our doctoral programs, as if just some simple courses in statistics and so on are going to be the way that we produce new knowledge?

Inspired by the sense of possibility and generativity that Gergen's ideas presented, Cooperrider went on to pioneer his thinking – and sensemaking – around the idea of what he came to call appreciative inquiry. Bringing in the mystery – even the spiritual element of his work, which links to the third element of the sensemaker role: spiritual leadership – Cooperrider recalls:

I was excited by this idea of how...we increase the generative capacity of the field with more relevance, more rigor. How do we take seriously this idea that in the social world there really are no laws of human system behavior in the sense that X causes Y under all of these conditions? Literally, after 100 or 150 years of social science, there are no laws of human behavior in the strict sense of a law in physics like the law of gravity. So, maybe that means that we need a different kind of social science, not a science of prediction and control and repetition and replication, but a science that actually helps transform and create new patterns and advance new human possibilities in kind of an anticipatory theory, theory of what's possible.

With these ideas in mind, Cooperrider started seeking a 'generative capacity of theory construction and the development of new knowledge that makes a difference in the human condition of the world.' He recalls his ultimate conclusion:

We needed a dramatic shift from this metaphor that the world is a problem to be solved, organizational life is a problem to be solved, to reclaim a more inspired view of knowledge that maybe, maybe, the world, maybe human existence and social existence, is a miracle. It's certainly a mystery. It's constantly unfolding in ways that are emergent and creative and surprising. [...] That we live in the social sciences, our realities are much more permeable and transitory, and there is no firm ground to say that there is one law or a series of laws of human behavior that are going to hold across all cultures, across all time. If that's the case, why not reconceptualize science to help participate in creating new and better futures?

As he reconceptualized his approach to social sciences, Cooperrider also reframed – made new sense of – how human systems might be understood:

I felt like, instead of a mechanic who says 'Here's a problem in our engine under the hood of our car; you need to fix that engine in a mechanical sense,' maybe what we need is a reconnection with the miracle of life on this planet, where we see things again in living systems, alive and miraculous and filled with emergent potential. Basically, what I found is that organizations are not so much problems to be solved but they are living systems and universes of strengths that connect strength upon strength, that lead to one emergence after another, that the questions needed to shift. Instead of 'What's wrong with this picture?' we started asking questions about life. What is it that gives life to this living human system when it's most alive, when people are most engaged, when it's most symbiotically related to its larger constituencies and ecosystems? What is it that gives life to this living system when it's most alive?

Explicitly focusing on the life-giving qualities of organizing and thinking about the emergence of the positive organizational scholarship movement (with which Jane Dutton, Kim Cameron, and Bob Quinn are closely identified), Cooperrider highlights the element of spiritual leadership that certain of the intellectual shamans exemplify:

> So, the key question we started asking in every system was: what is it that gives life to this living system, this miraculous, this mystery, this ever-emergent system? What's happening when it's most alive? How can we use that information to engage people to imagine new propositions about the possibilities that lie in the future?

Note further the linking of the elements of wisdom – systems understanding (the true), moral imagination (the good), and aesthetic sensibility (the beautiful) – as Cooperrider describes his work with the Cleveland Clinic in more detail. Here he makes quite explicit the spiritual nature of his particular quest and illustrates the power of the way that story is told to shift understanding and, ultimately, action:

> At first they said, 'Well, where's all our problems?' But then I said, 'No, what I decided was to study everything that gives life to this social invention that you've given birth to and to seek and understand all the enablers, the whole context.' The more we studied the true, the good, the better, the possible in that system with real rigor, the more the system began to move in the direction of what we were studying. In other words, there was like a super-Heisenberg effect. The Heisenberg effect says, just by observing the particle in physics, that you actually shift the particle. Well, that same promise became so clear to me: that theory does create and take part in the creation of the future, that inquiry and change in

human systems are a simultaneous moment. They're not separate moments. First you do a research and then you change? No! Simply by asking questions of what gives life or, oppositely, all the companies that spend money on doing low-morale surveys? Those are not innocent-objective, detached kinds of inquiries or research like we have this scientific image of objectivity. It changes everything just by asking the question. This insight that we need to lift up into our secular pursuits the miracle of life on this planet – call it the sacred, call it the gift.

Another of the intellectual shamans who acknowledges the spiritual element of his sensemaking work is Raj Sisodia, whose work on conscious capitalism attempts to reshape the way capitalism and its core principles are framed. Although he was not spiritual in his younger days, that aspect has emerged into his life and work as conscious capitalism developed. In the late 2000s Sisodia became interested in the art of living when his sister gave him a book by Sri Sri Ravi Shankar called *The Guru of Love*. The book shifted his thinking, and he recalls:

At the same time I was thinking about these issues from a business standpoint, and that way of thinking started to seep in, the idea of responsibility; what do you take responsibility for? That's one of the tenets in the art of living: the idea of focusing on the right actions, and not being wedded to the outcome. I found a lot of parallels in what [the companies profiled in his jointly authored book *Firms of Endearment*, which argues that companies that treat their stakeholders well outperform others] were doing with what is generally being prescribed from the ancient wisdom, at that time of the ancient wisdom of India.

What really flipped a switch for me was when the book came out, and I shared it with one of my professors in India. I had gone back for my twenty-fifth reunion. He was our most impactful professor twenty-five years ago. He taught us strategy. He did his doctorate here [in the United States] at Harvard. So, when I shared the book with him, the next day he said, 'I'm really enjoying reading your book. Normally, I go to bed at eight, but I was up till eleven reading it.' So I said, 'That's great. That means a lot to me that you find the book interesting.' He said, 'Yes, but as I read it I realize it's nothing new.' I was a little deflated. I said, 'What do you mean by that?' He said, 'Well, everything you're writing here was written 4,000 years ago. It's all there. It's there in the Gita, the Bhagavad Gita, and in various other writings as well.'

With this insight, Sisodia appreciated the link between ancient spiritual traditions and the discoveries that he and his co-authors had made in recognizing that good and meaningful relationships are a core element of success. Having had the explicit link to ancient wisdom traditions made clear, Sisodia goes on:

That really opened my eyes, because this had never been a part of my education. Growing up in India we were never exposed to the actual wisdom of that philosophical tradition. All we got were the rituals, the religious aspect, but not the spirituality. [. . .] I would ask, 'Why are we doing this? What's the meaning of this?' Because I knew there had to be some symbolic meaning as to why you did those things, but nobody could explain that, because they didn't know. My parents didn't know. My grandfather didn't know. Nobody knew. [. . .] So I grew up with this sense of, here's a religion that's just all pretty pictures and these nice-looking gods. It was just empty ritual and never a sense of the wisdom.

His professor's comment triggered a shift in Sisodia, a spiritual journey, which, combined with reading and retreats, brought the connection to spiritual leadership closer. His work started to gain more visibility around the *Firms of Endearment* work and moved him toward the development of ideas of conscious capitalism. In 2013 Sisodia published a book with Whole Foods CEO John Mackey by that title. Sisodia relates a bit more about how his insights emerged:

I also found that, when I started giving a lot of presentations on this subject, people would actually come up multiple times, many times, and say, 'This is a spiritual talk, what you're describing here. What you're saying here, this whole message, is a spiritual message.' It wasn't overtly a spiritual message, and neither was it something I was trying to do covertly, but yet it was in there. The principles were deeply embedded in there. So that has become kind of a more explicit thing for me now, to understand and try to integrate, because I think what we've tended to do in the past is separate the world of work from the world of personal life and personal spirituality. There doesn't need to be a compartmentalization, that really the way you are needs to be reflected in how you work, and, when you do that, all of these positive things result.

In one sense, the intellectual shaman as sensemaker/spiritual leader is always on what the great mythologist Joseph Campbell would have called a quest.[23] Perhaps it is that constant questing – for new ideas, information, connections – that explains the insatiable curiosity that seems to characterize intellectual shamans. Phil Mirvis is someone who has both written about consciousness-raising in executives and is always on a quest for interesting new experiences. Indeed, Mirvis calls himself an 'experience junkie,' and designs, contributes to, and writes about his experiences. In that sense, he is an explicit and consummate sensemaker. Putting the two elements of questing-and-being together with the sensemaking or storytelling, Mirvis comments:

I think [questing and being] are two sides of the coin. As an experience junkie, I'm constantly looking for stimulation... 'Let's see what's going on here. Wow, that's interesting!' Being comes in living an experience, pulling it together, seeing how it might be useful, getting people engaged in storytelling about what is happening to them. This makes experiential learning more purposeful and more personal. Questing is fun, it's sexy, it's interesting. Being involves me internalizing experiences, living in the moment, and then writing about my lessons.

Similarly to Sisodia, Bob Giacalone talks about an incident that triggered his transition to a more spiritual way of being, also a part of his sensemaking role. Early in his career Giacalone experienced a toxic work environment, and also had a student threaten his life because he had given a grade of 'C.' Stressed, he got into a minor accident on the way home from work one day – and the sense of a lack of awareness that had caused the accident triggered a major change for Giacalone. He recalls what happened next:

> I went back to my office over the next week or so, threw out all my data, and spent five years reading. I read radical biology, Rupert Sheldrake. I read physics, I read religion. I read spirituality. I read stuff that was mysticism. I read great thinkers. I just spent five years reading, and I had to figure out where I was going, because it was something that happened to me then and it was a minor accident. That's what's so weird about it. Something shook me up at the core, and I don't know what it was. I still don't know what it was. But something came out of that, and what came out of it was this five years of thinking. I had so much backlog of information I could keep writing. So it didn't affect my career very much.

The incident, combined with all the reading, shaped new insights and ways of thinking about the world for Giacalone – and ultimately reshaped his way of being in the world and how he makes sense of – and translates for others – his research. He continues:

> This was 1994, so I was thirty-seven, and so I just read an awful amount, and began to synthesize. I started thinking about ethics very differently. I started to understand the concept of systems, started to think about the world not from my point of view but from how I was connected to everything. Suddenly everything I believed no longer made sense. It was just bizarre. All the things I thought

were true weren't anymore. I saw myself as part of everything, rather than apart from everything. [...]

I started to think to myself, 'God what's this all about?' I had been very materialistic, very driven by getting status and power... I wanted to prove to everybody that I was worthy. That's what it really comes down to. You hate to say that, but it's true. [...] So I wanted all this stuff, and in 1997 I was offered an endowed chair, endowed professorship, at University of North Carolina at Charlotte, and I took that job and bought my McMansion. I had prestige and I had all the things I had worked for since I graduated. The bottom line was that within a month of having them all I wanted to give them all back. I began to see that something weird had happened that all those things didn't make me happy. It happened very suddenly.

Giacalone goes on to recount how his sensemaking, triggered by the accident and other events, plays into his work today:

It's impacted me enormously, in the classroom in particular, because I go to the class, and what I try to do all the time with my students is say, 'Ethics is not what you think it is.' I talk about it from a standpoint of systems theory, from religious standpoints, from spiritual standpoints, and from behavioral standpoints. What I tell my students all the time is that, if they leave my class the same as all other classes, I failed. When you leave a class in calculus, you should know how to do more problems at the end. You should have more answers at the end than you had at the beginning. But, in my class, they'll know I succeeded if by the end they have more questions than answers, and that it will be the questioning that saves them. It'll be a question that saves them.

The University of Michigan's Bob Quinn makes explicit the links between the spiritual/sensemaking leadership provided by the master teachers that he studied, discussed in Chapter 5, and their calling to become teachers. The explicitly spiritual link is also evident for some, but not all, of the intellectual shamans. Some of the intellectual shamans, though not explicitly expressing a spiritual orientation, instead focus on a bigger purpose than self, understanding and meaning-making, and their sensemaking.

Shamans are frequently told that they need to 'dream the world into existence' (see Chapter 8 for more on this topic), and, in Quinn's remarks, we can see much the same process operating for the master teachers as for intellectual shamans themselves. Taking on, in a sense, a similar role of guide and facilitator as Quinn's teachers in his own work, Rice University's Marc Epstein makes sense of how business can best be developed in Africa using the language of some of the trainees he has worked with. He notes a similar facilitation of learning and a self-evolutionary role that the teachers Quinn describes used as a core element of how businesses in Africa need to be developed. Epstein remembers how a talk he gave helped potential leaders in Africa make sense of how to begin rethinking transformation of the continent through entrepreneurship:

> I gave a keynote address in Nairobi...and there were representatives from a lot of the countries in Africa. In every case, people came up to me and said, 'This is exactly right. What this is about is entrepreneurship. Long term, it is not [about] foreign aid. [Foreign aid] is helpful as stopgap, but that is not the solution, and it is also not the solution to wait for Toyota to come in and build a factory and hire 10,000 workers. The solution is the same solution that has worked all over the world. We need small businesses to start up. Start-up is one- and two-people firms that go to three and to five [employees], and to ten, and then to twenty and to fifty. Some of them will stop and some of them will grow to 100 and 200, and one of 100 will grow to 500 [employees]. That is the way you folks in America grew up, and that is the way we are going to have to do this. So what we really want is [that] you to help us learn how to be entrepreneurs.' So that is some of the work that I have been doing.

Words are not enough, however, as Epstein relates:

> We developed this training for illiterate and innumerate adults,
> and now we have developed training for primary school children.
> You might say, 'Why primary school children?' A large percentage of
> the people [in Africa] never get past primary school. They go in
> and they become subsistence farmers or traders, so they are going to
> go into business when they are ten or twelve or fourteen or fifteen
> years old. They are not going to finish school. In many of these
> countries, it is 85 percent of the population who are going to go and
> become these traders. They are not going to be in the formal job
> sector. So, if you want them to succeed, you'd better teach them
> entrepreneurship. And you'd better teach it when they are in grades
> three, four, and five.

Themes of authenticity – i.e., being true to one's self in life and work, a deeper purpose that leads to healing, and wisdom – are common as intellectual shamans speak about their work. Jane Dutton has struggled to make sense of the success of her career as a woman in a male-dominated field. Below, Dutton examines how her feminine sensibility helped her when she took a (spiritual) leadership role within the Academy of Management by creating connection and identity in that big professional organization:

> I've come to understand that part of why I find resourcefulness so
> interesting is that I associate it with being a woman or a girl, female.
> I make use of the everyday stuff and make it into things. I'll give you
> an example. When I became division chair at OMT [the
> Organization and Management Theory Division of the Academy of
> Management], I learned to trust my everyday experience. My sense
> was that there wasn't much of an attachment that I had to OMT, the
> division. At the time I was studying identity, so [this idea] wasn't
> completely disconnected intellectually. I thought, 'OK, from the
> time I was a little girl, what did people do to feel connected to stuff?'
> So we just started playing with practices and artifacts and little

things that...would bring more joy to people when they encountered OMT. [For example], we made OMT 'the place to be.' It's still the tag line, and every year OMT has an artifact. We created these 'Above-and-Beyond the Call of Duty Awards,' and now every other division has ABCD Awards for reviewers.

Explaining the rationale behind simple and inexpensive artifacts that helped create connection, the awards, Dutton implicitly highlights her own spiritual leadership, which emphasizes helping people feel valued, connected, and as though they belong wherever they are. Some of this spiritual leadership involves creating rituals and connections among people, some involves the framing, storytelling, or sensemaking elements discussed earlier, and some is symbolic; some of it involves creating or tapping into important networks that provide insight, support, and engagement. Dutton comments:

> POS [positive organizational scholarship] for me is a giant example of this [approach]. Many years ago I felt that our field was really silent about relational perspectives and that the way that we were talking about relational stuff was pretty dead and pretty structured. So I just invited colleagues, and said, 'Do you want to start a book club?' It was a reading club on relational perspectives. For almost three years we just read and talked about relational perspectives. Then we did goofy things, again, like little rituals at our meetings. We would do sharings at the beginning, and we would do personal reflections. It involved taking the practice of what we were doing professionally into the personal domain, using the formal practices about what you're supposed to do, then embellishing them with things that were more meaningful symbolically.

Below, Dutton describes the origin of her highly acclaimed work on compassion in organizations, and in this description highlights not only a link to Peter Frost but also how the sensemaking process itself works, sometimes, as in this case, simply because someone has the temerity to name something for what it is – i.e., to tell a new story:

I'll give you another example. There are rich gardens, more playful and full of life. So, when Peter Frost and I started to do this compassion work together, we were in San Diego [at the Academy of Management meeting]. [. . .] We felt like this phenomenon of compassion is so much an important part of the human experience, and there weren't any stories of that in our field, but there were tons of stories in our own lived experience. [Peter] was wrestling with cancer, and we had had a real trauma in our family with our daughter [who had been badly injured by a babysitter]. There was a very personal sense that we wanted to do some work with this idea, but we didn't want to do it the same old way. So we created the compassion lab, then we set up certain principles and practices that were about trying to cultivate more joy, more enjoyment, more enrichment of the experience.

Dutton, with typical modesty, downplays her role as spiritual leader and sensemaker. Below, she elaborates how her 'midwife' role has enabled whole new fields and areas of research to be born as a result of her (and others') sensemaking:

If you were to look at the residue on the road behind me, I would say the best part would be that they were like little gardens that at times were really alive, and I'm just one of the tillers. This is sort of like being a gardener or midwife. [. . .] It's like looking in the crevices and letting the stuff come up from the crevices, trusting the universe that it will grow. That's not an uttered command; we just have to cultivate the conditions, and [new insights and ideas] will come.

Note that, as many of the other intellectual shamans reflect on their work, they do so with a humble realization that they did not operate alone. Networks, like-minded others, and supportive friends and family are crucial to developing and implementing new ideas and insights.

Intellectual shamans as scholars and writers engage with their sensemaking through their writing. The University of Michigan's Andy

Hoffman has written an autobiographical account of his work as a builder's apprentice when recently out of college. He explains the importance of living authentically:

> In the book [*Builder's Apprentice*] I'm really trying to instill in people the idea of a vocation or a calling. When I made the jump from a Harvard acceptance to being a carpenter, a lot of people around me were saying, 'You're out of your mind.' But I had to take control of my life. That is such an important thing that many of us do not do. Many of us, I think, live for other people. We teach kids to [live for others] when we teach them to build résumés at a young age. The question I hate the most is 'Will that look good on a résumé?' It is a horrible question. What you're telling somebody is 'Don't follow your inner compass. Do what looks good to other people.' That's a terrible thing to teach people.

Hoffman applies much the same philosophy to himself in his academic career, taking personal and intellectual risks, and following his own lights.

> I'm doing work on climate skeptics. [...] I wrote an academic paper that I could have sent it to an 'A'-level journal. But they would have done two things. First, they would have forced me to take the empirical question and make it secondary to the theoretical question... Second, they would have taken three or four years to publish it. It would be guaranteed to be irrelevant...by design! So I decided that, even though that would look great on my resumé, I'm not going to do that. I sent it to a second-tier journal that allowed me to leave the empirical question as primary, and it came out in about four months. The idea is that that's only the beginning. I got it out but have more work to take the paper's ideas to a broader community.

Hoffman has bridged the gap to practice by becoming something of a public intellectual through his work on climate change skeptics, moving from sensemaking in academia to doing so for the general public. Continuing the conversation about his climate change skeptics work, Hoffman adds:

> It's been written up in blogs for *The New York Times*, *Time* magazine, *Scientific American*. I've been on *Talk of the Nation*. I'm going to be on the Canadian Broadcasting Network next week. I'm really proud that I am now moving in the direction which I always wanted to be in: that of a public intellectual. I think that we've too few academics doing that.

In becoming a public intellectual on the issue of climate change, Hoffman is putting the larger purpose of educating the public ahead of his personal interests in traditional career advancement. He is also working to tell his truth, his story, to a broader audience. Education, which is a core element of the work of all intellectual shamans, is explicitly related to leadership, and, I would argue, spiritual leadership. Etymologically, the word 'education' is derived from the Latin *educo* – to lead forth, raise up – and *duco*, meaning 'I lead, I conduct.' Education, then, whether in the classroom or in the court of public opinion, is inherently linked to sensemaking and to leadership, and, ultimately, to what shamans do in their roles as spiritual leaders. Hoffman elaborates on the role of the public intellectual:

> Navel-gazing [which is what critics call some academic work] is benign enough. But on some issues – and climate change is one of them – the relative absence of the academic voice in the public debate actually does society a disservice, because it cedes the space to some pretty absurd opinions from the demagogues out there.

The path of intellectual shaman as spiritual leader is not without risks, as Hoffman notes the risks associated with such leadership:

> I have a new folder in my e-mail file for climate skeptic hate mail. At first that stung, but now I recognize that this is the price of being engaged in the debate, and not everyone has to agree with me. If they're responding to me, then I'm saying something that strikes a

chord. I'm saying something important, and that's gratifying and encourages me to go further.

Hoffman identifies the sensemaking roles of academics as intellectuals:

> There's a huge difference between an academic and intellectual. I find academics boring. I find intellectuals exciting. Following intriguing ideas is what intellectuals do. David Brooks in his book [*Beyond the Brain*] just spent years talking to brain scientists and psychologists. He just immersed himself. Then he did what we do, and that's find patterns and pull it all together and make sense out of it. That's what a good academic does. That's what a good intellectual does, but an intellectual makes it accessible and relevant to a broader audience. He or she joins the public debate and changes minds. Not all academics do that.

The University of Michigan's Jim Walsh also tries to ensure that his children and his students alike lead authentic lives. He states:

> I sometimes draw a little Venn diagram for my kids as we talk about finding a life course. Of course, this isn't about plugging a few values into an equation and – presto! – you have life worth living. But, still, it gives you something to think about as you make life choices. I start by drawing two little circles: what do you love? What are you good at? We look at whether there are points of intersection. For example, in my case, I love to run, but I'm not all that good at it. While I was actually pretty good at math, I never really loved it. The challenge is to reflect about intersections. As I thought about work, I realized that I am really curious, love to learn, love talking to people. Am I good at it? Who knows? Actually, that's an odd question. What is the 'it' in this case? But the question can get you thinking about where curiosity, learning, and engaging others are all somehow valued.
> Ever so slowly, I found myself drawn to academics. Then you might draw two other circles as you start to think about work. These

are secular and sacred questions. The first is: can I make a buck doing it? After all, you do need to support yourself and your family. Then you ask, 'Can you make a better world doing it?' I found myself looking for that sweet spot between doing what you love and what you are good at, and then making money and making a better world. I ask my kids to put this kind of thinking in the back of their minds too.

Walsh spoke earlier about his journey from psychology and cognition to strategy and governance and then to his quest to understand how business can best serve society. But there is another journey too. This one is more about learning your craft, and then finding – and staying in – that sweet spot. He speaks candidly about what it took for him to become a professor, once again highlighting commitment, passion – and the support of key people:

> Moving from SUNY–Albany to Columbia to Chicago to Northwestern and from repairing bridges to processing disability claims to selecting stockbrokers was its own journey. Once I found myself in what seemed to be the right place a different kind of journey unfolded. I pretty soon knew that I had found work that I loved (or could grow to love); I knew that I could make a living; and I also knew that professors can absolutely make the world a better place. But, man, oh man, learning how to be an academic, to be good at it, was another story. I think the tagline for the game Othello is 'A minute to learn, a lifetime to master.' Academics is 'A lifetime to learn, a lifetime to master.' Of course, that is its fundamental allure, but, still, you don't have much time to get up to speed and become worthy of your students' attention and your early paychecks.
>
> What I am about to say could sound pretty self-aggrandizing but, really, it applies to everyone. Someone has to say it out loud. I do not know anyone who has mastered their craft without working incredibly hard and with some real discipline. It took me a while to develop those traits. [. . .] You need to learn how to teach and do research. I learned that this is hard work. It takes incredible time and discipline.

Two things changed my life. The first is that I started running, and eventually ran what was to be the first of many marathons over the next thirty years [starting in 1979]. Training for and then running a marathon is all about hard work and discipline. You cannot run a marathon based on the equivalent of an all-nighter, staying up all night cramming for the next day's exam or, in this case, race; you cannot get an extension or an incomplete for your shoddy preparation; you cannot finesse your way through the event with a winning smile and personality. You have to train every day for months and months and then really concentrate and perform on race day. I love the purity of it. Anyway, running changed my life.

Then, of course, Sue Ashford, my wife of now thirty plus years, changed my life too. I met her a year after my first marathon. Among her many fine qualities, I can say unequivocally that she did not need to run a marathon to learn the value of hard work and discipline. Of course, she has her own interesting story and compelling academic biography to tell, but suffice it to say that, when we met, she already knew all there was to know about discipline and hard work. She was, and still is, an inspiration and role model for what you can accomplish when you put your mind to something. She is incredible.

To the point about the importance of supportive networks of friends and families, Walsh adds:

Speaking of Sue, I need to make another obvious point here. There will be no heroes' journeys in this book of yours. No one does anything alone in this world. I am incredibly grateful to Sue and to so many others who have helped me on every step of my journey. I've mentioned some already. There are so many others. In fact, some of the people you profile in your book are among them.

Then there is the question of finding and staying in what Walsh calls 'the sweet spot.' Notwithstanding how important his 'make a better world' orientation is, Walsh found that he had to periodically take stock to keep from drifting away from that kind of aspiration.

For a curious person, research is incredibly seductive. Once you kinda sorta know what you are doing, the whole world opens up before you. You can ask and answer any question that pops into your head. You may start with a broad question – or maybe 'broad quest' is the better word – but, after a while, your questions can get narrower and narrower as you pursue them.

In his own journey, Walsh began by looking at how individual leaders' mental models blind them to the decision environment and harm the firm. Then he looked at group mental models and the psychology of influence around them, then broadened his perspective to organizational mind and memory, realizing:

On the one hand, it's great to see new questions open up right before your eyes, but, on the other hand, you can find yourself go deeper and deeper into, say, the world of psychology when you are ultimately motivated and trying to connect this work to the world of affairs – a world that recedes from view as you look at these other important questions. So, I moved to governance.

But the same thing happened there. I began by looking at what I thought was the most interesting agency theory prediction, that mergers and acquisitions pruned the world of managerial deadwood. Not finding real evidence to support that idea, I dug deeper and deeper. Before I knew it, I was looking at different kinds of restructuring activity and different kinds of financing arrangements. That is all fine, but I was going deeper and deeper into the world of governance and further and further away from what mattered to me in the first place. [. . .] Every now and again you have to ask yourself if you are doing what you really want to do. Just because you can do something doesn't mean that you should do it.

Hard as it might be to find that 'sweet spot,' the real challenge comes when you get there. You need to have something to say. Walsh tells two stories to illustrate how important it is to find what he calls 'voice.' One, as an editor, tells a vicarious lesson, and the other, as an author, tells a direct lesson.

> At the end of the day, scholars are supposed to have something to say, but, oddly enough, it took me a while to find my voice. I was so busy reading and chronicling the literature to document what others had already said about my topic that I could get lost trying to say what I wanted to say. I first saw this in others' writing when I served as an *AMR* [Academy of Management Review] associate editor. I can't tell you how many papers I saw that had loads of references, and even some boxes and arrows diagrams, but, honestly, I could not figure out what the author was trying to say. My job as editor was to help authors find their voices. It really helped to help others do that.
>
> My law review experience really helped me too. I love to read law review articles. They are, in essence, two papers. The work 'above the line' [above all the footnotes] is all about the author's point of view. That is where you find the author's argument, his or her voice. Then 'below the line' is where you find all of the detailed connections to past work and the references. The format forces you to establish a clear narrative in your paper. You need to say something. I'd like to think that I got a little better articulating my own voice over time. Of course, my reviewers and editors helped me do that too.

Learning to relate a story, a narrative, with an authorial 'voice' is an important element of the sensemaking process that intellectual shamans go through. Walsh articulates the relevance of that voice, and the difficulties that even very bright and articulate people can encounter in making the transition to using the voice that allows sensemaking to happen in both writing and teaching:

> You really do need to learn how to write with confidence. Even as you put your first word on paper, you know that everything you will say can and probably will be criticized. There will always be books and articles that you have not discovered, much less digested. There

will almost surely be alternative explanations and boundary conditions to identify. Learning how to articulate your point of view and write with some power takes some time, or, at least, it did for me.

He adds:

The same thing can happen in the classroom too, by the way. You can spend way too much time thinking about how you want the class to unfold, forgetting that in many ways teaching is all about sharing who you really are with your students.

Implicitly, Walsh recognizes the link between authentic voice, sensemaking, and the capacity to heal:

I want our students and, sure, even the colleagues we see every day to walk away from our time together with a sense of confidence that they can proactively engage the world and make a difference, even when our lives can be uncertain and even scary at times. I hope I have the humility to know that I don't have all these answers. But, for a fact, I know that we can help each other find them.

SENSEMAKING, LEADERSHIP, AND WISDOM

Spiritual leadership and sensemaking are part of what Nancy Adler calls the 'art of leadership,' which she defines as 'hope made real.'[131] Putting together intellectual shamans' capacity for systems understanding and moral imagination with their aesthetic sensibility that the world needs to be made right, we come to the idea of wisdom, to which we will return in Chapter 8.[60] Bob Giacalone's path toward this goal has been somewhat tortuous, though it allowed him to learn and grow, as all intellectual shamans must if they are to assume their spiritual leadership roles. The path to spiritual leadership, sensemaking, and wisdom means overcoming fear, finding authentic voice and self. It also involves creating new forms of understanding, and making linkages that others do not readily see. Giacalone's story also speaks to the power of not only finding voice but being authentic in saying what needs to be said, when that something makes connections others haven't made – and, fundamentally, makes sense of a difficult world.

Such sensemaking can also create connections among people, ideas, and the world that might not otherwise be made. Giacalone relates what happened after the paper on transcendent management education, discussed earlier, was accepted. At the annual meeting of the Academy of Management and the board meeting of the *Academy of Management Learning and Education* journal, where the paper was eventually published, he recalls:

> I walk in, and what was the *AMLE* editorial meeting had just ended. [The editor] walked up to another editor and said, 'This is the guy who wrote the paper I was telling you about.' I'm thinking, 'Wow! This is, like, very unexpected.' He sat there and just told me how much he loved the paper. As you know, and I know, you don't get that from editors very often. [. . .] Then he said something that was very interesting. He said, 'When I read the second draft of your paper, I cried.' I thought, 'Wow, wow!' – and, this was not an ego thing. It had nothing to do with 'Gee, I'm so wonderful.' It had to do with the fact there was an internal definition of how I saw the world that I brought out and that other people got. There's something affirming about that, not because it was a pat on the back but because someone out there understood. I think we live in the world where very often there's a degree of loneliness that we face, and for a minute that went away. You know, there was a connection.

Critically important, however, is not just the sense that the intellectual shaman can make of the world through his or her writing, teaching, and research, but the role that these things can play in shaping a better world. Giacalone articulates the power of sensemaking and its attendant spiritual leadership as he concludes his story:

> But, most importantly, I think that what happened there was I got to understand that it wasn't about me. The reason that people were responding was because I was not talking about me. I was talking

about something bigger. I was talking about a bigger picture and a bigger world view. There was something exciting about that, something exciting about 'less me, more you,' something wonderful about that... I understood that clearly: that success had nothing to do with me but a lot to do with us. That was a very pivotal moment when I made that realization.

The words of Ian Mitroff, reflecting the view of sensemaking, spiritual leadership, storytelling, and wisdom that we have been thinking about, close this chapter. Mitroff, who has extensively studied the relationship of spirituality to management and business, talks about his roots in pragmatism in ways that are evocative of spirituality in the sense of the search for ultimate purpose, meaning in life, and wisdom. In doing so, he also articulates the role of spiritual leadership on the part of the intellectual shaman:

> Pragmatism is the definition of truth; truth is that which makes a difference in the quality of one's life. It makes an ethical difference. So, in pragmatism, truth and ethics are inseparable. [...] Truth is not something in a journal, but [something that] makes a difference, an ethical difference, whatever your theory of ethics. [...] In pragmatism, the true, the good, and [the] beautiful are inseparable.

Taking these ideas into practice, Mitroff continues, explicitly discussing sensemaking in organizations, such as mental hospitals, in which, instead of curing patients, the setting can actually exacerbate symptoms. He notes:

> It's like reading the psychodynamics of mental hospitals, where actually they can intensify the symptoms of the patients who are incarcerated. So you've got to really understand, and then formulate in as non-threatening way as you can. So, when I talk to clients, I have to modulate anger, and have to be very patient, and proceed very slowly and gingerly, and take a lot of time, build up trust, confidence. Because there are too many barriers that you have to get through, and the fear and the anxiety are so great that you can be

kicked out at any time. I've been kicked out because I've gone too quickly to push buttons. I've learned that you have to be firm but gentle, firm but supportive. You have to be understanding. There are only people struggling to get through the mess of everyday life.

As he puts these ideas together, and making the link to spirituality, leadership, and wisdom explicit, Mitroff adds:

It's a different mission, to put it mildly (to use that term); it's a different spiritual mission. The point is, in today's world, you need high cognitive, emotional, spiritual [capacities], you need multiple IQs, and that's what we need to develop as leaders. We need leaders who are developed as best we can in organizations that are really, really developed along multiple interdependent dimensions facets of reality and humanity.

7 The *intellectual* shaman

The aim of art is to represent not the outward appearance of things, but their inward significance.

Aristotle

INTELLECTUALS AND SHAMANS, AFTER ALL

In previous chapters, we have investigated shamanism – what it means to be a shaman. If we are to talk about *intellectual* shamanism, however, we also need to think about what the first word – 'intellectual' – means and implies in a context of intellectual shamanism. Here we explore the nature of the work that intellectual shamans do within management disciplines. While the particular work would differ depending on the nature of the discipline of the intellectual, I would argue that intellectual shamanism can exist within any discipline. It can also exist outside specific disciplines, as it tends to be transdisciplinary. This chapter focuses on the intellectual aspects – the work – of intellectual shamanism as it is exhibited by management scholars.

An intellectual fundamentally can be described as someone who uses the mind creatively, or, as Wikipedia defines the term, uses intelligence in either a professional or individual capacity. A list of synonyms for the noun 'intellectual' comes up with numerous examples. These synonyms include, among others: alchemist, *bel esprit* (a witty or clever person with a fine mind), exponent (someone who interprets or explains), mentor, doubter or skeptic, synthesizer, theorist, student, scholar, thinker, creative thinker, illusionist, seer, visionary, wonderer, and wise and trusted guide and advisor. As shaman, the intellectual is a sort of alchemist – another synonym – who is, in a sense, trying to turn straw into gold. The intellectual shaman, that is, takes the straw of theories, practices, and research approaches that do not work as well as they might and attempts to convert them into something that does work, works better, or suits its time and context better.[1n]

Aside from the sometimes negative connotations occasionally applied to intellectuals in some societies (particularly, perhaps, the United States) – i.e., as eggheads, brainiacs, highbrows, and the like – most of the synonyms have positive connotations that well describe the work of intellectual shamanism. Intellectuals are frequently, though not always, academics, though the terms are not synonymous. A. C. Grayling has written about the difference between academics and intellectuals. Grayling argues that 'curricula go stale without [the] enquiry' that is associated with research and thinking. He also critiques modern academia's emphasis on rankings and specialization as potentially killing the life of broad inquiry, curiosity, and transdisciplinarity that is needed for true intellectuals to thrive – and that intellectual shamans thrive on. Reflecting on the 'corporatization' of the university, in 1997, Grayling argues:

> For if providing liberal education remains part of the university's task, the need remains for scholars who are also intellectuals – as creative, inspired and engaged in the connections between their callings and the wider world, as are the members of that main body of intellectuals who choose literature, the arts, journalism and life outside the university. In the new climate of research ratings, the cultivation of intellectual virtues, and the organic rather than forced pace of enquiry, is discounted. So the intellectual scholar, a person occupying a place apart, is a rarer creature now, even though there are many more universities. And that is because the universities are no longer genuinely Sunday places in the social fabric, fostered for the value they might produce, and permitted to be answerable to their own high standards as communities of minds. By industrialising the university and measuring it by the same criteria as govern Monday's world, the idea of a place apart, for reflection and the cultivation of intellect, becomes increasingly lost to view.[138]

Even earlier, Noam Chomsky had written about the 'responsibility of intellectuals' in *The New York Review of Books*. Writing in 1967 in the context of the Vietnam War, Chomsky notes the seeming truism, now often sadly 'not so,' that '[i]t is the responsibility of intellectuals to speak the truth and expose lies,'[139] while – like Grayling – noting the pathologies of the then emerging 'scientific' approach to the social sciences. For Chomsky, that meant that some controversial and emotion-laden ideas seem to have become 'simply unthinkable, unworthy of consideration. More accurately, these possibilities are inexpressible; the categories in which they are formulated (honesty, indignation) simply do not exist for the tough-minded social scientist,' who is following norms that Chomsky labels 'pseudo-scientific posing [that] reaches levels that are almost pathological.'[139]

Writing explicitly about public intellectuals in 2013, Grayling attempts to capture a definition that encompasses the breadth of the term – and, I believe, also captures some of the essence of the intellectual element of intellectual shamanism. Taking as public intellectuals people such as Norman Mailer, Susan Sontag, and Noam Chomsky, among others, Grayling concludes, 'They have very little in common other than intelligence and engagement, and the fact that they speak out. These three things, accordingly, might be taken to capture the essence.'[140] These characteristics – intelligence, engagement, and speaking out – also characterize the intellectual shamans, albeit sometimes the speaking out is within discipline-based and academic circles rather than in more public venues, in the sense of attempting to influence public policy or the public conversation, as Grayling would have it.

In this chapter, I explore the work that is associated with intellectual shamanism within the management disciplines. Obviously, the work of intellectual shamans will vary in nature depending on the disciplines involved, but I am hopeful that some general sense of what it is that *intellectual* shamans do in management may guide understanding of a more general phenomenon of intellectual shamanism in different disciplines. Arguably, intellectual shamans differ from traditional academics, who may not have the breadth of interests and curiosity, engagement, or willingness to speak out that intellectual shamans have, whether they actively serve as public intellectuals or not.

The work of intellectual shamans does not generally follow today's expected academic script of making small twists on existing academic theory or empirical work, or trying to find 'gaps' in the literature that can be reasonably readily resolved conceptually or empirically. Instead, intellectual shamans are academically entrepreneurial, intensely curious, and generally, though not always, interested in what are called 'wicked problems.' Through their roles as healers, described in Chapter 4, they also evidence healing and common good orientations. Intellectual shamans thus have a tendency to pioneer ideas or new ways of thinking and doing the work of the management intellectual in their fields. Simultaneously they bridge across multiple 'worlds' (notable in the connecting role discussed in Chapter 5). Thus, their work tends to be systemic and holistic, transdisciplinary, and multi-level or multi-sector. They are characterized by a seemingly insatiable intellectual curiosity and desire for constant learning, persistent in pursuing their own instincts and interests, yet are frequently quite humble about their own contributions. Further, as the sensemaking role articulates, they evidence a need to make sense of the world as they see it, often interpreting it for others.

Below we look at three notable characteristics of the scholarly work of intellectual shamans: an orientation toward what are known as wicked problems, unasked questions, or new framings of old questions that have the potential to shift existing paradigms, rather than what Thomas Kuhn has called normal science;[62] a pioneering/intellectual and risk-taking orientation that is future-oriented; and a systemic, holistic, and humanistic approach to much of their work.

SYSTEMIC, HOLISTIC, AND HUMANISTIC

As must be obvious by now, much of the work of intellectual shamans is systemically and holistically oriented, and frequently crosses disciplinary boundaries. Further, there is a humanistic underpinning that surfaces in much of their work because of the ways in which it addresses bigger questions facing humanity that are associated with healing – i.e., the service to something beyond the self that can be conceived as some form of the greater good. We have already seen this systemic, holistic, and multidisciplinary approach discussed in the work of scholars such as Dave Brown, Paul Shrivastava, Jane Dutton, Bob Quinn, and Stuart Hart, among others.

For individuals intrigued by unasked or unanswered questions, curiosity combines with an insatiable desire to learn, passion, and systems understanding. For individuals such as the intellectual shamans, systemic problems are what complexity theorists call natural attractors (in physics, they are called strange attractors). David Cooperrider's words highlight exactly this type of attraction, while also providing a rationale for his healing orientation. Cooperrider, thinking about challenges in his early work to develop appreciative inquiry, emphasizes his holistic approach and a positive future orientation, and previews the orientation toward wisdom to be discussed in Chapter 8:

> The biggest challenge I faced early on was the sense that if we're not studying what's wrong with the human systems then we're being Pollyanna-ish, and we're turning our eye from a troubled world. The sense that I had at the time was that, no, the study of the true, the good, the better, the possible is going to be exactly what we need to create, kind of, the capacity for transcending those issues that people are so concerned about.

Appreciative inquiry, like many of the ideas of intellectual shamans, takes a different tack from simply solving problems. Instead, it has a future-looking inclination that attempts to move toward something new – a different way of viewing the future that could result in a positive-sum game or win-win, rather than simply fixing what is broken. Evidencing the curiosity and constant learning that characterizes intellectual shamanism, Cooperrider continues:

One of the challenges has been to hold a position that says that there is another way [than applied science] and it requires another theory of change. That change is not just about moving from a negative two to a zero, but there could be another kind of change dynamic that moves from a plus two to a plus twenty, to a plus 200. Kind of saying, 'OK, I want to take that perspective to its logical conclusion.'

When I sat down with [management thinker] Peter Drucker shortly before he passed away, he wanted to hear all about the logic of appreciative inquiry and the experiences we were having into how inquiry into life creates change. At the end of that conversation I said to him, 'But, Peter, you've written more about leading and change and entrepreneurship and good leadership than anybody in history. Can you put it in a nutshell?' He said, 'David, it's easy. The task of leadership is to create an alignment of strengths in ways that make a system's weaknesses irrelevant.'

Like many of the intellectual shamans, Cooperrider took the nugget that Drucker offered as a seed for thinking about the nature of appreciative inquiry work and growing that work. It is this capacity for intellectual generativity that characterizes much of the work of intellectual shamanism. Cooperrider elaborates:

I took that down and underlined 'irrelevant.' 'The task is to create an alignment of strengths in ways that make a system's weaknesses irrelevant.' Well, what a curious phrase: 'make it irrelevant'! That leads to all kinds of questions, like: OK, for a positive theory of change, why would strength connected to strength propel change? We know that strengths perform, but the idea that strengths transform – well, what does that mean in terms of the elevation of strengths and working new configurations of strengths and new combination effects of strengths? We didn't have a good language for this kind of change that moves from a plus two to a plus twenty to a plus 2,000.

Cooperrider reflects a similar learning orientation in one of three meetings he had with the Dalai Lama. During the last session, which included business leaders, Cooperrider asked the Dalai Lama how he would change business schools for the twenty-first century if anything were possible. Cooperrider relates the insight and his own learning from what the Dalai Lama offered, particularly around the need for a more holistic perspective in leaders and managers:

> The Dalai Lama was humbled by the question, I think, in some ways. He scratched his head and said, 'Management. Well, management. First of all, let me just say that I can't manage a thing. If I were to try and manage things, I would mess it all up.' He was laughing and saying to the business leaders, 'You guys, this is your field; you know a lot more about this than I do.' But then he went into this tremendous discourse and conversation around the need for a radical reorientation from our preoccupation with the self to our concern for the other, and for a view that recognizes this fundamental human relatedness, this fundamental interdependence of all of life.
>
> I came away from that realizing that *that's* what our management schools need to be about in a leadership sense: about a reawakening to this fundamental interdependence, this fundamental intimacy of all relatedness, to all of life, and to reawaken that sense of how special a gift that is. When we do that, it changes management education; it changes the language of corporate social responsibility, for example.

Typically, this insight applies far more broadly. Cooperrider illustrates this breadth in continuing to make connections to related areas of study and interest. Indeed, he takes a holistic approach, making what can only be called a spiritual link to his own work of appreciative inquiry:

> In one of the sessions I did with executives in Brazil, I was talking with them, and they were saying that good management for the future needs to take responsibility for the whole. We were using this language of corporate responsibility, responsibility for the whole.

One of the executives said, 'This language of responsibility for the whole isn't right. What happens if we replace the word "responsibility" for the whole with "intimacy" with the whole?' I thought a lot about that, and [realized] that's getting at what I think. We need to reawaken that fundamental intimacy with the whole, that it's irreducible, that it's the foundational starting point. When you start thinking about the intimacy with the whole, think about how just even the language – how different that is than responsibility for the whole. It invites a different kind of conscious relationship when you see that fundamental intimacy or interdependence with the whole. So I think that's a really important agenda for schools of leadership and management.

Recognition of these interdependencies is common in the work of intellectual shamanism. Indeed, acknowledging both the whole and the interdependencies among elements of the whole is core to holistic or systems thinking. Raj Sisodia, for example, places his perspective on the emergence of conscious capitalism in the broader perspective provided by an historical and developmentally based lens. Sisodia explains the emergence of some of the ideas associated with conscious capitalism, a holistic and still relatively novel approach to business, as follows:

Conscious capitalism is a logical part of our journey as humans towards higher consciousness in all things. In some areas more than others, but in general, we are becoming more conscious about what's right, what's wrong. We are becoming fully awake. We're recognizing all the impacts of our actions. We are understanding the long-term consequences, and we're starting to adapt to that.

In the domain of business, for too long we have accepted some of these narrow ways of thinking. Really, these were sort of foisted on business and capitalism by the critics of capitalism. The very word 'capitalism' comes from Karl Marx. It was used as a pejorative. Economists came in and they took that idea of pursuing self-interest just to make their mathematical models work. They said, 'OK, business is simply about maximizing profits.' When you have that kind of single objective function, you can create elegant models, so those got written into textbooks and taught, and businesspeople started to learn those in college. Then they started to think in that way.

Sisodia places this thinking into a developmental context to illustrate how ideas about self-interest and greed in economic and business thinking have supplanted more humanistic ways of thinking about business, humanity, and society. He continues, highlighting the negative role that economics-based thinking plays, while also noting the positive developments that businesses have brought to many societies. In thinking about the system as a whole, Sisodia also recognizes the interconnectedness that exists among various aspects of societies with respect to sustainability:

[This perspective on economics] became sort of a self-fulfilling prophecy. Yet it was deeply lacking, because economics is such a rich, multidimensional human undertaking. To reduce it down was very harmful, [along with] notions of selfishness as a virtue. Selfishness can never be a virtue. Self-interest is different from selfishness, likewise 'greed is good,' etc. All the [ideas], like the 'invisible hand' hypothesis, are used to justify 'greed is good,' to selfishness [being] good, etc. – all of those things. [This perspective] ultimately became self-defeating, where businesspeople essentially conceded the argument that business is inherently selfish and self-serving, but basically said, 'Well, yeah, because of the invisible hand it works. So, it's OK for us to be selfish and greedy. That ultimately works out for everybody.'

So [selfishness] became a necessary evil in the minds of many, including those who practiced it. There's sort of a lower level, almost of self-esteem, associated with [such economics-based thinking]. Intellectuals and others always look down on business in every society, almost, around the world. Minorities that were very good at business were kind of persecuted and not respected. Yet, if you step back and look at the impact that business has had on the world, especially modern capitalism in corporate form, in the last two centuries, it's been quite dramatic, of course. Also, per capita income and all of those kinds of things, [including] life expectancy, after being flat for thousands of years, shot up in the last two centuries. However, it happened at the expense of many other things, because we didn't recognize the interconnectedness and all the resource issues, the land issues, the water, consequences on the environment. But now that our consciousness has been raised in those domains, I think we are capable of figuring out how to gain the benefits of this without actually having the devastating impact and the unsustainable long-term impact on the planet.

As with Cooperrider's perspective, Sisodia's view of his work verges on the explicitly spiritual. He reflects on the core purpose of businesses through the lens of conscious capitalism. Sisodia provides insight for creating not only meaningful businesses by applying a holistic lens – but also a meaningful life:

One of the books that really was transformational for me was Viktor Frankl's *Man's Search for Meaning*, which I was given by a friend at the age of fifty, three or four years ago. I wish I had discovered that book when I was fifteen. I thought it was a really impactful, transformational way to think about life, and that happiness cannot be pursued. Happiness ensues. It's the outcome of living a life of meaning and purpose; all the things about that are incredibly powerful. I've made that kind of a centerpiece also of my work in this domain of conscious capitalism. Just like human beings pursue happiness, businesses pursue profit. But profit cannot be pursued. Profit ensues. That's the outcome of the exact same things: living a life of meaning and purpose, or having a higher purpose as a business; and loving without condition, building a business on love and care; and the third is finding meaning in suffering, which is, basically, growing from adversity. So those principles to me apply exactly in the world of business.

Sisodia elaborates, further exploring the purpose of business – and also his own growing awareness of the spiritual nature of his intellectual pursuits:

> For example, I taught strategy for twenty years, marketing strategy, but strategy in general, without using the word 'purpose.' Never occurred to me. If it had occurred to me or somebody had asked me, I would say, 'Well, the purpose is to make money. That's the purpose.' The purpose of business is to make money, so you don't need to ask that question. Now you just figure out how to make it. That's the strategy. Now I realize how hollow that is. The money is the outcome. So, unless you have that guiding purpose as, sort of, that animating spirit, it's like a machine. What makes a machine come alive is really that soul, that spirit. That's their purpose. In a way, for me, I think I came alive around that time, because I suddenly discovered some kind of animating purpose. Before that I was just going through the motions.

These ideas also reflect, importantly, on leadership, as well as leadership development, as Sisodia explains:

> So, you cannot have a conscious business without a conscious leader. It starts with that. So the first thing is about raising consciousness of leaders, and that's a big challenge in and of itself. Part of it says, when you select people to be leaders, you must look for certain attributes and traits, but then, unlike intellectual IQ, emotional and spiritual intelligence can be grown, can be enhanced. It requires intentionality and a willingness to learn and grow. So we need people who are continuously learning and growing and evolving. Conscious capitalism is about bringing the highest level of consciousness to the world of business, so it's a living organism that we are creating now. It's a self-organizing, self-managing, self-feeling and learning organization, or organism. How do we create the conditions in which it continues to grow and evolve on its own, including the people that are within it?

A similarly broad form of questioning characterizes the work of Tima Bansal, who is addressing questions of the foundational paradigm that shapes modern businesses operating in a global context in which sustainability issues threaten the future of humanity. Shaping her own work holistically and openly acknowledging the moral imperative to shape a better world that fuels her interest, Bansal reflects on the challenges that her broad perspective on issues of sustainability, growth, and business present:

> What's wrong with the business paradigm? Everything about the business paradigm is fueling this tragedy of the commons. It's not just, as Garrett Harding wrote in the '60s, about a common space. Our common space now is the Earth – a tragedy of the Earth. I can't in good conscious anymore go into a classroom or spend my days researching issues or ideas that will propagate more growth. As a strategy person, what we care about most is profits and growth. I can't do that anymore. I can't in good conscious feel good about that. So, what I hope to do, then, is to understand organizations, and it's still very much subscribed to business and organization. I'm not anti-business. I just don't think that the business goal that we have right now is a foundation on which we can build a set of prescriptions that will lead to a better society, whereas it did hold true in the 1960s, or '40s, or '30s. When the economy was first being developed it did make sense at that time. It doesn't make sense now under a new set of resource constraints. It's our obligation as academics to fill those gaps.

Bansal gives a sense of how her vision of a better world has grown in scale and scope as she has struggled to deal with the issue of sustainability with respect to the current business paradigm. She also notes the need for multidisciplinarity as the complexity of the issue itself grows, and for including important dimensions into management thinking that are not currently addressed well – or at all, in some cases. She once again highlights the need for like-minded others to fully develop the work:

Where I want this to go is finding a new paradigm for business. I don't think I can do that. I'm not doing that alone but as a collective. [...] Even the research that I'm doing right now – it started as institutional theory and a resource-based view [of the firm], but what I'm doing now is looking at the dimensions of time and space – or 'scale,' I guess, is a better word. Time and scale, because I think that those are really critical in business, and they're almost completely absent.

Even the word 'sustainability' is about time. Very simply, it is that one looks at how time has manifested in organizations, strategy, or finance, or whatever it might be, by discounting time. So we actually [typically] discount the future, whereas sustainability is actually valuing the future so that future generations can live the same lifestyle that we do. There's immediately a paradox. What I think we need to do is to introduce time, but explicitly, in organizational decisions beyond just discounting it. Price is actually an indicator. Certain price erases time. I think the market mechanism is actually the culprit. It doesn't mean that we get rid of markets, but I think that we have to introduce time dimensions into markets that don't already exist. Then we started looking at time-based compression, ...how globalization and financial markets are leading to the accelerated compression of time and space.

Then there's the scale aspect to it. As organizations get bigger and bigger, their scale gets so enormous that we can create changes that defy our ability to resolve them. [...] So organizations need to match the scale of the issue, the environmental resource issue. These are very different concepts than the concepts that we often think about in business. I don't even know what the touch points are to current theories, but I do know that there are theories within geography and biology and ecology that help us out a lot. And I think that they can inform business.

The systemic, holistic, and multidisciplinary approach used by intellectual shamans is often made necessary because much of the work of intellectual shamans tends to be pioneering, as I discuss below.

PIONEERING, RISK-TAKING, AND ENTREPRENEURIAL

In addition to its holistic, systemic, multidisciplinary nature, the intellectual work of intellectual shamans also tends to be oriented toward new ideas, rather than simply rehashing old ones or making small twists on an existing body of work. There is, then, a pioneering element in at least the more recognized work of these individuals. Of course, some of their papers and studies do follow more of what Kuhn calls normal science than what he terms paradigm-shifting.[62] But, on the whole, the body of work – or, at least, the work most recognized and applauded – that intellectual shamans produce leans more toward paradigm-shifting work than normal science. As a consequence, their work tends to be somewhat academically entrepreneurial, risk-taking, and sometimes pioneering.

David Cooperrider's work on appreciative inquiry exemplifies all three of these aspects of the work of intellectual shamans. He recalls attempting to introduce ideas about appreciative inquiry at the Academy of Management meeting, at which management scholars gather annually:

> When I first started talking about appreciative inquiry in a 1984 talk at the Academy of Management, it was hard to speak about the positive in organizational life. We were embedded [in] and dominated by psychology, for example, [in which] out of the last 44,000 journal articles in the field of psychology 98.9 percent were on human defects, human deficiency, what's wrong with the human beings – studies of anger and fear and co-dependency and anorexia and so on. Less than 2 percent of our studies had to do with human strengths and human capacities, like 'What good are positive emotions, like hope and inspiration and joy?'
>
> When I was doing this talk at the Academy, I raised the question: what happens to our inquiry if we shift our root metaphors? On the one hand, we could say we had the image that organizations at their root are problems to be solved. Or we might say that organizations as

living human systems are miracles of human existence, that we don't have explanation of what gives life to living human collection organizational systems. When I said that we could shift from the world as a problem to organizational life as a miracle or mystery, people laughed. Maybe it came across as awkward, or maybe I said it funny, but to begin to imagine that organizations should be treated with that respect as centers of almost a sacred expression of what we're capable of a human being – people thought it was a joke, and they laughed. I didn't know why they were laughing. So I just kept on going.

Consider the risk that Cooperrider took in putting this perspective forward to a largely unreceptive audience. His perspective was novel and had the potential to shatter the dominant strain of thinking about organizations in ways that were unfamiliar and that listeners were, apparently, not ready to accept. Recall that her early whistle-blowing led to threats on Judi Neal's life. Not all risks taken by intellectual shamans are life-threatening, as Neal's were, though, occasionally, there are other types of very real risks. Defying the long-held (though collapsing) 'standard' that management research is a science that is completely objective, some academics openly acknowledge their own role in the research process and walk the tightrope between the discovery and creation of new knowledge by spanning the boundary between practice and scientific rigor. In these pursuits they resemble the others who work at the interstices between organizational types, or within enterprises and contrary to 'type' – individuals known in circles beyond academia by different names.

MIT's John Van Maanen's early work – work that has continued for much of his career – was based on his participant observation of the police training academy and later the work of police. After actually going through the police training academy, Van Maanen recognized his affiliation with what he terms 'hoi polloi on the ground' rather than the managers with whom most other scholars in his field were interested. He was particularly interested in doing his pathbreaking work on police officers (or 'cops,' as he calls them), at a time when there was not much interest in the subject or in his preferred research method, ethnography. At one point Van Maanen was almost sent to jail as a result of his research. He tells the story as follows, in talking about obstacles in his work:

> I've had a lot of people probably watching my back. Sure, I almost went to jail over a suit that was filed in Seattle in my police work, where I was present to a beating. A newspaper picked it up and reported it. I was friends with the reporter. The reporter then told the grand jury that was investigating the case, or the reporter wrote a profile of this incident. It was called a Skid Row Squad of police, and happened to be the squad I was with. The reporter then was sued by the police for defamation of character by the police union. The reporter said, 'Well, no, this is a truthful account, and Professor Van Maanen was there.' Actually, there's a paper of mine called 'The moral fix' that sort of gives the details of this, but the court then subpoenaed me to appear and to bring all my field notes and all my tapes..., of interviews, and turn it over to the court.

Taking a stand that required significant courage and risk, Van Maanen refused to turn his data over. He remembers:

> I said, 'No'; I wouldn't do that. I would be happy to testify, but I wouldn't turn over any of my research material. They then turned around and filed a criminal contempt of court charge against me. That was where the case was, and I was defended by the American Sociological Association and MIT lawyers. They all said, 'Look, you're not going to win this.' I don't know what I'd have done, but, as it turned out, the cops...asked for preliminary judgment from the district court judge in Seattle, and the preliminary judgment was that they didn't have a case. So it became moot, and they stopped coming after me. That was a little scary...

Thinking about the value of ethnographic or participant observation research, Van Maanen believes that much work that is considered pathbreaking is actually based, as his own work is, on experience and observation; the 'scientific' norms of the academy mean this experience base is disguised in the interests of 'objectivity.' The result is that, as Van Maanen says, 'everything is generalized. [...] It's all acontextual. And I find that unfortunate.'

Taking strong stands, as Van Maanen did, demands self-knowledge and self-confidence, and no small degree of courage. Another MIT professor, Otto Scharmer, is explicit about what is needed for risk-taking of the sort that he has done in his career, with the development of what he calls 'theory U,' a theory of large-scale as well as individual and group change, and in following a career path that is not that of the typical academic. A senior lecturer at MIT, rather than a tenure track faculty member, Scharmer took a risk in moving from Germany to MIT without a future track and knowing that he would have to fund his own position.

Discussing some of the important 'places' that represent significant life episodes, Scharmer mentions the innovative and unusual university he attended. There, a group of professors who were unsatisfied with the pace of reform in universities and the first class of fourteen students, among them Scharmer, collaboratively developed the curriculum. Perhaps more importantly, they jointly created the intellectual space that challenged and allowed for growth. Recalling this experience, Scharmer notes:

> That was the greatest thing on Earth, because, basically, the dean says, 'OK, so this is student-centric learning. So it's on you guys now. So these are the principles. And you basically kind of dream up your own stuff, and we support you in that. Just go out and make it happen.' [...] That was a great opportunity for me, that life gave to me, because, yes, I would have loved to have, kind of, maybe more famous faculty members there, and some of them came in there as visiting faculty and so on, What was the most valuable in this university time is to have the opportunity ourselves, that, basically, by being handed a blank slate, there is no history, [and there were]

very high expectations, very high visibility, like key people from industry watching you, and from the critical part of the intellectual community; and then go out, do it.

Explaining the impact this experience had on him, and his ability to take future intellectual and life risks, Scharmer says:

This was so empowering for me, because before that I had the same intentions, but I was in a public system where no one was really interested in doing anything different. I'm still the same person, but now I'm in a context, in a place, where everything that I dreamed of, that I thought a university should look like, suddenly was very relevant. So that was a huge gift for me.

Scharmer tells a similar story that reflects his risk-taking and entrepreneurial spirit in relating how he came to be at MIT, not in a traditional tenure track faculty position but, rather, as senior lecturer funding his own position:

So, in my dissertation I read [Peter Senge's book] *The Fifth Discipline* and other articles from [Edgar] Schein and [William] Isaacs [his work on dialogue] and so on. They all came out of what was then the MIT Learning Center. I thought, 'That's the place I want to go. That's where I see the new stuff happening. That's where I see the possibility to create something new. It's applied, it's practical. It's intellectually novel, to some degree. It also is relevant to the main challenges that we have. There's a feeling that you can bring in some elements of deeper humanity there.' [...]

When I interviewed here at MIT they said, 'We like what you do, but we're in a hiring freeze. So we can't pay you a thing. Could you get your own funding?' I was in a situation where I was already maxed out with my credit cards. I needed to pay back my student loans. I had good offers in Germany, but I thought, 'That's really what I want to do.' That's what my heart told me. So I, of course, said 'Yes,' and thought, 'Well, somehow I will figure this out.' Then, of course, it turned out to be the gateway to how I developed the first interview project. So, . . .this risk-taking certainly also applies to my own path, but, if I think about it, for me it never felt like blind risk-taking.

For me it had to do with confidence. For example, what made me very confident, saying 'Yes'? They ask you, 'Can you bring your own funding?' I said 'Yes' because I had the confidence it would work out. The reason why I had the confidence is that throughout my student years I had taken similar risks, and it always worked, when you put your full mind into it. I was working very closely with the dean, the founding dean of the Witten/Herdecke University, and I watched how he moved into the new entrepreneurial situation, and how he had the confidence to say 'Yes' to something where I knew he didn't have the answer yet. I saw that he was very relaxed and confident in that, and it always worked out.

So, in coming to MIT with relatively uncertain prospects compared to many faculty, Scharmer gained – and took – the freedom to follow his own instincts about the work he needed to do. For him, the risks involved made sense, as he explains:

For me, what looks like risk-taking from the outside from the inside really has to do with confidence, and with being acutely aware. Kind of connected with your inner sources of knowing, and being really attentive to what happens in your environment and to the doors that are opening up, and to connecting with them.

Others of the intellectual shamans also took significant risks in their careers, both in terms of how they lived their lives and conceptually. We have already seen how Dave Brown, for example, made significant career jumps simply to follow his interests or his heart, and Marc Epstein has done much the same thing over the course of his career. This passion for pioneering work and willingness to take risks also is reflected in the content of the work of the intellectual shamans. Take Brown as a case in point. Brown served as executive director of the Institute for Development Research, which he jointly ran with his wife, Jane Covey, for twenty years while at Boston University, before he left his full-professor position there to join the Hauser Center at Harvard Kennedy School. The IDR tackled large-scale change issues, such as helping the World Bank attempt to change public enterprises, and with the World Health Organization to reorganize ministries of public health. Then the IDR began developing case studies of non-governmental organizations working on empowerment to build local capacity for decision-making. Highlighting, as many of the intellectual shamans do, the sense of being 'lucky,' or in the right place at the right time, as well as a willingness to take a chance on opportunities and what psychologist Carl Jung would have called synchronicities that presented themselves (also characteristic of intellectual shamans), Brown recalls:

> What were we learning from these NGOs that went against sort of the traditional wisdom in OD [organization development]? It turned out there was a lot. So we began to develop a set of ideas about how...you work with NGOs, development NGOs, to build their capacity, and how that differed from standard OD. Not by good management, but mostly by good luck, just about the time that we were beginning to publish some of this stuff USAID [the leading US government aid agency] decided they needed to get into the organizational capacity-building of NGOs. They started looking around for who knew something about this. Well, it turns out that's a small cell in the matrix. There were very few people that knew anything about it, and we had published some stuff, and they said, 'Oh, let's talk to these folks.' So we began to get some [US]AID contracts to do this stuff.
>
> About the same time we got a Ford grant to run a program for leaders of Asian NGOs. Basically, the idea was to bring two or three key leaders from NGOs in six Asian countries to Boston for a month to talk about their strategies, to talk about their relations with donors and agencies like the World Bank or USAID, to talk about leadership, their personal leadership development, and to talk about

the evolution of the civil society in their countries. So we brought people from India, Bangladesh, Sri Lanka, Indonesia, Thailand and the Philippines. For five years, once a year, we'd have a month-long program with these leaders.

This somewhat opportunistic risk-taking led to pioneering insights for Brown and Covey in the development arena. In addition, the link to actual on-the-ground experiences and practice that shaped his research was central.

> Now, that had a number of impacts. One is, we learned a lot about the challenges facing those NGOs. We also built relations with key players that continue today. All of a sudden, IDR was connected in Asia in a way that few other organizations were. We began to amass this sense of what...it take[s] to do strategy for various different things. That worked; the funding from [US]AID got us connected with US international NGOs, and we were also connected through this project with the Ford project with the national ones. Then, in south Asia, we got a grant from Ford India to start working on how...the sector evolve[s], what...it take[s] to have a strong civil society as a whole in a country.

Taking advantage of this chain of circumstances, combined with hard work and a willingness to continue learning in a context of uncertainty, provided the grounding for doing pioneering research work of the sort that few others, at the time, were tackling. Brown explored his strategy, such as it was, in pursuing these lines of inquiry with respect to his work in the IDR. His willingness to allow the ideas to emerge as they needed was necessary to do this type of pioneering work.

> IDR was an organization that brought together a bunch of people who shared a set of values and engaged each other in building ideas that were highly relevant to a number of issues. The fact that Jane and I built it together, and that it was the two of us, plus a bunch of other people who were fellow travellers, was really [what made it] an

exciting project. We had no idea what we were doing! We were making it up as we went along all the way. We were almost always out on the edge of our competence, and frequently way the f**k over the edge. I could identify some ideas that got generated out of that that then had implications down the road and got picked up and developed and so on. IDR was partly ideas, but it was also very much relationships and engagement, and part a process, I guess.

This process of discovery is what many theorists today would call coevolution: working with clients and others to coevolve ideas in an action-learning setting, rather than going into the setting with pre-existing ideas to test out. Brown elaborates on the process that allowed new insights and ideas to emerge:

One of the things that we found ways to do was co-invent a lot of ideas with other people. Just for example, we did this project on scaling up the impact of NGOs in collaboration with a couple of associates, one of them at Brown and one of them in India, and eight Indian NGOs that one way or another had had impact way, way beyond their size and resources in India. We did case studies of those NGOs and brought them all together to have a conference about what [was] really important here. The resulting paper built on some work that [Brown University's] Peter Uvin had done, but it also built on the work of all those people to take a new look at these issues and identify a new paradigm for understanding what was going on out there.[141] It was a very exciting process to see these happen.

Brown had numerous similar experiences over the course of his career, as he reflects being constantly on the edge of chaos:

This [approach] was taking practice and turning it into ideas that then go back to affect the practice. So there was this kind of interchange that nobody knew where it was going to come out. It was a long way from controlled experiments. But it ended up influencing the participants in the process, some of whom were predominantly practitioners and went out and practiced in a different way, and some of them were predominantly academics, and who went out and 'academized' in a different way.

Curious, passionate, boundary-spanners with a thirst for learning, inspired by new ideas, knowledge, new ways of thinking, and experiences, intellectual shamans enjoy learning for its own sake as well as its potential for making a difference in the world. Much of their work seems fueled by a curiosity that leads them to work at the edges of existing knowledge, exploring new territory, rather than delving more deeply into what is already known. Just a few examples of this intense curiosity help illustrate how it results in work that is, from external perspectives, often considered pathbreaking or pioneering. Tima Bansal discusses the insatiable curiosity that has driven her interest in tough questions:

> Inspiration... There's this intellectual curiosity. I think everybody has their strengths. My strengths are probably that I tend to be analytical; that's also a weakness, but I'm really curious to the point that I used to drive my parents crazy, asking 'Why?' I really am always curious about how things work, and so another aspect of my work is I like working with junior scholars, because they have this curiosity that's not dogmatic. It's more creative. I love being with people who are asking questions and trying to answer them, and not motivated by the pragmatic outcomes but are more motivated by just really good conversations.

Paul Shrivastava reflects a similar passionate sense of curiosity, which has resulted in the innovative bent to his work, and currently fires his foray into the relationship between art and management. This curiosity leads to a multidisciplinary orientation, because, as is well known but not always practiced in academia, real issues and problems are not bounded by disciplines. As Shrivastava notes below:

> I would say that a good general handle on my motivation is this intellectual quality. I don't know where I got this from, but I feel intensely curious about things, and I'm not satisfied by answers that

come from, sort of, dogmatic, discipline-bound [ways of thinking]. I find those to be limiting of questioning [sic]. I try to just pursue the next step. OK, maybe it's not in our field, but this question needs to be answered, and opens up some new areas. It takes time to learn enough about that new area to make sense of it, but, to me, that is very gratifying, because my intellectual frame expands and I feel this is a kind of maturing, especially with age, and I found it very, very worthwhile.

This strategy of constant learning and expanding the boundaries of interest to satisfy curiosity has the potential to open up new lines of thinking – in conjunction with the tenacity needed to so such work when it seems only a few people are interested in a topic. The University of Michigan's Kim Cameron illustrates these elements in talking about some of his work, and in particular an article in the works when he was interviewed:

> What I think has happened to me is that I have been interested in taking some of what are normally considered to be traditionally psychological variables and seeing whether or not they are (a) applicable and (b) impactful in organizations. So [we have done] a study of positive energy in leaders of business units. The question is, . . .'When I interact with you, what happens to my energy? Am I uplifted, elevated? Are you life-giving to me? Or are you life-depleting, exhausting, difficult, or, in other words, negatively energizing?' What we are trying to do is measure positive energy of leaders. [. . .]
>
> In fact, this article is trying to show how to scale positive energy, to scale different shades from all kinds of other concepts, and then show the impact of positive energy of the leader on individuals and on organization performance. There are some of these psychological variables like positive energy, but the question is: can you see it in an organization, and does it have impact on the organizational level? I don't want to give up the 'O' in the POS [positive organizational scholarship], mainly because nobody is paying attention. [. . .]

Anyway, positive psychology...is focused on positive attributes of people – positive emotions and positive institutions. The trouble is [that] nobody – literally nobody – in psychology is studying positive institutions or positive organizations except for us. So we are not going to give up on the 'O' part.

This work on energy within the POS domain is not the first time that Cameron's interests and curiosity have led him into challenging new domains. Beginning with a problem-centered dissertation that addresses the issue of assessing the effectiveness of colleges and universities and studies organizational decline in higher education, Cameron then joined the University of Michigan, where he became interested in what was going on in the automobile industry in Detroit. He recalls how his curiosity led to innovative work that ultimately was defined as organizational downsizing:

> I came to Michigan, and had just done all this research on decline, organizational decline, in higher education. I got to know somebody who happened to be the number two guy at General Motors, Bill Hoaglund. He came over and gave a talk, ...and I talked to him one day and I said, 'I would really like to do some research on this topic. I just am interested in on subject of decline.' He said, 'We are not declining.' I said, 'Well, I just noticed in the newspaper last week you announced a 40,000 people layoff.' He said, 'That is not decline; that is downsizing.' I said, 'OK, well, I want to study downsizing then.' So I began about a twelve-year odyssey of studying downsizing. The auto industry was an easy target since it is close, and they were downsizing a lot. Almost everybody thought downsizing was going to be a temporary phenomenon and, as soon as we got through the late '80s, then it would be over and everything would get back to normal; but downsizing has become a non-stop change phenomenon – I think probably the most implemented change strategy in history.

In the typical 'one thing leads to another' way of the consistently (and insistently) curious, who are also willing to seize new opportunities as they come along, Cameron eventually moved on to consider the opposite issue: flourishing. He relates the story:

> Downsizing led me to an interesting conclusion: about 80 percent of organizations that downsize deteriorate in performance. They, in fact, lose productivity, lose profitability, morale goes down, conflict goes up, innovation collapses, communication channels get restricted, leadership anemia occurs, threat rigidity response, and so on. All of those things combine. I call them the dirty dozen. It is a cutesy way to talk about twelve things that occur in organizations, but performance almost always deteriorates. However, that still leaves 10 or 15 percent of organizations that don't deteriorate but, rather, flourish after downsizing. After a dozen years or so of research I began forming an impression. I had no data, but I began forming an impression that one of the major differences between those 10 or 15 percent [of] organizations that flourished and...everybody else (...most of them) that didn't was (and the word I used back then was) they [had] embedded or institutionalized *virtuous* practices.

Talking about virtuous organizations is not without risks. Cameron continues, in a story reminiscent of Cooperrider's efforts to introduce appreciative inquiry to an academic audience:

> Now, here is the problem with that. The word 'virtuous' or 'virtuousness' in academic settings is not easy to swallow. Too philosophical, too religious, not legitimate. It is not rigorous, not empirical. But this was now about 1995 or so. I had an opportunity to give a presentation at the Academy of Management on downsizing. Simultaneously I had just been asked and accepted this opportunity to go be the associate dean at BYU [Brigham Young University]. So I took a risk at the Academy and gave a presentation arguing for the idea that virtuousness differentiates winners from losers when you think about downsizing. My rationale was, 'Look, if I get laughed off the stage, if people say "This guy has lost his mind," it is OK,

because I am going to become an administrator, and I won't do that scholarly stuff anymore, anyway. I will be illegitimate, but it won't matter.' Well, about six months later somebody called me up and said, 'Hey, I was in your talk at the Academy; do you know about [the Templeton] Foundation? [It] is funding research on forgiveness in organizations, and. . .one of the things you talked about is that organizations that downsize people tend to forgive, don't hold grudges. They essentially forgive the harm.'

Following his stint at BYU, Cameron returned to Michigan with this idea still in his head, but having had no time to do research while serving as an administrator. The Templeton Foundation renewed his contract, because it wanted to work with an organizational specialist, but required that the research be completed within two years. This was around 2001, before much was being done organizationally on POS, and Cameron remembers the skepticism he faced – along with the power of connecting with like-minded people, in this case two other individuals studied as intellectual shamans, Jane Dutton and Bob Quinn.

When I came back to Michigan, people began asking me, 'Hey! It is nice seeing you again. What are you doing? What is your current work?' I would start to talk about forgiveness in organizations, and their eyes would glaze over. People think, 'What in the world has happened to you, Cameron? Are you an idiot? What has happened to your rigor?' Except that my friend Jane Dutton had just finished doing, or was in the midst of doing, research on compassion in organizations. Jane had had one of her children abused by a babysitter, and that, as you would expect for a mother, is a very traumatic experience. Well, she had a joint appointment in psychology and in business. Her psychology colleagues essentially said, 'Hey, look: bad things happen, lady; get over it.' Her business school colleagues were enormously nurturing, supportive, empathetic, compassionate. That triggered in her the idea that organizations themselves may have a very different perspective with regard to compassion, but she created a compassion lab with a bunch of doctoral students to talk about and then eventually to do research and write on the idea of compassion. Some of those doctoral students are still doing it.

Then my friend Bob Quinn had just written a book called *Deep Change*. It has to do with internal deep-changing your nature and your identity and the way you think about yourself. We were sitting, talking to each other, saying 'One of the things that glues us together is that we are doing research on something that we care deeply about, that it is more than just scholarly research, a set of research questions. This is a set of issues or phenomena that is what you want society to illustrate, to exemplify. It is what you want your children to develop; it is the stuff that we care deeply about.' So we said, 'Well, let's figure out a way to learn from each other.' (I am making these stories short.) That led to the creation of a center called the Center for Positive Organizational Scholarship. Actually, that was before we had ever heard of Marty [Martin] Seligman [founder of the positive psychology movement and past president of the American Psychological Association] or anybody in the positive psych world. [. . .] That then started this whole trajectory on positive organizational scholarship, and my own work primarily is focused on the question 'Can you detect or measure virtuousness in organizations?' because everybody knows forgiveness.

Pioneering ideas are, by definition, ahead of their time, and often, too, they are oriented toward building a better future rather than analyzing the past. These qualities, as with flourishing, energy, business as an agent of world benefit, and positive organizational scholarship, have a tendency to be somewhat abstract and less readily assessed through traditional empirical means than are more tractable ideas. Because of these qualities of the ideas with which they work, intellectual shamans can sometimes be viewed as seers.

Seers can be prescient, often seeing things or making connections before others have been able to grasp the need for change, or seeing things differently from others, who may accept the current norms or common wisdom. Indeed, it is this capacity that makes them seers. They are not always the best day-to-day managers, but it is often their vision (as in companies) that drives initiatives and ideas forward. Many of them tend also be entrepreneurial, starting new initiatives or in other ways pushing the boundaries. One person who has pushed boundaries – and is still doing so – is Bocconi University's Maurizio Zollo, who is currently heading up the GOLDEN for Sustainability global research initiative on how companies move toward sustainability. Zollo recalls how an earlier project called RESPONSE took shape and how it shaped his vision of what research was – and ultimately influenced the emergence of the GOLDEN project:

> In that project, which is code-named RESPONSE, we studied nineteen multinational companies in depth for about three years with interviews – we did about 430 interviews, and about 1,000 questionnaires [were] completed. It was a very interesting project. We started changing the way that we were thinking about research, really going inside the organization, understanding how managers think about issues, how they frame it and how they then act.
>
> We also did something very innovative, entrepreneurial. We wanted to also understand the effectiveness of learning and educational processes aimed at bridging this gap, because it's not enough to study the gap and the factors that create it. You also want to understand something about how to bridge this gap. So we did field experiments with four companies, big companies: IBM, Microsoft, Shell – really big multinationals. The experiments were about measuring the impact of different types of management education approaches. [We wanted to] say something about whether, by educating managers in the standard approach in the classroom environment, you actually can get real change in the mindsets of managers and the way that they think about problems...

What was shown by the RESPONSE project's results, which assessed, among other factors, traditional classrooms against meditation techniques, was contrary to expectations. In Zollo's words:

> We found out that, actually, the standard [classroom-based] approaches have no impact whatsoever on change, on change in the company, or in managers' mindsets. . .or decision-making processes. [. . .] More importantly, [there were] not many changes in the psychological antecedents of those decisions. We measured things like emotional traits, value systems. We don't expect value systems to change a lot, but, actually, compared to what we saw in the other approaches, the meditative and even stress management actually had some really interesting changes. Meditation was the one that had by far the deepest changes, not only in decision-making but also in the psychological antecedents, particularly the development of positive emotions. The reaction of negative emotions was just incredible – very, very strong. Much stronger than we expected.

Zollo is also exploring what he terms 'neuro-scientific management': actually using neuroscience approaches to study differences in the brains of entrepreneurs and leaders as they make decisions. Simultaneously, he is working on GOLDEN, which he believes may be the world's largest-scale organizational learning research project to address the issue of how companies are attempting to make a transition toward greater sustainability. His words describe both the challenges and the excitement of being on the cutting edge of a new way of thinking about research – a 'space' that is quite typical for intellectual shamans. Zollo comments on this innovative project, which involves numerous collaborators and companies from settings around the world:

> GOLDEN is by far the most – the most experimental, the most innovative, the most ambitious – . . .crazy thing I've done so far. It will probably be one of the most crazy things I will do in my life, so I want to make sure that it works out well. I have all the incentives

aligned, I think. It is about studying how companies learn to change themselves, to transform themselves in fundamental ways, connected to their *raison d'être*, to why they exist, to what they can do, to what...their purpose [is], their strategies, how they should be conducting their business, how they should compete and collaborate. Obviously, [it is about] how the culture of the organization should evolve toward a model of sustainable enterprise, so it's about innovation in business models toward sustainable business models basically. So [it is] toward embedding notions of sustainability across all the various functional activities, of the firms and across levels.

A project of this magnitude comes with challenges and the need to break existing paradigms, which Zollo recognizes, and which are similar to many of the challenges faced by other intellectual shamans.

There are a number of taboos that we're breaking with this project. One taboo is that you're not supposed to mix inductive and deductive research designs, and, of course, we're trying to do that, to do both if we can. Another – not a taboo but, really, a practical constraint – is that either you do large-scale but very superficial quantitative analysis, or deep case studies but with very few companies. Here we're trying to do very deep data collection inside the company, throughout all the main functions, also looking at subsidiaries in different countries and so on. So, really deep and longitudinal, with sustained access for about three years. At that same time trying to do that with a fairly large number of firms, 100 to 150 firms across the world, – key regions of the world, across [industry] sectors. [...]

Now, doing that across industries and across cultures, across the institutional context, is fantastic, because, clearly, it allows us to not only understand the processes inside the firm but also see how firms try to figure this out: what are the barriers, what are the enablers? But also try and understand the impacts of all these processes, and [get] the role of the context right – the role of the industry context, the role of the cultural context, the role of the institutional context – in facilitating or inhibiting the learning and change processes inside firms.

Tackling such a big set of questions with such a large-scale project is unusual, and GOLDEN at this writing is still emerging and developing, but it is this 'on the edge of chaos' notion of taking on big issues that intellectual shamans thrive on. In the last section of this chapter, I focus explicitly on what are known as wicked problems, which is where the hearts and minds of intellectual shamans gravitate.

WICKED PROBLEMS AND UNASKED QUESTIONS

Wicked problems are at the heart of many of the issues in intellectual shamans' work, as must be obvious by now. Wicked problems are complex problems with no clear solutions. By their nature, they have multiple stakeholders, are difficult to define, because each stakeholder has a different take on what the problem is and how it should be dealt with, and are generally intractable.[119,120] They tend to span across boundaries, are poorly formulated, and have numerous potential pathways to resolution.[120,142] Because of these characteristics, wicked problems do not lend themselves to ready solutions, deductive logic, neatly defined theories, or traditional, quantitatively oriented empirical research. They demand more holistic or systemic approaches, the asking of new questions, and sometimes even what Thomas Kuhn has called paradigm shifts.[62] Many social and even organizational problems can be considered 'wicked' because they have these characteristics. They represent the opposite of what, as Dave Brown suggests, most academics today focus on.

> I'm constantly somewhat startled at my intellectual trajectory,
> which has really been from small groups in social psychology
> to...'Change the world.' Experience clearly has not given me good
> sense, and my aspirations don't seem to have been subdued much.
> I think the natural tendency of academia is to know more and more
> about less and less, till you know everything about nothing.

Ed Freeman, for one, recognizes the complexity or 'wickedness' of human-centric problems, especially in the context of businesses; regarded as deeply human enterprises, they deserve consideration as the complex and somewhat chaotic entities that they actually are. Freeman comments:

> David Newkirk, a colleague of mine, and I have written a couple of papers about [the idea that], fundamentally, we get business wrong. Business is a human enterprise. Business isn't the physics of money. It's not some repeatable phenomenon for which there are covering laws, as philosophers would say. Business is a deeply human enterprise. Unless you get that right, all the other stuff doesn't matter. And business schools get that wrong, for the most part. We get it wrong from this, sort of, dominance of the narrow economic and finance models. I have to be careful here. There's a lot of critique of that, but if I were to give you certain economists to read – Kenneth Arrow, Thomas Schelling, or even James Buchanan and Amartya Sen - you wouldn't find business as an ahuman [sic] activity at all.
>
> But, for the most part, we have this narrow idea of what a business is: primarily as a physics of money. Look at the language: it is 'human resources.' C'mon! As someone said, the problem with human resources is you can't make a sentence with a subject. The human resources went for a walk. It just doesn't work. Even worse is human capital. Social capital and human capital. I once said to a colleague, 'Where are the people?' 'Oh, they're human capital.' Oh, no, they're not!
>
> So, what happens is this prevalence of a kind of narrow thinking. By the way, in the real world, that's not what happens! In the real world, there are real human beings in companies. That, again, goes back to this idea that you've got to start with experience, not with theory, and then bridge practice. You start with the experience.

Arguing (as other intellectual shamans would, such as Henry Mintzberg, Dave Brown, Ian Mitroff, and Nancy Adler, to name a few) that starting with experience would provide better insights into the very human enterprise of business, Freeman elaborates problems that he elsewhere calls 'physics envy,' which cause social scientists to try to avoid the more holistic and 'wicked' nature of human and social issues:

> Then what happens is, you take the so-called soft areas –
> organization behavior, strategy, ethics, that sort of stuff; now they
> need to prove themselves in terms of making their disciplines hard.
> You don't have to be much of a Freudian to understand how trying to
> get bigger data sets and harder data, and that sort of stuff, you
> know... There's a pretty primitive thing that most people don't see.
> You don't have to be much of a feminist to see that this mania with
> rationality is a way to try and make masculine most of business.
> There are other critiques other than this psychoanalytical one, but
> business schools get all this stuff wrong.

Moving away from the narrow thinking embedded in much research, intellectual shamans instead focus on more complex problems embedded in the social realities of the world and businesses. Ian Mitroff also critiques the narrowness of the academy, as well as disciplinarity and overspecialization. Thinking about the systemic nature of problems, Mitroff argues:

> We need an educated populous more than ever, given the
> overwhelming problems, and that's where the jobs are. You have to
> have a technical education, but you also have to have an education
> in the humanities. They need to be combined. I would totally break
> down the divisions between schools and departments. They're
> dysfunctional. It's an eighteenth-, nineteenth-century way of
> organizing knowledge. I would organize universities around
> problems, like home abuse, addiction, and child abuse, global
> warming, whatever... But Russell Ackoff said it best: 'Nature is not
> organized the same way universities are.' The university is a
> dysfunctional organization, but it doesn't know it.

Mitroff further explores the wicked nature of social problems:

[Academia and its organizations and associations need] the proper
organization and frame of mind to really confront the problems that
we face, [which] are enormous. In Russ Ackoff's terms, what we face
are messes. A mess is a whole dynamic system of problems that are
so interconnected that you can't take the problem out of the mess
without destroying the system, like the financial mess, the
education mess. All these messes are now interconnected. So, we
don't face isolated little problems that you break apart via
reductionism. But you have to understand practice systems,
methodology systems, thinking philosophy of science.

ESADE Business School's Josep Lozano takes a similar perspective on the need for holistic approaches within management education. Lozano provides insight into how he thinks better management
education might be developed:

One of the worst problems of our academic educational reality is
fragmentation. I'm strongly interested in understanding education
as creating bridges between organizations, creating bridges
between disciplines, creating bridges between ideologies and
mindsets, or religions, and so on. This idea of education as a creator
of bridges and connections is crucial for me. It's amazing how
things change, just giving people the opportunity to listen and talk
with other people coming from different frameworks. By itself, that
creates change. Thus, for me, dialogue implies not speaking
beforehand but being attentive and receptive, and listening. If there
is something that we need today it is to learn how to listen, to
create a real space for dialogue. 'Dialogue' is another word that is
really important for me. If you create a real space for dialogue,
honest dialogue, changes happen. This idea of fighting against a
fragmented approach to education, and understanding education
that's creating these kinds of bridges, is something that's really
important for me.

WICKED PROBLEMS AND THE SEARCH FOR A BETTER WORLD

Wisdom, I have argued elsewhere, combines Aristotle's three elements of the good (moral imagination,[128] or the capacity to see the ethical issues in situations and issues), the true (a reasonably accurate systems understanding), and the beautiful (application of aesthetic sensibility to the situation) in the service of the greater good.[59,60] Part of what it means to be an intellectual shaman, in my view, is to be on a quest for such wisdom, whether this quest is articulated as such or not. Although most of the intellectual shamans interviewed would not claim wisdom, their words suggest that many are indeed on this path.

For stakeholder theorist Ed Freeman, 'getting business right,' as discussed above, provides a positive lens on business activities and the issues that understanding them bring up. Reprising one of the opening quotes to this book, I quote Freeman again below:

> I think [there will be problems] until we get business right. It's a deeply human enterprise. It's how we create value and trade with each other. It's how we create meaning for each other. It's how we spend a third to half our lives. Until we come to see that as a human activity full of emotion and rationality and spirituality and sexuality and connection with others, until that's in the center, not at the edge: imagine if financiers had to *prove* to us that people who have (I want to get this right) convex utility preferences for money were really human beings too, so they had to make the human case for their theory, rather than other people having to make the economic case for theirs. I think the world would be a much better place.

Bob Giacalone takes a similar stance around the dominance of materiality, with respect to scholars working on what is important (as opposed to what is relatively easy) – a stance he also applies to his teaching of business ethics, and what is important in life:

> The dominant ideology of materialism is the ideology that says: what counts in life is what you can count. The dominant ideology, the

ideology of power, of status, of money, of influence; I refer to it as a *Supermarket Sweep* life. Oh, *Supermarket Sweep*! I wrote this in one of my articles once. *Supermarket Sweep* was a stupid game show. It was the dumbest game show ever. You'd be asked questions, and if you got them right you'd get points, which translated to seconds. Then you were given a shopping cart with X number of seconds, and your job was to throw in as much stuff – it didn't matter whether you liked it; the most expensive stuff you could – into that cart, and you were against two or three other contestants. At the end, the person who won the game was the one who had the most at the checkout line.

This is the life we're living. It's *Supermarket Sweep*: throw crap into your shopping cart and run around like a mad person, accumulating things you don't need and don't want. You may not even like them, but keep going at it. Do it faster and faster. Accumulate points, so you can run through the aisle for more seconds of your day and then come out on top again. Got me? We spent more money and got more things than everybody else, and that is the most destructive mindset that we've got. It pervades everything. It pervades everything: more status, more power, more influence, more toys!

Giacalone talks about why such materialism is problematic:

It's never enough, and it creates a hunger. People mistake that hunger for meaning. But, point of fact, it has nothing to do with meaning; nothing at all. It has to do with the hunger that's created by an addiction cycle. The culture loves that addiction cycle, because, if you don't buy, the people at the top of the food chain can't go out and get the things that they think make them happy. So, ultimately, the people at the top of the food chain, all the rich people. . ., are victims just like everybody else. Nobody comes out of this alive. Not with their soul intact. We destroy lives like this. That's the mindset I think that's being perpetuated in business schools. I think that if we don't change that we will be complicitous in the wreckage of the world as we know it.

In developing conscious capitalism, Raj Sisodia, of Babson College, agrees with Mitroff and Giacalone about the need for an academic community that is engaged in the real problems of the world to convey a set of attitudes that, as David Cooperrider might say, value the life-giving or generative aspects of business rather than simply the material and financial. Sisodia illustrates how this approach needs to be part of the move toward a better world:

> I've never agreed with [academics sitting on the sidelines of practice]. I've always felt the world of practice needs to be very much part of our domain, which means what we do in research has to be relevant, and what we also learn in our research needs to be communicated. There's a tag line that I really love, from this company that I worked with called Pivot Leadership, which does executive development. It says: 'Better leaders = better world.' It tells you what they do and why they do it. They're in leadership development. Why are they doing it? Because better leaders make for a better world!

Sisodia elaborates:

> Better business makes for a better world! If we can help impact business practice in a positive way, that's what the development piece [of conscious capitalism] is about. Trying to create practical tools, like an assessment tool that companies can use to look at where they are today on all of these different dimensions; where the gaps are, how...they compare to some of the best, and what they can do. Then we're trying to come up with intervention programs: purpose search, future search, more stakeholder integration. How do you do those things? My vision with the Conscious Capitalism Institute is that we have three planks: research, education, and development. We would like to deepen our understanding of this philosophy (I really think of it as a philosophy of business) and flesh it out much more than what we have so far.

Many of the intellectual shamans carry similar ideas into their work, focusing holistically and qualitatively on the wicked problems that beset humanity and their social/business systems and trying, in their various ways, to make the world a better place. David Cooperrider highlights the evolution of his own thinking as he moved toward a considered understanding of both the complexity and the promise of human systems and ways to better appreciate what he calls the miracle of life:

> For me, it was the writing of a dissertation, I think chapter two, called 'Appreciative inquiry into organizational life,' that laid out the initial vision and theory. [...] I can remember when I started following where the logic was going, this shift, and how this kind of secularized view of the world had taken hold. I started to really grapple with the shift from the world as a mechanical problem to be solved versus the world as this living miracle, this miracle of life on this planet. I realized that, if we really operated from that stance, that everything we see would be different. All the questions we would ask would be different.

Cooperrider also recalls the emotional impact that this realization had:

> It was in the writing of that, I remember, there were moments where I had tears. We didn't have computers then. I had a yellow notepad, and there were tears flowing down my face onto the paper, realizing: ...why don't I feel that all the time? Why don't I feel this miracle of life on this planet? Why haven't I told [my wife] Nancy's father, for example, who was dying of cancer at that time, all the positive qualities I saw in him? Why wasn't I able to share my deepest appreciations and love? What was the social construction, or hypnosis, or cultural blinders that we were on, where we couldn't see the beauty and goodness and gift of life all around us anymore? Where we had, kind of, become so pragmatic that we were not asking these kinds of questions?

Cooperrider's inspiration came as spiritual rebirth of the sort we witnessed earlier for many of the intellectual shamans, at a time when he had isolated himself in his parents' cabin for a month to write his dissertation. It also arises from what can only be called an aesthetic appreciation of life itself, providing a spiritual perspective. Like others who live this path toward wisdom, the idea of appreciative inquiry pulled Cooperrider into action:

> I was just completely alone with this work. It felt like a relationship was being born, where relationships make demands on you. This topic was making some demands on me, saying, 'Take this seriously. Follow where the logic is leading and lift this up, in as clear and pure a form as you can.' So, it was really personal in that sense, a personal reopening of the heart. I started thinking: maybe let's call it the cognitive power of love, that we just aren't going to see it if we don't – if we aren't in love with it. If we don't have that respect for the world, we're not going to see those miraculous sparks or moments that give us the material out of which to paint a new picture of the future.

In particular, Cooperrider paints a picture that highlights how design or aesthetic sensibility is an important element of wisdom (which I explore further in the next and final chapter):

> Like an artist pulls together the various colors and materials, the paintbrush, the canvas, the red colors, the blue, the green, yellow, and so on, and out of that material they're able to paint a picture and give a gift to the future. It begins with valuing, it begins with love, it begins with an open heart. It begins with a beginner's mind, to see things as if we're seeing it for the first time.

8 Sage: the work of wisdom

He will speak these words of wisdom
Like a sage, a man of vision
Though he knows he's really nothing
But the brief elaboration of a tube.

Leonard Cohen, 'Going home' (2012)

SAGE: INTELLECTUAL SHAMANS' WORK OF WISDOM

Intellectual shamans serve as sages – wise men and women. Indeed, in a sense, they are the wise elders of their various communities, for wisdom typically comes with maturity. The sage is a person of wisdom and clarity who realistically understands the systemic implications of situations and events. The intellectual shaman as sage is a seer who appreciates the beautiful and design elements, sees 'what is' holistically and systemically, and understands the moral implications inherent in any situation, combining the aesthetic sensibility, moral imagination, and systems understanding in the service of the greater good that it takes to attain wisdom.

The term 'sage' is often used to refer to the 'wise old man,' yet the word applies equally to the wise woman. It is applicable to the intellectual shaman who uses his or her work to make some things in the world better. Sages are the elders of most communities. It takes time, experience, knowledge, and insight – i.e., maturity – to develop the wisdom, and the breadth of its perspective, that is associated with being a sage.

Wisdom, as I have noted above, is the capacity to integrate three capabilities – moral imagination (the good), systems understanding (the true), and aesthetic sensibility (the beautiful) – into future-oriented actions and decisions focused on achieving the greater good or a better world.[59] In assessing the work and words of intellectual shamans, it is difficult to separate these three elements, as they are integrated in their approach to their worlds and to their work. Philosopher Ken Wilber, articulating a similar relationship without the link to wisdom, notes in a commentary that the good relates to the realms of 'we,' or how we treat each other, in his four-quadrant framework; the true relates to 'objective,' or science-based observations, that we understand as 'reality,' or the 'it' and 'its'; and the beautiful relates to the self-expressive and emotional, or 'I,' elements.[143] Philosophers have long sought this integration of the good, the true, and the beautiful, and I believe that it manifests in individual lives – and in the work of intellectual shamans – as wisdom used in the service of the greater good.

In prior chapters, we have already looked at the intellectual shaman's commitment to the greater good and a better world (e.g., a theory, field, or practice) when addressing the healing orientation inherent to intellectual shamanism. Below we look explicitly at how the three core aspects of wisdom, manifesting as the good, the true, and the beautiful, are integrated in the worldviews of intellectual shamans, then consider some explicitly 'shamanic' experience that some of the intellectual shamans evidence.

As we consider wisdom in intellectual shamans, we will also note the importance of the role of 'seer,' in the sense of the prophet or visionary looking to the future. Being a seer is embedded in each of the three capabilities associated with wisdom: moral imagination, systems understanding, and aesthetic sensibility. Seeing also implies a future orientation that, when combined with healing elements, helps to confirm the role of the intellectual shaman as a healing force. Let us begin with the exploration of moral imagination as expressed by intellectual shamans.

WISDOM: INTEGRATING MORAL IMAGINATION, SYSTEMS UNDERSTANDING, AND AESTHETIC SENSIBILITY

Before we look explicitly at how intellectual shamans integrate the good, the true, and the beautiful, it is helpful to explore the three elements of wisdom in more detail.

Moral imagination, a concept developed by business ethicist Patricia Werhane, is the expression of 'the good': the capacity to see and understand the ethical implications in a situation, decision, action, or system.[128,130] Moral imagination, the good, involves reflective capacities, including self- and other-awareness, an ability to see the mental models that are at play in a situation, and an understanding that situations are morally embedded. It also implies a willingness to consider alternatives to the current situation even in the face of uncertainty and to formulate ideas beyond immediate experience.[144] In terms of the role of seer, moral imagination allows insights about possibilities that do not yet exist, while weighing those possibilities against a moral lens,[130] and helps to avoid the problem of 'moral muteness,'[145] or the inability to see ethical consequences in actions, decisions, and situations that can otherwise result in 'blind spots'[146] or wearing blinders[127] around ethical issues. Such moral imagination is integral in a definition of wisdom offered by management theorist Russell Ackoff, who notes that wisdom is the capacity to think through the consequences of one's actions[147] – essentially, to use moral imagination in decisions and actions that have consequences.

Intellectual shamans face the ethical underpinnings of the issues with which they deal directly and explicitly. Often they are quite open in addressing the ethical issues, which too often go unspoken, in a way that integrally links ethical to other elements. They thereby avoid what Ed Freeman calls the 'separation thesis': the idea that ethics can somehow be separated from practice, research, ideas, or management.[148]

To achieve wisdom, the intellectual shaman incorporates systems understanding, the true, a reasonably realistic understanding of the situation or system and its dynamics into his or her thinking – a capacity that Senge has termed systems thinking[118] and that Wilber associates with science.[143] Werhane has also made an explicit link between moral imagination and systems thinking. She argues that in systems thinking the concept of the system as a whole is comprised of interdependent and interrelated parts, other 'wholes,' and their patterns of interaction and relationships.[129] Systems understanding enables the intellectual shaman to understand both the whole and the parts – i.e., to recognize that elements constituting the whole are called 'holons,' entities in which parts that are themselves whole make up bigger wholes (e.g., individuals as part of departments that, in turn, are part of divisions in companies that, in turn, are part of the whole company, which is itself part of an industry, and so on).[149] This way of understanding also provides insight into the dynamics at play in complex systems.

We saw that problems of interest to intellectual shamans tend to be 'wicked' and that intellectual shamans' research approaches are generally holistic, rather than atomistic or fragmented. Such holistic approaches transcend disciplinary boundaries and are problem-centric – or more positive, as Cooperrider has eloquently noted. Systems understanding is needed to cope with the complexity of wicked problems or messes.[147] Because they are generally problem-oriented (versus theoretically driven), intellectual shamans' work is grounded in experience and observation, moving from observation to theory rather than the reverse. They tend to observe the patterns of interrelationship inherent in multi-level, multidisciplinary phenomena, focusing on understanding the dynamics and complexities rather than simply the nuances.[150] Abstraction helps intellectual shamans make sense of what they observe and translate it for others.

There is one more element of wisdom: aesthetic sensibility, or the beautiful. As Paul Shrivastava points out, an artistic or design sensibility helps create new insights, organization, and visions that can reshape the world – one that links us closely to emotions and sensory experiences.[151] It is this aesthetic sensibility, a combination of mind (intellectual), body (sensory), and heart (emotional, experiential) commitments, that generates passion,[151] and also enhances the capacity to view situations holistically.[152] Aesthetic sensibility underscores the intellectual shaman's passionate commitment to his or her work and the creativity attendant to generating new insights and ideas.

Indeed, Nancy Adler, who is an artist as well as an academic, has explicitly developed the idea that the arts can provide novel ideas and insights for businesses and in other important domains.[131] Ed Schein, also an artist, agrees, noting that 'art and artist stimulate us to see more, hear more and experience more of what is going on within us and around us.'[153] Aesthetic sensibility has other important functions, also articulated by Schein, including 'broaden[ing] the range of perceptions and feelings that we allow ourselves' and 'forc[ing] us to look at what we normally avoid because it is disturbing, anxiety provoking, politically incorrect,'[153] and it also stimulates the broadening of skills, behavioral repertoire, and response flexibility, not to mention enhancing creativity.[153]

Intellectual shamans, looking at whole systems, are often able to see not just the complexity and dynamics of those systems, and their wicked problems, but also the design features, and even the beauty (or lack thereof), of ideas, of creativity, of new concepts and insights. Notably, there is a certain beauty in wise decisions, innovations, and insights that can make witnesses respond from an aesthetic perspective – respond to elements that John Dewey articulates as balance, harmony, and rhythm, which generate a form of equilibrium (for a while at least) and which somehow resolve tension, creating order and coherence[154] out of what seemed to be chaos.

Wisdom integrates all three elements of the good, true, and beautiful, because they offer different ways of understanding, all of which are needed to come to wisdom.[143,151] The combination of moral imagination, systems understanding, and aesthetic sensibility not only draws out the core features of a situation, permitting new insights, but also allows for the development of emotional or sensorial, ethical and moral, *and* reasonably accurate and truthful accounts of what is seen. Of course, any insight is necessarily culture- and time-specific and can eventually be changed, but intellectual shamans hone the capacity to bring these three elements together into their work to meet the demands of the current world.

Raj Sisodia evidences this integrated and systemic approach in discussing the origins of conscious capitalism:

> I had a vision for what I was calling the Institute for New Capitalism. It was so close. It was a convenient acronym, because it stood for INC, like 'incorporated.' The idea was that here is a way of thinking about business in a holistic fashion, with all these elements that are part of it, that seems to not only work better, because these companies actually are financially more successful, but all of that doesn't come at [an] expense. So it's not based on any kind of exploitation or misleading. It's actually a win-win value creation approach that is very powerful. It doesn't seem to be all that well understood when there are people talking about stakeholders, there are people talking about purpose, and so leadership etc., but putting it all together into some kind of an integrated whole seemed like a good thing to do and something that really excited me.

Sisodia also notes that these ideas developed when he was exploring his own spiritual roots through an approach called 'the Art of Living.' Note in particular how moral imagination seems to have been stirred as he began conceiving of what has become conscious capitalism:

> So, I was starting to get exposed to that [spiritual practice of the Art of Living]. At the same time I was thinking about these issues from a business standpoint. That way of thinking started to seep in: the idea of responsibility. What do you take responsibility for? That's one of the tenets in the Art of Living: the idea of focusing on the right actions and not being wedded to the outcome and so forth. I found a lot of parallels in what these companies [profiled in his jointly authored book *Firms of Endearment*] were doing with what is generally being prescribed from the ancient wisdom, at that time of the ancient wisdom of India, which is what I was being exposed to.

As this way of thinking developed, Sisodia began also to consider taking the risk of becoming a public intellectual – and in his way trying to make the world better. He recalls trying to accomplish this goal by writing opinion pieces for *The Wall Street Journal* – and the highly negative reaction his efforts, which apparently made them uncomfortable, engendered from some colleagues. For example, he had written a *Wall Street Journal* opinion piece, of which he was very proud, criticizing the merger of Disney and Capital Cities/ABC, because of the huge premium that had been paid – and because research suggested that such mergers frequently do not work out well. Sisodia recalls his colleagues' reactions:

> One of my senior colleagues, . . .a chaired professor, . . .came over to my office. I thought he was going to say 'Congratulations.' He came over and said, 'What the hell are you doing?' I said, 'What do you mean?' He said, 'Why are you writing for *The Wall Street Journal*?' I said, "Well, I thought this thing was happening, and I had something to say about it. There's some theory and other things that relate to that.' 'That's not your job. That's not your job to write. You're not a journalist. Your job is to do research.' Then I got an e-mail from a friend of mine. . . He said, 'Congratulations, but you realize this is academic suicide?' OK. I think I had just gotten tenure or I was about to get tenure or something, and I heard them and I said, 'I just don't agree. I don't agree that we should be sitting in our ivory tower and just sort of doing whatever we do. I mean, things happen out there. Why not engage?' Why not? But that is such a mindset. That's pervasive.

Sisodia goes on to make a direct link to systems understanding:

> When 9/11 happened, that semester I was actually sitting in on a class at MIT in system dynamics with John Sterman, who's the head of the systems dynamics [unit]. [. . .] The class was happening on Tuesday and Thursday. So, that morning (this was only the second week of the semester, I think, so maybe the third class, September 11th). . ., when I went into class, one tower had been hit and nobody knew what was going on. When I came out both towers were down

and the world had changed. When I came back to class on that Thursday, two days later, John basically said, 'OK, let's set aside what we were going to do. Let's analyze this from a systems standpoint. So, here's this event that happened. . .'

He said, 'We understand that every event is an outward manifestation of an underlying system at work, and that system has been there for a while. There are a whole bunch of things. So let's try to understand what that system was that led to this particular event. Then, what are the likely responses that we might have to that, and what will be the consequences of those responses, and so forth? What would be a systems way of understanding this and how it needs to change?' [. . .] A very sophisticated model, and it came out with some clear policy implications as to what should and should not be done.

Sisodia wryly notes what happened next:

Afterwards I went up to him and said, 'John, why don't you write this for *The New York Times* or someone? Why don't you put this analysis out there? Because these decisions are being made as we speak.' He said, 'Oh, no. That's not my job.' He refused to get involved in that sort of public. . .debate around that issue.

The University of Pretoria's Derick De Jongh describes some of his own work on corporate responsibility and responsible leadership in similar ways. In his case, the aesthetic piece, which is frequently connected to emotions, is expressed as what he terms 'heartset,' the emotional connection that we have doing something in the world. Talking about his shift from the University of South Africa to Pretoria, De Jongh explains:

I reached the point in my life where I thought, 'OK, the field of corporate citizenship has evolved tremendously, but somehow something is missing in all of this.' The thing that was missing is that there was a compliance mindset. . . With corporate citizenship and corporate responsibility, and a very powerful corporate governance practice and framework, what companies started doing is they saw citizenship as nothing else than just complying with the rules of the game.

There were a lot of mindset commitments, but not a lot of heartset commitments. It's the heartset that was the factor that became clear. That is, why are people *really*, and companies *really*, doing this? Is it because they need to make the Johannesburg Stock Exchange Index? Is it because they want to win yet another report or award? Is it because legislation requires them to do that? There was a significant gap in moving from compliance to real behavior. It was just blatantly clear that it's a leadership issue. It's fundamentally challenging the very purpose of business. It's fundamentally saying 'It's all good and well that we've got all these fantastic standards and guidelines and codes of conduct and so on, but all of that means nothing if there's no significant shift in the values of the business, in the culture of the organization, in the leadership shift of a business, in a critical review of the purpose of an organization.'

De Jongh elaborates on the aesthetic – emotional – piece, what he calls the 'heartset,' that would engage responsible leadership in businesses fully in serving the world in different ways:

The heartset is really much deeper. It's much deeper, which organizations seem to find very difficult to cope with, because, once you talk about a heartset, suddenly you talk with a much deeper introspection and a reflection from within. [You begin] to say, 'But the way that we've conducted ourselves in our business up until now – is it really in the very best interest…?' So that's the difficulty. The heartset takes a different element in an organization to make that change than merely to say 'All right, we complied with GRI [the Global Reporting Initiative], we sat on the New York Stock Exchange Dow Jones sustainability index, blah, blah, blah.' That's where it becomes difficult.

Both Sisodia and De Jongh understand the implicit design (artistic) complexities associated with defining the purpose of businesses differently for the future from how it has been defined up to now. They also recognize that a different leadership mindset will be needed for an uncertain future, particularly when, as De Jongh states below, they recognize the systemic implications of change and the difficulties of effecting system change from within:

> We already talk about a next generation of leaders that we need to embody with a new set of principles and understandings (if I may use the word 'heartset' again) to retrofit somebody – if you can retrofit a human being. How do you retrofit somebody in a leadership position today who's been trained and is a product of a particular system? They might be an economist or an accountant or an MBA graduate at Harvard or wherever. They've been taught in a particular paradigm. You can't expect them to fundamentally challenge the very system that supports them, when they feed off that system. How can you kill the system that feeds you by coming up with a radical view on what the purpose of business is? It's very difficult for the current generation of political, private-sector, society leaders. It's very difficult for them to fundamentally challenge the dominant paradigm. It takes a lot of courage. It takes a lot of conviction. It's just not so easy.

Paul Shrivastava, whose research specifically involves aesthetic rationality, concurs with Sisodia and De Jongh about the emotional component of aesthetics integrated into wisdom through the sense-making process, noting:

> [With] aesthetic rationality, we saw this sensemaking process as largely a cognitive process where [people gained] a sense of what was happening by connecting pieces of information and understanding them fully. In our view of aesthetic rationality, which we claim is also operating in organizations, there is an emotional component to this sensemaking. It has nothing to do with how you understand, what kind of information you have. It has everything to do with your internal state, with your emotional life, with your level of comfort

with certain kinds of things that are happening in your environment. We feel that this emotional rationality is ignored in organizations, but it is a very constitutive part of the standard rationality. We're trying to stretch the conventional view of sensemaking to incorporate those emotional interests that actually, in our view, form the glue for all of this together. Maybe, in thinking about vision, one can give more space to an emotional element that gives that vision an anchoring, and also other enduring motivation that comes with emotional engagement.

Bill Torbert, known for his developmental theory of both individuals and organizations, takes a similar systemic approach to thinking about the challenges facing leaders, describing the developmental process in moral, aesthetic, and systemic terms, once again illustrating the integration needed to come to wisdom. Torbert says of leaders and his own work on developmental theory:

One of the reasons I've come to like developmental theory is that it has a quite precise definition of what different transformations look like, and why they represent a change of form, and qualitative change of forms. It's, if you will, a genetic change rather than a phenotypical change. When you think about it, it seems almost impossible. It's like the caterpillar not just becoming a butterfly, but then the butterfly becoming something equally different, then that goes on four or five more times. Yet that's what it seems to me human beings have the capacity to be. Very few human beings have poked their heads out beyond the butterfly stage, let's say. Each of these stages has a whole underlying logic of how to deal with the world best. Most of them assume that the world is the way you're seeing it. They don't say, 'I'm in an action logic, and the world can be seen in different ways, and I'm looking at it this way.' [The action logics] actually dictate the way you see the world, and you assume everybody else is seeing it the same way. They may be pretending not to, because they're so sneaky, the opportunist [one of the action logics in Torbert's system] would say. But, anyway, you think that's the way the world is. But one way in which transformations become more and more inclusive is that eventually you become aware that you're actually engaged in these things, and you can start to name them and see them happening.

Torbert's ideas about action logics and development can be used in parallel with the idea presented above that wisdom requires holistic and encompassing ways of thinking systemically, and incorporates the aesthetic and moral dimensions as well. Torbert explains how action logics work in a way that helps shed light on the orientation to wisdom that is evidenced by the intellectual shamans:

> It's always very difficult to see the one [action logic] beyond yourself, because your assumptions are rooted in that. Although you've excavated other assumptions you used to make, there's still some more basic assumptions left. For example, most scientists assume that what they are really engaged in is nailing down the world and getting the facts of the world straight so that we actually know the truth. But, in the science I'm doing, you become more and more aware of how little you know about the truths, so it really is quite a different kind of science. It evokes fear in the hearts of those who thought their vision was to know everything. This takes you to realizing that you know less and less, even as, of course, you're learning more and more. But you're aware that there's an even bigger universe you haven't, sort of, really gotten in on yet.

Torbert argues that more developed ways of thinking, analogous to what I have called wisdom, are

> [t]ruly [like modern quantum physics]. There really are analogs – the whole antimatter business where, suddenly, that's most of the universe. It really is getting bigger in a qualitative sense. I guess the idea (and it's hard to know [because] all the words lead to questions about what those words mean) but. . .a transformation is when the framework itself changes. It's what we call a double-loop feedback. Most human beings just process single-loop feedback, at best, but,

according to these developmental theories in my work, it would be possible to systematically seek transformation, to seek double-loop feedback, and even triple-loop feedback. This [is a] kind of ongoing awareness, where you're not simply stuck in one part of yourself, like your mind, but you're actually aware of multiple territories at once.

Torbert concludes by stating his vision, which has evolved and matured over time:

Probably, after fifteen years, I could have said it this way: that, through repeated transformations, humans can learn to love so powerfully that the balance of power shifts from the predominance of coercion, and other forms of unilateral power, to the predominance of mutual power. That's my vision, or one way of saying my vision.

In a similar vein, David Cooperrider discusses how his approach to appreciative inquiry, a systemic approach that deliberately incorporates design elements and moral imagination to build a better world, and that integrates theory and practice, can be used to shape the future:

I started to really look carefully then at the way inquiry itself creates the future, the way theory constructs potentials for the future, the way knowledge interrupts this habit – the status quo that opens up new possibilities. That's why I'm so excited about this perfect interplay between theory and practice, because theory *is* practice. There's no way that it's separate in human systems. Simply building a theory of the Cleveland Clinic [research that he did early in his career] began to shift attention, the language, the agendas, the way groups talked, the inquiry itself. It's true: the questions we ask determine what we find. What we find sets the stage for how we begin to conceptualize the future. That sets the stage for what we talk about and how we coordinate our actions. So I became very interested not just in this relationship between inquiry and change but, specifically, in the relationship between [change and] appreciative inquiry – that is, inquiry that searches for the true, the good, the better, the possible: everything that gives life in human systems, and how powerful a creative act that is.

Cooperrider makes a direct link between the aesthetics of design and the creativity integral to his work, referencing conversations he has had with management guru Peter Drucker:

Today we know that [inquiry is] a real part of the creative process. So you go into a design firm like IDEO [a design and consulting firm based in Cambridge, Massachusetts, that has pioneered ideas about what is known as design thinking], and the first phase of the designer's mind is an inspiration phase that leads to more ideation [sic]. [Management thinker] Peter Drucker was very much of an appreciative inquiry theorist. His first powerful piece of work was his study of General Motors. From that he gave birth to images of the characteristics and practice of managers. It led him to realize that management is one of the most noble professions in the world; that, in a society of organizations, organizations are healthy to the extent that their institutions are healthy, and those institutions are healthy to the extent that they have managers that can help lift up the capabilities of that system. [...] Then that led to his theorizing about the noble profession of management. I don't think it's an accident he was an aesthetic theorist. He was an artist-theorist. His first position wasn't in the field of management. It was in the field of art history, and he was a connoisseur of Japanese art. I think there's a real relationship between valuing and creating.

Nietzsche had a phrase that said, 'Valuing is creating: hear it, ye creating ones! Valuation itself is the treasure and jewel of the valued things.' There's an interesting double word definition, a double definition with 'appreciation.' If you look in one direction, it means to value those things of value, to see what gives life – to celebrate, for example, the best in our son or your daughter. So it means valuing. But it also has an economic definitional attribute, and it means to appreciate in value, as in 'The stock market has appreciated in value.

The economy has appreciated in value.' There is a really interesting interplay between our capacity to appreciate and the capacity of the world around us to appreciate getting value. Appreciation appreciates!

Karl Weick, though not an artist (except with respect to his writing), nonetheless acknowledges the important role of aesthetic sensibility in providing what we can call a space for reflection, even though he has no explicit reflective practices. Note the integrative quality of Weick's sensibility about jazz – and even train travel:

> Jazz – music, jazz, just reading about it, listening to it, watching it, trying to think about it – really is. . .a kind of oasis, where things just fall together or draw together in the sense of intensity and emotion and feeling and evolution and streaming and interplay. All of those kinds of things are just like right there in very well done jazz. An interlude of just savoring that is just magical almost.
>
> I don't fly much. I don't fly pretty much at all. So I take a lot of trains to different places, and you've got a lot of time on your hands. Somehow, [there is] the sheer pleasure of staring out a train window or writing notes as you're going along or free-associating or whatever. It's not an escape; it's just a more vivid kind of presence, and it goes on for a while. It's got rhythms of stopping and starting at stations. It's got the sounds of wheels and all that. You know what that's like? Anyway, I sound like a country and western songwriter with something about whistles in the night! But, anyway, those are as close as I get to what I think may be implied in a concern with spirit, with renewal, with non-thinking or extra-thinking kinds of activities

Tima Bansal, dealing with the problematic issue of sustainability, also offers a systemic view laced with ethical understanding and a design sensibility that integrates all three elements of wisdom. Note that, while she denies having an ethical orientation with respect to ecological matters, she goes on to discuss the tragedy of the commons and comes back full circle to an ethical orientation despite the disclaimer:

> In a way, the two worlds – social and environment – are different, in that the social issues (when you think about literacy, gender, poverty – those sorts of things) really pull at your heartstrings. They're things that are deeply important, but they're almost ethical. How can I allow people to go hungry or without good health care while I'm having a good life? So, that's almost an ethical position. But the environment – there's more of an antagonistic aspect to it, in that I don't feel that I can't consume natural resources because somebody else is living worse or better than I am; somehow, there's no ethical sensibility that I have. It's more that the environmental movement now, at least for some people like me, is really motivated by the tragedy of the commons, in that we've now reached our limits to growth and are going to see catastrophic failures. Those catastrophic failures are just humankind. It's mankind – it's just our consumption.

Bansal moves on to consider the inherent design issues in thinking about how our current economic and other institutions, and our teaching, which have created the problems she has identified, need to shift:

> [It's about the] social embeddedness of institutions. [. . .] We have a science behind climate change. We know it's happening. Well, why in the world aren't we doing something? That's because of social embeddedness. It's the fact that all my colleagues are teaching stuff that they don't believe in, but that they've been told to teach. How do you change mindsets? It's not because they're evil people. Far from it! So, yeah, we need to change social institutions, and that's the obstacle. How do you extract people from doing the things that they've always done in the way that they've done them, expect to do them?

In an even more fundamental critique of social science as it is practiced today, Ian Mitroff argues not only that the wicked problems of system issues are difficult to understand but that there is, effectively, a co-creation process that exists between the one who would study and understand the system and the system itself. Mitroff also links in the idea of spirituality, related to moral imagination, and an aesthetic sensibility:

> One of my favorite sayings is from the great British poet T. S. Eliot, and it is 'Humankind cannot bear much reality.' That kind of sums up all of social science in one fell swoop. On the other hand, I do believe that [as Ken Wilber's approach to spirituality and other developmental streams indicates] people have enormous potential for growth, that they can overcome trauma, they can overcome so many obstacles in their life if they really want. But you've got to really want it. [...]
>
> When you ask somebody like me 'What's your motivation?', it cannot be separated from my being. My being is my motivation. So, it's like in philosophy: the question has to be reformulated so that I can even answer it. [...] I'm talking about the deeper purpose of universities and learning and living. I'm talking about the ultimate; that's why...I am not religious but (I don't even like the word 'spiritual') I believe deeply in something, whatever it is called – 'God.' [...]
>
> Stephen Hawking once said, 'Suppose we have this grand physical equation that explains everything, but [does not] breathe life into the equation?' It's one thing to write the equation, but – and that's what most physicists don't understand. They think they can explain everything in science in completely natural terms. They don't understand I'm not a creation, because that's just loopy and dopey, but what is it that gives the continuity and the orderliness and intelligibility of the universe? Orderliness and intelligibility are concepts that are derived from religion. Most scientists don't know that.
>
> When you look through a telescope you don't see the concepts of orderliness. You see things. But Immanuel Kant had no doubt

that all knowledge starts with empirical experience, but it does not all arise there. What is built into our minds so that we can have orderly experience? That's not found in experience. There's something in the mind that gives order, it co-participates. It's not just a passive show, passing by. That's why realism is a flawed philosophy. But you've got to know this. If you don't know this, then your research is deeply flawed, which it is in most people.

We put the order in there. I use one of Singer's [Edgar Arthur Singer, Jr., was a philosopher at the University of Pennsylvania] examples...; suppose you had an intelligent, reflective wine glass. I put to students: what would it ask? Why am I here, what's my purpose? For Singer, it said, 'Why is it no matter what is poured into me?' It always has the same shape. Aha, I'm supplying the shape. So, containability is a property both of the glass and the wine. Well, our minds are like the wine glass; because of our hardware, software, we're able to get stuff in from the outside world and shape it via our perspective. [...]

People have different wine glasses, so to speak. We all have to have a wine glass, and Kant showed that, in order to have experience, you've got to have a file system, you've got to have logic, you've got to have a clock, you've got to have a ruler – all of those, because those are all part of the experience. It happened there; it's a ruler. It's happened then; that's the clock. It's a 'this' versus a 'that.' That's the logic, and that's in the mind. The mind imposes; we would not have found causality in nature, so says Kant, if we had not imposed it via our minds. Causality is not necessarily in the nature of things. Apparently, we've got to know that, because, if you don't, then you think data and theory are value-free. Baloney! No such thing. You don't observe anything without presupposing some theory or notion of what it is you want to observe and why it's important, how much money and time and effort you're going to expend. [...] So, yeah, this is knowledge for humanity.

THE SHAMANIC SELF: DOING WORK THAT ASKS BIG
QUESTIONS AND IS DEEPLY PERSONAL

The shamanic self, as we have seen in the work and lives of the people interviewed for this book, can be a powerful way of making a difference in the world for academics. In our era, shamanism, particularly intellectual shamanism, shifts away from the magico-religious practices aimed at the supernatural that characterize shamanism in indigenous cultures. *Intellectual* shamanism emphasizes the work of healing, connecting, and sensemaking for a better world, in realms associated with ideas, theories, research approaches and methods, and within management disciplines and in management practice. The ultimate aim is to make some of these things better in some way – to do something good for the world beyond the self.

One key characteristic is that intellectual shamans connect ideas in new ways that allow for greater insight or helpful innovations conceptually, practically, and methodologically. For the *intellectual* shaman within the management academy, on whom this book focuses, this work is intellectual in nature and has to do with research, theory, practice, and action. For intellectual shamans, and, I believe, for any shaman, there is also an element of becoming fully who one is meant to be: finding and living out, to the best of one's ability, one's purpose, which demands walking through the fears and risks that are associated with following one's one light instead of doing what others or societies in some way suggest.

Shamanism is about finding and using your power – and taking necessary risks to do so. I have argued that finding your power means finding your purpose, and using that purpose in the service of something (good) beyond the self. Purpose and power have different manifestations and are different for different people. There is a spiritual element to the search for purpose and passion, and, for some of the intellectual shamans more than others, there is a more direct expression of such spirituality. The search for meaning and purpose in intellectual shamans is mostly secular, albeit, for some individuals, the search for meaning connects directly to a religious background or explicit spirituality.

The 'shamanic self' manifests itself in this search, which can be expressed as purpose, passion, spirituality, meaningfulness, or in other ways that individuals attempt to use whatever their specific gifts are, through healing, connecting, and sensemaking roles. In each case, the search leads to a sense of one's strengths: power. Key is finding how to use that power for what Buddhists call 'right work' beyond the self. Using the power that comes with such insight is where the capacities to heal, sensemake, and mediate realities can be found, when these capacities are used for good, to serve the world. When shamanic power is used appropriately, it is directed for healing purposes, for insight and knowledge, for helping the self and others makes sense of things. To do otherwise leads one to the darker path of the sorcerer, as 'dark' shamans are known in traditional cultures. The core of shamanism is finding balance, and there are any number of ways that balance can be achieved intellectually and in other aspects of the work of intellectual shamans.

Intellectual shamans find balance for themselves through their work in many different ways, often taking them to today's cutting edge of thinking, research practice, and insight. These are frequently places where more traditional academics might not willingly go, but toward which the intellectual shamans are, in a very real sense, called.

Paul Shrivastava talks about this sense of calling in describing his current work, on the nature and impact of passion for work. Note that he describes his current work holistically and without some of the more 'scientific' trappings that would prevent that holistic approach, albeit he is doing so rigorously through a hands-on, in-depth process of trying to understand individuals' experiences with passion. Shrivastava, in describing his work on passion, is also, in effect, describing intellectual shamanism and its gifts:

> I don't think passion is something that is constant and stays.
> It endures over time. [...] I'm most interested now in engaging
> community and sustainability and all these issues with passion.

I'm actually interested in understanding how passion emerges. What is it that people get passionate about, and how can we use that passion to change human nature relations? I'm not so interested today in a scientific understanding of the world or a scientific understanding of organizations and their productivity and profitability. I am interested in understanding how passion is experienced by people and how that passion can help us to create a new relationship with daily humans, their organizations, and nature.

Shrivastava continues:

The passion part has two parts to it. One is an internal sense of who I am, myself identically, and the rich the buried internal selves that we carry with us. It is psychological, it is emotional, it is personal, it is subjective, etc. But I also find that passion has another outlet, which is collective. It's in the form of a collective consciousness. You can't be passionate in isolation and in a vacuum. Passion is something that connects us to the outside world and to nature. So, to me, it has both of those elements: internal as well as the external.

Shrivastava makes the link to a more fundamental rationale for his interest in how passion arises, as a core element of the human condition:

I think the passion thing emerged from the entrepreneurial experience [that I had with an educational enterprise]. It was less connected to sustainability, when it hit me that this is a very key driver of human activity. Subsequently, after I discovered its importance, I started to apply it to sustainability, because I think sustainability is such a huge challenge that if we think about it we need some kind of enduring, more motivational system within humans and within organizations. I think trying to get them passionately engaged could be the way to become more sustainable.

Intellectual shamans are often inner-directed, rather than externally driven by social, academic, or other forces. For a minority of them, this inner direction comes in the form of what can only be called guidance. Judi Neal exemplifies this aspect of intellectual shamanism in discussing the aftermath of her whistleblowing experience early in her career:

> In the middle of this crisis, I continued to read things about spirituality, and before they were more philosophical. [...] All of a sudden it seemed like everything I read gave meaning to the crisis I was in. It helped me to understand why these things were happening and how I was supposed to respond. It gave me an anchor and direction, meaning and purpose.

This experience shaped how Neal came to define her work life, as she was pulled more strongly toward understanding the intersection of work and spirituality. She recalls:

> As I began to get more trusting about being guided in my life, this came out of that kind of sense of trust. I went to a conference, the Institute for Noetic Sciences conference in Chicago in '94, and people were asking me, 'Why are you here? What are you interested in?' I told them I was interested in the intersection of spirituality and work. The more people I talked to, they kept saying 'You know, I'm a therapist, and I'm interested in spirituality in therapy.' Or 'I'm a nurse and I'm interested in spirituality in nursing.' Whoever I met, they were saying 'I'm really interested in the intersection [of spirituality] in my work.' So I would ask them, 'Well, what are you doing? They would start to tell me stories about how they actually integrated spirituality in their work.

From this beginning, Neal began doing some of the early work and presentations about spirituality at work, starting an organization called Spirit at Work, discussed earlier, and later moving on to be the first director of the Tyson Center for Faith and Spirituality in the Workplace at the Sam M. Walton College of Business, University of Arkansas, from which she has now retired. She had already retired early from the University of New Haven when the opportunity in

Arkansas came up, simultaneously with meeting the man who is now her husband. Torn between accepting the offer and the new relationship, Neal recalls the synchronicity involved in her desire to accept the job in Arkansas while continuing a relationship that had begun in New England. The awakening of her interest in the then cutting-edge topic of spirituality and work had deep roots for Neal, who had also had a near-death experience that heightened her sensitivity to such issues. She describes the experience:

> I have to go back to an older story. When I was twenty-four I gave birth to my second son, and in the process, somewhere in that night, I hemorrhaged seriously and had to be rushed to the emergency room, and had a near-death experience. In that near-death experience, I had just this incredible experience of being one with God, which was a real shock because I was an atheist at that point. I had given up. I had really given up on religion and God, and just couldn't believe that there was a God because of some horrible things that were happening to me and in the world. All of a sudden, there I was in God's loving presence, and wanting to go back to be with my child and thinking, 'That never happens. That's breaking cosmic rules.' But I asked God to be sent back, and was sent back.

Realizing, with the help of her brother, that the experience had been very real, Neal was nonetheless left with more questions than answers: 'I'm just this twenty-four-year-old housewife with no college education and no self-esteem. What am I supposed to do? I felt like I was supposed to save the world. That's why I was sent back, and I didn't know how in the world this housewife with a new baby could do that.' Some ten years later Neal read a book called *Life after Life*, which helped her normalize her experience. She continues:

> My sense was that I was part of what I call the 'peaceful army'; that there's a whole bunch of us who have a sense of mission and vision. We may not all know what it is. For a while I thought it was all the people who had near-death experiences. Then I realized, no, no,

that's just one way to get your sense of mission. There are many millions of us who have a sense of mission and who have a commitment to making the world a better place.

Another of the intellectual shamans who is deeply and explicitly spiritual is the University of Michigan's Bob Quinn, who is Mormon. Quinn's career has been about helping people and organizations change, as his seminal book *Deep Change* reveals. Quinn remarks, 'There was a time – for example, when I started to write *Deep Change* – where I had reduced everything I knew to one sentence: "Deep change or slow death." I felt that sentence was full of power and potency, but most people listen to that and say "Big deal."' He reveals how his passion to understand and help people with change came about when he was just an undergraduate student, having just returned from a difficult year as a missionary for his Church, with an undetermined future path, and discovered that

> I was mostly failing, but I threw myself at it, committed myself to it, and continued to fail, but discovered that, if I went through extensive self-change, things started to happen. [...] It's almost unimaginable how demanding it was: a personal change process, of just purifying out all the normal assumptions that a twenty-year-old can make, and then – boom! – it was this powerful transformation. Suddenly I had a voice that was powerful and spiritual, and people started listening and changing their lives.

His transition to college as a twenty-year-old was difficult, however, until a friend recognized that Quinn was sleeping all the time because he was depressed. Quinn recalls:

> So here I was, a twenty-year-old, helping adults make these dramatic changes in their lives, because I had changed me. It was so sacred, it was unspeakable. The stories were incredible. But I came home to be a sophomore in college. They said, 'Here's your 101 this book, and your 101 that book,' and I was so depressed. So I said, 'What am I going to do with my life?' I was sleeping all the time. This guy said,

'You're not tired, you're depressed.' So I started looking for the answer. What do I major in? I prayed about it, fasted about it. No answers.

Guidance came in a flash of insight.

Then, one day, I'm walking across campus, and lightning strikes me, and the lightning is a new question. The question is, 'Up until now, what's the most meaningful thing you've ever done in your life?' Now, it was like a micro-micro-second instantaneously; with the formulation of that question, was the answer. The answer was, it's when I've talked to someone and said some things that have caused them to change their lives in a way that they would never retreat from their forward progress. It would change them forever. That's the most meaningful thing I've ever done.

With a new 'voice in his head' saying 'Major in change!' (a major that did not then exist), Quinn began a new strategy of not taking classes but taking professors – any great teacher he could find.

I would take any class that would give me insight into change. So I would obtain classes from all over the place. I would never again take a class; I would only take professors. That is, I would only take great teachers, and I would do whatever it took to worm my way into the classes of great teachers. I would go to public lectures – unthinkable notion. . .; who would do that? I would read books that weren't assigned.

Note the power of following purpose in what Quinn describes, as he concludes:

Suddenly, in answering the question, I'm going to major in change; I've committed to know change. It crosses boundaries. I formally majored in sociology, but I was now an active consumer rather than a passive consumer of education, which most students never do. I got a master's in organizational development, which was just being born because it fit the criteria. I went on and did the PhD, and for the

rest of my life I studied change, practiced consulting in change.
I wrote papers and books about change. The topics could vary, but
they all wove back to the notion of changing the human condition,
having the power to do that. It was very much a calling – right? It was
very much, but it wasn't about a specific activity, like teaching or
being a consultant. . .; it was changing human potential.

The idea of changing human potential, though expressed differently, is familiar to the University of Michigan's Jane Dutton, who has
done extensive work in recent years on compassion in the workplace
and is, along with Quinn, Kim Cameron, and others, a founder of the
positive organizational scholarship movement. Dutton recalls her earlier days feeling something of a misfit at Michigan, before she began
working closely with Quinn and Cameron, and what a revelation POS
was for her – and them. She relates the story:

> [POS] is such an important part of my life, by far the most
> meaningful thing. . . I and others are just trying to use whatever grace
> and legitimacy we're given from the fact that we're here [at
> Michigan] to do something that we really think is useful. [. . .] It's just
> such an example of how the discourse, the language, can change.
> How you experience a community. It's not the people; it's 'What are
> the conversations we're having?' Now we've been having
> conversations for ten years that have been really meaningful.

Dutton continues, relating some of the origin story of the POS
movement's first conference, where she and Quinn risked doing things
very differently. Part of the shamanic self is learning to go where
instinct and a certain sense of flow take you, taking advantage of
opportunities that present themselves and seem synchronistically
'right.' Dutton explains how what Otto Scharmer calls 'letting come'
evolved into what became the POS movement:

> At [the first POS] conference we did this thing the last day. It was a
> day-and-a-half conference, so it was the last half-day. I said to Bob
> Quinn, 'This will never work, Bob. Let's not do this.' He said, 'Ah,

just trust me, Jane.' I've learned that when people say that, you go – and he was so right! He put people in random groups and said, 'All right, you have an hour to create a symposium or a PDW [professional development workshop for the Academy of Management annual meeting submission process], and then you have to present it to the group by the end of the day.'

It was what I thought was an impossible, possibly alienating, charge, but, damn it, if people didn't do a great job! It was so stunning what people put together, half doctoral students, half faculty, from different parts of the university. [These were] people who didn't know each other. People came up with great things. That was in December, so they all got submitted to the Academy, and I think nine out of twelve got accepted. So, between this period of having this idea that maybe we should do something [about POS] and actually getting a lot of feedback that in fact it could be useful and creating some toehold in the academy, it just sort of seemed like this was supposed to happen.

Experiences such as Dutton's finding her purpose around issues of compassion and POS are lasting and transformative. Such experiences have what I can only call an 'energy' or vibration around them that serves as what physicists would call a strange attractor. They provide a sort of glue that keeps the intellectual shaman engaged, energized, and hard-working over long periods of time. Dutton comments, 'You know, that was ten years ago, and I feel still as much energy about it.'

Otto Scharmer expresses much the same sentiment:

I nourish myself through enjoyment. I enjoy what I do, and that's what's nourishing me. It's as simple as that. I think that's number one. [...] Yes, I do a lot of other things, ...but the number one thing for me is basically following your heart. Then do something that really inspires yourself. Try to develop the connections you have with other people so that this something keeps nourishing you. This has to do with the economics of energy. So there's the normal energy economics, and then there's more intentional or spiritual economics of energy, when it comes to your purpose. So, normal tasks or jobs – . . .we are tired in the end.

But then there's other work; when we do it, the more we do it, the more energy we have. It's the other way around, and that's what I mean. It has to do with purpose. It's not just an intellectual purpose, of course. It's like a purpose that you find through your heart. It's, kind of, this 'Do what you love, love what you do,' this kind of enjoyment. If what you do really has this high quality, then you have the benefit. Although you do a lot, and people expect you to be exhausted (and sometimes, of course, you are), but actually you are nourished even more.

Notable also is the sense of flow – the 'allowing' of the opportunity to emerge that permits new things to evolve – that is at the core of what happened to Quinn, Dutton, and Neal. The University of Virginia's Ed Freeman concurs:

> I think life is about how you take, in part, advantage of the serendipity that unfolds before you. Think of your life as a canvas, which you created in much the way the artist does. There's a wonderful book by Alexander Nehamus called *Nietzsche: Life as Literature*. It's about a sort of Nietzchean view of how you create your own life. I find that to be a very empowering way to really think about, to be open to new experiences and to make it up as you go along.

This kind of 'allowing' of serendipity to take the lead at turning points is something that many of the intellectual shamans have experienced. Freeman holds black belts in tae kwon do and is a serious musician and songwriter, as well as a renowned academic. He elaborates his sense of both the opportunistic nature of some developments, their spiritual underpinning, and this sense of allowing. Growing up as an Evangelical Southern Baptist, reading philosophy, Freeman ultimately identified as, in his words, 'a kind of unbeliever' in traditional religions (ironically, he is currently also a professor of religious studies at the University of Virginia). Through becoming adept at martial arts, he also began to turn toward meditation and Buddhist thought. He wryly comments:

> People ask me now, and, depending on the circumstances, I say either, 'Well, I'm an atheist' or 'I'm a Buddhist.' Sometimes I say both, and let them puzzle that out. I guess spirituality can mean a whole bunch of things. That's the way I see it. Certainly in martial arts, and certainly in music, there are moments of what Csikszentmihaly would call flow, in which you are one with the universe. That's the only way to see that. As an intellectual enterprise, Buddhism has the best (I think) explanations [for that]. But, again, it's the experiences that are of interest.

Freeman explains:

> Sure, [experiences of connection with the universe, or flow] come in lots of places, and then you try and create them. I've found, interestingly enough, the place where they come as sort of flow moments, if you go with that metaphor, is songwriting. Where, as strange as it sounds, it feels like you've sort of tapped into some stream and they just come, the songs just come in. Some of them are crap, but some of them can be pretty good. To me, they come bunches at a time, come three-quarters time. That's a little bit the way writing goes. It's a little bit like we find more of those things [happening], I think, the more you're open to it. It's a hard thing to teach, a hard thing to even talk about. You never talk about that in business school, for God's sake! That's too bad.

McGill University's Henry Mintzberg explicitly reflects a similar quality of 'dreaming' the world you want into existence in thinking about how his life and work have evolved over time:

> I always thought, if I wrote an autobiography, it could be titled *Dreams I Never Could Have Dreamt*, because my life has been, kind of, charmed. In the case of my academic career, I never dreamed that

I could be successful. I certainly was ambitious and hoped for success, but, no, I never anticipated any of this.

It was by following his instincts and interests that Mintzberg became successful as an academic, and much of that instinct has to do with an ability to diagnose organizations:

There's a science fiction book about a guy who goes crazy because, when people are cutting the grass, he can hear the grass screaming. Well, I've never read it, but when I walk into an organization I can smell what's going on. . .in an instant. I can feel if this place is well run, badly run. I really have the sense of that, and sometimes other people are, like, 'Why are you complaining about this place?' I say, 'Well, if you feel that way, here it is.' I can tell what's going on behind the scenes with that guy, and everybody else. So I sort of have a knack for it. [. . .] I'm never interested in micro-behavior. I mean, I'm interested in everybody else, but I'm not a psychologist. I'm not drawn to that. I was never interested in macro-behavior. I think economists sit in the clouds and don't know what's happening on the ground. Organization is in between. It kind of suits my personality, I guess, in the sense that you can get in and see things in more of a structural than a personal way, yet you can do tangible things. I love being influenced by what's going on, on the ground, and organization studies gives you a chance to see what's going on, on the ground, at the same time that you can kind of abstract into a collective kind of thing.

The University of Michigan's Andy Hoffman talks about his circuitous path to finding his own way in the world, including 'allow-ing' both passion and serendipity, along with a willingness to take advantage of opportunities that presented themselves, to play a role. Talking about finding purpose in life by following his interests and passions and 'allowing,' Hoffman notes:

I am motivated by the idea that we have a purpose and a set of skills and gifts, and that we should use them to the benefit of society as best we can. That's what I'm trying to do. I never thought about [career turns] as risks, but they motivated me to go down this path, I think, accidently. I don't think it was by design, but without having an angle in mind you just go with the journey, and when a door opens you go through it if it seems like the right door at the moment. My path has been circuitous and it may seem random, but I was open to the possibilities around me, and I think those make the most interesting lives.

Of course, openness to serendipity and 'allowing' does not mean 'going with the flow' in the new age sense of the phrase. Rather, it means having the wisdom to see the opportunity in a new situation and being willing to both take advantage of it and undertake the decisions, actions, and hard work needed to realize that opportunity. Hoffman continues:

> I'm always excited about hearing people taking hard right turns in their life, like a friend that was at the Harvard Business School and queued up to be the CEO of his parents' corporation. At the last minute he said 'This isn't for me,' and quit to become a cop in LA. I love stories like that; stories of people just taking control of their lives and taking them where they want to go. I have to believe that, at the end, that's where you derive the most satisfaction. You live the life you wanted to live. The most regret comes when I made decisions – and we all do – to satisfy somebody else. It's either their expectations, their assessment of me, and that's unfortunate.

Hoffman talks about the risks he took going into the sustainability arena before it had become the popular topic that it is today. Though not a theoretically oriented person, Hoffman had significant mentors who taught him to write academic papers, but initially he was turned down for academic jobs because people thought he was too focused on the natural environment – because he was taking the risk of following his passion.

Going into an area like the environment... It's hot now. I'm really amused by this. When I came out [of the doctoral program], I got turned down for a job at [an institution] where they said, 'We really love your stuff on institutional theory, but we think you're too focused on the environment.' People were afraid of the environment. When I was here at MIT [where the interview was conducted, and where he received his PhD], I would go to people to be on my committee, and they'd say, 'I would love to do that, but I'm not going to do it until I'm tenured. It's too risky.'

His view is tempered by practical considerations, however, which may suggest the limits of such allowing and following of one's passion, not necessarily for himself but for others, as he continues:

Being driven by a desire to focus on what mattered to me took me towards the environment. I would not say to someone 'Follow your heart and everything will work out,' because I could have picked an issue that mattered to me and no one else. But I also I had a strong ambivalence towards academia. If I didn't get tenure, I really didn't care. I really didn't, because I knew that I could get a job in practice in a heartbeat; therefore, it freed me up to break some of these rules, some of which I think are pretty bogus. 'Don't do books!' I actually think that's a myth. I think books really made my career.

DREAMING A BETTER WORLD

The core work of shamans, whether intellectual, traditional, or in some other line of work, is to dream the world you want into existence. But this dreaming is far from daydreaming, as we have already seen. It can entail significant risk and demands talent and hard work, as well as an orientation toward building a better world. In other words, it is about making a (positive) difference in the world and being willing to do what is necessary to accomplish that. But there is also a sense in many of the intellectual shamans of having simply been lucky – a luck that combines with hard work, risk-taking, and synchronicity to help them dream their particular worlds into existence.

For David Cooperrider, appreciative inquiry represents that kind of dreaming the world into existence. Note in the following how important the framing of an inquiry is to its eventual outcome as he sees it. While Cooperrider calls this 'framing the social construction of reality,' it is, in essence, what shamans would call dreaming the world into existence. Illustrating how this process works in practice, Cooperrider observes:

> What sustains me now, and what sustained me early on, is that we become what we study. It's almost like a nutritional excellence program. If we're flooding our body with nutritional excellence of things that give our body maximum nourishment in life, then it has an impact on our whole system. The same thing [is true] with inquiry. What gave me strength and support was choosing these topics that gave me an open doorway into realities that I wouldn't have seen before. [...]
>
> So I decided to start studying these things, and, like food, it filled my body and my mind and my heart with such capacity that it provided all the support I needed just simply doing that. For example, when I started this study on business as an agent of world benefit, what does it look like, where is it happening? Well, once you declare that topic, all of a sudden reality starts shaping itself; people send you articles. Pretty soon my whole office was filled with materials that I had never read before; all of these materials giving me more hope about our future than anything I'd ever studied before.

Cooperrider gives a concrete example of this unfolding process, elaborating:

> I was on my way to Israel to give a talk on business as an agent of world benefit... On the way I stopped in Amman, Jordan, during early moments of the bombing of Iraq. You can imagine the tensions at that moment. Here I am, I'm in Amman, Jordan, and I'm meeting with the former prime minister... That next day I woke up, and there are headlines in the paper saying there was a terrorist plot that

was to let go of a biological weapon intended to kill 150,000 people in Amman. That hit me hard, and I could feel the edge that the world was on. So, on my way to Israel the next day, I changed the topic of my speech and I decided to talk about business and peace. I had never talked about that before and I didn't have much background.

The speech went OK, and afterwards an elderly man in his mid-eighties came up to me and said, 'David, let me introduce myself. My name is Stef Wertheimer [a German-born Israeli business industrialist, humanitarian, and former politician, who has started a number of industrial parks in Israel and elsewhere]. Your proposition is right on target. Business is a force for peace.' I had started my speech with 'Where's the peace going to come from in this part of the world? I don't think it's going to come from the lawyers. I don't think it's going to come from our military. I don't think it's going to come from our paralyzed senates and governments. Could it be that business could be the most important force for peace?'

Wertheimer invited Cooperrider to meet him the next day at his helicopter to visit an area of the Galilee region called Tefon. Flying through this area, with the Mediterranean to the left and through deserts to hills, where all they could see were a few goats but no natural resources, the pilot landed in a beautiful setting that Cooperrider describes as having magnificent homes, beautiful museums, parks, recreation spaces, schools – all placed in the middle of the desert in the hills. Cooperrider continues:

> We're landing, and he starts telling me this story of how he gave birth to his entrepreneurship center there, an industrial incubator. They've given birth to over 300 businesses in the last ten years that now account for over 10 percent of Israel's export GNP [gross national product]. Then he started telling me the key point of this whole experiment was to bring people together. So everything is co-owned. It's all coexistence: of Arab and Jewish co-ownership of the schools, co-ownership of the businesses, co-ownership of the parks and the museums, and so on. Here I am in this part of the

world, where everyone – all of the media, the negative media – says it's intractable, the hatred, the bitterness, the fear, the ancient animosities will never be resolved. Yet here's this amazing world-class story right there that I had never heard about before. It wasn't just business philanthropy. It wasn't charity. It was real, solid business.

Cooperrider's appreciative inquiry, as applied to businesses as a positive benefit to the world (what he and his colleagues term business as an agent of world benefit), has all the characteristics of dreaming a better world into existence. Here is how Cooperrider frames what this initiative is ultimately attempting to accomplish:

> What gives me strength? It's literally that I am taken to a new level every time I do one of these appreciative inquiries. My sense of hope about what we're capable of as human beings, my sense of the goodness, fundamental goodness in human beings, of what we're capable of collectively, goes up each time I do one of these interviews. In a study on business as an agent of world benefit, we've gathered over 2,000 stories. We've taken it to the largest appreciative inquiry project we've ever done. We've taken the appreciative inquiry questions, what I call unconditional positive questions, and put them out on a website where anybody in the world can download the questions, and then go into their communities or their villages or the cities and find stories of business and society innovation that helps us begin to think in new ways about a twenty-first-century relationship between business and society.

Paul Shrivastava, who works on aesthetic rationality, gives another example of how entrepreneurs, guided by their own lights, operate from a similar shamanic place. He tells the following story about individuals he calls passionate entrepreneurs, who like intellectual shamans follow their own lights as they attempt to build their businesses. A stubborn form of vision is central to the persistence necessary for success, even in the face of advice to the contrary. Shrivastava comments:

> They do have a vision of where their organizations can go. They have a very intense sense of hope that keeps them engaged, and it is sometimes a very unrealistic one. But they don't listen to anybody else; they just want to do it. I don't think it is a kind of special knowledge, because many times...they hold onto it very intently, and they're kind of obstinate, almost, in giving it up. But whether it is a sort of a revelation – that I'm not 100 percent sure of.
>
> Many of them, actually, don't have specialized knowledge. The one guy who was right next to me [in an innovation lab], his product was making small rubber magnets that go on refrigerators. [...] That was his business, but it was not high tech or something that required great new knowledge or a special way of working. But he was committed to the idea that he wanted to be the best, to make his magnets for Disney, and for Penn State, and for all the big guys. He would do anything, even if some business was not financially rewarding. He had an option that was more financially rewarding and he would not follow what our finance professors would tell him to do. He would follow his passion for Disney: 'I want to get into Disney! Disney's where it's at! I'll do it even if I lose some money.' Eventually he ended up being very successful, where he followed that passion.
>
> Now, you could call it a vision or whatever. But I don't think it comes out of some revelatory cognitive innovation. It is a state of emotion, it's a mood of the person, and I saw [it] constant[ly] across everybody, regardless of how sophisticated or unsophisticated their products were.

Dreaming a better world, as intellectual shamans do, applies beyond their theorizing and organizational impacts. It also applies to their thinking about teaching and the classroom. Jim Walsh illustrates the application of this thinking to his teaching:

I was first exposed to the demands and power of teaching at Dartmouth. They take their teaching very seriously there. Honestly, I am so grateful that I was able to begin my career at Tuck [the Tuck School of Business]. I managed to survive in their classrooms, but I sure didn't leave Hanover as any kind of great teacher. I did leave with a set of values and reflexes that helped me grow over the next twenty-plus years, though. I learned that you need to be yourself and that you need to teach for transformation.

I've also learned over time that I much prefer to connect with my students as individuals and not as some kind of large mass. I have some skill at managing a class of, say, seventy-five or eighty people, but I'm always trying to figure out a way to make the experience more intimate somehow. I want to know people by name, and, more than that, know who they are, how they think, what they care about, and more. [...]

I started to teach undergraduates a few years ago. Speaking of transformation, that experience has transformed me. [...] When our daughter went off to college, I decided to see what it would be like to work with people who were her age. That's when the real power and responsibility of teaching became apparent to me. Of course, twenty-two-year-olds are in a very different place than twenty-eight-year-olds, thirty-eight-year-olds, or forty-eight-year-olds. They are still very much in formation (if I can use that word). I really do believe that you can change lives for the better if you can earn their trust. It's exhilarating. It's truly exhilarating. It's been a journey, but, to get where I am now, I had to develop another skill. Much like with writing, I needed to develop the confidence to be myself in the classroom. Parker Palmer talks about this very phenomenon in his book *The Courage to Teach*. I needed to find that courage, or, maybe more to the point, I needed to learn that I needed to find that courage.

Walsh relates this teaching experience to personal authenticity – being himself – and finding the voice he needs to speak from that place, whether it is in the classroom or in his academic writing. He elaborates:

> I spent way too many years trying to learn how to operate in front of a room, to learn class management skills, and – I hate to say it – to try to teach cases by somebody else's standards. It finally dawned on me that, no matter what I did (or did not do) in class, I survived because I was being me – even as I worked hard to almost suppress the real me, as I fiddled about with board preparation in the good old days, or building snazzy PowerPoint decks more recently. I always cared. I think my students picked up on those good intentions.
>
> At the end of the day, teaching is all about sharing yourself with your students. Do that and they will reciprocate. The class I developed for the undergraduates is, in essence, my own intellectual journey. I try to be alive and present in the class and share my (I'll even say it) my love for my students. Do that, and we all come alive! It is beyond wonderful!

Coming around to this sense of authenticity, to being fully one-self and living one's one life with purpose, teachers such as Jim Walsh and, as we will see below, Maurizio Zollo, along with most of the other intellectual shamans, find ways to help their students do much the same. Zollo discusses how he approaches this idea, not from a content perspective but, as with Torbert and Scharmer, from the place of inquiry. Zollo notes:

> If you we want to build leadership skills, you have to allow individuals to go through a deep transformation, personal transformation, deep inquiry. You have to give them the opportunity to. . .to really face themselves and deeply go inside, touch the foundational elements of their self, and eventually emerge as a different human being. I think we have that responsibility if we want to nurture and develop corporate leaders. We don't do that; we shy away from it. First of all because we don't quite understand it, and again, we don't feel comfortable. It's difficult for instructors as well, for us.

The University of Michigan's Jane Dutton views her shamanic skills as helping others to 'birth' their work. She explains:

I see their greatness. [...] I don't have a hard time imagining everybody as quite amazing, in this life. [...] I have more of an appreciative stance. It doesn't carry over to other parts of my life. So it's that I see stars in everything. For whatever reason, in this field, since the time I was a student, I could see something that I thought was really wonderful in everyone's work. [...] It's just something that comes. My seeing that way means that people experience me differently. Then I have the job of the relationship, and whose relationships really have enabled me to do quite well professionally, but it was never about that. [...] It's not that everyone is the same, but I've never seen anyone that doesn't have something to offer, ever, in our field.

AND SO – WHAT ABOUT YOU?

The pathbreaking work of many of the intellectual shamans speaks to some of the ills of today's academy – and of the world more generally. In the complexities of the modern world, approaching issues and problems from a single discipline's perspective – or from that of a single idea or theory – provides only limited potential for breakthroughs and insights. Perhaps it is the disciplinary focus of so much of today's academia that underlies the numerous complaints that there are fewer big ideas, big breakthroughs, new ways of thinking today than in the past. Overspecialization in the world of wicked problems that we actually face provides barren ground for new ideas. As we have seen with the healing, boundary-spanning, and sensemaking orientations of intellectual shamans, bridging among different realms, wanting to make the world a better place, and having the courage to be one's self – fully – are crucial to the work of the intellectual shaman.

The shaman is a person of light – and the light shines out to the world in the form of ideas, insights, and a way of being in the world. The light attracts others to the person and his or her ideas and work.

The light is something that is inherent, and it can be developed over time. I believe that anyone willing to find and feed his or her own light can become a shaman in whatever world he or she chooses to function in.

The shaman is a person of power – used in the service of others or the world, something beyond the self. It is the power that is the source of light, I believe, and that power comes from recognizing and following a purpose beyond self-interest, and being willing to take the risks, outsider status, and challenges that come with following purpose to become, as we have seen, fully who you are. Thus, the shaman is a person who recognizes and accepts his or her own power, gifts, or abilities – and uses them for productive good in some way, in particular, as we have seen, for healing, sensemaking, and making connections among different realms. The shaman knows his or her purpose and is willing to live out that purpose by living life fully and helping others do so.

The shaman is a healer, connector, and sensemaker, particularly in the intellectual world. He or she takes the necessary risks, learns to understand the system, tries to bridge boundaries that others might avoid, and then attempts to make sense of all of it. These capacities are available to all of us, if we are willing to do the work and take the steps necessary to find our own, individual source of power – and put that purpose to work to serve the world in some way.

Being an intellectual shaman can sometimes mean stepping out on intellectual or other cliffs willingly, because it is what must be done to embody purpose. Misused traditional shamanism can result in harm; shamans on the dark side are often called sorcerers. The same is true of the intellectual shaman if the light goes dark while the power remains. Ideas matter. Words matter. Practices matter. Questions and inquiries matter. Great damage can be done via theory, research, teaching, and practice that offer prescriptions or insights that are wrong or harmful. Conversely, great good comes when ideas provide strength, a future orientation to making the world better and healing what needs to be put right. This is the core work of intellectual shamans.

Seeing things in new ways, making connections across boundaries, and making sense of what has been seen: these skills are desperately needed for dealing with the systemic and 'wicked' problems of the modern world, even within the more narrowly construed world of academia. This seeing can happen only in the context of holistic thinking, a questioning of accepted views, and the courage to stake out a claim of one's own based on new ways of connecting what has been learned. Just as the Newtonian view of a mechanical world gave way in physics to the mysteries of the quantum view, so in academia – and other arenas in which policy, strategy, and systems thinking are important – single-disciplinary, fragmented, and atomistic thinking needs to give way to the more holistic thinking and acting that we have seen in the work of the intellectual shamans profiled here. Purely theory-based research needs to give way to observation- and experience-based research grounded in the world of practice, problems, or issues that need attention.

The shamanic experience is nothing if it is not about transformation: both personal transformation, the transformation of those persons the shaman attempts to heal, and the transformation of the world, so that it is a better place for all. For intellectual shamans in the management academy, transformation is of disciplines and fields, organizations, management practice, research approaches, and the classroom. Shamans, as the great mythologist Joseph Campbell demonstrates, can and do go through personally transformative experiences and sometimes mix the dream that they wish to bring into being with reality. Indeed, their claim might well be that what is experienced in their dream of something better is exactly the path of transformation.

The world needs more intellectual and other shamans today. Academia needs more intellectual shamans in all disciplines. We all, I believe, have the capacity – the light – within ourselves to become shamanic in our own ways if we wish.

Maybe everyone doesn't want to be a shaman, intellectual or otherwise. The path to intellectual shamanism can be tortuous and winding. The road is not always easy. The 'call' to shamanic practice can be decidedly difficult, fraught with crises and risks. A lot of hard work, some mentoring by others, and a degree of careful listening to 'hear' and 'see' when you are in the right place for becoming yourself are necessary. The reward is great, however. Finding and living your purpose. Living a rich and meaningful (academic) life. Doing your bit to serve the world.

Everyone's particular path is unique. Though I firmly believe that everyone has the power to become shamanic in the senses that the intellectual shamans demonstrate, with their lives and work, not everyone may wish to do so or feel the call in that direction. At its core, becoming shamanic means accessing the power and wisdom that is inherently within you (or that you can access from elsewhere) and using that power in the interest of something beyond the self. That something beyond the self helps to heal some piece of the world, bring together ideas, people, or interests that might not otherwise be brought together, or make sense of the world in new ways.

Newer, more junior scholars, in particular, may fear that the path to intellectual shamanism is not without significant career risks. Indeed, when I have talked about this work with more junior academics, one common response is 'I can't do that or I'll never get tenure! I need to publish (a lot) in the "right" journals, the ones that my university says matter because they have the right impact factor. I need to have the right number of citations. I need to do work that will get accepted to these mainstream journals – and what I'm really interested in is out of the mainstream. Maybe I'll wait till I get tenure, or full professor, or my family is grown, or... Then I'll take the necessary risks.'

The problem is that the day for taking risks may never come! The goal for too many scholars today becomes the equivalent of the deeply flawed notion that 'maximizing shareholder wealth' is the purpose of business – something that is inherently meaningless and that inspires little passion. In my view, this path is a prescription for burnout, work of little significance or impact on the 'real' world, and, ultimately, frustration. As a famous advertisement says, 'A mind [and, I would add, 'heart'] is a terrible thing to waste.'[1n]

We have seen, in the lives and work of intellectual shamans, that intellectual shamanism means starting from an inquiry, a question, an idea – and following that idea to its implications, even when that means questioning what everyone 'knows.' We have seen that intellectual shamanism in the management academy means starting with observations of practice, the much-vaunted 'real' world, and seeing where those observations take you. We have seen that there is indeed risk involved: papers and ideas that might not be accepted immediately by the 'best' journals, if you are working outside the mainstream, and many other potential problems. On the other hand, if as a scholar you are doing work that deeply engages you, that you believe is important, and about which you are passionate – then isn't it likely you will be both a happier person and a better scholar? Isn't it just possible that you will yourself serve the world in ways that are completely unexpected? And isn't it just possible, even in today's academic culture, dominated as it is by citation count and impact factor concerns, that your work (if it is good – and that is an important caveat) will get you noticed in some of the same ways that the intellectual shamans in this book became noticed?

So, yes. Intellectual shamanism is a risky business, and demands being a bit of a maverick, stepping outside the accepted canon, the accepted intellectual pathways, and finding out what really matters to you, now and in an ongoing way. It means following your scholarly instincts about significant questions that can help our troubled world work better. It means finding your passion, or, as the mythologist Joseph Campbell said, your 'bliss,' and following it – because that is what you have to do to truly become fully who you are and to do your particular healing, connecting, and sensemaking work. In the end, there is another, more significant risk among the possible career risks of intellectual shamanism, and that is the risk to yourself and your fully human purpose of *not* following your way of dreaming the world into existence.

One final quote from Otto Scharmer highlights the path of intellectual shamanism. Scharmer says, in talking about personal transformation and his work of theory U for transforming to a sustainable and equitable world,

That does not mean everyone becomes an Ed Schein or Henry Mintzberg. That's not the point. Because it is not about. . .Otto becoming another Ed Schein. It's Otto becoming Otto, and the next person becoming his own thing. It's not really replicating what other people did. What this real intention is that what people bring differs from person to person. I would say, ideally, the ultimate goal of education should be that we create environments where, if you have. . .a million students, you have a million different student journeys, different study tracks; where it's not manufactured. . .but where the curriculum is really reassembled and aligned around the entrepreneurial intention of what people bring into their student years.

That goes beyond. . .the old distinction of disciplines, and it also goes beyond just problem-solving, or we need ecological problem-solving or this or that. It really connects more with the deeper entrepreneurial capacity that I think is dormant in every human being. I see that in companies, in governments, in NGOs. There is so much more in creative potential that you can experience working with [people at different stages]. This potential is not activated in the way we structure universities [or businesses, governments, or societies] these days. [. . .] If we reinvent the university [or businesses, societies, or governments] of this century, we can create similar conditions for many more students.

If we reinvent education, if we reinvent universities, if we reinvent organizing, if we reinvent societies, economics, and sustainable enterprise of all sorts, we can perhaps tap the potential within human beings to reinvent our relationships with each other and change our world for the better. We have to dream a new world into existence.

In my view, we as shamans, intellectual and other, can and need to retell our own cultural myths in ways that allow for sustainability and equity, that bring us closer together, not farther apart, and that allow 'enough' for everyone to thrive. Ultimately, that is the healing work of shamanism in today's world. The world needs us to act as shamans, as healers, sensemakers, and connectors who, each in our unique way, find our power and our purposes – and to live those purposes out in the service of a better world.

> We are all shamans.
> We can all be shamans.
> The power is within us if we only realize it.
> To realize it, we have to live it.

Dream the world that you wish to see into existence.

Notes

1 THE INTELLECTUAL SHAMAN

[1] For many years I was involved with a program developed at my home institution, Boston College, called 'Leadership for Change', that attempted to provide a basis for developing managers and leaders as change agents with a social purpose. One of our core colleagues in that endeavor was Robert Leaver, founder of the New Commons think tank in Providence, Rhode Island, who always used to ask participants this core question: how will you serve the world? I am deeply grateful to Robert for providing this seed question.

[2] I want here to acknowledge that the metaphor of light comes in part from informal conversations with Jim Walsh, one of the people profiled in this book, who has stated multiple times that he is attracted to people who seem to have a certain inner light.

[3] More information about John Myerson, his writings, and other work can be found at http://life-arts.com.

[4] For more details on Peter Frost's career and contributions, see http://ssb64. devl.sauder.ubc.ca/Faculty/People/Hidden_Faculty_Members/Frost_Peter.

[5] A short methodological note: quotes are directly from transcribed interviews unless otherwise indicated and are verbatim, except for the removal of unnecessary verbal ticks or speech mannerisms, such as 'I mean,' 'you know,' too many 'ands,' starting sentences with 'like,' and similar phrases when they would otherwise interfere with the telling of the story.

2 THE PATH TO INTELLECTUAL SHAMANISM: BECOMING FULLY WHO YOU ARE

[1] Bob Sutton discusses this paper in a blog entitled 'Work matters,' posted at http://bobsutton.typepad.com/my_weblog/2009/12/the-asshole-john-van-maanens-classic-article-on-police-officers.html, viewed January 16, 2013.

[2] Sutton, 'Work matters' blog, viewed January 16, 2013.

[3] James March is the Jack Steel Parker Professor Emeritus at Stanford University and the Stanford University School of Education. Renowned for his work with Richard Cyert on the behavioral theory of the firm, and with others for articulating the 'garbage can' model of organizing, March is one of the most influential management scholars, who spent much of his career before joining Stanford at Carnegie-Mellon University.

3 BEYOND THE SELF: POWER OF PURPOSE

[1] Source: http://jamespwalsh.com/biography.html.
[2] Source: http://jamespwalsh.com/biography.html.
[3] Freeman, www.consciouscapitalism.org/purpose.
[4] See www. mintzberg.org.

4 HEALER

[1] See www.oatshoes.com/about/ for more company details.
[2] Malcolm Gladwell outlines the idea that 10,000 hours of practice in any discipline, particularly guided by knowledge masters and with a degree of discipline, are needed to master it.[107]

5 CONNECTOR

[1] Rev. Dale White of South Africa was executive director of the Wilgespruit Fellowship Centre (1965 to 1993); a priest at various Anglican congregations in Soweto (1957 onwards); executive trustee: Fellow Trust (1984 to 1999); special pensions board member: government of South Africa (1997); chairperson of St Gregory's College, Kwa-Zulu Natal (1992 to 1996); executive committee member of the South African Council of Churches (1984 to 1988); United Religion's initiative – South African representative (since 1997); member of the Council of Parliament of World Religions (since 1999); and chairperson of the Interdenominational Committee for Industrial Mission (1968 to 1988). He was influential in challenging the injustices of apartheid in South Africa.
[2] Stephen Bantu Biko (1946 to 1977) was an anti-apartheid activist in South Africa who was killed while in police custody, and he is considered something of a martyr for the anti-apartheid movement.
[3] See http://goldenforsustainability.org.

⁴ Complete disclosure: Phil now knows that I was the anonymous reviewer on his *Academy of Management Learning and Education* 'best paper' about consciousness-raising in executives.

⁵ See www.youtube.com/watch?v=cqNYF92dlEw.

7 THE *INTELLECTUAL* SHAMAN

¹ Definitions from www.thefreedictionary.com/Intellectuals, viewed July 24, 2013.

8 SAGE: THE WORK OF WISDOM

¹ This quote comes from an advertising slogan begun by the United Negro College Fund, starting in 1972 and still used to this day.

References

1 Egri C. P., Frost P. Shamanism and change: bringing back the magic in organizational transformation. *Research in Organizational Change and Development.* 1991; 5: 175–221.

2 Frost P., Egri C. P. The shamanic perspective on organizational change and development: theory and techniques for instruction and practice. *Journal of Organizational Change Management.* 1994; 7(1): 7–23.

3 Waddock S. A. *The Difference Makers: How Social and Institutional Entrepreneurs Created the Corporate Responsibility Movement.* Sheffield, UK: Greenleaf; 2008.

4 Neal J. *Edgewalkers: People and Organizations that Take Risks, Build Bridges, and Break New Ground.* Westport, CT: Praeger; 2006.

5 Perlman B., Gueths J., Weber D. A. *The Academic Intrapreneur: Strategy, Innovation, and Management in Higher Education.* New York: Praeger; 1988.

6 Pinchot III G. *Intrapreneuring: Why You Don't Have to Leave the Corporation to Become an Entrepreneur.* New York: Joanna Cotler; 1985.

7 Bornstein D. *How to Change the World: Social Entrepreneurs and the Power of New Ideas.* New York: Oxford University Press; 2007.

8 Roberts D., Woods C. Changing the world on a shoestring: the concept of social entrepreneurship. *University of Auckland Business Review.* 2005; 7(1): 45–51.

9 Alvord S. H., Brown L. D., Letts C. W. Social entrepreneurship and societal transformation. *Journal of Applied Behavioral Science.* 2004; 40(3): 260–82.

10 Prahalad C. K., Hammond A. Serving the world's poor, profitably. *Harvard Business Review.* 2002; 80(9): 48–57.

11 Drayton W. The citizen sector: becoming as entrepreneurial and competitive as business. *California Management Review.* 2002; 44(3): 120–32.

12 Henton D., Melville J., Walesh K. The age of the civic entrepreneur: restoring civil society and building economic community. *National Civic Review.* 1997; 86(2): 149–56.

13 Levy D., Scully M. The institutional entrepreneur as modern prince: the strategic face of power in contested fields. *Organization Studies.* 2007; 28(7): 971–91.

14 Myerson J., Greenbaum R. K. *Riding the Spirit Wind: Stories of Shamanic Healing.* Framingham, MA: LifeArts Press; 2003.

359

15 Myerson J., Robbins J. *Voices from the Other Side of the Couch: A Warrier's View of Shamanic Healing*. Framingham, MA: LifeArts Press; 2008.

16 Myerson J., Robbins J. *Death Grip on the Pommel: A Warrior's Journey to Grace*. Framingham, MA: LifeArts Press; 2012.

17 Krippner S. Psychology of shamanism. In Walter N. M., Fridman E. J. N. (eds.) *Shamanism: An Encyclopedia of World Belief, Practices, and Culture*, vol. I. Santa Barbara, CA: ABC-CLIO; 2004: 204–21.

18 Woodworth W., Nelson R. Witch doctors, messianics, sorcerers, and OD consultants: parallels and paradigms. *Organizational Dynamics*. 1979; 8(2): 17–33.

19 Charbit R., Kiefer C. Insight and wisdom: new horizons for leaders. *Reflections*. 2004; 5(9): 1–9.

20 Eliade M. *Shamanism: Archaic Techniques of Ecstasy*. Princeton University Press; 1964.

21 Eliade M. Recent works on shamanism: a review article. *History of Religions*. 1961; 1(1): 152–86.

22 Harner M. *The Way of the Shaman*. New York: HarperOne; 1990.

23 Campbell J. *The Masks of God: Primitive Mythology*. London: Arkana; 1991.

24 King S. K. *Urban Shaman: A Handbook for Personal and Planetary Transformation Based on the Hawaiian Way of the Adventurer*. New York: Fireside; 1990.

25 Villoldo A. *Courageous Dreaming: How Shamans Dream the World into Being*. Carlsbad, CA: Hay House; 2008.

26 Villoldo A. Healing and the four levels of existence. *Explore*. 2008; 4(2): 140–7.

27 Villoldo A., Krippner S. *Healing States: A Journey into the World of Spiritual Healing and Shamanism*. New York: Touchstone; 1987.

28 Villoldo A. *The Four Insights: Wisdom, Power, and Grace of the Earthkeepers*. Carlsbad, CA: Hay House; 2006.

29 Hoppál M. Shamanism: an archaic and/or recent system of beliefs. In Nicholson S. (ed.) *Shamanism: An Expanded View of Reality*. Wheaton, IL: Quest; 1987: 76–100.

30 Krippner S. Conflicting perspectives on shamans and shamanism: points and counterpoints. *American Psychologist*. 2002; 57(11): 962–78.

31 Boyer L. B., Klopfer B., Brawer F. B., Kawai H. Comparisons of the shamans and pseudoshamans of the Apaches of the Mescalero Indian Reservation: a Rorschach study. *Journal of Projective Techniques and Personality Assessment*. 1964; 28(2): 173–80.

32 Fabrega H., Silver D. B. *Illness and Shamanistic Curing in Zinacantan: An Ethnomedical Analysis*. Stanford University Press; 1973.

33 Walsh R. Shamanic experiences: a developmental analysis. *Journal of Humanistic Psychology*. 2001; 41(3): 31–52.

34 Basilov V. N. Chosen by the spirits. In Balzer M. M. (ed.) *Shamanic Worlds: Rituals and Lore of Siberia and Central Asia*. New York: M. E. Sharpe; 1997: 3–48.

35 Sandner D. F. Introduction: analytical psychology and shamanism. In Sandner D. F., Wong S. H. (eds.) *The Sacred Heritage: The Influence of Shamanism on Analytical Psychology*. London: Routledge; 1997: 3–11.

36 Van Ommeren M., Komproe I., Cardeña E., Thapa S. B., Prasain D., de Jong J. T. V. M., Sharma B. Mental illness among Bhutanese shamans in Nepal. *Journal of Nervous and Mental Disease*. 2004; 192(4): 313–17.

37 Findeisen H. *Schamanentum: Dargestellt am Beispiel der Besessenheitspriester nordeurasiatischer Völker*. Stuttgart: W. Kohlhammer; 1957.

38 Krippner S. Trance and the trickster: hypnosis as a liminal phenomenon. *International Journal of Clinical and Experimental Hypnosis*. 2005; 53(2): 97–118.

39 Csikszentmihalyi M. *Good Business: Leadership, Flow, and the Making of Meaning*. New York: Penguin Books; 2004.

40 Csikszentmihalyi M. *Finding Flow: The Psychology of Engagement with Everyday Life*. New York: Basic Books; 1997.

41 Csikszentmihalyi M. *Creativity: Flow and the Psychology of Discovery and Invention*. New York: Harper Perennial; 1997.

42 Krippner S. The epistemology and technologies of shamanic states of consciousness. *Journal of Consciousness Studies*. 2000; 7(11/12): 93–118.

43 Weick K. E. *Sensemaking in Organizations*. Thousand Oaks, CA: Sage; 1995.

44 Weick K. E., Sutcliffe K. M., Obstfeld D. Organizing and the process of sensemaking. *Organization Science*. 2005; 16(4): 409–21.

45 Aldag R. J. Bump it with a trumpet: on the value of our research to management education. *Academy of Management Learning and Education*. 2012; 11(2): 285–92.

46 Bartunek J. M., Egri C. P. Introduction: can academic research be managerially actionable? What are the requirements for determining this? *Academy of Management Learning and Education*. 2012; 11(2): 244–6.

47 Egri C. P. Introduction: toward a more balanced perspective on academic contributions. *Academy of Management Learning and Education*. 2012; 11(2): 302.

48 Greve H. R. Correctly assessing the value of our research to management education. *Academy of Management Learning and Education*. 2012; 11(2): 272–7.

49 Ireland R. D. Management research and managerial practice: a complex and controversial relationship. *Academy of Management Learning and Education.* 2012; 11(2): 263–71.

50 Northcraft G. B., Tenbrunsel A. E. Publications, contributions, and the social dilemma of scholarly productivity: a reaction to Aguinis, Debruin, Cunningham, Hall, Culpepper, and Gottfredson (2010). *Academy of Management Learning and Education.* 2012; 11(2): 303–8.

51 Martin R. The price of actionability. *Academy of Management Learning and Education.* 2012; 11(2): 293–9.

52 Pearce J. L., Huang L. The decreasing value of our research to management education. *Academy of Management Learning and Education.* 2012; 11(2): 247–62.

53 Adler N. J., Harzing A. When knowledge wins: transcending the sense and non-sense of academic rankings. *Academy of Management Learning and Education.* 2009; 8(1): 72–95.

54 Lorsch J. W. Regaining lost relevance. *Journal of Management Inquiry.* 2009; 18(2): 108–17.

55 Giacalone R. A. Academic rankings in research institutions: a case of skewed mind-sets and professional amnesia. *Academy of Management Learning and Education.* 2009; 8(1): 122–6.

56 Ghoshal S. Bad management theories are destroying good management practices. *Academy of Management Learning and Education.* 2005; 4(1): 75–91.

57 Scharmer C. O. *Theory U: Leading from the Future as It Emerges.* Cambridge, MA: Society for Organizational Learning; 2007.

58 Adler N. J. I am my mother's daughter: early developmental influences on leadership. *European Journal of International Management.* 2008; 2(1): 6–21.

59 Waddock S. Wisdom and responsible leadership: aesthetic sensibility, moral imagination, and systems thinking. In Koehn D., Elm D. (eds.) *Aesthetics and Business Ethics.* Dordrecht: Springer-Verlag; 2014: 129–48.

60 Waddock S. Finding wisdom within: the role of seeing and reflective practice in developing moral imagination, aesthetic sensibility, and systems understanding. *Journal of Business Ethics Education.* 2010; 7(1): 177–96.

61 Hollander E. Conformity, status, and idiosyncrasy credit. *Psychological Review.* 1958; 65(2): 117–27.

62 Kuhn T. S. *The Structure of Scientific Revolutions.* University of Chicago Press; 1996.

63 Frost P. J. Creating scholarship and journeying through academia: reflections and interpretations from the field. *Journal of Applied Behavioral Science.* 1989; 25(4): 399–418.

64 Maslow A. H. Self-actualizing people: a study of psychological health. In *Personality Symposia: Symposium # 1 on Values*. New York: Grune & Stratton; 1950: 11–34.

65 Bellah R. N., Madsen R., Sullivan W. M., Swidler A., Tipton S. M. *Habits of the Heart: Individualism and Commitment in American Life*. Oakland: University of California Press; 2007.

66 Novak M. *Business as a Calling: Work and the Examined Life*. New York: Free Press; 1996.

67 Palmer P. J., Rudnicki S. *Let Your Life Speak: Listening for the Voice of Vocation*. San Francisco: Jossey-Bass; 2000.

68 Conklin T. A. Work worth doing: a phenomenological study of the experience of discovering and following one's calling. *Journal of Management Inquiry*. 2012; 21(3): 298–317.

69 Adler N. J. Going beyond the dehydrated language of management: leadership insight. *Journal of Business Strategy*. 2010; 31(4): 90–9.

70 Adler N. J., Hansen H. Daring to care: scholarship that supports the courage of our convictions. *Journal of Management Inquiry*. 2012; 21(2): 128–39.

71 Mingers J., Willmott H. Taylorizing business school research: on the 'one best way' performative effects of journal ranking lists. *Human Relations*. 2013; 66(8): 1051–73.

72 Willmott H. Journal list fetishism and the perversion of scholarship: reactivity and the ABS list. *Organization*. 2011; 18(4): 429–42.

73 Mourkogiannis N. Purpose: the starting point of great leadership. *Leader to Leader*. 2007; 44: 26–32.

74 Quinn R. E., Rohrbaugh J. A spatial model of effectiveness criteria: towards a competing values approach to organizational analysis. *Management Science*. 1983; 29(3): 363–77.

75 Quinn R. E., Cameron K. Organizational life cycles and shifting criteria of effectiveness: some preliminary evidence. *Management Science*. 1983; 29(1): 33–51.

76 Quinn R. E., Hildebrandt H. W., Rogers P. S., Thompson M. P. A competing values framework for analyzing presentational communication in management contexts. *Journal of Business Communication*. 1991; 28(3): 213–32.

77 Gardner K. Commentary on 'Reflections on Sullivan and the language of psychiatry': the times of David McK. Rioch. *Psychiatry*. 2003; 66(2): 104–7.

78 Dik B. J., Duffy R. D. Calling and vocation at work: definitions and prospects for research and practice. *The Counseling Psychologist*. 2009; 37(3): 424–50.

79 Pinquart M. Creating and maintaining purpose in life in old age: a meta-analysis. *Ageing International*. 2002; 27(2): 90–114.

80 Meyerson D. E., Scully M. A. Tempered radicalism and the politics of ambivalence and change. *Organization Science*. 1995; 6(5): 585–600.

81 Meyerson D. *Tempered Radicals: How People Use Difference to Inspire Change at Work*. Boston: Harvard Business School Press; 2001.

82 Neal J. Edgewalkers: walk on the leading edge. *Personal Excellence*. 2010; 15(11): 9.

83 Dow J. Universal aspects of symbolic healing: a theoretical synthesis. *American Anthropologist*. 1986; 88(1): 56–69.

84 Money M. Shamanism as a healing paradigm for complementary therapy. *Complementary Therapies in Nursing and Midwifery*. 2001; 7(3): 126–31.

85 Achterberg J. *Imagery in Healing: Shamanism and Modern Medicine*. Boston: Shambhala; 1985.

86 McClenon J. Shamanic healing, human evolution, and the origin of religion. *Journal for the Scientific Study of Religion*. 1997: 36(3): 345–54.

87 Keeney B. P. *Shaking Out the Spirits: A Psychotherapist's Entry into the Healing Mysteries of Global Shamanism*. Barrytown, NY: Station Hill Press; 1994.

88 Villoldo A. *Shaman, Healer, Sage: How to Heal Yourself and Others through the Energy Medicine of the Americas*. New York: Harmony Books; 2010.

89 Winkelman M. *Shamanism: A Biopsychosocial Paradigm of Consciousness and Healing*. New York: Praeger; 2010.

90 Wolf F. A. *The Eagle's Quest: A Physicist Finds the Scientific Truth at the Heart of the Shamanic World*. New York: Touchstone; 1992.

91 Wolf F. A. *The Spiritual Universe: One Physicist's Vision of Spirit, Soul, Matter, and Self*. Needham, MA: Moment Point Press; 1999.

92 McClenon J. How shamanism began: human evolution, dissociation, and anomalous experience. In Houran J., Lange R. (eds.) *From Shaman to Scientist: Essays on Humanity's Search for Spirits*. Lanham, MD: Scarecrow Press; 2004: 21–58.

93 Meyer J. W., Rowan B. Institutionalized organizations: formal structure as myth and ceremony. *American Journal of Sociology*. 1977: 83(2): 340–63.

94 Cameron K. S., Dutton J. E., Quinn R. E. *Positive Organizational Scholarship: Foundations of a New Discipline*. San Francisco: Berrett-Koehler; 2003.

95 McClenon J. What is to be done: evaluating the ritual healing theory. Paper presented at forty-seventh annual convention of Parapsychological Association. Vienna, August 5, 2004.

96 Parsons T. On the concept of influence. *Public Opinion Quarterly*. 1963: 27(1): 37–62.

97 Walsh J. P. Presidential address: embracing the sacred in our secular scholarly world. *Academy of Management Review*. 2011; 36(2): 215–34.

98 Corbin H. *Mundus Imaginalis: or, The Imaginary and the Imaginal*, trans. Horine R. Ipswich, UK: Golgonooza Press; 1976 [1972].

99 Seligman M. E. P. *Flourish: A Visionary New Understanding of Happiness and Well-Being*. New York: Free Press; 2011.

100 Seligman M. E. P., Csikszentmihalyi M. Positive psychology: an introduction. *American Psychologist*. 2000; 55(1): 5–14.

101 Cooperrider D., Laszlo C. Innovation's new frontier. *Leadership Excellence*. 2012; 29(3): 14.

102 Zandee D. P., Cooperrider D. Appreciable worlds, inspired inquiry. In Reason P., Bradbury H. (eds.) *The SAGE Handbook of Action Research: Participative Inquiry and Practice*, 2nd edn. London: Sage; 2008: 190–8.

103 Cooperrider D., Whitney D. *Appreciative Inquiry: A Positive Revolution in Change*. San Francisco: Berrett-Koehler; 2005.

104 Cooperrider D., Whitney D., Stavros J. M. *Appreciative Inquiry Handbook*. San Francisco: Berrett-Koehler; 2003.

105 Cooperrider D. *Appreciative Inquiry: An Emerging Direction for Organization Development*. Champaign, IL: Stipes; 2001.

106 Rader M. M. *A Modern Book of Esthetics: An Anthology*. Austin, TX: Holt, Rinehart & Winston; 1973.

107 Giacalone R. A. A transcendent business education for the 21st century. *Academy of Management Learning and Education*. 2004; 3(4): 415–20.

108 Gladwell M. *Outliers: The Story of Success*. New York: Back Bay-Books; 2008.

109 Schein E. H., Kampas P. J., DeLisi P. S., Sonduck M. M. *DEC Is Dead, Long Live DEC: The Lasting Legacy of Digital Equipment Corporation*. San Francisco: Berrett-Koehler; 2004.

110 Schein E. H. *Helping: How to Offer, Give, and Receive Help*. San Francisco: Berrett-Koehler; 2009.

111 Movva R. Myths as a vehicle for transforming organizations. *Leadership and Organization Development Journal*. 2004; 25(1): 41–57.

112 Laughlin C. D., Throop C. J. Imagination and reality: on the relations between myth, consciousness, and the quantum sea. *Zygon*. 2001; 36(4): 709–36.

113 Tillich P. *Systematic Theology*, vol. III, *Life and the Spirit: History and the Kingdom of God*. University of Chicago Press; 1963.

114 Schutz A. Symbol, reality and society. In *Collected Papers*, vol. I, *The Problem of Social Reality*, ed. Natanson M. The Hague: Martinus Nijhoff; 1964: 287–356.

115 Campbell J. *The Inner Reaches of Outer Space: Metaphor as Myth and as Religion*. New York: Harper & Row; 1988.

116 Dutton J. E., Dukerich J. M. Keeping an eye on the mirror: image and identity in organizational adaptation. *Academy of Management Journal*. 1991; 34(3): 517–54.

117 Bradley M., Schipani C. A., Sundaram A. K., Walsh J. P. The purposes and accountability of the corporation in contemporary society: corporate governance at a crossroads. *Law and Contemporary Problems.* 1999; 62(3): 9–86.

118 Senge P. M. *The Fifth Discipline: The Art and Practice of the Learning Organization.* New York: Doubleday; 1990.

119 Churchman C. W. Guest editorial: wicked problems. *Management Science.* 1967; 14(4): B-141–B-142.

120 Rittel H. W., Webber M. M. Dilemmas in a general theory of planning. *Policy Sciences.* 1973; 4(2): 155–69.

121 Sidky H. A shaman's cure: the relationship between altered states of consciousness and shamanic healing 1. *Anthropology of Consciousness.* 2009; 20(2): 171–97.

122 Csikszentmihalyi M. *Flow: The Psychology of Optimal Experience.* New York: Harper Perennial; 1991.

123 Gilding P. *The Great Disruption: Why the Climate Crisis Will Bring On the End of Shopping and the Birth of a New World.* New York: Bloomsbury Press; 2011.

124 Loeb E. M. Shaman and seer. *American Anthropologist.* 1929; 31(1): 60–84.

125 Dixon R. B. Some aspects of the American shaman. *Journal of American Folklore.* 1908; 80: 1–12.

126 Howard A. Paradexity: the convergence of paradox and complexity. *Journal of Management Development.* 2010; 29(3): 210–23.

127 Bazerman M. H., Chugh D. Decisions without blinders. *Harvard Business Review.* 2006; 84(1): 88–97.

128 Werhane P. H. Mental models, moral imagination and system thinking in the age of globalization. *Journal of Business Ethics.* 2008; 78(3): 463–74.

129 Werhane P. H. Moral imagination and systems thinking. *Journal of Business Ethics.* 2002; 38(1): 33–42.

130 Werhane P. H. *Moral Imagination and Management Decision-Making.* New York: Oxford University Press; 1999.

131 Adler N. J. The arts and leadership: now that we can do anything, what will we do? *Academy of Management Learning and Education.* 2006; 5(4): 486–99.

132 Whyte D. *Crossing the Unknown Sea: Work as a Pilgrimage of Identity.* New York: Riverhead Books; 2002.

133 Noll R., Achterberg J., Bourguignon E., George L., Harner M., Honko L., Winkelman M. Mental imagery cultivation as a cultural phenomenon: the role of visions in shamanism [and comments and reply]. *Current Anthropology.* 1985; 26(4): 443–61.

134 Austin R. D., Devin L., Sullivan E. E. Accidental innovation: supporting valuable unpredictability in the creative process. *Organization Science*. 2012; 23(5): 1505–22.

135 Norgaard R. B., Baer P. Collectively seeing complex systems: the nature of the problem. *Bioscience*. 2005; 55(11): 953–60.

136 Mirvis P. Executive development through consciousness-raising experiences. *Academy of Management Learning and Education*. 2008; 7(2): 173–88.

137 Gergen K. J. *Toward Transformation in Social Knowledge*. Thousand Oaks, CA: Sage; 1994.

138 Grayling A. C. Intellectual or academic. *Prospect*. January 20, 1997; 15–16.

139 Chomsky N. The responsibility of intellectuals. *New York Review of Books*. 1967; 8(3): 16–26.

140 Grayling A. C. Do public intellectuals matter? *Prospect*. April 24, 2013; 14.

141 Uvin P., Jain P. S., Brown L. D. Think large and act small: toward a new paradigm for NGO scaling up. *World Development*. 2000; 28(8): 1409–19.

142 Batie S. S. Wicked problems and applied economics. *American Journal of Agricultural Economics*. 2008; 90(5): 1176–91.

143 Wilber K. Why do religions teach love and yet cause so much war? Beliefnet. June 15, 2004.

144 Abowitz K. K. Moral perception through aesthetics engaging imaginations in educational ethics. *Journal of Teacher Education*. 2007; 58(4): 287–98.

145 Bird F. B., Waters J. A. The moral muteness of managers. *California Management Review*. 1989; 32(1): 73–88.

146 Bazerman M., Tenbrunsel A. Blind spots. *Leadership Excellence*. 2011; 28(3): 5–6.

147 Ackoff R. L. On learning and the systems that facilitate it. *Reflections*. 1999; 1(1): 14–24.

148 Freeman R. E., Wicks A. C., Parmar B. Stakeholder theory and 'the corporate objective revisited.' *Organization Science*. 2004; 15(3): 364–9.

149 Koestler A. *The Ghost in the Machine*. New York: Macmillan; 1968.

150 Cabrera D., Colosi L., Lobdell C. Systems thinking. *Evaluation and Program Planning*. 2008; 31(3): 299–310.

151 Shrivastava P., Ivanaj V., Ivanaj S. Sustainable development and the arts. *International Journal of Technology Management*. 2012; 60(1): 23–43.

152 Elm D. R., Taylor S. S. Representing wholeness: learning via theatrical productions. *Journal of Management Inquiry*. 2010; 19(2): 127–36.

153 Schein E. H. The role of art and the artist. *Reflections*. 2001; 2(4): 81–3.

154 Dewey J. *Art as Experience*. New York: Perigee Books; 1980.

Index